THE
EASTER
RISING

MICHAEL FOY & BRIAN BARTON

SUTTON PUBLISHING

This book was first published in 1999 by
Sutton Publishing Limited · Phoenix Mill
Thrupp · Stroud · Gloucestershire · GL5 2BU

This new paperback edition first published in 2004

Reprinted 2004

British Library Cataloguing in Publication Data
A catalogue record for this book is available from the British
Library.

ISBN 0 7509 3433 6

Typeset in 11/12pt Photina.
Typesetting and origination by
Sutton Publishing Limited.
Printed and bound in Great Britain by
J.H. Haynes & Co. Ltd, Sparkford.

CONTENTS

ACKNOWLEDGEMENTS

We owe a considerable debt of gratitude to Walter Grey, formerly a member of the English Department at Methodist College, Belfast. Walter has been a close associate since the book's inception and made readily available his encyclopedic knowledge of Dublin. In addition, he directed us to a number of important sources, read the manuscript and suggested a number of revisions. He was also responsible for drawing the maps. His constant good humour, encouragement and erudition enlivened many discussions during the writing of the text.

We also thank Stewart Roulston of the History Department at Methodist College, who proofread every chapter; Alistair McCullough, Head of Modern Languages at Methodist College, who translated a considerable volume of German material into English; and Terry McBride of the Linenhall Library, Belfast, who translated several passages from Irish into English.

In particular, Brian Barton would like to thank Margaret Lamont of Methodist College for typing his part of the book, and Valerie, his wife, for painstakingly proofreading it. Michael Foy would like to thank two enthusiastic amateur historians from Carrickfergus, who read and commented on the book as it was being written: his mother Mrs Beatrice Foy and Ivan Johnston, also Colin Kirkpatrick of the Technology Department at Methodist College for his assistance throughout with the computers and e-mailing as well as working on the index. Lastly, he would like to express his gratitude to his headmaster, Dr Wilfred Mulryne, who granted and funded a sabbatical term at Merton College, Oxford, where much of the research for the book was undertaken.

ACKNOWLEDGEMENTS

In addition, we both wish to thank the trustees, archivists and staff at the many archive centres which we visited when conducting our research for their invaluable assistance, in particular those at the National Library of Ireland; the Allen Library, North Richmond Street, Dublin; the Archives Department, University College, Dublin; the Manuscripts Department, Trinity College, Dublin; the Public Record Office, London; and the Bodleian Library, Oxford. Every effort has been made to trace the copyright holders of the various primary sources used: in the instances where this search has been unsuccessful, we offer our most sincere apologies.

Finally, we owe a deep debt of gratitude to our publishers, Sutton Publishing, especially to our editor, Jenny Overton. We are also extremely grateful to Edmund Ross, Grafton Street, Dublin, who expertly reproduced the photographs used to illustrate the text.

Michael T. Foy and Brian Barton
2004

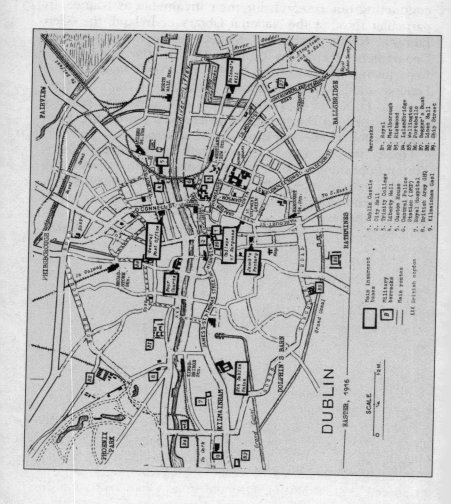

1

THE PLANNING OF THE
EASTER RISING: PART ONE

The Easter Rising of 1916 was planned and executed by a secret revolutionary organisation, the Irish Republican Brotherhood (IRB) and, in particular, a small Military Council of its leaders, Tom Clarke, Sean MacDermott, Patrick Pearse, Eamonn Ceannt, Joseph Plunkett and Thomas MacDonagh. In 1916 they also formed an alliance with the radical socialist James Connolly who had established an Irish Citizen Army for the purpose of setting up a workers' republic but ultimately made common cause with this group of conservative nationalists in an attempt to overthrow British rule in Ireland.

Their serious preparations for a Rising began only with the outbreak of the First World War in August 1914 but, in a sense, a rebellion had been over half a century in the making, ever since the foundation of the IRB in 1858. There had been, of course, previous attempts by revolutionaries to establish an Irish republic, all of them unsuccessful. Inspired by the French Revolution and the rebellious American colonies, the Society of United Irishmen, led by Wolfe Tone, had sought to unite 'Catholic, Protestant and Dissenter' in an alliance to sever the connection with England. Their uprising in 1798 assumed serious proportions in various places, including Ulster where for the first and last time Catholics and Presbyterians joined in political action. Many thousands died and the rebellion was put down with great severity. Other risings in 1803 and 1848 were miserable failures but, like 1798, they left behind potent symbols and memories and the republican revolutionary tradition was never completely eradicated. The extensive 'Fenian Conspiracy' of the IRB threatened much more, but it, too, failed ignominiously in 1867.

With no realistic prospect of revolution in the next decades, the IRB supported the Home Rule movement led by Charles Stewart Parnell and the associated agitation for land reform organised by Michael Davitt's Land League. They saw this as the best available strategy for weakening British authority in Ireland. However, even that limited programme collapsed with the fall of Parnell in 1891 and the defeat of the Second Home Rule Bill in 1893. But while the IRB stagnated at home its American sister organisation, the Clan na Gael, initiated a dynamiting campaign in British cities. For five years London's inhabitants lived under daily threat as explosions occurred at the Tower of London, London Bridge, left-luggage rooms and tunnels in the underground railway system. In the end that campaign petered out as a result of police arrests of the operatives.

'The bold Fenian men' of the ballad celebrating their actions were the generation who preceded the makers of the Easter Rising of 1916. On the Supreme Council of the IRB Tom Clarke, with years of penal servitude behind him, was the living link with that time and the prime instigator of what was to follow now. In the early years of the new century a rejuvenation of the IRB occurred alongside a cultural and intellectual renaissance in Irish nationalism, which owed much to disillusion with the party of Parnell's successors. With Home Rule blocked by a decade of Conservative ascendancy between 1895 and 1905, many nationalists, especially of the younger generation, diverted their energies into organisations such as the Gaelic League and the Gaelic Athletic Association, both of which in turn became recruiting grounds for the IRB. Within the IRB a younger, dynamic element was determined to bring a new sense of purpose and vitality to the organisation by purging the elderly, moribund, and in some cases corrupt leadership.

The process was begun in Belfast by a partnership between Denis McCullough, the son of a veteran republican, and Bulmer Hobson, a talented political organiser and journalist. Between them they completely overhauled the IRB in Ulster with a considerable degree of ruthlessness.[1]

In 1908 Hobson transferred to Dublin to carry on the task of restructuring the IRB on a national basis. In the capital he worked with two allies, Tom Clarke and Sean MacDermott, and the story of Irish republicanism up to the Easter Rising was largely shaped by the fluctuating relationships between this triumvirate. Their association began harmoniously but ultimately imploded spectacularly into mutual loathing and an enmity which knew no cease. They were a most unlikely team. Hobson came from a Quaker family and had been educated at Friends' School, Lisburn, in the Protestant heartland of Ulster. His study of Irish history caused him to gravitate towards militant Irish nationalism and Wolfe Tone came to be his political inspiration. When Hobson left school in 1899 he dedicated his life to an 'endeavour to bring the English occupation to a timely end. I spent the next sixteen years engaged in that enterprise.'[2] Hobson was a prolific journalist with an austere, intellectual and rather priggish personality, a formidable propagandist with considerable organisational ability. He had a predilection for establishing clubs and societies, constantly seeking 'a line of action which was neither abject surrender nor futile insurrection'.[3] Once he found that course it was pursued with great single-mindedness and a self-righteousness and inflexibility that were always likely to lead to friction within any organisation of which he was a member. Not that Hobson was the only Irish republican with such characteristics; there were more than enough to go round.

Tom Clarke, who had been born in 1858, was raised in Dungannon in County Tyrone before emigrating to America.[4] There he became involved with the Clan na Gael which eventually sent him to England on a hopelessly incompetent bombing mission. The operation had, in fact, been infiltrated from its very inception by British agents and Clarke's inevitable arrest was followed by a sentence of penal servitude for life. There was usually no hope of release until twenty years had been served and his incarceration was to be a Calvary of 'relentless savagery'[5] and emotional desolation. He endured a regime of perpetual silence, intellectual starvation and minimal material comfort. Every inmate was only a number to the prison authorities and Clarke witnessed comrades disintegrate slowly into madness. He therefore employed every stratagem to prevent himself being reduced to a mental vegetable, practising mathematical calculation and constant meditation on the lessons of the misbegotten enterprise which had brought him to this situation. Clarke's salvation came suddenly in 1898 when he was released as part of a government amnesty and though he left prison physically wizened and prematurely aged, his revolutionary commitment was undiminished by fifteen terrible years. To Clarke his future course was simplicity itself: he would start all over again. The long years of imprisonment, however, meant that he re-entered civil society socially inept, paralysingly shy and with a harsh, unforgiving attitude to those whom he believed had betrayed the republican cause. Even Bulmer Hobson would eventually find that out to his cost.

After a brief spell in America, Clarke returned to Ireland in 1907 and his life was transformed as he discovered status, power and admiration. His co-option on to the Supreme Council of the IRB located him at the very centre of Irish republicanism and made him an icon to younger revolutionaries who were humbled and awed by the sacrifices which he had made for the cause. Clarke also discovered a talent for political manipulation which more than compensated for his distaste for public oratory and the limelight in general. Much of his activity took place at the tobacconist's shop which he opened in Parnell Street and which served as the public front for his subterranean activities. For many republicans the premises became almost a shrine and a friend of Clarke's noted well the emotional power which it exerted.

The store was of a size that did not permit more than half a dozen men to stand in front of the counter at a time. There was just about enough space between the counter and the wall for two men to walk in together. Along the wall were arranged all of the important Dublin and Irish newspapers, weekly and monthly periodicals, and so forth. Behind the short and narrow counter was a large assortment of brands of tobacco, cigars, pipes and cigarettes, with a side line of stationery. The window was occupied mainly by a cardboard representation of an Irish Round Tower, advertising the Banba brand of Irish tobacco. Both the window and the store itself were brilliantly lighted, and the whole place suggested care and attention and spotless cleanliness.

But the store and its attractiveness were forgotten after the first glance at the man who stood behind the counter. Of medium height, with grey hair thinning away from the temples, with dark-blue eyes deeply sunken under shaggy brows and high cheekbones standing up in startling prominence from thin, sunken and emaciated cheeks, the general appearance of the man was keenness personified. Seemingly nearing the seventies, he was, nevertheless, possessed of a force and vigour that might well have been envied by men in their early thirties. The truth was that the man was in the prime of life. Brutality and confinement, however, had left on his features a mark that death alone could remove, but had been powerless to subdue the fire that glowed within and animated every thought and action of his life.[6]

In the personal and political sense, Clarke in Ireland was a man reborn. He made a happy marriage to Kathleen Daly, a member of a prominent Irish republican family. He also established the political friendship of his life with Sean MacDermott, a somewhat unlikely partnership which more than any other generated the dynamism that ultimately resulted in the Easter Rising. Although Clarke and MacDermott have never received the historical renown of people such as Pearse and Connolly, they were the key figures who, in the years before 1916, shaped the policies of the Irish Republican Brotherhood, promoted their favourites within it and drove out those they regarded as inimical to their single overwhelming revolutionary goal. MacDermott, who was twenty-six years younger than Clarke, was a farmer's son from County Leitrim who had worked as a gardener's assistant, a tram conductor and a barman. Politically, he had graduated from constitutionalism to revolutionary conspiracy and membership of the IRB, within which he had risen rapidly because of his high intelligence, enormous self-confidence, single-minded drive and organisational ability. In contrast to the reclusive Clarke, MacDermott was very gregarious, handsome with dark hair and blue eyes, extremely popular and very athletic until a devastating polio attack shortly before the First World War almost killed him. It left him a shadow of his former self, a crippled man who walked slowly, first with a crutch and later with a walking stick.

In many ways there could hardly have been two more dissimilar men than Clarke and MacDermott. One was physically old before his time, suspicious, introverted and virtually tongue-tied, while the other was sparkling, fluent and, until his illness, physically dynamic. However, they complemented each other perfectly and established an unshakeable bond in which Clarke treated MacDermott with almost paternal affection and MacDermott shared the older man's goals and his techniques of manipulation. It can also hardly have escaped MacDermott's attention that Clarke's favour was the route to the top in the IRB and while he idolised Clarke his loyalty was not slavish: at a critical moment on Easter Sunday, 1916, MacDermott was to devastate Clarke by voting against him on a matter of crucial importance.

Even with the revitalisation generated by Clarke, MacDermott and Hobson the IRB by 1911 still had only about 2,000 members. Nevertheless, rigorous screening meant they were talented, committed, energetic and ready should the political situation in Ireland change to the organisation's advantage. The breakthrough came as a result of the Ulster Unionist campaign against the Third Home Rule Bill of 1912 which was introduced by the Liberal government of Herbert Asquith. Ulster Protestant opposition, led by Sir Edward Carson, involved mass political mobilisation, the formation of an Ulster Volunteer Force (UVF) of tens of thousands of members and a massive gun-running operation at Larne, County Antrim, in April 1914. These developments radicalised the situation in Ireland and created destabilising political tensions which the republican leadership was determined to exploit. Hobson recalled that 'In the IRB we knew that Carsonism had opened a door that could not easily be closed again' and Tom Clarke always rubbed his hands with glee whenever he spoke of the UVF.[7]

Throughout 1912 and most of the following year John Redmond, leader of the Home Rule movement, issued constant public assurances that the Ulster Unionist campaign was mostly bluff and that Home Rule was certain to become law. But by the autumn of 1913 a growing sense of unease was developing within nationalist Ireland along with a feeling that an equivalent to the Ulster Volunteer Force should be created. Hobson was determined that such a mass organisation should be established, but knew well that it would be shunned by many were the fact to become public knowledge that it had emerged as a result of an initiative by the IRB. Republicans needed a respectable figure as a public front that would conceal the reality of deep penetration and control by Hobson and his associates.[8] He found the ideal candidate in Eoin MacNeill, the Professor of Early and Medieval History at University College, Dublin, who, in November 1913, had created a political sensation with an article, 'The North Began', which argued that the British government's failure to resist the UVF necessitated a similar force to protect the interests of nationalist Ireland. MacNeill's academic credentials and a reputation for integrity and political moderation had widespread appeal and Hobson prompted MacNeill's publisher, Michael O'Rahilly, to encourage the professor to form an Irish Volunteer Force. While MacNeill was unaware of the detailed background machinations which made him the focus of so much attention, he knew Hobson's general political leanings and the purpose for which he had been chosen. He was determined not to be a puppet, but to lead a movement that embraced the full spectrum of Irish nationalism. Accordingly he agreed to O'Rahilly's proposal and Hobson drew up the list of a Provisional Committee which launched the Irish Volunteers in Dublin on 25 November 1913. The Volunteers were presented as a broad non-party national organisation whose object was 'to secure and to maintain the rights and liberties common to all the people of Ireland'.

During the first six months of 1914 the Irish Volunteers mushroomed to over 150,000 members until John Redmond, the Home Rule leader, became so alarmed by its size and independence that on 9 June he demanded that the Provisional Committee accept twenty-five of his nominees. Hobson said the ultimatum 'came on us as a bombshell'.[9] To avoid a damaging public split he reluctantly favoured capitulation and on 15 June 1914 he persuaded MacNeill and a majority to agree to Redmond's demands. Even so, there were convulsions within the Provisional Committee and a minority of seven, including MacDermott, dissented. Events had moved so rapidly that Hobson had been unable to consult Clarke and MacDermott. They were appalled at what they regarded as unmitigated treachery and very soon the triumvirate was ripped apart. At a meeting in Clarke's house, Hobson ran straight into a 'storm of hysterical abuse and accusations of having betrayed the movement'.[10] Clarke directed a vitriolic tirade at Hobson and then staggered him by suddenly inquiring, 'How much did the Castle pay you?' This was the most appalling allegation which could have been directed at a member of the IRB and it resulted in an irreparable rift. Hobson resigned every office in the organisation which would bring him into contact with Clarke and MacDermott, including his seat on the Supreme Council.

What had occurred was in effect a *coup d'état* by Clarke and MacDermott. Hobson knew that he was abdicating control of the IRB to his two former colleagues, but he was not prepared to cause a schism and, anyway, he was physically and emotionally exhausted. Angry and bitter, he never spoke another word to Clarke, whom he also blamed for his dismissal as Irish correspondent of the *Gaelic American*, his sole source of regular income. Clarke, for his part, gladly reciprocated the animosity and from now on always referred to Hobson as the devil incarnate. Hobson was still forced to work with MacDermott on the Provisional Committee of the Irish Volunteers, but their exchanges were formal and restrained. There was also an unpleasant personal undercurrent to their dealings because Hobson attributed MacDermott's attitude to a polio victim's jealousy of a fit and active person. Hobson was also hurt at his abandonment by members of the IRB whom he had helped and even initiated, such as Patrick Pearse who, while he thought 'they have been too hard on Hobson',[11] made no attempt to save him from Clarke and MacDermott's wrath. Pearse now went on to Hobson's list of enemies and was thereafter damned as ungrateful, unstable, arrogant and overweeningly vain.

Although the triumvirate's collapse had been precipitated by a sudden rancorous dispute, a deeper issue lay at its heart. What had really divided it were two different visions of the IRB's future direction, especially when it was at last in a position to influence political developments in Ireland. Hobson's preferred course was based on the lessons which he drew from history – and especially the unsuccessful Rising of 1867. This fiasco had occurred despite the well-founded doubts of many IRB leaders. Several hundred poorly armed rebels with no clear military objective had marched to Tallaght, on the outskirts of Dublin, where they wandered aimlessly in the snow and cold before piling into pubs and houses. They had been rounded up and when they were marched back to Dublin they did so with their hands in their trouser pockets; the buttons had been removed to prevent escape. Hobson heard the story in Clarke's shop from a survivor and 'Some of those present . . . laughed at the story of the prisoners; they thought it funny. I was filled with rage at the thought of decent men being so humiliated because of stupid and inept leadership.'[12] By now he was convinced that England's tremendous military and economic resources doomed any ill-thought-out rising by untrained men who lacked experienced and talented leadership. Success could only come through strengthening the IRB's infrastructure, building up its membership and constructing a broad nationalist movement, a popular front of like-minded allies, which would eventually overthrow British domination. Hobson adhered absolutely to the IRB's constitution of 1873, which forbade the Supreme Council from initiating a rebellion until it had the support of the mass of the Irish people. So also did many members whom he initiated into the organisation and who asked for an assurance that they would not be dragged into a futile rising. Hobson's programme reflected the man: patient, logical, sober, responsible, bureaucratic, evolutionary and long-term in his thinking.

Clarke and MacDermott, by contrast, were daring, impatient, romantic gamblers who were driven by a great fear. In a sense their *Weltanschauung* was a mirror image of that of the Ulster Unionists whose detestation of Home Rule they shared and for an identical reason. Carson's followers dreaded a nationalist-dominated Dublin parliament which they believed would ultimately lead, either through erosion or persecution, to the extinction of their British way of life in Ireland. Conversely, Clarke and MacDermott were convinced that Home Rule would lead to Redmond accommodating Ireland permanently and comfortably within the United Kingdom. The result, they believed, would be the ultimate disappearance of a distinct sense of Irish identity and the inhabitants of Ireland becoming effectively West Britons. While Home Rule promised greater formal freedom, the reality would ooze away. Clarke and MacDermott were the products of a Europe obsessed with the rise and fall of nations, one in which a gloomy Kaiser could muse in 1914 that the great question for Germany was 'To be or not to be'. They shared the same anxiety for Ireland and were convinced that unless decisive action was taken in the near future it might be too late to arrest the ongoing assimilation of the Irish people into a greater British entity. With these views they could hardly regard Hobson as anything but defeatist. Indeed, to them he appeared anxious to postpone revolution indefinitely and as fundamentally lacking an appetite for war. Clarke and MacDermott were also elitists who deemed that they knew best the interests of the Irish nation and were not going to be constitutionalised out of insurrection. They also possessed a Leninist distaste for sharing power, a compulsive need to control any organisation within their orbit and drive out those who dissented. They believed that they were creators and sole owners of the Irish Volunteers and even before the rift of June 1914 were sceptical of Hobson's more pluralistic outlook. He, for his part, regarded them as 'narrow partisans, inclined to distrust anybody who was not a member of our small organisation. They were very suspicious of my co-operation with men like MacNeill . . . who belonged intellectually and socially to a different world.'[13] They might just have been prepared to accept a puppet as head of the Volunteers and MacNeill was in some respects an ideal candidate for this, especially as he was a useless politician; but MacNeill was simply not prepared to play the role of titular leader.

Although Hobson had been ostracised from the Supreme Council, he remained influential within the IRB as Head of the Dublin Centres Board. He was also Secretary of the Irish Volunteers, to which organisation his struggle with Clarke and MacDermott was transferred. An incessant battle now existed between his determination to keep the Volunteers a broad national movement and Clarke and MacDermott's resolve to forge it into a sword to smite England. It was a subterranean struggle because Clarke and MacDermott, having been defeated over Redmond's demands, were never again prepared to risk an open showdown with their former ally. Instead, over the next two years, their policy was to infiltrate the upper echelons of the Irish Volunteers with their protégés and slowly strip MacNeill of effective control. Their intention was to engineer a silent coup in which MacNeill would be left in place as titular leader but operational command would be exercised by IRB loyalists. Clarke and MacDermott knew that Hobson understood their intentions and conspiratorial methods and for the next two years, as he sought incriminating evidence, they and their supporters responded with plausible deniability, perpetual evasion, pained indignation and absolute mendacity. The split of June 1914, then, lit one of the slowest-burning fuses in history. But when it eventually detonated in April 1916, just before the Rising, it did so spectacularly. In the meantime, just as Hobson believed would happen, Redmond's nominees were consistently outmanoeuvred and the original Provisional Committee retained effective control of the Irish Volunteers until the outbreak of the First World War.

That war was a seminal event in Irish history. It involved more combatants and casualties than all subsequent conflicts in Ireland combined and it also changed utterly the political situation in the country. Initially, the people appeared gripped by pro-war sentiment as patriotic crowds in Dublin waved Union Jacks, wrecked shops owned by German immigrants and wildly cheered soldiers departing for the western front. By the end of 1915, 86,000 men had been recruited, having been encouraged to join by press campaigns, good wages and separation allowances. Irish soldiers had won seventeen Victoria Crosses. But the war quickly crystallised the differences between the two nationalist traditions in Ireland. Redmond saw the conflict in broad and generous terms, as an opportunity to unite Protestants and Catholics in a common cause. He hoped this would create a national consensus and that Ireland's participation in the war effort would eradicate pre-war political differences and lead to the implementation of the Home Rule Act, which was now on the statute book but suspended until the end of the war. To militant separatists this was a further extension of the process of seduction by which the Irish race was sleepwalking to extinction. A future Irish prime minister, Garret FitzGerald, remembers the apocalyptic fear of his father.

Our first reaction of jubilation soon gave way to a condition very close to despair. There were reports of the success of recruiting, of Volunteer bands marching to the station to see off their comrades who had volunteered for service in the British army. The movement on which all our dreams had centred seemed merely to have canalised the martial spirit of the Irish people for the defence of England. Our dream castle toppled about us with a crash. It was brought home to us that the very fever that had possessed us was due to a subconscious awareness that the final end of the Irish race was at hand. For centuries England had held Ireland materially. But now it seemed she held her in a new and utterly complete way. Our national identity was obliterated not only politically but in our own minds. The Irish people had recognised themselves as part of England.[14]

Such differing outlooks could not easily coexist within the Irish Volunteers and internal tensions were stoked by Redmond's speech to a cheering House of Commons on 3 August 1914. In this he pledged the Irish Volunteers to the defence of Ireland and urged the British government to concentrate on the war against Germany. Many members of the Provisional Committee, of course, were opposed to any support for the British war effort and their patience cracked when Redmond, in a speech on 20 September 1914 at Woodenbridge, County Wicklow, urged his audience of Irish Volunteers to go 'wherever the firing line extends'. The uneasy truce that had existed within the organisation since June 1914 now collapsed. On 24 September, MacNeill and the original leadership expelled Redmond's nominees and he retaliated by establishing the rival National Volunteers, to which over 90 per cent of the 180,000 members defected. While MacNeill retained most of the officers and the Dublin rank and file, his 11,000 supporters were a geographical rump, restricted outside the capital to a sporadic presence in the south and west; it had a lop-sided profile which actually became more pronounced in the eighteen months before the Rising. But their weakness was not as great as it initially appeared, because Dublin had now become the power centre of Irish nationalist politics. It was here that the political agenda was set, where party conventions and great public rallies took place, and headline events such as the labour troubles of 1913 and the foundation of the Irish Volunteers itself occurred.

Clarke and MacDermott were overjoyed at a schism which ended the threat of the Irish Volunteers' emasculation by the Home Rule movement. Although only a small number of members had remained loyal they were the most committed and determined and in their view the only ones worth having. MacNeill now became President of an Irish Volunteer organisation which was controlled by an Executive, containing, among others, Hobson and MacDermott. It also acquired, in December 1914, a Headquarters Staff. Previously the Irish Volunteers had been perceived largely as a political weapon to pressurise the British government into enacting the Third Home Rule Bill. It lacked weapons, experienced officers, training facilities, instructors and equipment of all kinds; many Volunteers did not even possess a full uniform and made do with caps, belts and puttees. The new Headquarters Staff set out to create a credible military organisation which was indispensable to Clarke and MacDermott's vision of a revolutionary sword. IRB members were quickly infiltrated into key posts, including Patrick Pearse as Director of Organisation, Joseph Plunkett, Director of Military Operations, Eamonn Ceannt, Director of Communications and Thomas MacDonagh, who was appointed Director of Training.[15]

In 1915 a gradual decline took place in mainstream nationalist support for the war which had been generated initially by sympathy for Catholic Belgium, the prosperity it brought to rural Ireland and the expectation of a short struggle. It was muted now by the reality of a seemingly endless war of attrition in which casualties mounted incessantly and the wounded became a common sight in Dublin. Furthermore, the fear of conscription increased, especially after its partial introduction in Great Britain in 1915. Most army recruits were urban labourers and artisans motivated not by patriotism but by good wages and security of employment. David Fitzpatrick has described how, for many young sons of farmers, 'rural Ireland's wartime prosperity accentuated their reluctance to abandon butter for guns. Fear of "press-ganging" swept villages in Kerry: the advent of a motor car with lights sent the lads into hiding until news came that it belonged to a doctor.'[16] There were also general complaints about the political conduct of the war. The inclusion of Carson in a coalition government which Asquith formed in May 1915 outraged many nationalists. They were further alienated by the War Office's insensitive rejection of Redmond's advice to create Irish brigades with officers chosen from the National Volunteers. Yet at the same time it had authorised the formation of a 36th Division from the UVF with its own officers and its own emblem, the Red Hand of Ulster. At the same time the IRB shrewdly manipulated anti-recruiting and anti-conscription campaigns through public meetings and the press. While Redmond's National Volunteers lapsed into terminal decline, the Irish Volunteers forced their way to the forefront of public consciousness by their drive, their commitment and their uncompromising hostility to the war effort. The police noted the organisation's success in widening the popular base of the anti-recruiting movement:

It soon became apparent that a spirit of disloyalty and pro-Germanism, which had hitherto been confined to a small number, was spreading. . . . Another object these parties had in view was to establish themselves in Irish politics in opposition to the Parliamentarians, and their anti-recruiting policy found favour with farmers' sons and others, who from selfish or unpatriotic motives were determined to remain at home.[17]

IRB organising for a Rising which required military plans, weapons and men had already begun in mid-August 1914 when its Supreme Council decided, in principle, to revolt before the end of the war.[18] It had then devolved organisational responsibility on to its executive, which was effectively a two-man show consisting of Clarke and MacDermott. They initially relied on a short-lived and shadowy Advisory Committee which had been established in October 1914 and comprised Irish Volunteer commandants and vice-commandants who were members of the IRB, such as Joseph Plunkett. This committee, whose very existence was concealed from MacNeill and Hobson, produced plans for a Dublin rising, but Clarke was unhappy with both its report and the security implications of its unwieldy size. He and MacDermott then allowed the committee to lapse and passed its plans on to be refined by a smaller successor group consisting of Ceannt, Plunkett and Pearse. While the last two were only recent recruits to the IRB they held important office in the Irish Volunteers on both the Executive and the Headquarters Staff. They were also students of military affairs. Their membership of the new planning group bound them closely to Clarke and MacDermott and its small size facilitated the two men's control.

In 1914 Eamonn Ceannt was a clerk in Dublin Corporation's Treasury Department. A 33-year-old product of the Christian Brothers School in North Richmond Street, a veritable revolutionary seminary, he resembled Clarke in his distaste for intellectual ideas and debate, his dour, distant and taciturn exterior and his uncompromising belief in physical force. He had been talent-spotted and sworn into the IRB by MacDermott, who encouraged him to become involved in the Irish Volunteers from its inception, and his loyalty to Clarke and MacDermott and the whole revolutionary enterprise was absolute.

Joseph Plunkett, born in 1887, was a thin, pale, delicate, shortsighted but intelligent and ambitious young man. His well-off father was a Papal count descended from the seventeenth-century Irish martyr, Blessed Oliver Plunkett, and the family house was situated in large grounds in the suburb of Kimmage. Throughout his life, Plunkett was plagued by health problems, and botched surgery on what might have been tubercular glands in his neck left him with appalling scars. By the First World War one Dubliner described how Plunkett's appearance was as 'emaciated as the Spanish saint in his prison cell at Toledo'.[19] Plunkett, who had been educated at Belvedere College in Dublin, had developed strongly nationalist and Catholic sympathies, which he propagated through a journal that he established and edited, *Irish Review*. He possessed considerable literary talent, wrote poetry and read widely. But he was also a man of action who had joined the Provisional Committee of the Irish Volunteers. Although he had voted to accept Redmond's takeover in June 1914 he joined the IRB soon afterwards. His absolute commitment and desire to play an important historical role through a dramatic act before his imminent death eerily resembled the outlook of Princip and his Black Hand Gang conspirators at Sarajevo in June 1914.

Pearse, born in 1879, was the son of an English monumental sculptor who had come to Ireland in the 1860s. After university, where he studied law, he concentrated on education and the Irish language. In 1903 he became editor of the Gaelic League's journal, *An Claidheamh Soluis*, and five years later he attempted to put his ideas into practice by founding St Enda's, a boys' boarding school of about a hundred pupils. Pearse was a firm but fair and well-respected headmaster but many people found him distant, driven, obsessional and somewhat repellent. He seemed unable to unwind or indulge in small talk and he developed an ascetic lifestyle; he abstained from tobacco and alcohol and certainly nobody ever accused Pearse of being the life and soul of a party. By now in his mid-thirties, he had become rather stocky for someone just over medium height. Possessed of dark hair, grey eyes and a pale complexion, he was extremely interested in the impression that he made on people. One not uncritical admirer noted that;

Those who knew him at his home, with his family, or alone with his pupils or his brother, would never remember him as anything other than the quiet young man full of nothing but the business of his school. But outside, some might have said that Pearse was vain – a bit of a poseur.

He was very neat, a lot of people would say he was very finicky about his clothes. His hair was always sleeked down, never out of place. He liked to make an impression through his appearance. In St Enda's, he was always the soberly suited schoolmaster, his tie always at the right angle. At other times when he wore his green Volunteer uniform, which was perfectly tailored, his slouch hat with the brim bound to the crown was always firm and straight on his head, never rakish. It made him look very intent and serious.[20]

Pearse's journey to physical force republicanism and the firing squad had been slow and somewhat tortuous. Although he was a convinced separatist, he had still appeared on a Home Rule platform as late as 1912 in the belief that devolution was the best available stepping stone to independence. But his personal circumstances and frustrations helped drive him in a radically different direction and his biographer Ruth Dudley Edwards has noted how cramped, bored and trapped he had become as the headmaster of a minor school in perpetual financial difficulties. Increasingly he yearned for a public stage commensurate with a man of his perceived abilities and he steeped himself in the writings of Irish revolutionaries such as Wolfe Tone, another disenchanted barrister and frustrated man of ambition. As Dudley Edwards remarks: 'A craving for action came to dominate Pearse's thinking, and combined with his literary and oratorical gifts it made him an object of interest to revolutionary groups.'[21] The IRB recognised Pearse's rising public profile and his widening circle of contacts, and although Clarke was lukewarm about his previous political moderation, MacDermott persuaded him to allow Pearse to give the oration at an important republican commemoration. Clarke was impressed and remarked, 'I never thought there was such stuff in Pearse.' Even so, Pearse had still to prove the seriousness of his intent and to accept the immense implications of membership of a secret society, but in December 1913 he committed himself and was sworn in by Bulmer Hobson. On the face of it, the conspirators were a diverse group of men varying in educational background, social status and age. But they shared a fanatical commitment to the separatist ideal, great energy, determination, cunning and ruthlessness; they also had a blinkered belief in the righteousness of their cause and actions which banished all self-doubt. In addition they brought to their task considerable powers of deception and manipulation, resilience, supreme indifference to their own lives and, in their own different ways, daring imagination; they were dreamers impatient to change the course of history.

At the end of May 1915, while MacDermott was serving a short prison sentence for anti-war activities, Clarke upgraded the planning group of Pearse, Plunkett and Ceannt into a formal Military Committee. The new committee's existence, though never its activities, was later revealed only to the Supreme Council of the IRB and its small and absolutely secretive nature satisfied the autocratic Clarke's need for total control and tight security. He had learnt a bitter lesson in prison and was determined never again to be involved in any enterprise whose members were unable to keep a secret. When MacDermott was released in September 1915, he and Clarke joined Pearse, Plunkett and Ceannt on what had now become a Military Council and became personally involved in the executive planning for a Rising.[22] By now, particular attention was being paid to weapons acquisition and John Devoy, the head of the American Clan, had requested an arms shipment from the German ambassador in the autumn of 1914. Even before a reply came, possible landing places were being sought in remote areas of the south and west, such as Kinsale Harbour and Tralee Bay.

The Military Council knew that the Germans had to be convinced face to face of its seriousness, and Plunkett, whose need to convalesce provided ideal cover for continental travel, was dispatched on a clandestine mission which lasted from April to July 1915. It involved a circuitous journey through Spain disguised in a moustache and beard; and then to Italy where he had to engage in endless counter-surveillance manoeuvres. Finally, in Switzerland, he had to face a 23-hour journey by rail to Berlin. In Berlin the Germans put Plunkett in contact with a fellow Irishman, Sir Roger

Casement, who for six months had been attempting to strengthen ties between Germany and Irish revolutionaries.[23] Casement had been born near Dublin in 1864, the son of a British army officer and a Catholic mother, and for twenty years had been a member of the British Foreign Service. He had acquired an international reputation for his exposure of European colonial exploitation in Africa and South America and was regarded as an utterly selfless humanitarian idealist whose life was dedicated to the salvation of the underdog. But Casement was a highly strung individual, temperamentally unstable, naive and completely lacking in political judgement. Despite his impeccable establishment background, Casement's increasing interest in the Irish situation caused him to gravitate to involvement in nationalist politics. He became a member of the Provisional Committee of the Irish Volunteers. His diplomatic career had taught him to think in international terms and he became increasingly attracted by the potential of a German–Irish alliance as a means of securing an independent Ireland.[24]

Casement visited America in July 1914 and when the First World War broke out the German embassy transmitted to Berlin a paper by him which argued that the British enemy could be undermined in vulnerable possessions such as Egypt, India and Ireland. Casement urged the Germans to make a declaration in favour of Irish independence and to establish an Irish Brigade of thousands of Irish prisoners of war and launch an invasion of Ireland with several thousand reservists conveyed from the USA to the west of Ireland in German cargo ships. Once landed, they would assist a rising by Irish Volunteers. Casement's document was closely scrutinised by the German General Staff and Foreign Office and they approved his suggestion that he should travel to Germany for direct negotiations.[25] Casement had also skilfully persuaded the leaders of the Clan na Gael to support his mission to Germany politically and financially. Devoy and the Clan Directorate were attracted by the prospect of active collaboration with the German government, though Devoy harboured deep reservations about Casement's suitability, temperament and judgement.[26]

Initially, Casement had considerable success and in November 1914 the Germans announced their support for Irish independence, but this only generated entirely unrealistic expectations in Casement. He believed, mistakenly, that it heralded active and decisive intervention in Irish affairs and was disheartened shortly afterwards when General Stumm of the German General Staff told him that, in view of Britain's naval superiority, it would be pointless even to attempt to send soldiers or arms to Ireland. A further setback came after the Germans agreed to the establishment of an Irish Brigade in December 1914. Recruitment figures were abysmal because most of the Irish prisoners of war were Home Rulers, few had ever heard of Casement and those who met him regarded him as a traitor who was attempting to persuade them to assist a Protestant country which had attacked Catholic Belgium. At the peak in June 1915 only fifty-six men had enlisted and a disillusioned Casement described the prisoners of war as 'recreant Irishmen . . . cads and cowards'.[27] His relations with the German authorities deteriorated seriously as they came to distrust his judgement and he came to appreciate Berlin's lack of real commitment to Irish independence. The German leadership had hoped that the raising and deployment of an Irish Brigade would create difficulties for England in Ireland and, in some measure, divert troops from the western front.

Casement and Plunkett shared the same broad ideological outlook; they sought an Irish rebellion and German assistance. Accordingly, during Plunkett's stay in Berlin the two men co-operated in composing a 32-page memorandum for submission to the German government.[28] This document, which became known as the Ireland Report, described the contemporary Irish situation, the various Irish nationalist organisations, the structure and activities of the Irish Volunteers, political attitudes in Ireland and the strength of the British military and police forces. It also contained a description of the French intervention in the 1798 Rebellion in Ireland, the lessons to be derived from that episode and the means by which Germany could most effectively assist a future Rising. The Ireland Report is crucial to any understanding of the intentions of the Military Council and the lengths to which it was prepared to go to secure German assistance. It dispels the long-held belief that Plunkett was engaged in simply an arms procurement mission and makes clear that the purpose of his journey was much more radical. What Plunkett hoped to secure from the Germans was a commitment to send a large expeditionary force to Ireland which would land simultaneously with the start of a rising. Thereafter the military campaign would become a joint enterprise between it and the Irish Volunteers. The document began by stating that;

It has been recognised by the Volunteers Headquarters Staff ever since it took control that in the present unarmed, unequipped, partly trained state of the organisation, it would be impossible to bring any considerable military operation to a successful issue without help from an external source. Even the plan for dealing with Dublin depends on relief coming, or a diversion of the British opposition being brought about by the end of a week, or at most, ten days. Moreover, when they considered that their forces were, owing to the nature of the Volunteer movement, spread out all over Ireland and in contact with and penetrated by considerably larger British forces, they decided that it would be impracticable to prepare a general mobilisation for concentration on any given point.

Plunkett and Casement then outlined British military resources in Ireland which would have to be defeated if the rising were to be successful. The Military Council had located the main army establishments at Finner in Donegal, the Curragh in Kildare about 20 miles from Dublin, and camps at Buttevant, Mallow and Fermoy in County Cork, as well as small garrisons in Belfast, Dundalk, Mullingar and an artillery depot in Athlone. It also believed that there were 5,000 troops stationed permanently in Dublin, part of a force which, in March 1915, it had estimated at 37,000 troops, with the largest concentration in Munster. These were supplemented by an estimated 12,000 armed members of the Royal Irish Constabulary. The council's sanguine assessment of the enemy forces was that;

> British forces in Ireland are not an army nor even a garrison at present. They are a number of small scattered garrisons and many large training camps. They are not equipped for the occupation of the country much less to resist invasion. Those units that are intended for immediate service receive their equipment, munitions and stores in England when they leave Ireland on their way to the front.

In view of these British weaknesses, they argued that 'Ireland could almost be taken by a *coup de main*', and went on to present a detailed and cogent analysis of the conduct of a successful military campaign whose unmistakable objective was the complete destruction of British political and military power in Ireland. Once Ireland had been liberated the Military Council clearly envisaged itself as the new rulers of an independent Irish Republic. Plunkett and Casement conceived a rising as a three-pronged but integrated military operation. Its elements were to be an Irish Volunteer seizure of Dublin, a German naval invasion which would land a military expeditionary force in the west of Ireland and a rebellion in the west by Volunteers and untrained local sympathisers which would be armed and led by the invaders. The Military Council had made preliminary plans for the destruction of British transport facilities at selected railway bridges, canals and viaducts, the seizure and occupation of Dublin by Volunteer battalions, the arrest of British officials and military officers, the stationing of guards at banks and British commercial interests and the possible appointment of a military governor in the capital. With these arrangements in place, the two men argued that 'the project begins to assume the appearance of feasibility as far as the internal campaign is concerned'.

However, the key to success was a German force of 12,000 soldiers to be brought to the west of Ireland by ships which could navigate the unfortified River Shannon and seize Limerick, which Plunkett believed had few, if any, British defenders. The document argued that a massive amphibious landing also bringing 40,000 rifles for the Volunteers would receive an ecstatic welcome from Limerick's 50,000 inhabitants. It would also have an electrifying impact on Ireland as news was disseminated quickly by messengers in motor cars and would be the signal for a nationwide revolt. It would provoke a serious rising in the west where many Volunteers and civilians in Kerry and Clare would flock to Limerick to join the Germans and also be the signal for the Military Council to seize the capital.

Once the Germans had landed safely, Plunkett and Casement visualised their officers creating a German–Irish force to which they would bring leadership and professional military expertise while the rebels would contribute numbers, enthusiasm and geographical knowledge. This army would be required to occupy territory and towns, defeat British military forces and divert pressure from the rebels in Dublin, the final destination of its military operations. These would commence once the Germans had converted Limerick into a base 'as impregnable as the Dardanelles', and then with their Irish allies had started to penetrate the rest of the country. Limerick was an ideal place to begin because of its central position on an extensive railway network whose lines ran south and east. It was also 'the south strategic end of the chief strategic line of Ireland, the line of the Shannon and Lakes' and threatened Athlone, 100 kilometres away, 'the chief strategic node' and 'the principal British artillery station in Ireland'. 'Whoever holds the line Limerick–Athlone is master of the whole of the west and a great portion of the south of Ireland.' Plunkett and Casement argued that to neutralise an early British counter-attack, the railway lines between Patrickswell and Charleville and from Cork to Tipperary would have to be severed at various points. At the same time the town of Tipperary would be occupied, the Shannon mined from Tarbert to Foynes and small German forces stationed in Limerick and along the line of the Shannon from Limerick to Killaloe.

A large German–Irish force could then advance on Athlone and because there were few, if any, British troops in Connaught Plunkett believed that the town and its vital bridge over the Shannon would fall quickly. The way would now be open for an advance on Sligo before a British flank attack could be organised. At this stage the insurgents would have control of the whole of Connaught, its resources and population – as well as a potentially war-winning asset, the well-protected harbours of the west of Ireland. By the spring of 1915 the Germans were aware that England was mobilising its military and industrial resources for total war and had become the motor of the Allied war effort. They had attempted to cripple this process in February 1915 by initiating a campaign of unrestricted U-boat warfare in the waters around the British Isles. In their memorandum Plunkett and Casement offered an enticing inducement to the Germans which would have made their submarine campaign even more effective. In return for a German expeditionary force to Ireland, the new rulers of an independent Ireland would provide the German navy with naval bases in the west of the country from which U-boats could sever England's Atlantic lifeline. Among the prizes that the document dangled in front of the Germans were Valentia Harbour, Bantry Bay, Dingle Bay, Ventry Harbour, the Blasket Islands and Killary Harbour, where 'the biggest battleships in the world can ride at anchor'. A further bait was the prospect of occupying the British naval base at Lough Swilly:

The base is very lightly held as no attack is or has been anticipated, and the land defences appear to be more or less precautionary in nature. The forts, of course, are intended to prevent an attack by sea. If the Shannon–Sligo line was strongly held by the German–Irish forces, it might be easily straightened northwards and extended to the Donegal Highlands. In such a case an attack from the land side would become feasible. A favourable result would entirely alter British naval strategy and provide an Atlantic base for the German fleet.

In relation to the land campaign, Plunkett and Casement envisaged a 50-kilometre advance by the German–Irish force from Athlone on Mullingar to take control of the midlands and the country's cattle supply before an easy 70-kilometre march towards Dublin. They also speculated on possible British counter-measures. They predicted that since most troops were concentrated in County Cork, they would attempt to move east by Waterford to seize the line from Tipperary to Portarlington. Simultaneously the Curragh garrison might attempt to break rebel control of Dublin. But they believed that because the British army was top-heavy with cavalry and virtually bereft of artillery, it would advance on Maryborough in Queen's County and link up with forces moving from Cork. The garrison at Finner in Donegal was regarded as 'hopelessly inadequate to force the line of the Shannon and would therefore come south to assist in the effort against Athlone'. At the same time the British would attempt to land large reinforcements at places such as Lough Swilly in Donegal, Dundalk in County Louth, Malahide in north County Dublin or somewhere in east Cork or Waterford. While subsequent developments would depend on circumstances, they speculated that it was 'likely that the first conflicts might develop on the lines Limerick–Tipperary and Mullingar–Tullamore'. Even before the British encountered large German-Irish forces their transport facilities would be sabotaged as they attempted to move through a countryside 'eminently suited to a kind of guerrilla or irregular warfare', 'in which the individual rifleman in cover could be of great value' and whose walls, hedges and ditches made cavalry mostly redundant.

To convince the Germans of the seriousness of their proposals and the realistic prospects of success Casement and Plunkett presented a detailed analysis of a previous naval expedition to the west of Ireland by an enemy of England in a major European war. This was the French invasion fleet under General Humbert which landed at Killala Bay in County Mayo after the 1798 Rebellion in Wexford and Wicklow in the south-east of Ireland had already been crushed and only a few scattered bands of rebels were still holding out. Humbert's army consisted of only 1,200 troops and four pieces of artillery and he brought no weapons for any Irish rebels who joined him. But despite these handicaps, the Franco–Irish force descended on Castlebar, the capital of Mayo, and defeated the British garrison. It then advanced rapidly on Collooney in County Sligo where it won a second victory, after which Humbert marched rapidly towards and across the River Shannon. His army managed to reach Ballinamuck in County Longford before it was finally surrounded and overwhelmed by the British commander-in-chief, General Lake.

The document argued that even though the French expedition arrived 'in the air' with very inadequate resources and no definite plan of operations, it had still performed impressively. Humbert had advanced well over a hundred miles through enemy-occupied country before surrendering and his force had;

> taxed the whole military resources of the government to prevent Humbert reaching Dublin, right across Ireland. Had Humbert come with 12,000 men instead of 1,200 and with a supply of arms and ammunition for the hardy and brave men that were so ready to risk their lives and homes by joining him, he could have armed the whole region west of the Shannon and unquestionably have held the greater part of the island and established a provisional national government with a headquarters that would have attracted all that was best in Ireland. He came however six months too late and then with insufficient forces and no plan of campaign or arms and munitions for thousands of men ready to join any force at all.

Plunkett and Casement acknowledged that the situation in Ireland had changed since 1798 and that, in some respects, English control was even stronger, with an efficient railway system and an armed police force. Nevertheless, they argued that the strength of resistance had increased correspondingly through the Irish Volunteers, which could lead an effective rebellion and render considerable assistance to a German expeditionary force. They concluded by maintaining that 'a successful military landing in Ireland would have political consequences of the first magnitude abroad; and if the force landed were sufficiently strong to seize, say, Athlone and the line of the Shannon, the task of expelling it and overcoming a joint force of armed Irish and invaders would tax the military and moral resources of Great Britain to the utmost'. An Irish rising would develop into an event of world importance which would transform the whole course of the European war in Germany's favour.

Plunkett's memorandum provides a unique insight into the attitudes, intentions and aspirations of the Military Council. It also has implications for the 'Blood Sacrifice' theory of the Easter Rising which postulates that it was an heroic but doomed protest which the leaders accepted would end in inevitable defeat. It argues that the members of the Military Council sought a posthumous victory in which the nation would come to recognise their sacrifices and give retrospective approval to their actions. To this end they choreographed their own executions after a creditable military performance so as to rouse the slumbering consciousness of the Irish people. In religious terms, the Rising and the death of its leaders were supposedly crafted as a political crucifixion in which Clarke, MacDermott, Pearse and the others would eventually be transformed into martyrs who had laid down their lives to ensure the resurrection of their people. In the process a short-term defeat would be turned into a long-term triumph through a renewed and irresistible campaign of resistance at the end of which national independence would finally be achieved.

There is no doubt that the cast of mind which a blood sacrifice would entail was represented on the Military Council in the persons of Pearse, Plunkett and, later on, Thomas MacDonagh. These were literary men whose writing was infused with religious symbolism, but the revolutionary enterprise was driven most of all by Clarke and MacDermott, the two senior directors of the IRB and very practical and down-to-earth men. Pearse, Plunkett and MacDonagh were junior partners and they operated under the disciplines of an organisation in which rank and position were all-important and the commands of superiors were to be respected. It is clear that Clarke and MacDermott were able to contain the restless and somewhat excitable energies of their subordinates and focus them on this world rather than the next. The Ireland Report indisputably reveals the Military Council's plans as optimistic, coherent in relation to land warfare and directed to achieving a military victory by overwhelming the British forces in Ireland. The military campaign was designed to culminate in a victory parade down O'Connell Street by Irish Volunteers and Prussian grenadiers with crowds cheering and throwing flowers as bands played 'A Nation Once Again' and 'Deutschland Uber Alles'. When the victorious soldiers passed the Post Office they would salute the members of the Military Council which would now have reconstituted itself as the new government of an independent Irish republic. What emerges from any study of the Ireland Report is the wealth of hard detail which the Military Council had assembled, a definite belief that, given the right circumstances, a quick victory over the British was both desirable and attainable. It also contained an elaborate and coherent description for a nationwide revolt to achieve that victory and goes far to explaining why the military knowledge of Plunkett was held in such high regard by the other members of the Military Council. Above all, there is the striking boldness and daring of the whole scheme and the lengths to which the leaders of the IRB were prepared to go to realise their vision of a militarily successful Rising. The radical step which Clarke and the others were prepared to take was, in effect, to join Turkey and Bulgaria in aligning an independent Ireland with the Central Powers against the Allies in the First World War.

Plunkett and Casement submitted the Ireland Report to Captain Nadolny of the German General Staff who transmitted it to his military superiors and the Foreign Office. If the General Staff had taken the Ireland Report at face value it would have given an invasion of Ireland serious consideration. Disappointingly for Plunkett and Casement, it reacted with extreme caution. It knew nothing about Plunkett, and the Irish Brigade of his co-author was floundering badly. Furthermore it understood, even if the Military Council did not, the enormous changes which had occurred in naval warfare since the eighteenth century and the extent to which the Royal Navy would make an amphibious expedition to Ireland a hazardous and potentially disastrous undertaking. The fate of the Dardanelles expedition later in 1915 can only have vindicated the Germans in their rejection of the Irish Report's proposals. When Plunkett left Germany in late June 1915 he did so without concrete promises of any kind from the Germans. It is often stated that while in Berlin he had met the Chancellor, Bethmann Hollweg, and secured a promise that Germany would send an arms shipment to the west of Ireland to assist a rising. But there is no evidence that Plunkett ever met Bethmann Hollweg, and every indication that the German army and naval authorities had vetoed military assistance to the Irish revolutionaries. Almost a year was to pass before their scepticism was overcome and a definitive decision was taken to risk German personnel on an arms mission to Ireland. A subsequent request by Devoy in October 1915 for 'a small quantity of arms' to be delivered to the west of Ireland was pigeonholed by the German Admiralty which reacted with the same lack of enthusiasm it showed for Plunkett and Casement's request in June 1915.

While Plunkett returned to Ireland with no definite promises of German support and left Casement at the end of June 1915 in a deeply depressed state, it is clear that his mission had not been a complete failure. Unknown to an increasingly marginalised Casement, Plunkett had been conducting parallel negotiations with the General Staff and the Foreign Office. These had clearly been productive and enabled Plunkett to bring back assurances of German interest in assisting the Military Council. But these would only be made good if the IRB were able to prove that its revolutionary enterprise was a serious undertaking and that Plunkett was not simply another of the fantasists who turned up in Berlin with promises that they would bring down the British Empire. The one thing which would convince the Germans of this was the fixing of a definite date for the start of an Irish rising. The Germans had clearly decided to steer a course between an immediate promise to provide material assistance to the Military Council and a definitive rejection of its pleas. Whatever their reservations about the unknown Plunkett, it would have been unwise not to keep him in play in case the IRB's plans proved to be serious. In that event minimal German assistance in the form of an arms mission might have an immense impact on the political situation in Ireland, as had the Larne gun-running of April 1914. Even if the projected Irish rising failed an insurrection would distract the British government from prosecuting the war in France, divert troops to put it down, undermine the unity of the British state and weaken the Allied claim to be the defender of small nations. Plunkett returned, not with definite promises, but a commitment that matters would change if the Military Council in the months to come proved itself to be serious in intent. Such a promise can only have emboldened it and given even greater urgency to its planning and preparations. In particular, the scouting of the harbours in the west of Ireland, which will be described later, must have been undertaken in the hope that German assistance would eventually be given.

Plunkett's prolonged absence was known to moderates on the Volunteer Executive, but he returned to Ireland with a cover story of frustration and disappointment. Sean Fitzgibbon, the Director of Recruiting, wrote:

I had always regarded Plunkett as rash and unbalanced. He came back from Germany in 1915. Bulmer Hobson told me what Plunkett was saying; that he had conferred with Germans of staff rank. The Germans told him they were not interested in Ireland. Plunkett said that all the German talk of will to win was bluff; that in reality they were trying to arrange a compromise peace with Britain. He gave the impression that his visit abroad had made him sane. I want to stress that he was not sent to Germany either by the Volunteer Executive or with the aid of its funds. I am now of the opinion that his moderation was a pose assumed to deceive.[29]

The encouragement from Germany prompted the Military Council to begin detailed examination of where an arms shipment might arrive. In September 1915, Pearse sent Diarmuid Lynch, the secretary to the executive of the Supreme Council of the IRB, to the south-west of Ireland to reconnoitre Tralee and canvass the local Volunteer leadership about possible landing places. He was unanimously recommended to select Fenit Harbour in Tralee Bay where the light railway would be able to speedily transfer rifles to Tralee.[30] German weapons were of vital importance to any Rising in view of the limited arsenal which the Irish Volunteers had managed to accumulate. The organisation was perennially short of money and had only managed to finance two gun-running operations at Howth in July 1914 and Kilcoole in August 1914. More weapons had been secured after the ban on arms importation had been temporarily lifted in August 1914 and an American loan had secured 10,000 Martini Enfield rifles. A small proportion of these was retained after the split with Redmond in September 1914 and more were brought over by defectors from the increasingly moribund National Volunteers. There were also purchases from soldiers, thefts from the British Army ordnance stores in Dublin and occasional smuggling. Michael O'Rahilly, Director of Arms, also popularised the use of the single-barrelled shotgun loaded with buckshot, a weapon that proved its power and effectiveness during Easter Week.[31] Ammunition and explosives were stolen from the Arklow munitions factory in County Wicklow and from railway wagons and colliery magazines in Scotland. Despite all these efforts the Irish Volunteers in January 1916 still possessed only about 3,730 arms, including rifles, shotguns and revolvers.[32]

In addition to military plans and weapons, the Military Council needed fighters and for this control of the Irish Volunteers was indispensable. By 1915 Pearse, Plunkett and Ceannt held membership of the Military Council, the Volunteer Executive and the Headquarters Staff. The Military Council also controlled the four Dublin Volunteer battalions through their IRB commandants, Ned Daly, Thomas MacDonagh, Eamon de Valera and Eamonn Ceannt. Its supporters had also become Volunteer commandants in Cork, Kerry, Limerick and Galway and most of the provincial organisers were also members of the IRB. MacNeill suspected almost nothing of the extent to which he was being undermined, while Hobson was constrained by his IRB oath of secrecy.

The Military Council took enormous care to shroud its activities in 'almost impenetrable secrecy'.[33] But though no written records of its deliberations were kept and every member was subsequently executed, it is still possible to reconstruct much of its planning for the Easter Rising. The Military Council always remained a small, tightly knit group whose membership expanded from three to five during 1915 and then to a maximum of seven by the time of the Rising. It operated on the basis of absolute confidentiality, since previous Irish rebellions had been destroyed from within through carelessness, betrayal or infiltration by British agents. So even prominent IRB leaders such as Denis McCullough, President of the Supreme Council, and Diarmuid Lynch, the secretary of its executive and a close friend of MacDermott, were excluded from knowledge of its activities. James Connolly, who joined in January 1916, shared its members' obsessive secretiveness. When a member of his Citizen Army who was involved in stealing gelignite required an operation for appendicitis, Connolly approved surgery only when a doctor assured him that any dangerous revelations by the man would be dismissed as delirious rambling. The Military Council met only in discreet locations where it was protected from police surveillance or raids by guards and scouts. It convened most frequently in the backroom of Houlihan's, a basketmaker's shop in Amiens

Street.[34] But it also met at Clontarf Town Hall, whose librarian was an old associate of Clarke, in a closed restaurant in Henry Street, which was owned by a trusted supporter, in private houses such as Ceannt's and, most famously and finally, at Liberty Hall on Easter Sunday, 23 April 1916.[35] In addition to general planning sessions, individual members were assigned specific tasks. MacDermott, for instance, was responsible for obtaining information on Dublin's telephone and telegraph manhole system. He did so by using IRB members who were employed by the Post Office as clerks and outdoor servicemen who surveyed and sketched every manhole in the city.[36]

A fascinating description of how the Military Council developed a project is provided in a memoir by an IRB member called Patrick Daly.[37] In 1916 he was in MacDonagh's 2nd Dublin Battalion of the Irish Volunteers and was also employed as a carpenter at the Magazine Fort in Phoenix Park, the British army's main weapons armoury in the city. MacDermott had recruited Daly as a spy to provide intelligence on the fort's layout, its garrison strength and the location of keys, tools and equipment. By Palm Sunday, 16 April 1916, the Council had decided that one of the Rising's first dramatic acts would be an attack on the fort. On that day, at a meeting at Clontarf Town Hall attended by most of its members, it commenced detailed planning of the operation. Over the course of an hour Daly was questioned on such matters as the best method of surprising the guards and the number of men who would be required. Tom Clarke was particularly interested in knowing the relative merits of an attack in daylight or in darkness. A debate then occurred over whether to seize the fort's armaments for use in the Rising or to demolish the whole complex in a titanic explosion. MacDonagh, who had recently joined the Military Council, favoured seizure but Clarke and MacDermott successfully argued for detonation. Clarke also demonstrated that the passage of time had not dimmed his youthful knowledge of dynamiting techniques. Daly then provided information on the ammunition, oil and tool stores and the keys in a glasshouse in the guard room. He also suggested a stratagem for gaining entry to the fort based on his knowledge that on Sundays footballers often passed its gates, watched unsuspectingly by the guards. Daly believed that Volunteers posing as a soccer team could get close enough to surprise and overpower the defenders. Clarke was delighted with the idea and the Council instructed Daly to assemble a team. It also approved his proposal to use in the attack officers from the Fianna, the republican boy scout organisation. MacDonagh, his commandant, then promoted him to lieutenant, a post senior enough to enable him to recruit for the operation. Next day, on MacDermott's orders, Daly took a plan of the fort to Liberty Hall where Connolly was concerned that the Fianna members needed extra muscle and added some hefty men to the team. MacDonagh, whom the Council had left to finalise arrangements, told Daly on Wednesday 19 April to convene a team meeting at which final sanction was given by the leadership and a rendezvous arranged for Easter Sunday. Daly's account also confirms that, of necessity, outsiders had to be given some information, but were never allowed to see the whole picture and have the innermost secrets revealed to them. Among them were the provincial leaders in Kerry who, in the months before the Rising, were informed of the proposed German arms shipment. Likewise, in January 1916, Irish Volunteer commandants in the south and west were informed secretly by Pearse of the military dispositions they were to make once a rising had begun. And in either late December 1915 or January 1916 the Military Council took a momentous step by finally fixing the Rising for Easter 1916.[38] But even the Supreme Council was not informed of the decision at its last meeting in Clontarf Town Hall on 16 January 1916. At this session MacDermott blandly proposed only that the Supreme Council should reaffirm its decision of August 1914 to rise 'at the earliest possible date'. The original choice of date for the Rising was Good Friday, but that was subsequently altered to Easter Sunday. It had been realised that a Friday mobilisation of large numbers of Volunteers, many of them civil servants leaving their place of employment, might alert the British authorities that something more dangerous than routine manoeuvres was in progress.[39]

While the Military Council refined the general plan, battalion commandants instructed their officers to gather intelligence on their areas of operations, select outposts and ready their men psychologically and militarily for urban warfare. De Valera, commandant of the 3rd Dublin Battalion, meticulously reconnoitred the district surrounding Boland's Mills, while his officers identified garages, stables and factories, and food, clothing and medical stores.[40] There were also night classes on street-fighting techniques, including the construction of barricades, cutting passages through buildings, loopholing walls, sandbagging windows and firing from roof-tops. In the weeks before the Rising the tempo of activity was to increase as commandants conducted a final recruitment drive and attempted to secure more arms. During Holy Week rifles were moved into Dublin or removed from storage places in the city and transferred to dumps prepared for use by Volunteers at the start of the Rising. These included one cache which had been located among hundreds of coffins in a church vault.[41]

2

THE PLANNING OF THE
EASTER RISING: PART TWO

While in many respects the Military Council's plans were progressing satisfactorily, at the end of 1915 and in early 1916 it feared that it might be outflanked on two fronts. First, some Council members believed, without any justification, that the British were considering implementing the Home Rule Act. But if such a step did take place it would rob republicans of any credible justification for a rebellion against future prime minister John Redmond. A second and more realistic apprehension derived from the threat posed by James Connolly, the trade union organiser and socialist revolutionary.[1] Connolly had risen to national prominence through his Transport Workers Union's involvement in the great Dublin Lockout of 1913 and although the labour movement lost that particular dispute Connolly ended up as leader of the union. Even more important for the future, he became commander of the Irish Citizen Army, a small force of 200 men which had been established during the dispute to protect workers in clashes with the police. Connolly's power base in Dublin, henceforth, was at Liberty Hall, the headquarters of both the union and the Citizen Army. When socialist internationalism failed to prevent the outbreak of the First World War, Connolly's disillusionment became discernible. Increasingly he was attracted by the idea of a national uprising against British rule in Ireland. Connolly was rather dour and distant, but he had formidable political talents, fanatical determination, drive, organisational ability and considerable verbal and written powers of persuasion. While never a flamboyant orator, he had conquered a speech impediment and become an effective public speaker through his capacity to argue a detailed and well-structured case. However, his movement had reached the limits of its growth in a conservative country with a small industrial working class and a powerful Catholic Church bitterly opposed to socialism. By the end of 1915 Connolly's frustration had led to increasingly strident demands for action and to threats that if nobody took the lead then he would act with his tiny Citizen Army. He was very concerned that some sudden change in the fortunes of war might lead to a British victory and leave the revolutionary movement high and dry.

In his speeches and his articles in *Workers' Republic*, Connolly tried to expand his support by appealing over the heads of the leadership of the Irish Volunteers directly to the rank and file. His clear intention was to create a situation where the Volunteer Executive and Headquarters would be sucked into supporting an uprising which had been precipitated by radicals in the lower echelons of the organisation. Hobson recognised the dangers of such a strategy and persuaded MacNeill to confront Connolly at Volunteer Headquarters on Sunday 16 January 1916.[2] They were appalled by Connolly's candid confirmation that he was prepared to use the Citizen Army to attempt to create a nationwide chain reaction and warned him that they would never be dragged into such a venture. Pearse, who was also present, was equally appalled, though for very different reasons. He now informed the Military Council that Connolly was spiralling out of control and that his actions risked precipitating massive British repression before its own plans had been completed. The Military Council decided that it had to move quickly to neutralise Connolly and three days later, in circumstances which are still mysterious, he vanished from Liberty Hall in the company of two IRB members. He was brought to a brickworks in the suburb of Dolphin's Barn and in the course of three days' negotiation with

Pearse, MacDermott and Plunkett, Connolly learnt of the Military Council's existence and its plans for a German arms shipment and a Rising. In return for abandoning his own insurrectionary plans Connolly was offered an alliance between the Irish Volunteers and the Citizen Army, and a place on the Military Council. Connolly accepted eagerly because, in exchange for a few months' delay, he had the promise of certain action by a far larger number of men than he could ever hope to put in the field. The Military Council, for its part, was delighted that it had eliminated the constant concern about a premature strike by the Citizen Army and could concentrate absolutely on refining its plans for a Rising.

By the end of January 1916 those plans were well advanced. They were a modified version of Plunkett's memorandum to the Germans in 1915. The centrepiece remained the Irish Volunteers' seizure of Dublin, which in turn would inspire the rest of the country and transform the insurrection into a truly national affair. The provincial Rising would still be initiated in the west where the Volunteers were relatively strong, but precipitated now by the anticipated arrival of a large German arms shipment. The original destination of this shipment, which had not yet been given final approval by the Germans, had been Limerick, but about the end of January 1916 this was changed to Fenit, probably at the request of the western Volunteer leaders who had always favoured the latter. A probable factor in the change was that whereas Plunkett in 1915 had believed that at most Limerick had only a small British army garrison there, one Kerry Volunteer leader in 1916 had estimated it as 1,000 troops.[3]

Dublin's central importance to the Easter Rising is obvious. The rebellion was planned there and the headquarters of the Irish Volunteers and the Citizen Army were located there, as were the homes of the members of the Military Council. It was here that a rising would begin, an Irish Republic would be declared and a Provisional Government based. The general outline of the insurrection in the capital had been decided by the time Connolly joined the Military Council. For months past its Volunteers had switched their training to the handling of explosives, bomb-throwing and classes on street-fighting, though Connolly's assiduous study of urban warfare in European cities would have brought much useful advice. He especially stressed the need for highly motivated men of initiative, capable of employing unorthodox methods against an enemy superior in numbers and firepower. He also rejected the traditional use of barricades with static defenders firing at oncoming troops and cavalry, arguing that these would be annihilated by the British. He proposed instead unmanned barricades to frustrate cavalry charges and slow up advancing troops, who would then be decimated by concealed Volunteers. These defenders should loophole buildings and knock down parts of walls to slip from building to building and rain down rifle fire on an enemy trapped in the open. This method had a mobility that was vital since a static defence would be pinned down and eventually overrun. Connolly stressed that urban warfare was a lethal battle of wits in which an insurgent occupying a house who was unwary enough to answer a telephone would probably be cut down by rifle fire directed by the caller on the other end of the line.[4]

In Dublin the four Volunteer battalions were to seize a series of strongholds in the city centre sufficiently close to one another to form an inner defensive cordon. They would also threaten rail and road communications along which would travel British reinforcements heading for the city centre. The Provisional Government would occupy the GPO in O'Connell Street. Ned Daly's 1st Battalion would occupy the Four Courts, a large classical building which lay on the direct route of troops coming into the city centre from the Royal Barracks, a short distance further up the Liffey. Daly's seizure of North King Street to the rear would also neutralise the route of troops coming from Marlborough Cavalry Barracks on the north-western edge of the city. MacDonagh's 2nd Battalion was to occupy Jacob's biscuit factory, which was less than three-quarters of a mile from both Portobello and Richmond Barracks on the southern rim of the central city area. De Valera's 3rd Battalion would take Boland's bakery close to Beggar's Bush Barracks and cover the road and rail routes to Kingstown, a port to which the British would almost certainly rush troops from England. Ceannt's 4th Battalion's occupation of the South Dublin Union was designed to threaten Richmond and Islandbridge Barracks. In addition it was intended to seize railway stations such as Kingsbridge, the terminus of the line from Cork and the south; Broadstone, from Athlone, Galway and the west; and Amiens Street which connected with Belfast and the north. It was also intended to take control of the capital's telegraph and telephone system.

That the Military Council did not plan to seize either Dublin Castle or Trinity College has caused endless debate. The Castle was the nerve centre of British rule in Ireland and Connolly had conducted Citizen Army manoeuvres in its vicinity during the winter of 1915/16. It is often argued that the Council missed a wonderful opportunity on the first morning of the Rising when the small number of guards was exposed. However, the Military Council was concerned with the problems not of seizure but of occupation, and decided, no doubt with some reluctance, that the complex of buildings was too extensive to be held by the men. Furthermore, the Castle contained a military hospital and protecting and feeding the sick and injured as well as guarding many prisoners would have over-stretched resources.[5] Trinity College was not seized, but there are indications that it was originally a target because it features on a list of strongholds to be occupied by de Valera's 3rd Battalion, only to be excised, suggesting a late abandonment.[6]

The Dublin Rising is often depicted as a siege in which encircled defenders endured as long as possible an onslaught by attackers who, after the initial surprise, always held the initiative. Yet enough is known of the Military Council's plans to indicate that its strategy was considerably more imaginative, aggressive and optimistic. It clearly hoped that the German navy would be able to prevent troop reinforcements arriving from Britain, having seen the consequences of submarine warfare after the sinking of the

Lusitania on 7 May 1915, off the coast of Ireland. The liner, which had been attacked by a U-boat, went down with the loss of over 1,000 lives, and the Military Council clearly envisaged similar attacks on British troop ships during the Rising. In April 1916 the Military Council was to demand the dispatch of a U-boat to Dublin Bay when the Rising began.[7] This submarine, which existed only in the Council's imagination, appears to have assumed an almost talismanic significance for its members. During Easter Week in the Post Office Pearse caused wonderment to some of the garrison by his constant assurances that the U-boat would soon appear. If the U-boat failed, then Volunteers would attack reinforcements when they disembarked, as de Valera's 3rd Battalion planned to do at the port of Kingstown. If the British garrison in Dublin could be isolated, then Volunteers in north County Dublin and surrounding counties might be able to exert pressure on it before being joined by mobile relief columns coming from the Rising in the West. In this scenario, then, the inner city cordon can be seen as a trap, designed to lure the British on until they were squeezed between the rebel strongholds in the city centre and the large numbers of provincial Volunteers on the outskirts exerting increasing pressure as they pushed forward to relieve the inner cordon. In that event the Rising was envisaged as ending with the capitulation of the British army leadership, not that of the Provisional Government.

As Plunkett had envisaged, the rising in the west was to be co-ordinated with that in Dublin and the Military Council had to hope that the German arms landing would incite a popular and convincing uprising in which the Irish Volunteers would be joined by large numbers of enthusiastic civilians. The German rejection of an expeditionary force vexed the Military Council, which was reluctant to abandon its dream of support from the best army in Europe. It tried, unsuccessfully, in April 1916 to bounce the Germans into supplying at least a token force. It told them that it required officers to accompany the arms shipment, anticipating that even a small number of experienced and superbly trained men would provide leadership in the west and give shape and direction to the rebellion there as well as electrifying the country as a whole.[8]

The western Rising was planned to erupt suddenly as Volunteers, triggered by the seizure of Dublin and the arrival of the arms ship at Fenit, surprised and overwhelmed police and soldiers in a pre-emptive strike.[9] As soon as the German vessel landed, news was to be transmitted to Tralee, where Austin Stack, the Kerry commandant, would mobilise his men, occupy the post office and take control of telephone and telegraphic communications. At the same time roadblocks would isolate the town from the outside world to prevent pro-British sympathisers alerting Cork and Limerick. Once Tralee was under full control he was to dispatch a goods train to Fenit to receive the German arms. Simultaneously other Volunteer units in places such as Listowel, Castleisland and Killarney would prevent British forces disrupting the Fenit landing by capturing police and troops in the open, isolating their barracks with sniper fire or destroying them with fire and explosives. If, as was likely, the British authorities in Cork and Limerick discovered that communications with Tralee had been severed and sent out reconnaissance units, the Volunteers in Cork and South Kerry were to intercept them on the main roads or sabotage the railway lines with explosives. The German weapons were for use by the Volunteers in Kerry, Cork, Limerick, Clare and Galway and were to be distributed quickly throughout the west. When the train carrying them from Fenit arrived at Tralee, some would be removed for the Cork and Kerry Volunteers, while the rest went to Limerick, then across the Shannon by boat and on by rail to Clare and Athenry in Galway. Once mobilised, the Volunteers in the western counties would eventually link up with each other to occupy a line running from the Shannon through Limerick and east Kerry to Macroom in County Cork.

Ulster was to play no part in the Rising because the Military Council feared a sectarian war in the province. Denis McCullough, the President of the Supreme Council of the

IRB, was to be told by Pearse and Connolly in March 1916 to assemble his men in Dungannon and march to join up with Liam Mellows and the Galway Volunteers. He was sceptical about the prospects of undertaking an exhausting journey of over 200 miles during which he was ordered not to fire a shot, even though the most direct route passed a strong British garrison in Enniskillen, County Fermanagh.[10]

The Military Council clearly hoped that if British forces were overwhelmed and the Provisional Government established effective control, then it could defeat any attempt to reconquer Ireland. Almost certainly, it would have revived Plunkett's offer to make Ireland a partner in the German war effort with its ports available for naval operations in the Atlantic and making the Irish Sea a new theatre of war, with a potentially crippling impact on Britain. If Ireland were able to hold out until the end of the war she would then be an independent nation, but if the Rising developed less favourably then the western Volunteers might at least be able to hold the line of the Shannon to receive the Provisional Government and those men who had broken out of Dublin. In those circumstances the joint force might be able to conduct a campaign of guerrilla warfare.

Both Connolly and the Military Council, of course, concealed the new situation from public knowledge, and Sean Fitzgibbon noticed at the next meeting of the Volunteer Executive that;

> Pearse, obviously in great stress of emotion, and speaking very tensely, said that he and MacDermott had induced Connolly to take no action without the aid of the Volunteers. I asked Pearse if he had given any promise or had pledged the Volunteers. Pearse said 'No.' His right knee kept quivering as he spoke. He kept raising his right foot slightly, tapping the ground with it, like a horse pawing as he answered my questions. He was lying, for at that time the date of the Rising had been decided upon.[11]

Hobson, for his part, didn't believe a word of the entire charade. During the next three months an increasingly desperate power struggle took place at the top of the Volunteers between him and the members of the Military Council. The battle was waged behind closed doors away from the gaze of the rank and file and the general public who had no inkling that serious policy differences existed within the leadership. Although Hobson had allies such as J.J. O'Connell, the Chief of Inspection, he often felt that he was carrying an intolerable burden. He was also frustrated by his inability to secure incontrovertible proof of the activities of his opponents who consistently outmanoeuvred the moderates by their unity of purpose, energy and complete unscrupulousness. Nor was it easy to obtain decisive action from MacNeill; it was often 'easier to convince [MacNeill] . . . that nothing could be done than it was to spur him into positive action'.[12] For example, in February 1916 MacNeill agreed to summon a special Volunteer convention to lay down policy but then changed his mind and opted for a private meeting with Pearse, Plunkett and MacDonagh who reacted with hurt innocence and gave him unqualified assurances about their loyalty. Their ability to subvert the Volunteers from within was greatly assisted by MacNeill's frequent absences from Headquarters where an overworked Hobson despaired of a regime of organisational indiscipline. When Hobson, in early April 1916, demanded that all important orders should be signed by MacNeill, Pearse and his associates simply voted for the motion and blithely continued as before.[13]

MacNeill, as Chief of Staff, displayed a remarkable capacity to ignore incriminating evidence. In late 1915 in Limerick he learnt, accidentally, that Pearse, on his own initiative, had issued important orders to Volunteer officers and had even instructed Michael Colivet, the Limerick commandant, to 'hold the line of the Shannon in the event of actual hostilities'.[14] MacNeill declined to investigate the matter further. When he was subsequently warned by an American correspondent of a planned Irish rising, he lamely told MacDermott and wrote about it in *Irish Volunteer* in the expectation that the publicity would frustrate any such venture.[15] This drift and indecisiveness at Volunteer Headquarters in the early months of 1916 suited the Military Council very well. So also did a developing anxiety, which it helped generate, that the British government intended to provoke and then disarm or suppress the Irish Volunteers. In the face of this atmosphere of crisis and apparent threat Volunteer unity became paramount. This, in turn, enabled the radicals to explain away any activities which looked suspiciously like preparations for a rebellion as purely precautionary and defensive measures to protect the organisation from attack. This indeed was invariably the line taken by Pearse when he was challenged at Executive meetings.[16]

The Military Council never doubted its moral right to deceive for the higher good of the nation Executive moderates, rank-and-file Volunteers and even members of the IRB. Nevertheless, it understood that future generations would debate the morality of manipulating into battle men who had not explicitly given their consent. It no doubt justified its behaviour by the impossibility of seeking open approval for rebellion. Also it believed that every Irish Volunteer by 1916 accepted that, in certain circumstances, he would engage in conflict with British forces and the overwhelming majority had come to accept its inevitability. In such circumstances it seemed to the Military Council that the issue of rebellion had been reduced to a matter of timing rather than principle between 'extremists' and 'moderates'. Furthermore, some moderates were in practice as radical as the extremists, including The O'Rahilly.[17] Michael O'Rahilly, universally known (at his insistence) as The O'Rahilly, had been born in 1875, the scion of a prosperous Kerry family. He had a peripatetic and varied past and at one stage had emigrated to America before returning to Ireland where he became involved in advanced nationalist circles which led to his becoming manager of the journal of the Gaelic League. He had something of a taste for the melodramatic but his open and ebullient personality appealed even to his political opponents who recognised his generosity of spirit, tenacious loyalty and absence of personal rancour. In August 1914 he had advocated seizing Dublin Castle, proclaiming Home Rule and inviting Redmond to become President of Ireland. Although The O'Rahilly refused to join the IRB, there was clearly no inflexible line separating him from Pearse, whom he in fact eventually joined in the GPO during the Rising. Similarly MacNeill, in the crucial days before the Rising, was to conclude a short-lived alliance with representatives of the Military Council and even after it broke down he was only just dissuaded from donning his Volunteer uniform and joining the rebels when the Rising began.

The Military Council went as far as it dared to psychologically condition the Volunteer rank and file to the inevitability of revolution by having Pearse give a series of brilliantly ambiguous speeches. For instance, in a lecture in February 1916 to a Dublin company, Pearse deftly walked a tightrope, hinting at possible eventualities while taking care not to alert the British authorities.[18] He galvanised his audience by openly advocating separatism and talking about 'being called into action', yet he also cautiously stressed that it would be wrong of him to tell Volunteers 'that they might soon be called into action'. His speech then 'succeeded in conveying the desired idea to those who were ready to be impressed by it but at the same time in minimising the full and immediate purport of his remarks to others'. By constant repetition, Pearse gradually effected an almost unconscious transformation in the outlook of many Volunteers away from a defensive cast of mind to an offensive one. One Volunteer officer recalled that 'At no time was it stated at any of our meetings that we were to engage in an insurrection, with or without assistance, but very definitely an atmosphere was cultivated which pointed towards the uprising'.[19] Another officer, Oscar Traynor, has described a meeting of Dublin Brigade officers shortly before the Rising at which the heightened sense of anticipation was almost tangible.

Patrick Pearse was wearing his greatcoat of volunteer green and a slouch hat when he entered the room. His brother helped him to take these off. Pearse then approached the head of the table and, after a short time, was introduced to the Volunteer officers who had already spoken. Patrick Pearse rose amidst dead silence, stared over the heads of the Volunteers assembled in the room, and paused for almost one minute before he spoke. The first words he uttered sent a thrill through all present. The words were somewhat as follows: 'I know that you have been preparing your bodies for the great struggle that lies before us, but have you also been preparing your souls?' These words made such a deep impression on all present that there was complete silence for a considerable period. Following this, Pearse went on to urge the Volunteers to do everything possible to prepare themselves for the great struggle ahead. Most of us left that meeting convinced that in a short time we would find ourselves in action.[20]

The Military Council also cunningly manipulated its opponents' self-deception and exploited the anxiety of the British government and the Executive moderates to cling to any hope that Ireland would remain peaceful and reasonably stable. As a result of this desperate optimism they failed to recognise the many small changes which had cumulatively altered the political situation in the country. Connolly encouraged his opponents' wishful thinking by his strategy of 'wolf, wolf, wolf'.[21] He had the Citizen Army conduct endless exercises in the vicinity of Dublin Castle and Wellington Barracks and even advertised them in advance on a blackboard outside Liberty Hall. Eventually the authorities became bored and lost interest. For his part, Pearse sought to lull the Irish administration into a false sense of security by toning down public displays of extremism by the Irish Volunteers. He proscribed the tricolour and insisted on a flag with a plain gold harp on a green background, a design which was identified with conservative nationalism.[22] He also arranged a brilliant deception of the ever-suspicious Hobson by encouraging Liam Mellows, an Irish Volunteer organiser, to pose as Hobson's eyes and ears in the provinces and an enthusiastic supporter of his gradualist policy. Whenever Mellows came to Volunteer Headquarters he cultivated Hobson who came to believe that he could trust Mellows to warn him of any dangerous developments outside the capital. Hobson never suspected until it was too late that he had been comprehensively duped and that Mellows had already been chosen by the Military Council to lead the Rising in Galway.[23]

By March 1916 the radicals had succeeded in depicting British policy towards the Irish Volunteers as aggressive and provocative. On the Executive moderates and extremists alike had become incensed by what appeared to be systematic harassment of the organisation. There was the arrest of Volunteers under the Defence of the Realm Act, constant police surveillance, closure of militant newspapers, imprisonment and deportation of organisers such as Mellows and pressure on employers not to recruit extremists. Tension was ratcheted up even further by a violent confrontation in the town of Tullamore, King's County on 20 March 1916. Fighting between pro- and anti-war nationalists ended with supporters of 'separation women' attacking the Irish Volunteer Hall in the town and, as the crowd stampeded up the stairs, a Volunteer, Peadar Bracken, fired over their heads.[24] When the police arrived and threatened to search for arms there was a scuffle in which Bracken fired at an inspector and wounded a sergeant in the ensuing mêlée before he fought his way down the stairs and escaped. Thirteen Volunteers were subsequently arrested and charged with attempted murder, though they were eventually released on a legal technicality.

The shots at Tullamore were, in a sense, the first shots of the Easter Rising. Although the affair had not been deliberately engineered, its timing and manner were wonderfully helpful to the Military Council, because outraged moderates on the Volunteer Executive now endorsed resistance measures. The Executive responded to Tullamore by declaring that government raids would be met by 'resistance and bloodshed' and MacNeill warned that Volunteers would 'defend our arms with our lives'. Events and propaganda had created a perception of a coherent and aggressive British policy which was completely at variance with reality. Augustine Birrell, Chief Secretary for Ireland, was a cultured and civilised politician who got on well with mainstream nationalist politicians, but his reputation for indolence was well deserved and he was frequently absent in London. The day-to-day administration of Ireland was the responsibility of his under-secretary, Sir Matthew Nathan. He was highly intelligent, hospitable, prodigiously hard-working, 'a model public official'.[25] But his sense of loyalty and obedience to his political masters made Nathan reluctant to pressurise Birrell whose mandate since August 1914 had been to keep Ireland quiescent while the British cabinet concentrated on winning the war. Accordingly both men's policy was simply to contain the Irish Volunteers. Even in that limited ambition they constantly discovered the narrow limits of their seemingly sweeping emergency powers. At a conference in Dublin Castle on 17 March 1916, for instance, Nathan, Major-General Sir Lovick Friend, the army GOC, Ivor Price, the British Intelligence Officer in Ireland, the Irish Attorney-General and police representatives examined proposals to frustrate the Volunteers.[26] They worked through a list of options but, because of political expediency or legal complexity, rejected internment, action against organising instructors, Tom Clarke's reincarceration under his old sentence and even the banning of night manoeuvres. After weighing 'the comparative disadvantages of a suppression of the movement with the risk of some bad collisions and of allowing it to continue and possibly grow stronger', Nathan was more impressed with 'the difficulties of the former course'; but he took comfort in his belief that the Irish Volunteers were still being restrained, though he was giving them 'a good deal of rope'.[27]

This complacency, which embraced most, though not all, of the British authorities in Ireland in the eighteen months before the Rising was reinforced by Redmond's advice to allow the Irish Volunteers to wither away. When Field-Marshal French, Commander of Home Forces, mentioned that information had been 'received that certain parts of Ireland are in a very disturbed way – an insurrection had even been suggested in the public press', Nathan replied, reassuringly, that, 'though the Irish Volunteer element has been active of late, especially in Dublin, I do not believe that its leaders mean insurrection or that the Volunteers have sufficient arms to make it formidable if the leaders do mean it. The bulk of the people are not disaffected.'[28] On 13 April an upbeat Nathan informed Birrell that 'Things are getting better for the moment. . . . We are at last getting some information as to what is going on here – for the first time since I have been in place.'[29]

The Inspector-General of the RIC, Sir Neville Chamberlain, did not share this optimism and his reports to Birrell and Nathan contained increasingly stark warnings about the Irish Volunteers. In February and March 1916 he asked 'whether this force, so hostile to British interests, can be permitted to increase its strength and remain any longer in possession of arms without grave danger to the State'.[30] He urged them to consider arresting the Volunteer leaders, who he said were 'in readiness for a German landing at an early date'. They were 'a pack of rebels who would revolt and proclaim their independence in the event of any favourable opportunity'. He went on to warn that;

If the speeches of Irish Volunteer leaders and articles in Sinn Fein journals have any meaning it must be that the force is being organised with a view to insurrection, and in the event of the enemy being able to effect a landing in Ireland the Volunteers could no doubt delay the dispatch of troops to the scene by blowing up the railways and bridges, provided the organisers were at liberty to plan and direct the operations.

Chamberlain's detectives had planted among the Irish Volunteers two spies, 'Granite' and 'Chalk', who provided mixed signals about the organisation's intentions. On 27 March 1916 Granite reported no present danger of a rising because 'Standing alone, they are not prepared for any prolonged encounter with the forces of the Crown and the majority of them are practically untrained'.[31] Instead, he believed they were concentrating on stockpiling explosives and this was 'the real danger' – apparently warning of a renewal of the dynamite campaign of the 1880s. More alarming, Chalk believed that 'the young men of the Irish Volunteers are very anxious to start "business" at once, and they are being backed up strongly by Connolly and the Citizen Army and things look as if they were [sic] coming to a crisis'. . . While 'The heads of the Irish Volunteers are against a "rising" at present . . . the rank and file say that if they wait until the war is over they will all be shot'.[32]

With exquisite guile the Military Council solved the problem of how to commence the Rising with the unopposed appearance of large numbers of Irish Volunteers on the streets of Dublin. The strategy was to present the organisation's Easter manoeuvres as purely training exercises which were announced publicly and well in advance on 8 April by Pearse in his capacity of Director of Organisation. He even had them approved by MacNeill and the entire Volunteer Executive. Similar exercises had taken place at the same time the previous year so those of 1916 could be presented convincingly as a routine operation. Also their stated purpose, 'to test mobilisation with equipment', was reassuringly anodyne. In addition, as masterly camouflage, each commander was ordered to submit to Pearse before 1 May, 'a detailed report upon the manoeuvres carried out by his unit', implying a peaceful exercise and a subsequent leisurely review by Headquarters Staff.

By the middle of April 1916, Hobson was convinced that the radicals were about to engineer a confrontation between the Volunteers and the government. Having failed to neutralise Pearse and his associates inside the organisation he decided on a new and risky tactic by going public with his concerns. At a Dublin concert on the evening of Palm Sunday, 16 April 1916, Hobson gave a coded warning about 'precipitate action which could ruin the Volunteers'. A *frisson* of concern glided around the auditorium and one of the audience noted:

> One could feel that he was treading on dangerous ground. There was a certain breathlessness in the hall. One could see glances passing between those who were probably aware of what decisions had already been taken. When it was all over there were groups talking earnestly, some denouncing him and others praising his speech. On the following days that speech was a general subject of conversation. Opinions differed, from those who thought that it was a timely word of caution, to those who thought that it was black treachery. It was quite clear that those who knew most about the plans regarded it as disastrous.[33]

Such a public revelation of the tensions between Hobson and the radicals was an extraordinarily risky action by a member of the IRB and the next day the Military Council decided to deal with him, but nearer the Rising.[34] Its meeting on Monday 17 April, however, was mostly devoted to approving the draft of the Proclamation of the Irish Republic which was to be announced on the first day of the Rising. It also ratified the Provisional Government, whose members would sign the Proclamation and who coincidentally were also the seven members of the Council. Finally, it approved the circulation of the so-called Castle Document, an exercise in disinformation apparently devised by Plunkett, which purported to reveal a British plan of mass arrests, including the entire Executive of the Irish Volunteers. This Castle Document was read out on Wednesday 19 April 1916 at a meeting of Dublin Corporation, which guaranteed widespread press coverage. It electrified the political atmosphere in the capital and created fears of an imminent crackdown by the authorities. Soon the headquarters of the Irish Volunteers resembled a fortress whose occupants were frantically preparing for an onslaught by enemy forces.

One Volunteer, Desmond Fitzgerald, records that when he visited Pearse he found;

what seemed to be an enormous amount of surgical dressings were brought into one of the offices, and members of the women's organisation were called in to arrange for the making of field dressings and this work was treated as of immediate urgency. Members of the inner circle came in and out, and when there they retired into a room to hold secret conferences. Bundles of a leaflet which purported to be a secret order of the British that had been decoded were brought in and were being sent through the country for distribution.[35]

MacNeill was completely hoodwinked and convened an emergency Executive meeting to respond to the apparent threat of hostilities. It declared a state of alert and warned the rank and file to be prepared to resist government suppression. This was a psychological readying and a most convenient smokescreen for the Military Council as it initiated the final stage of its own plans.

For many months the Council had guarded its secrets, but it always knew that eventually it would have to share them with senior officers of the Irish Volunteers and the Citizen Army. The Council had delayed this as long as possible to avoid a leak either to the Executive moderates or to the British authorities. Not until the evening of Spy Wednesday, 19 April, when public attention was distracted by the uproar over the Castle Document, did commandants learn that the Rising would commence on Easter Sunday, 23 April, at 6.30 p.m. in Dublin and at 7 p.m. in the provinces. At the same time individual Volunteers received instructions to carry out specific acts of sabotage. Some senior officers, including de Valera, were informed in coded messages from Pearse which were brought by couriers. Others were told in person, such as Diarmuid Lynch who learnt the news from Sean MacDermott over a lunch in a restaurant. Connolly, however, preferred to brief his Citizen Army commanders personally at Liberty Hall. There he detailed their roles, revealed the existence of the German arms shipment and warned them to maintain absolute secrecy until the following Sunday.[36] The circle of knowledge widened further as battalion commandants briefed their senior officers. De Valera met those of the 3rd Dublin Battalion on Good Friday evening, 21 April, and outlined the positions to be occupied at the start of the Rising and the stores which would be waiting for them. He also tightened security by assigning them bodyguards, armed Volunteers who were to accompany them night and day.[37]

Yet even now the British authorities did not make an intelligence breakthrough about the Military Council's plans. While it is true that those people who had been informed on Spy Wednesday had been carefully vetted and sworn to secrecy, even many ordinary Volunteers sensed that momentous events were imminent. It is amazing that a British intelligence system that had infiltrated and broken many previous Irish rebellions and whose legendary efficiency aroused paranoia among Irish revolutionaries, failed so dismally over such an extended period. Even after Spy Wednesday only one clue reached Dublin Castle before the morning of Easter Monday and it came from a most unlikely source – a member of the Military Council itself, Thomas MacDonagh.

MacDonagh was a poet and literary scholar who, in his posthumously published *Literature in Ireland*, had sought a distinctive Irish note in those before him who wrote in English. He was conscious of the profound change whereby, in relatively recent times, his nation had moved almost completely from its own language into another. While he normally wrote in English himself, it could be said that ultimately he took up arms for the spiritual liberation of a country becoming ever more deeply assimilated and anglicised. Like other poets in the Europe of his time, he could happily contemplate war for a just cause:

> . . . the joy that laughs and sings
> Where a foe must be withstood.

MacDonagh had been appointed to the Military Council in the second week of April 1916. On the face of it the expansion of its membership at such a late stage, when planning for a rising was virtually complete, is puzzling. It almost certainly derived from a concern to ensure that, while the irreconcilable Hobson had long been written off, MacNeill should not be alienated if humanly possible. It was desirable to keep some channel of communication open to the Chief of Staff in case last-minute problems emerged and MacDonagh's function was to act as a link to his colleague at University College, Dublin.[38] MacNeill himself recognised that the younger man was 'to some extent as an intermediary between that section [i.e., the IRB in the Volunteer Movement] and myself'.[39]

MacDonagh's friends knew this engaging, idealistic side of his personality but it was open to question whether MacDonagh was suitable for the role he was now undertaking. Joining the leadership of the Irish Volunteers at the very start, initially he was a protégé of MacNeill, but his involvement in public parades and manoeuvres gradually moved him in the direction of revolution. He rose to membership of the Volunteer Executive and joined the Headquarters Staff as Director of Training. In addition he became Commandant of the 2nd Dublin Battalion and eventually also Commandant of the entire Dublin Brigade. By early 1916 MacDonagh was aligned with the radicals with whom he had close personal connections: Plunkett was his best friend and Pearse had employed him to teach at St Enda's. MacDonagh certainly looked the part – tall, clean-cut and good-looking, with short curly hair – but he lacked the steely purpose of a natural revolutionary and was at heart an insecure, gloomy, solitary young man. His temperamental instability led to erratic and melodramatic behaviour. During a lecture in the spring of 1916 he startled students by producing a large revolver from his pocket, laying it on the desk and remarking, as if to himself, that 'Ireland can only win freedom by force'.[40] After he joined the Military Council, MacDonagh's brittle character and perpetual oscillation between euphoria and depression made him a loose cannon. Furthermore, by the middle of Holy Week he was in a heightened emotional state and speaking with a lack of caution which would have appalled someone like Clarke. The police spy, Chalk, reported that;

> Professor McDonagh on issuing the Orders on Wednesday night last said: 'We are not going out on Friday, but we are going out on Sunday. Boys, some of us may never come back – Mobilization orders to be issued in due course.'[41]

The exact circumstances were not described, but on Wednesday 19 April, as noted, the Military Council revealed its plans to senior commandants and if MacDonagh, as seems probable, spoke to Volunteers who were not absolutely trustworthy then it was a remarkable indiscretion on his part. Fortunately for the Military Council his words did not alert the Irish Administration. Chalk's report of 22 April lacked explicit detail and it was still working its way through the bureaucracy when the Rising began. Nevertheless, MacDonagh's behaviour was sufficiently reckless to make one wonder what might have happened had he been a member of the Military Council from its inception. Chalk's report was a solitary glimmer of light in the black hole that was British intelligence in Ireland in 1916. It is difficult to disagree with Leon O'Broin's assessment that;

> Of all the division in the Volunteer Executive, of all the moves and countermanoeuvres, the Government knew absolutely nothing and this is all the more extraordinary because so many people, including some on the fringe of things, knew that a revolt was due to take place. . . . The British intelligence system in Ireland had failed hopelessly.[42]

However, while the government was ignorant of the imminent danger, the Executive moderates in the Volunteers at last learnt of the Military Council's intentions. The leak, ironically, was the responsibility of the Council itself. It had decided to risk involving in its plans J.J. O'Connell, the Chief of Inspection, and Sean Fitzgibbon, the Director of

Recruiting, both moderates and allies of MacNeill and Hobson. For the Military Council to take these men, even partially, into its confidence seems inexplicable, but it wanted their services because O'Connell had the best military mind in the Volunteers and Fitzgibbon had successfully organised the Kilcoole gun-running in August 1914. In addition, it suited the Council to have both men out of the capital in the days before the insurrection, especially since that would increase MacNeill's isolation and remove Fitzgibbon from his post as vice-commandant of de Valera's 3rd Battalion. And the deception was skilfully done. Fitzgibbon recalled that;

On Saturday before Palm Sunday, Kent [i.e. Ceannt] called on me as I was having breakfast. He was an official in the City Treasurer's Office. He said he had taken a day off and would walk in with me. If a man was asked to do a job in the Volunteers he invariably agreed. Kent asked me if I would go down the country to handle a job. I agreed and asked what it was. He said it was to land guns from Germany in Limerick and Kerry. I had landed guns successfully at Kilcoole, the week after the Howth gun-running. He wheeled his bicycle and we walked in to work. On the way I asked, 'Does MacNeill know?' 'No,' replied Kent, 'but he will be told by Pearse tomorrow. You are to go to Pearse in St Enda's tomorrow night and he will give you funds.'

Late on Sunday night I went to St Enda's and well remember the dark walk up to the house – a horrible place. I saw Pearse and said to him, 'Have you told MacNeill?' 'Yes,' replied Pearse. 'He fully agrees.' 'Without any *arrière pensée*,' asked I. 'Without any *arrière pensée*,' replied Pearse. This statement was a lie.[43]

The mendacity and skill of the exercise were impressive. Fitzgibbon was given only a certain amount of information – that an arms shipment would arrive in the west of Ireland. Fitzgibbon had no objection to that since he had already helped organise one such operation. What he was not told was that it was an integral part of a Rising that was to coincide with the landing. O'Connell, for his part, was ordered to lead the Volunteers in south-east Leinster, allegedly with MacNeill's authority. The Military Council had taken an audacious gamble, but in the frenzied atmosphere of the Castle Document affair and MacNeill's bellicose response, Pearse's assurances to the two men had considerable credibility. The members of the Military Council were gamblers; the gun-running was a gamble and so, of course, was the Rising itself. Their gambles had paid off so often that one final deception must have seemed well worth the risk. And it almost succeeded, because Fitzgibbon headed west to liaise with the commandants in Kerry and Limerick.

O'Connell, however, was dubious and decided to verify the information with Hobson at Volunteer Headquarters on Thursday 20 April.[44] When he arrived at ten o'clock in the evening his news confirmed Hobson's own suspicions. At an earlier IRB meeting one member had revealed to Hobson details of instructions which he had received to sabotage a railway line on Easter Sunday.[45] At last, very late in the day, Hobson had found his smoking gun and he was determined to act while there was still time. He and O'Connell drove out to Rathfarnham and at 11 p.m. they managed to bring MacNeill to the door in his pyjamas. When they told him what they knew, MacNeill immediately grasped the outlines of an insurrection. The group then went to confront Pearse after midnight in a 'long and stormy interview'[46] at St Enda's during which Pearse nonchalantly admitted the truth and dismissed MacNeill's warning that he would do anything he could to prevent a Rising, short of informing the government. Everything was in place, Pearse told them; it was time for a fight that would take place on Easter Sunday and he advised MacNeill to reconcile himself to that inescapable fact. MacNeill became increasingly incensed by Pearse's attitude and told him that his dishonesty would be responsible for any catastrophe that befell the Irish Volunteers. But he was airily brushed aside by Pearse who indicated that the IRB had been using him ever since the creation of the Irish Volunteers and it was now, in effect, dispensing with his services, like an aged retainer being told that he was surplus to requirements. Hobson's incandescent interventions were also rebuffed by Pearse, who radiated indifference and condescension amidst all the acrimony and seemed like a man who had risen far beyond their timid and petty considerations.

The group now returned to MacNeill's house having had its worst fears confirmed. The three men were also very conscious of how little time was left to prevent the Rising – only until Sunday's manoeuvres. O'Connell was sent on the early train to Cork on Friday 21 April to demobilise the Volunteers in Munster. Hobson went to Headquarters to draw up cancellation orders for the Easter Sunday exercises, but also started a bonfire of incriminating documents in case the government learnt of the recent developments. Meanwhile, Pearse had reconsidered MacNeill's threats and along with MacDermott and MacDonagh cycled out to Rathfarnham early on Friday morning to continue discussions with the Chief of Staff. It was now clear to them that MacNeill could do immense damage to their plans and they brought something with which to change his mind – his own words. According to Sean Fitzgibbon:

> At the end of March 1916 a conference on policy took place at MacNeill's house with people of Headquarters Staff present. Some one of the war party asked MacNeill, 'Would you fight if you got a large supply of arms?' He at once replied, 'Yes.'[47]

A casual inquiry, or a trap set by men who knew that such a large supply of arms would soon be on its way? Whatever the correct answer to this question, MacNeill's reply was now to prove very useful when they arrived at his house at 8 a.m. MacNeill later recalled:

> I was awakened and told that Sean MacDermott was there to see me. I sent word to him to come up to the bedroom; he came immediately, and I sat up in bed talking to him. He disclosed to me for the first time that a ship with arms

from Germany was expected at that very time. It will be remembered that in a previous conversation I had said to him that the importation of arms for the Volunteers was the one thing of importance. This part of the scheme coincided with my view. It was of course evident to me that in the circumstances a landing of arms from Germany meant an immediate challenge to the English government and I said to MacDermott, 'Very well, if that is the state of the case, I'm in it with you.'[48]

With MacNeill apparently mollified and co-operative, the Military Council appeared to have regained control of events although Hobson still remained to be dealt with. MacDermott sent dispatches to Munster ordering commandants to proceed with the Rising and ignore any instructions brought by O'Connell. MacNeill now had to deal with Hobson; he knew Hobson would never emulate his own political somersault. He sent a message telling him to put the countermanding orders on hold since he now feared the Rising had to take place, though he failed to mention his meeting with Pearse, MacDermott and MacDonagh. This was the moment when Hobson finally gave up on MacNeill and accepted that all the months of imploring, chivvying and cajoling had been in vain. Exhausted and depressed, he acquiesced and waited for a personal explanation which never came.[49] Even so, the Military Council was determined to isolate the notoriously irresolute MacNeill from Hobson's influence and the latter's arrest was discreetly executed by armed men on Friday evening when Hobson arrived for a hastily arranged IRB meeting in Phibsborough. Hobson had been rightly suspicious of the sudden invitation, but went along from a mixture of intellectual curiosity and a desire to escape the unbearable strains of recent days which had left him an angry, defeated and frightened man.

I felt that I had done all I could to keep the Volunteers on the course which I believed essential for their success and that there was nothing further I could do. My principal feeling was one of relief. I had been working under great pressure for a long time and I was very tired. Now events were out of my hand.[50]

Provided he kept the location secret, Hobson was allowed to tell MacNeill of his arrest and, with no real conviction, that it was up to him to prevent the insurrection. Whether the message was delivered is unclear, but Hobson's detention did quickly become known to his frantic fiancée, who feared he would be shot, to The O'Rahilly and also to MacNeill, who told Fitzgibbon, 'I've been lied to and misled.' 'They've kidnapped Hobson,' said MacNeill on Good Friday. 'They may kidnap you,' said someone. 'If they do they'll get this,' said MacNeill, taking a revolver from his pocket.[51] However, his dissatisfaction did not extend to breaking off his recently concluded pact with MacDermott and Pearse and when the Military Council convened on Friday afternoon at Houlihan's shop in Amiens Street for a final overview session everything appeared to be back on track. Afterwards the leaders dispersed, as arranged, to safe locations around the city. Some, like Pearse and MacDermott, stayed in private houses, Plunkett went to the Metropole Hotel and Connolly remained in his fortress at Liberty Hall. Clarke did not leave his wife until Saturday morning, when he transferred to Fleming's Hotel in Gardiner Place, after warning her to preserve the appearance of normality by opening the shop as usual. All were now guarded permanently by squads of young Volunteers who had orders to resist to the death, a security measure initiated by Clarke when he learnt that he was under intensified surveillance by detectives who had occupied premises opposite his shop.[52]

The members of the Military Council probably hoped to recuperate from the hectic strains of recent days. But any problems up till then were trivial compared to those which erupted on Saturday and Sunday 22 and 23 April, and brought their enterprise to the brink of collapse. The crisis was initiated by events in Kerry, the destination of the German arms shipment. This assistance, which had been rejected by the Germans when Plunkett was in Berlin in the spring of 1915, had at last become reality. Their scepticism had been overcome by the Military Council's decision to set Easter 1916 as the date of the Rising. This decision was transmitted to Berlin by the German Embassy in America which also dispatched a submission from Devoy projecting an Irish Rising which would be successful if it received 25,000 to 50,000 rifles, some machine guns and field artillery as well as some senior officers. He predicted that such a rebellion would tie down 500,000 English troops. Devoy's proposal was backed by Captain Nadolny of the German General Staff who, on 22 February 1916, inquired of the Admiralty Staff 'whether the Irish revolutionary movement might be given assistance through means other than the delivery of weapons supported by U-boats'.[53] The key to overcoming the resistance of the naval arm to assisting the Irish revolutionaries was the agreement of the Supreme Army Command to a consignment of weapons to Ireland. Once that had been accomplished, the feasibility of an arms mission to Ireland was discussed on 17 March 1916 at a meeting of representatives from the Admiralty Staff, the North Sea Section, the Naval High Command and the Imperial Navy Office. They decided that any shipment should consist of one vessel which would transport to the west of Ireland 20,000 captured Russian rifles, one million rounds of ammunition and explosives to be used for sabotage. The meeting concluded that;

The enterprise does not seem to be without hope. Even if the English succeeded in suppressing the rebellion quickly, and censorship will try to prevent this becoming known, then we can still count on a strong moral effect. The fact that such a widespread rebellion could have occurred in Ireland, that in spite of the blockade the German Navy could have supplied the necessary means, must also make a lasting impression on Ireland's allies. All participants in the discussion share the view that the attempt must be made to fulfil the urgent wish of the General Staff, which for its part hopes that a substantial force will be tied up in Ireland, far from the European mainland.[54]

In this final phase of preparations for the arms shipment, Casement had been sidelined. His relations with the Germans were appalling and he only learnt of the imminent Rising and the limited German assistance via Robert Monteith, an Irish Volunteer organiser who had made his own way to Germany to join up with the Irish Brigade. Casement was enraged and filled with almost paranoid suspicions that his hosts had induced a hopeless rebellion in order to divest themselves of their Irish commitments. He had 'always been opposed to any attempted revolt in Ireland unless backed by strong military help'[55] and was now convinced that he had been duped by a country whose rulers had only been using Ireland for their own selfish ends rather than because of an idealistic dedication to a small nation's freedom. Casement lamented, 'Oh Ireland, why did I ever trust in such a government . . . they have no sense of honour, chivalry or generosity. They are cads. This is why they are hated by the world and why England will surely beat them.'[56] He now decided to return home in order to prevent a rising that he had never believed should take place without a realistic prospect of victory and that meant massive German assistance in terms of personnel and material. He concealed his intentions from the Germans by a pretence that he needed to go back to Ireland to prepare for the arrival of the arms shipment, but his request for a submarine to transport him was initially rejected. Later the Germans reversed their decision and told Casement that a submarine would be ready on 12 April for him and two members of the Irish Brigade – Monteith and Julian Beverley. This was three days after the arms shipment had departed German waters in a vessel called the *Aud*. The submarine in which Casement's party travelled was U-20 which had sunk the *Lusitania* but it quickly developed mechanical failure. The three men then transferred to U-19 which departed on 15 April and five days later passed the mouth of the Shannon, 5 miles off the coast.

At 12.10 a.m. on Good Friday, 21 April, the submarine reached the prearranged rendezvous point with the *Aud* but there was no sign of the arms ship, the anticipated pilot boat from Fenit or a reception party of Irish Volunteers. The *Aud* had reached the Kerry coast safely but its captain had weighed anchor several miles away from and out of sight of the submarine. The Volunteers had not expected either vessel before 23 April and had made no contingency plans for an earlier arrival. A few hours after arrival the three men clambered into a small boat and made their way to the coast. Casement and Beverley were soon taken prisoner by the local police though Monteith successfully evaded capture. The arms ship remained free for only a little while longer.

The *Aud*'s story is often presented as one which might have altered the course of the Rising, with endless speculation as to what might have happened if its cargo had been landed and had activated a major insurrection in the west. However, it is now clear that though the operation suffered bad luck, it was also affected by a lack of realism and inadequate planning.[57] It was further handicapped by a British military intelligence system which almost certainly sealed the vessel's fate even before it left Germany. As a result, the *Aud*'s chances of reaching Fenit, certainly of discharging its cargo, were close to non-existent. While the Military Council had been amazingly successful within Ireland in concealing its activities, the German connection had been discovered by British naval intelligence, which had broken German codes and knew in March 1916 of the arms shipment and an Irish rising. This knowledge appears to have been kept to a small military circle which included Kitchener, the Secretary of State for War, Field Marshal French, Commander of British Home Forces, and Major-General Friend, the Irish GOC. It extended also to Admiral Bayly and General Stafford who were both based at Queenstown in County Cork and who had direct responsibility for preventing any arms importation. Surprisingly and disastrously, neither Birrell nor Nathan appears to have been kept informed, possibly because the source of the information was deemed too sensitive to share with politicians.

In Queenstown, Bayly was waiting for the *Aud* with trawlers, a light cruiser and a destroyer patrolling the coast from the Aran Islands to Tralee. Stafford had been told on 16 April that the ship had left Germany disguised as a tramp steamer and he in turn had alerted the police in Limerick, Clare and Kerry.[58] He had also arranged for troops to picket main roads and move at short notice if the ship arrived and Irish Volunteers were mobilised to protect it. Between them Bayly and Stafford had ensured that either the ship would not reach Fenit or, if it did, the army would prevent a landing. The element of surprise on which the Military Council counted had already disappeared. The German arms were being transported in a 1,200-ton ship which had been disguised in the port of Lubeck as a Norwegian merchantman, the *Aud*, whose innocent voyage from Scandinavia to the Mediterranean was to take it along the west coast of Ireland. In reality its captain, Karl Spindler, was carrying a secret cargo of 20,000 captured Russian rifles. The *Aud* embarked on 9 April and followed a route between Norway and the British blockade line about 60 miles east of Shetland. By Thursday 20 April, as it approached the Kerry coast, the false cargo which concealed the arms and ammunition had been thrown overboard and by noon, 45 miles from Fenit, Spindler's crew was preparing for a successful end to its perilous voyage.

In fact the operation had been flawed from its inception, bedevilled by the profoundly unsatisfactory methods used by the Military Council and the German government to conduct business ever since August 1914. Direct contact by wireless had been non-existent and face-to-face meetings very rare indeed. Instead, both sides had relied almost entirely on American proxies, German diplomats and representatives of the Clan, and inevitably misunderstandings had occurred. The arms agreement provided for the vessel's arrival at Fenit between 20 and 23 April, a sensible flexibility in view of the problems of navigating in a war zone. But late in the day the Military Council had attempted, ineptly, to impose unilateral changes on the incredulous Germans who were informed that the Rising was now fixed for the evening of Easter Sunday, 23 April. Consequently, the Fenit arms should not arrive later than dawn the following day, German officers should be sent and a German submarine should be assigned to Dublin Bay once the Rising had begun.[59] The German navy refused the request for a submarine and the general staff rejected the dispatch of officers to lead an Irish Volunteer force of which they knew little or nothing. However, this entirely predictable response was never conveyed to the Military Council, which assumed that the mere act of dispatching its requirements guaranteed German compliance.

The Military Council then compounded its problems by attempting to change the date of the arms vessel's arrival from the period between 20 and 23 April. These dates had their origin in the period when the Rising was planned to commence on Friday 21 April. The change to Sunday 23 April meant that if the Germans stuck to the original schedule, it was possible that the vessel might arrive days before the Rising had commenced and alert the British to the insurrection. The Council then decided on a closer alignment of the dates of the ship's arrival and the start of the Rising. It sent Plunkett's sister, Philomena, to New York to have the Clan tell the Germans that the ship now had no leeway; it had to enter Fenit on the evening of Sunday 23 April to coincide with the start of the Rising.[60] The message was absurd and demonstrated a complete ignorance of the problems of naval communications. It required clockwork timing over large distances and took no account of the factors that could delay a ship navigating in a war zone or the weather complications that it might encounter. Not that any of this ultimately mattered, because the *Aud* had already left Germany and was not equipped with a wireless and the changes demanded by the Military Council could not have been communicated to the vessel.

What happened once Spindler approached Fenit is open to different interpretations. On one analysis he had been incredibly lucky to evade the trap which Bayly had set for him. But John de Courcy Ireland has argued persuasively that British naval intelligence had tracked him all the way and that a hole had been deliberately created in Bayly's screen to enable Spindler to reach land. The British intention was to set a trap which would draw into the open all those who had been involved in the smuggling operation and once they had been apprehended in a huge dragnet the pro-German sympathies and treasonous nature of the Irish Volunteers would be proven beyond doubt.

However, on the night of Thursday 20 April, when the *Aud* approached Fenit there was no reception party waiting for Spindler. The Military Council had assumed that he would not arrive until the following Sunday and no arrangements had been made in the event that the vessel might arrive early. It had been assumed, wrongly, that the Germans would have communicated the change of date to Spindler. Furthermore, MacDermott had vetoed a local proposal to have armed Volunteers in the area because he feared such activity would risk alerting the British. A local Volunteer, Mortimer O'Leary, who had been selected as the *Aud*'s pilot, had been told on Holy Thursday that a ship would be arriving at Fenit on Easter Sunday night.[61] However, he had also been told that it would be about 150 tons – a fraction of the *Aud*'s size – and because of this discrepancy he was not unduly concerned when he saw a large vessel in Tralee Bay that night. He records:

My sister, Hannagh O'Leary . . . took over the watch at midnight and I went to bed. About 2 a.m. she came and woke me and said the ship was burning a green light from the bridge. I jumped up at once and went to the window. The green light was not visible. I asked my sister if she was sure the light was green, not blue; she said it was green. A blue light was the ordinary signal for a pilot. At that time I knew nothing of a pre-arranged signal with a green light. . . . I watched the boat until dawn on Good Friday morning but did not see her make any signal during that period.

By Friday morning Spindler, after a dangerous and exhausting voyage, had become increasingly nervous about the failure to make any contact with his Irish counterparts. In John de Courcy Ireland's interpretation, he was under permanent surveillance by the British who were waiting for the landing operation to commence. But soon after 1 p.m. Spindler spotted HMS *Lord Hennage*, an armed trawler which had been summoned south from Galway, and he weighed anchor. This forced the British to spring their trap and during the afternoon, as Spindler steered a course into the Atlantic, where he hoped to commence raiding merchant ships, the *Aud* was shadowed by the *Hennage*. This continued until around 6 p.m. when the *Aud* was cornered by two British sloops and Spindler was soon heading in the direction of Queenstown accompanied by the three British vessels. On Saturday morning within sight of Queenstown he scuttled his vessel, which sank at 9.40 a.m.

The news of Casement's arrest had spread and the local Volunteer leadership dispatched a messenger to Dublin. He arrived at dawn on Saturday and informed Connolly, who convened the Military Council at 9.30 a.m. Every member attended except MacDermott, who had gone to see MacNeill to ensure his continued loyalty and, undoubtedly, to ferret out how much he was aware of events in Kerry. At this stage MacNeill knew nothing and MacDermott was delighted when he said he was now ready to fight and typed up for nationwide circulation MacNeill's order confirming the Rising. Later that morning Plunkett also came to Rathfarnham and MacNeill expressed his great relief that everything was finally settled, though he also expressed pessimism over the Rising's outcome. MacNeill hedged when Plunkett asked him if he was prepared to sign a Proclamation and the matter was dropped. This wariness saved MacNeill's life, because if his name had appeared along with the other seven signatories it would have committed him completely and guaranteed a firing squad at the end.

By early Saturday afternoon the Military Council had

learnt of the calamitous loss of the *Aud* which was to transform the Rising from a planned national insurrection into a predominantly Dublin affair. Even so, when Seamus Gubbins, an emissary from Limerick, arrived at the safe house in Hardwicke Street, he found MacDermott exuding a surface bonhomie which belied the enormous stress he was under. MacDermott was adamant that there was no going back now and with scant regard for the truth reassured Gubbins that more arms shipments were on their way from Germany.[62] However, a few hours later, when another Limerick Volunteer arrived with a suggestion that the Rising should be postponed, MacDermott's composure disintegrated completely. He was physically sick and shouted that delay was out of the question and that the Volunteers would fight even if they had only sticks and stones.[63]

At the same time MacNeill was visited by The O'Rahilly and Sean Fitzgibbon. Fitzgibbon had hurried back from Kerry, where he had been preparing for the arrival of the *Aud* – a mission undertaken, he believed, on MacNeill's behalf. He had left that morning after learning of Casement's capture and the sinking of the *Aud* and when he arrived back in Dublin he went immediately to The O'Rahilly's house.

He opened the door and the first thing he said was 'I've got to tell you that there's to be an insurrection in Dublin tomorrow.' He then told me that Hobson had been captured by the war party. 'Pearse speaks as if he thought he was the Almighty,' said O'Rahilly. He drove us to MacNeill's. MacNeill was at home. I asked him had Pearse been with him on Palm Sunday. He said, 'No.' I asked him had he [MacNeill] been a party to sending me to land arms. He said, 'No.' He was sitting in front of the fire as he spoke, holding in his hand an old Franco-Prussian war bayonet which he used as a poker. He jabbed it into the fire and said: 'Meet me at Seamus O'Kelly's house at 8 o'clock tonight, and I'll stop all this damned nonsense.' It was the first time I saw MacNeill really annoyed.[64]

MacNeill was indeed appalled at the full extent to which he had been deceived and manipulated, especially when Fitzgibbon told him that the Castle Document was a complete fabrication by Plunkett. He now felt morally justified in backing out and his resolve would have been strengthened by news that the *Aud* had sunk. At this crucial moment The O'Rahilly and Fitzgibbon had replaced Hobson as his emotional crutch and he embraced their assurances that the Rising still could and should be prevented. Once again he drew up countermanding orders which were to be issued after he had convened an evening meeting of available members of the Executive and Headquarters staff at the home of Dr Seamus O'Kelly, a friend who lived on Rathgar Road. The O'Rahilly and Fitzgibbon, meanwhile, went to tackle Pearse at St Enda's:

> Pearse met us on the steps. 'It's terrible, all this deception,' said he. 'It was all done for the best.' When he spoke he was perfectly cool, as if what he had done was of no importance. Nevertheless he gave me the feeling that he was sorry he had deceived me. 'Who ever comes to kidnap me, Pearse, will have to be first on the draw,' said O'Rahilly before we left.[65]

Later that night the two men went to the meeting at O'Kelly's home which was also attended, at different times, by MacDermott and Plunkett. The latter were furious that, despite all their efforts to by-pass, isolate, overawe and finally co-opt him, MacNeill was now threatening to slip the leash. After arguing against any climbdown, they left. They claimed that they needed to consult others but did not return, probably because they hoped that it was too late for MacNeill to back out or to do anything effective to frustrate their plans. But for once MacNeill had roused himself to decisive action and the crisis meeting at O'Kelly's house was not convened to debate or advise him but to hear what he intended to do. MacNeill now dispatched messengers such as The O'Rahilly throughout the country with countermanding orders for the

Sunday manoeuvres. Furthermore, MacNeill went to the offices of the *Sunday Independent*, the only Sunday newspaper published in Dublin, with a message for Irish Volunteers which was to be inserted in the next edition. It read:

Owing to the very critical situation, all orders given to the Irish Volunteers for tomorrow Easter Sunday are hereby rescinded and no parades, marches or other movements of Irish Volunteers will take place. Each individual Volunteer will obey this order strictly in every particular.

The order was skilfully drafted because while many of the rank and file would be puzzled by the reference to 'the very critical situation' the mention of 'other movements' was a coded message to those in the know that he was aware of the real purpose of the mobilisation and wanted nothing to do with it.

As the most influential Executive member available to MacNeill, The O'Rahilly carried a more explicit message to Volunteers in the west that the Chief of Staff had been completely deceived and all secret orders issued by Pearse and his associates had been cancelled.[66] The O'Rahilly had been suffering from a heavy cold and felt unable to drive through the night; nor did he want to be seen behind the wheel of his car since he had been served with an order excluding him from the south-west. Instead, he slipped into the back of a closed taxi cab at 10.00 p.m. on Saturday and set off into the darkness, a motorised Paul Revere in reverse gear, travelling with the news that the British were not coming after all and that the revolution had been cancelled. Four hours later he arrived in Limerick city and after a brief rest toured the counties of Limerick, Kerry, Cork and Tipperary. In each place he showed MacNeill's instruction to Volunteer officers and explained its background to these very confused men who had assumed that the Volunteer Executive was a united body. It was this mistaken belief and the associated inclination to obey orders from their superior officers which explains events that are otherwise surreal. James Ryan, for instance, had been dispatched to Cork on Good Friday by Sean MacDermott to deliver final instructions about the Rising in Munster to Commandant MacCurtain. Nevertheless, on his return to Dublin the following day he was reprogrammed by MacNeill, whose orders he unhesitatingly obeyed.

About ten o'clock that night I was summoned to a house in Rathgar Road, where I learned a number of members of the Volunteer Executive were in conference. After some time the door of the meeting opened and Eoin MacNeill appeared. He asked me if I had carried a dispatch the previous day and if I knew where to find the leaders there. I answered yes to both questions. Good! Well, I was now to go to Cork again, this time by motor car. It was urgent and I must deliver these dispatches as soon as possible. In his hand he held five or six slips, each in identical terms and signed by him. . . . They were orders cancelling the Sunday manoeuvres. . . . So now I gathered the Rising was not to be.[67]

MacNeill's change of mind sent a collective tremor reverberating through the Military Council, and MacDermott in Hardwicke Street was 'shocked beyond measure'[68] when MacDonagh told him at midnight. Shortly afterwards, Pearse and Plunkett arrived but it proved impossible to convene a full meeting because messengers who were sent to alert Clarke, Connolly and Ceannt could not secure admission. If they had been successful it might just have been possible to dispatch couriers to frustrate MacNeill's countermand and proceed with the Rising as originally planned. Instead it was decided, at about 2 a.m., to meet later that Sunday morning at Liberty Hall, though even now MacDonagh and Plunkett made a final attempt to swing MacNeill back into line. However, they found that O'Kelly's house was in darkness and MacNeill had gone. Later that morning MacDonagh did finally manage to get into Liberty Hall, where he found Connolly seething with anger, having already learnt from people in the building that county commandants were receiving countermanding orders. Connolly dispatched runners and by 7 a.m. Clarke and Ceannt had learnt of the scheduled crisis meeting of the Military Council.[69]

The Council's members slept little and MacNeill's countermand made disagreeable early morning reading that Sunday. To the incredulity of these experienced conspirators MacNeill had actually outmanoeuvred them, going over their heads to the Volunteer rank and file and bypassing the regular channels which they had long ago subverted. Over eighteen months of planning now appeared to be going down the drain and they reacted with all the outrage of professional gamblers who had been trumped by a rank amateur. MacDermott was virtually demented, weeping with frustration at MacNeill's 'betrayal' and ripping his pyjama top to pieces.[70] When he arrived at Liberty Hall turbulent scenes were occurring in the crowded passageways as emotional men shouted denunciations of the countermand, Sean Connolly, the Citizen Army commandant, wept and Henry Walpole, James Connolly's bodyguard, volunteered to shoot MacNeill.[71]

Some members of the Military Council had a breakfast of bacon and eggs cooked by Connolly's daughter, Nora, before the crucial session began at 9 a.m. Over the next four hours they wrestled with the central problem of how to overcome MacNeill's opposition. Abandonment or even lengthy postponement of the Rising was never considered because British suppression of the Irish Volunteers was now considered both inevitable and imminent. Even if, by some chance, government action against the organisation were avoided then MacNeill would almost certainly purge them and remove them from the power base which had made a rebellion feasible in the first place. In a mood of now-or-never all their discussions were focused on steadying their followers and re-scheduling the arrangements for the Rising. The only dissenter to this strategy was Tom Clarke who was terrified that his life's work was about to fizzle out. He argued fiercely in favour of sticking to the original plan, insisting that once the Rising began Volunteers would assume either that MacNeill's cancellation was a hoax or that it had been overtaken by events. But to Clarke's immense shock and distress at this critical juncture he stood alone, as men whom he had groomed and promoted rejected his advice. He was deserted even by Sean MacDermott who was not prepared to display blind loyalty when he agreed with the others that it was vital to buy time to examine the fall-out from MacNeill's countermand and devise methods by which it could be overcome. It was finally agreed that the start of the Rising should be postponed until noon the following day, Easter Monday, 24 April.

The Military Council now turned to finalising arrangements for the announcement of an Irish Republic. This would be done through a Proclamation which would be read out on Easter Monday at the Post Office in O'Connell Street. Most members of the Military Council would be located there, operating in a dual capacity as the Provisional Government and the Headquarters Staff of the Army of the Republic. The Proclamation was to be read by the President of the Provisional Government of the Irish Republic. This post was apparently offered first to Clarke in recognition of his services to and sacrifices for the republican cause as well as the respect in which he was held by his colleagues on the Military Council. But Clarke had spent a lifetime shunning the limelight and he declined the offer, though his pre-eminence was recognised by the fact that his signature had pride of place on the Proclamation. The post went instead to Pearse who had both the presence and the oratorical ability to make the historic address. Pearse was also appointed Commandant-General of the Army of the Irish Republic which would be created from the amalgamation of the Irish Volunteers and the Irish Citizen Army along with the auxiliary organisations, the Cumann na mBan and the Fianna. Connolly was appointed Vice-President and Commandant-General of the Dublin Division of the army.

Having reordered its timetable the Military Council now had to reassert its control over people and events for just another twenty-four hours. It was particularly concerned about the danger that local firebrands would ignore MacNeill's countermand and initiate premature local revolts. One such outbreak almost occurred in Dublin's 3rd Battalion, where de Valera initially instructed his officers to proceed as originally planned but then was persuaded to reverse himself and issue his own countermand order.[72] Even then one of his company officers decided to carry on and only backed down at 2.30 p.m. on Sunday when he received MacDonagh's official demobilisation orders.[73] Captain Simon Donnelly wrote:

> On receipt of Command. MacDonagh's dispatch steps had to be taken immediately to see that no men would concentrate at the point of mobilisation. If this had happened it was possible that some of G.H.Q. plans might have been divulged to the enemy as there was a chance that some of the later Volunteers who found their way to the mobilisation point might have been ambushed by enemy forces. However scouts were sent out and the demobilisation was very satisfactory.[74]

Pearse also publicly sent messages to local commandants confirming MacNeill's cancellation, though behind this smokescreen he immediately began secretly drafting, for later distribution, fresh orders which confirmed that the Rising would take place.[75]

After the Military Council's meeting word filtered through Liberty Hall that, while nothing would happen that day, hope was alive for the next day. At 4.00 p.m. the Citizen Army set out on a final, short practice route march which was virtually a dress-rehearsal for Easter Monday. Connolly led his men straight to Stephen's Green and on their return journey they passed so close to Dublin Castle that its guards hurriedly closed the gates. Afterwards, in front of Liberty Hall, Connolly gave what proved to be his last public speech in which he told his followers that they were not to lay down their arms until they had struck a blow for Ireland.[76] Afterward, the officers and section leaders received their final instructions and arrangements were made to reassemble next morning. Most Citizen Army members remained in the building overnight, but some were granted passes to return home. A heavy guard was maintained throughout that night both inside Liberty Hall and in the street outside.

The final loose end, a major one, with which the Military Council had to deal was MacNeill who had somehow learnt of its emergency meeting at Liberty Hall. MacNeill met provincial Volunteers who were in Dublin for a Gaelic Athletic Association convention and he sent a group of them to plead for an abandonment of the Rising.[77] After all that had happened the Military Council would probably have liked nothing better than to reacquaint MacNeill with Hobson. But the arrest and disappearance of the President of the Irish Volunteers was too dangerous a step, even for a group of such angry and desperate men who now felt themselves standing with their backs to the wall. Instead they arranged one final, exquisite deception designed to convince him that his actions and his appeal had won them over. In the afternoon Pearse sent MacNeill a letter which, while tinged with condescension towards his Chief of Staff, seemed to represent unconditional surrender.

> Commandant MacDonagh is to call on you this afternoon. He countermanded the Dublin parade today with my authority. I confirmed your countermand to the country as the leading men would not have obeyed it without my confirmation.[78]

When MacDonagh arrived, he knew that this would almost certainly be his last meeting with MacNeill and that his difficult assignment was to perpetuate Pearse's fraudulent assurances. Nevertheless he was able to conceal whatever qualms he might have felt and the deception of MacNeill was achieved with practised ease.

Sean Fitzgibbon, who was also present, recorded that;

> He, MacNeill and I walked around the grounds and talked. He was most friendly and assured us that everything was off. He was quite optimistic and said that all that had been intended was to occupy certain buildings as barracks and that the British would then come to terms with us.[79]

MacNeill did not disappoint the Military Council and his unquestioning acceptance of MacDonagh's bland assurances reveals both his political naivety and his bottomless gullibility. He had completely misread the character and determination of men whose submission he now assumed he had achieved. Even after the Rising, when he was fighting for his life, he was unable to come to terms with the fact that he had been comprehensively duped and instead blamed the government for his predicament. As he told his court-martial:

> I believe that the decision [to suppress the Volunteers] was the cause of the insurrection on Easter Monday. I have no doubt of it. Nothing else could explain it. The men who told me that I had compelled them to act as I wished them to act [i.e. to agree to countermand the rising] – those men I knew well. I will answer for them. They were men of honour. They were truthful and honourable men. They gave me that assurance on the evening of Easter Sunday. I have no reason to doubt it.[80]

It was as late as 1917, on his release from prison, before he knew of the existence of the Military Council, which had been completely concealed from him.

The O'Rahilly also believed that the Rising had been definitively cancelled. In the early evening he arrived back in Dublin from the west, exhausted but happy that he had, in the nick of time, delivered MacNeill's countermand. Even a chance encounter with Desmond Fitzgerald, a Volunteer friend, could not dampen his elation: 'I told him what I had heard at Liberty Hall, from which I gathered that the Rising was not abandoned, but he did not take it seriously. He felt that a disaster had been effectively prevented.'[81] Believing that all was now well with the world, MacNeill retired to bed. Across the city couriers were assembling at the Gaelic League offices in North Frederick Street under the protection of an armed bodyguard. At 8 p.m. Pearse arrived with dispatches which the couriers were to take to local Volunteer commandants throughout the country. The messages read: 'We start operations at noon today, Monday. Carry out your instructions. P.H. Pearse.' Some of the messengers left Dublin that night, others not till the Monday morning. Like MacNeill, Pearse now went to bed, but with totally different expectations of what the next day would bring. In churches across the city men who knew what was intended were attending mass to 'clean the slate'.

The day before, Saturday morning, 22 April, the Irish authorities were confident that the danger had passed. Friend, the Irish GOC, who knew much more than Birrell or Nathan, had gone to London on leave as soon as he knew of the *Aud*'s capture. To his immense embarrassment and to the detriment of his army career he was still there on Easter Monday when the Rising broke out. Also in London, to the ruination of his political career, was Chief Secretary Birrell who had attended cabinet and decided to remain until after Easter. The governance of Ireland then had been left in the hands of Under-Secretary Nathan who, on Saturday, was in an upbeat mood. He wrote to Birrell about the arrests in Kerry and the *Aud*'s sinking, and said that 'The Irish Volunteers are to have a "mobilisation" and march out from Dublin tomorrow but I see no indications of a "rising".'[82] Next day, before he had learnt of the MacNeill cancellation, Birrell replied cheerily in reference to Casement's capture, 'All this (particularly if RC is <u>the Prisoner</u>) is most encouraging. The march of the Irish Volunteers will not be conducted in high spirits.'[83]

On Saturday evening, Nathan met the Viceroy, Lord Wimborne, to discuss a response to recent events.[84] They were convinced that the government now held the initiative because of an erroneous belief that Casement was the prime mover in the conspiracy. Nor could they imagine that, after the loss of the *Aud*, any other plotters would persist with plans for a rising. Wimborne argued for the arrest and internment of Volunteer leaders, but Nathan did not commit himself at that stage. Early next morning Nathan was faced with conflicting signals. On the one hand he learnt that one of Casement's companions had spoken of a rising planned for that day, but on the other that MacNeill's countermand seemed to indicate that the crisis was subsiding with the Irish

Volunteers apparently in disarray and retreat. When he was informed that a large quantity of stolen explosives had been smuggled into Liberty Hall, Nathan proposed a raid on the building that night. But Wimborne pressed for more radical action such as the arrest of the Volunteer leaders and to this Nathan finally gave his support, provided Birrell approved. A telegram to this effect was sent to the Chief Secretary in London but did not reach Birrell until the following day. At 6 p.m. Nathan collected Colonel H.V. Cowan and Major O. Lewis, the most senior of Friend's staff officers, and they accompanied him to a meeting with Wimborne.[85] Cowan urged caution over the proposed raid on Liberty Hall which he thought might provoke strong resistance. To allow Cowan time to consult army and police officers about the wisdom of the operation another conference was fixed for 10 p.m at the Vice-regal Lodge. At this meeting, which was also attended by Edgeworth-Johnstone, Chief Commissioner of the Dublin Metropolitan Police, Price, the Military Intelligence officer, and Cowan, Wimborne supported Cowan's reservations about a raid on Liberty Hall and pressed forcefully for the immediate arrest of the Volunteer and Citizen Army leaders. But Nathan demurred because he wanted any arrests to be legally watertight and he had still not received Birrell's approval for such a dramatic step. By the time the meeting broke up at 11.30 p.m. it had been decided to await the Chief Secretary's verdict and in the meantime to prepare lists of those to be apprehended in any government swoop. The strains of recent days had told on Nathan and one close friend noted how quiet, grave and preoccupied he had become and how hard it was to raise his spirits.[86] On this Sunday, Percy Bick, a soldier based at Richmond Barracks, wrote one of the last letters to leave Dublin before the Rising. He wrote that 'Things are pretty quiet in spite of periodical alarms' but he warned that if the Volunteers 'start any trouble, it will be a serious matter and there will be bloodshed. I do not understand why they are allowed to go on spreading sedition. They should have been suppressed at their inception or at any rate at the outbreak of the war.'[87]

3

THE FIRST MORNING
OF THE RISING AND
ST STEPHEN'S GREEN

Easter Monday morning, 24 April, was a brilliantly sunny day as a sombre Nathan walked from his residence in Phoenix Park to the nearby Vice-regal Lodge for a brief meeting with Wimborne.[1] Afterwards he arrived at an almost deserted Dublin Castle at about 10.00 a.m. and was joined an hour later by Ivor Price, the Military Intelligence Officer. They discussed how to implement the previous night's proposals if Birrell authorised action against the Irish Volunteers and, indeed, the Chief Secretary's agreement to the arrest and internment of the organisation's leaders was already on its way from London. Nathan was still intent on avoiding a precipitate response. He opposed army and police raids at a time when the city was thronged with holidaymakers and he believed that time was on his side now that a rising had apparently been averted.

But from the early hours Irish Volunteers and members of the Citizen Army had been making their way to Liberty Hall, as had all but one of the Military Council. Tom Clarke, who had spent a last night with his wife Kathleen, left home after breakfast, accompanied by two armed bodyguards. Sean MacDermott also arrived on foot. Pearse and his brother cycled while Plunkett, who had recently had a serious operation on his glandular neck and was terminally ill, was

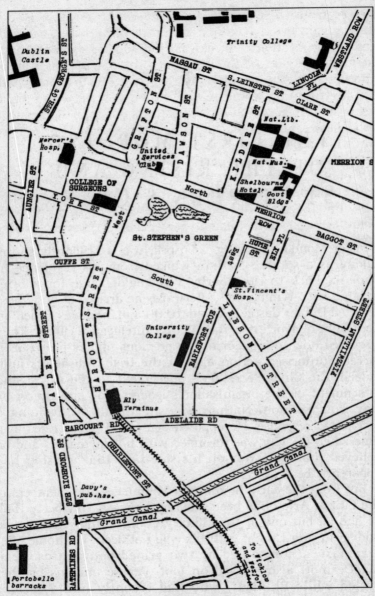

St Stephen's Green

driven from his apartment in the Metropole Hotel. MacDonagh was a battalion commander and designated to lead the occupation of Jacob's Factory, but he came to spend the final hours before the Rising with his fellow conspirators. Another battalion commander, Eamonn Ceannt, had spent Sunday night at home in the suburb of Dolphin's Barn composing mobilisation orders. He now sat at a table with a pistol before him, adding up the numbers who had turned out, while around him couriers came and went.[2]

Unlike the silent docks nearby, Liberty Hall was very busy on this public holiday. Much of the Citizen Army in their dark green uniforms had stayed overnight in the building but some who had been given passes were now returning. Irish Volunteer cyclists in their grey-green uniform were leaving with dispatches every couple of minutes while in one room a stockpile of bombs was being assembled from a large quantity of stolen gelignite. As a precaution against a last-minute government swoop, Connolly sent scouts to watch army barracks to verify that no unusual troop movements were taking place.[3] Inside Liberty Hall the first copies of the Proclamation were coming off the presses and one was proudly displayed by Connolly. But soon afterwards he sombrely presented a pistol to his daughter Nora who was returning to the family home in Belfast. Connolly then embraced her emotionally and gave her a salute.[4] At 11 a.m. The O'Rahilly suddenly appeared in a car laden with rifles. He had been tipped off that the Rising was definitely on and reasoned that 'If men are determined to have a Rising, nothing will stop them'. He was more hurt than angry at the deception perpetrated on him by the Military Council and with typical generosity had decided to join his erstwhile adversaries. They greeted him warmly but his resentful sister Anna did not reciprocate; she pinched Pearse on the arm and hissed, 'This is all your fault.' The O'Rahilly, however, was already warming to the task ahead and remarked to the flamboyant Citizen Army officer, Countess Markievicz, 'It is madness, but it is glorious madness.' He did not expect the Rising to last very long and was anxious to be present from start to finish.[5]

At 11.45 a.m. Bugler William Oman of the Citizen Army sounded the fall-in at Beresford Place outside Liberty Hall and as those inside surged out each man was handed two grenades encased in condensed milk cans.[6] James Connolly issued final orders to his officers and then shook hands with Sean Connolly who was to lead the Citizen Army occupation of the City Hall. James Connolly shouted, 'Good luck, Sean! We won't meet again'. and the column of thirty set off, with a number of women who had slipped in at the rear at the last moment.[7] As they crossed Butt Bridge and marched along Tara Street, College Street and Dame Street mocking cries of 'pop guns' came from civilians. The original plan was to occupy locations and attempt to prevent troop movements in and out of Dublin Castle and the Ship Street Barracks.[8] Among the buildings to be seized were the Evening Mail office, the Corporation rates building overlooking the main gate of Dublin Castle and a public house opposite the lower Castle Gate. Men were also to be placed on a viaduct overlooking the upper and lower gates of Ship Street Barracks. The main body under the command of Captain Sean Connolly was to occupy the City Hall where he was employed in the motor tax office and so was very familiar with the building and the surrounding area.

As Sean Connolly's force approached the City Hall at noon, Constable O'Brien who was on duty went to close the main gate of Dublin Castle but as he did so he was hit by bullets fired by Sean Connolly. An armed sentry nearby made as if to return fire but thought better of it and made for the guardroom. He was pursued by a squad of the Citizen Army who overpowered and disarmed the soldiers on duty in the guardroom and tied them up with their own puttees. Inside, Nathan and Price had been joined in their deliberations by A.H. Norway, head of the Irish Post Office, to discuss restricting the use to military personnel of telephone and telegraph services throughout much of southern Ireland. The three men were deep in conversation when suddenly shots were fired just below their first-floor window. Price later told the Commission of Inquiry into the Rising:

I was talking to Sir Matthew Nathan in his office not twenty-five yards from the gate when the firing commenced. I said 'They have commenced' and ran to see a policeman lying in a pool of blood and half a dozen Volunteers in green coats dashing about. I fired a few shots from a revolver and then they broke their way into a house on the opposite side. They could have done it as easily as possible [i.e. seized the Castle]. Twenty-five determined men could have done it. I think there was only a corporal's guard there at the time.[9]

Nathan instantly concluded that it was a rebel attack and alerted the small military garrison in Ship Street Barracks, helped close the gates at both the upper and lower Castle yards, and broke open the armoury to arm the constables on duty. At 12.30 p.m. military headquarters in Phoenix Park was informed of the rebellion and the Vice-regal Lodge was alerted. Nathan also dispatched a telegraph to Birrell in London. Meanwhile Connolly's force had occupied the City Hall. It was closed for the Easter holiday but Connolly's men were able to enter Exchange Court, a small *cul-de-sac* on the east side, and then go through some rooms into a basement and on to the ground floor of the City Hall. Connolly himself entered through a door leading from Castle Street but was killed within hours by a British sniper as he stood on the City Hall roof. His garrison remained in the building until Easter Wednesday when most members successfully evacuated in the face of an imminent British assault.

Another person who had left Liberty Hall before noon was Patrick Daly who had been designated by the Military Council to blow up the Magazine Fort in Phoenix Park.[10] Daly had arrived with his team shortly before 11 a.m and Connolly had stressed to him the crucial importance of entering the Fort at noon precisely. Daly and his men then cycled in twos and threes along the quays towards Phoenix Park and during the journey he collected a football in a shop. At the park they strolled towards the gate posing as a football team and throwing the ball from one to another. When Daly distracted the sentry by inquiring about the location of the soccer pitch, one of the Volunteers, Paddy Boland, jumped on the soldier and disarmed him. Daly and two other Volunteers then dashed through the archway to the guard room where the soldiers inside raised their hands and were made to face the wall. Daly then kicked in the glass door of a cabinet and grabbed the bundle of keys. But as he left another sentry, who had fired on Volunteer Gerry Holohan, was shot in the leg. By now Paddy Boland had wrestled his prisoner into the guard room where armed Volunteers were also guarding a Mrs Playfair, the wife of the commandant, and her two sons who occupied a house beside the guardroom.

Daly now made his way to the ammunition, paraffin, oil and tool stores and after securing entry dispatched another Volunteer with the keys to the guncotton store. Daly and his team now commenced smashing the ammunition store with sledgehammers and hatchets while paraffin oil drums were wheeled in to saturate the premises. After tin-can bombs had been distributed among the ammunition boxes most of the team cleared out while Daly and others lit the fuses and set light to the paraffin-covered boxes. When they departed they left the door half open to let in air and locked the outer iron gate while retaining the key. Then, to his chagrin, Daly learnt that the man he had sent to the guncotton store had been unable to get in and that part of the operation was reluctantly abandoned. He now went to the guard room and released Mrs Playfair and her two boys and warned them to leave the Fort immediately as it was about to blow up. He also freed the soldiers but warned them that they would be shot if they went in the direction of Islandbridge Barracks. His team then left the park and scattered, as previously arranged, and made off individually, every man for himself. Everyone got away safely and it was only the next day that he heard one of the Playfair boys had been shot dead at Islandbridge while running to an officer's house to tell of the attack. He was shot just as he reached the door.

ST STEPHEN'S GREEN AND THE COLLEGE OF SURGEONS

St Stephen's Green was the oldest and largest of Dublin's residential squares. It comprised 27 acres of open space and was over a quarter of a mile long on its north and south sides. Prominent at its centre was an equestrian statue of George II. With the passing of time, hotels, clubs, institutions and churches came to mingle with or replace its impressive eighteenth-century town-houses, and in 1880 it was opened as a public park with bandstand and ornamental lake. On the west side stood the substantial classical edifice of the Royal College of Surgeons in Ireland. Appropriately, close by was the birthplace of Robert Emmet whose reported words from the dock in 1803 had rung down through generations of Irish nationalists: 'When my country shall be free to take its place among the nations of the world, then let my epitaph be written.' The insurgents who occupied the Green and seized the College of Surgeons on Easter Monday, 1916, were responding to the same cause.

The occupiers came mostly from the Citizen Army and were commanded by Michael Mallin. He was a former silk weaver, British soldier and trade union organiser who had risen through the ranks to become Connolly's Chief of Staff. Nevertheless, the relationship between the two men was more formal than friendly and Mallin, who suffered from periodic recurrences of malaria which made him appear tipsy, had once been extremely hurt when his superior accused him of being drunk.[11] Despite his rudimentary education and rather dour personality, Mallin was regarded within the Citizen Army as capable and experienced, though during the Rising he also revealed himself as strategically unimaginative and organisationally deficient. He set off for Stephen's Green with only thirty-six men and supporting women's units, though the original plan had stipulated more than twice that number. Some of the company wore uniforms and carried rifles and shotguns, but others were distinguishable only by a bandolier. One member, Margaret Skinnider, had cycled ahead to scout for British troop movements, but to her relief and surprise she encountered only one bored policeman at the Green.[12] The column marched easily up Grafton Street in a mood of uncompromising determination and one member, Frank Robbins, recalls that at the top a young police recruit, 'annoyed by our singing of "The Peeler and the Goat", foolishly lost his temper and intervened. He was lucky not to lose his life for our lads were certainly not in the mood for interference from that quarter.'[13] At the Green Mallin's company closed the gates, posted guards and began expelling the public from the park. It teemed with mothers enjoying the sunny bank holiday weather with their children; some indignantly threatened to summon the police. To accelerate their departure the insurgents fired shots into the ground and even at one civilian who tried to resist. During the take-over an unarmed police constable, Michael Lahiff of College Street Station, who was on duty at Stephen's Green, was shot dead soon after noon for 'refusing to leave his post'.[14]

Soon afterwards, Mallin acquired a second in command with the arrival of Countess Markievicz, a colourful figure in green puttees, tunic, riding breeches, and slouch hat with ostrich feather; she invariably carried a weapon. Despite her foreign name, this exotic creature had actually been born in 1868 as Constance Gore-Booth. Her family estate was in Sligo and for the first forty years her lifestyle and attitudes were those of her class, including her presentation as a debutante at court. She later married a Pole, Count Casimir Markievicz, but as the marriage disintegrated Constance's energies became immersed in politics. By now the rebellious streak in her nature had set her on a course that entailed the shedding of almost every aspect of her former life except for her courtesy title and a refined upper-class accent. She became a nationalist, republican, socialist, revolutionary and finally a Roman Catholic, and was heavily involved in a plethora of militant organisations. In 1910 she founded the Fianna, a republican boy scouts group which was designed to give young men military training. She also became president of Cumann na mBan for republican women and by 1915 she was also helping to organise and train the Citizen

Army. Beneath her aristocratic hauteur, her undoubted theatricality and her considerable capacity for embroidering her own exploits, she possessed courage and flair, and certainly craved military action. When Markievicz arrived at the Green carrying a rifle she had just delivered medical supplies to Sean Connolly's Citizen Army garrison at the City Hall. Although she had originally been earmarked to liaise between Stephen's Green and the GPO, Mallin told her that he needed her to stay because he was short of followers. He now promoted her to be his second in command. A kindred spirit to Markievicz at the Green was Margaret Skinnider. She was a Scot of Irish descent who had developed powerful nationalist sympathies and had been summoned to Dublin by the countess a few days before the Rising.[15]

The activities around the Green had begun to attract the attention of civilians such as Douglas Hyde, the founder of the Gaelic League who later became the first president of Ireland. He had just cycled from his home nearby to purchase cigarettes and had initially dismissed the gunfire as car tyres being punctured, but his unease deepened when he saw gates closed at the Green and gardeners leaving early. He believed that Mallin's force might have been clearing the park for a military review until a vicious, shabbily dressed Fianna shouted an angry warning and pointed a gun directly at him. The youth was watched admiringly by a young girl with a bandolier whom Hyde thought 'looked as if she would have liked to kill' him. Eventually he departed, still mystified and unaware that he had witnessed the first minutes of an Irish revolution.[16]

Throughout Monday afternoon Mallin's company laboured to make the park secure with armed men placed at the railings or in the shrubbery along the entire north side; bystanders were moved on to prevent crowds gathering. A park kiosk was improvised as Mallin's headquarters, trenches were dug at the four main entrances and women established a kitchen and a first aid centre in a summer-house. The gates were blocked by park-benches, wheel-barrows, lorries, cabs and motor cars, and barricades were also constructed in adjacent streets. Shotguns, grenades and ammunition were distributed to the garrison from a handcart. During Monday the garrison was augmented by as many as twenty people who were anxious to participate in the Rising. They included Nora O'Daly, a member of Cumann na mBan who had drifted into the park and accepted Markievicz's invitation to stay, and Liam Ó Briain, a lecturer at the National University, who had been on his way to join his Volunteer company but accepted a challenge to 'come in and fight for Ireland'.[17] Although he was handed a shotgun, he spent the first afternoon digging trenches and dealing with frequent inquiries from mothers searching for their missing sons and daughters. Mallin and Markievicz, meanwhile, circulated around the Green with reassurances that everything was going well. Once the Green had been secured Mallin concentrated on establishing and fortifying outposts in houses and business premises in surrounding streets and manning them with sharp-shooters. Because of the public holiday, many of these buildings were unoccupied, including the Bank of Ireland branch in Stephen's Green East and the Winter Palace, a public house on the west side of the park. Most important, though, was the Royal College of Surgeons, a large classical edifice facing the park, and Mallin's immediate purpose in ordering its occupation in mid-afternoon was to seize its OTC rifles. Frank Robbins who led the raiding party just managed to prevent the caretaker slamming the doors shut and 'the gentle persuasion of a revolver at his throat managed the rest'.[18] While the caretaker and his family were locked into a room the insurgents searched the building but, infuriatingly, could not locate the weapons. Even so, Mallin ordered Robbins to hold the building and take up positions on the roof, where they ran up a tricolour.

A critical and surprising tactical blunder was that no attempt was made at any stage to occupy Dublin's premier hotel, the Shelbourne, a relatively high building with a view over most of the park. Before the Rising, Connolly had identified it as a potential garrison stocked with beds, food and barricading materials. The hotel was full to capacity with Irish and English racegoers, wartime officers on leave (many with their wives and families) and theatrical types. On Easter Monday most residents had left for Fairyhouse race-course, leaving a head porter who peeked out nervously at rebels constructing a barricade across the street, just outside the main entrance.[19] Mallin was anxious to provide additional defensive cover against an expected British assault and similar obstructions were going up on every side of the Green. During the afternoon Markievicz was in command on the west side as cars and wagons were commandeered. Sometimes the seizures were conducted with impressive diplomacy. On one occasion, the occupants of a motor were saluted by three armed and apologetic insurgents who requested them to step on to the sidewalk while the chauffeur was directed to drive to the barricade.[20] At other times less courtesy was displayed. From the roof of the College of Surgeons, Frank Robbins witnessed clashes between rebels and recalcitrant bystanders. The latter, 'presumably wives or relatives of Irishmen in the British army, were bent on making trouble for our men by prevailing on motorists and drivers of other vehicles to go by alternative routes. They also obstructed comrades who were detaining the vehicles. They lived in the vicinity and were aggressively pro-British.'[21] Furthermore, not every motorist was meekly compliant: one driver who attempted to recover his car from a barricade at the Shelbourne was warned off at gunpoint. Uncooperative tram drivers were also at risk, like the man who immobilised his vehicle by throwing away the control handle and was chased and fired on.[22] Robbins related another incident:

The driver proved to be an enterprising chap. He whipped off the control handle of the tram and changed to the other end, while the conductor reversed the trolley. It was the quickest bit of work on the part of two tramway employees I have ever seen. Detecting their intention, I as the officer in charge, gave the order to fire. We planned to frighten the tram crew, but not to kill and our widely aimed volley had no effect whatever. The driver and his mate were not to be frightened and undauntedly stuck to their post and drove the tram out of danger. We were furious at the loss of our potential barricade but we could not but admire the crew's adroit manoeuvre and their coolness in danger.[23]

Confrontations were made more probable by poor barricade construction. This tempted motorists to drive around or even through the barriers and Mallin's garrison does not appear to have received clear instructions as to how to respond. Furthermore, many rebels were young, inexperienced and undisciplined, like the boy of about twelve seen 'strutting the centre of the road with a large revolver in his fist'.[24] Inevitably civilians were seriously injured or killed, such as Michael Cavanagh, an elderly guest who was shot dead in front of the Shelbourne on Easter Monday afternoon. Although his vehicle of theatrical effects had been commandeered, he had been given permission to remove some luggage. But when he gripped the shafts to remove the lorry armed men appeared at the railings and told him to desist. Cavanagh appears not to have grasped the danger he was in or else he possessed a commendable but excessive dedication to the maxim that the show must go on because he ignored the increasingly vehement threats. When three warning shots were fired he dropped the shafts but then made the lethal mistake of approaching a group of ten armed men with a raised finger. A voice shouted repeatedly, 'Go and put back that lorry or you are a dead man. Go before I count four. One, two, three, four. . . .' Cavanagh was then fatally wounded in the forehead by rifle fire. A watching crowd was ordered to leave but several angry men carried Cavanagh over to the kerb and shouted, 'We'll be back for you, damn you.'[25] A St John's Ambulance Volunteer witness wrote of the effect on the crowd of bystanders. 'Women began to shriek and cry and kneel down to pray in the street, and the *vivandieres* with the rebels began crying and swearing and wringing their hands to be told by the rebels to go home and several of them were sent off.'[26]

Cavanagh was the most notorious and widely reported civilian casualty at the Green, but there were many other cases, included those reported to the police by the Shelbourne's assistant manager. There was the guest who was wounded as he went through the revolving door, another shot in the leg as he sat down for lunch and a third who was hit in the jaw by a bullet fired through the window of the large sitting room. In response the hotel's outer doors were soon closed and the guests transferred from the resplendent dining room at the front to a writing room at the rear. During the first day of the Rising the Stephen's Green Area acquired some of the characteristics of a battlefield, though most casualties were non-combatants. Mercer's Hospital nearby recorded 16 dead and 278 injured civilians during Easter Week, as well as 4 dead and 5 wounded soldiers. Hospital capacity in the area was quickly overwhelmed, prompting the St John Ambulance organisation to provide temporary casualty services at converted premises in Merrion Square and Harcourt Street.[27]

Prisoners were also taken at the Green on Easter Monday, including up to seven British servicemen. Most were speedily released because of a shortage of guards and suitable accommodation. A small number of civilians were imprisoned for much longer. These included Lawrence Kettle, chief of the Dublin Corporation Electricity Department, whose car had been seized at a barricade on Monday afternoon. Kettle was detained until the surrender as a suspected British informer because he had been seen entering a military barracks, though he had probably only been visiting his brother, an officer in an Irish regiment. Others were detained, first in the park bandstand and later in a greenhouse adjacent to the College of Surgeons. One policeman, Sergeant Hughes, was kept overnight on Easter Monday but shot after he was told he could leave, and lay unattended on the pavement for almost five hours before he was carried to hospital by some students. A British Red Cross worker was also detained because his medical skills were useful to the insurgents.[28]

On Monday afternoon a Citizen Army company of twenty-five men led by Captain Richard McCormick arrived at the

Green. Earlier it had not stopped at the park but continued on to attempt to establish a small number of strategically valuable outposts a short distance further south. These were intended to prevent, or at least delay, a British military advance north towards the Green or central Dublin. When McCormick's men entered Harcourt Street railway station they ordered the public to assemble on the platform. The situation then threatened to get out of hand when women and children among the day-trippers panicked and a group of men who had locked themselves inside the ticket office were forced out by a revolver shot through the door. Suddenly Robbins, who appears to have spent Monday permanently on the brink of shooting someone, saw;

a uniformed staff officer of the British army, obviously on holiday, looking out from the restaurant. My first impulse was to shoot. But seeing no visible side arms I called on him to surrender. He very foolishly ran behind the door banging it shut. The upper portion of the door was smoked glass. This helped to save his life, for on reaching the door I kicked it open, called on him again to surrender, while at the same time watching his figure as he flattened himself against the wall behind the door. He had no fight left. When he surrendered I handed him over to Captain McCormick.[29]

In another incident at the station an old man who intervened to dissuade an Irish soldier from discarding his uniform and joining the rebels, had his top hat blown off by rifle fire.[30] Then an attempt to block the line by overturning an engine had to be abandoned when the signalman blocked the points and there was neither time nor manpower to deal with the situation. Instead, some men scattered along the line and briefly took up position on two railway bridges from which they could attack any British troops advancing across Portobello Bridge. Another group of seven men had been sent to occupy Davy's, a public house on the corner of Richmond Street and Charlemont Mall, about half a mile from the Green. These premises were strategically important because they overlooked the entrance to Portobello Barracks as well as commanding both Portobello Bridge and the Rathmines Road. British troops from the barracks immediately launched a strong counter-attack by wheeling out a Maxim machine gun and after less than an hour they had forced the garrison in Davy's to retreat through a rear entrance.[31]

By the time McCormick returned to the Green Mallin's meagre force was well entrenched. Outlying streets were covered and the British army was still unable to mount an effective counter-attack. Later a squad containing Liam Ó Briain occupied and barricaded houses in Leeson Street and posted snipers on the roofs to guard the bridge over the Grand Canal. Well before dusk the crowds of curious onlookers had melted away and the traffic around the Green and adjacent thoroughfares had all but disappeared. Towards evening, Mallin went among the garrison with more assurances that the Rising was going well and the whole country had risen in support. Soon after midnight, in reply to an urgent request for reinforcements, he received twenty men sent by MacDonagh from Jacob's Factory. There was little shelter in the Green for Mallin's garrison on that first cold, damp night as it bedded down. Most lay on the open ground through the constant rain though some women bedded down in the summer-house and Markievicz retired to the car of Dr Lynn, the Citizen Army's medical director. Despite the discomfort, morale was high, no doubt in part because of Mallin's upbeat military assessments and also a young comedienne who had others laughing loudly at her comical complaints about British snipers disturbing her sleep. Skinnider recalled: 'We were all happy that night as we camped. . . . Despite the handicaps we were under with the lack of men, almost everything was going our way.'[32] But outside observers were much less sanguine and Douglas Hyde was convinced that the park would be evacuated during the hours of darkness. To him it seemed impossible to defend for any length of time; the trenches were too vulnerable to machine-gun and rifle fire from the tops of surrounding houses.[33]

Even so, most of the hours until dawn passed fairly uneventfully. There was some shooting at what might have been British troop movements, but the most serious incident occurred just before 2 a.m. when a column of shadowy figures were spotted moving along Leeson Street. The park sentries were tempted to fire, but could not be certain that the targets were not in fact fellow rebels – a wise restraint because they were indeed thirty Volunteers from the 4th Battalion on a midnight march to the GPO. These men, unknowingly, were doubly lucky because they also just missed decimation by British machine gunners who arrived soon afterwards to occupy the Shelbourne and the Hibernian United Services Club in Stephen's Green North. The troops had made their way from Dublin Castle to Trinity College and then moved as a 'noiseless column' along Kildare Street, undetected by the garrison in the Green, barely 30 yards away.[34] They had then crept into the hotel from the rear and posted guards at the entrance and snipers at every window. They also hauled a machine gun up to the roof and from there and the United Services Club they dominated the Green.

Mallin does not seem to have anticipated the threat on his northern flank and within an hour British fire-power from these newly acquired positions had ruthlessly exposed his vulnerability. At a stroke the viability of the Green's occupation was undermined and an entire day's effort nullified. From 4.00 a.m. on Easter Tuesday British guns raked the whole area along with supporting fire from troops stationed behind sandbags in Merrion Row. The women in the park's summer-house scattered for shelter behind an embankment while men in the trenches fled into the shrubbery. Although casualties occurred throughout the Green, a disproportionate number of the garrison had been concentrated opposite the Shelbourne.[35] Later that morning a civilian spectator, James Stephens, recorded the grim consequences of an uneven battle:

At the corner of Merrion Row a horse was lying in the footpath surrounded by blood. He bore two bullet wounds, but the blood came from his throat which had been cut. Inside the Green railings, four bodies could be seen lying in the ground. They were dead Volunteers. The rain was now falling down persistently. . . . A Volunteer stretched out on a seat just within the railings. He was not dead for now and again his hand moved in a feeble gesture for aid; his hand was completely red with blood. He was just a limp mass upon which the rain beat pitilessly and he was sodden and shapeless most miserable to see. His companions could not draw him in, for the spot was covered by the snipers from the Shelbourne.[36]

The officer commanding the Shelbourne estimated that eleven rebels had been killed but this appears to be an exaggeration. Stephens thought that he saw four bodies while Robbins believed that only a small number of men were killed and wounded.[37] Nevertheless, the unremitting machine-gun barrage forced the rebels to flee the gates and railings on the northern side of the Green and by 8 a.m. Mallin had accepted the hopelessness of his position. He now initiated a retreat to the extreme south-west corner of the park, as far away as possible from the Shelbourne. Although this area also had protective tree cover it only offered a temporary respite and Mallin soon ordered a general transfer to the College of Surgeons. The women went first with bullets 'flying everywhere and sending the gravel up in showers off the path', while wounded Volunteers were forced to take a circuitous route through the shrubs and bushes.[38] Not every insurgent evacuated the Green, because at noon on Easter Tuesday British snipers in the Shelbourne were still firing at men in the trenches, some of whom continued to operate covertly and sporadically throughout much of Easter Week. They also held prisoners in a glasshouse where they were brought food by the park superintendent. Nevertheless, as time went on the British penetrated the Green in increasing numbers and brought it more fully under military control. On Easter Tuesday the OC Shelbourne dispatched a search party to recover bombs, rifles, revolvers, and ammunition. Another party on Friday located and released a prisoner.[39]

But the pressure was not all one way and Mallin's snipers

shattered many of the Shelbourne's windows as well as frightening its residents. The hotel's entrance doors were now locked and barricaded and the lower windows shuttered, with mattresses placed behind them. Social life was transferred to smaller, less opulent back rooms where guests endured a claustrophobic existence of card-playing and fitful conversation while machine-gun fire overhead caused the chandeliers to tremble on every floor. Many eventually slept in the corridors or passed the time by covering for staff who had been warned by the rebels to stay away. During the Rising the Shelbourne became a metaphor for an Ascendancy class and a way of life that had been in retreat for decades, but now, suddenly, found itself in deadly peril. For a week its residents came to regard themselves as an oasis of civilisation in a violent land whose restless natives had finally slipped the leash. Surrounded though they were, the residents maintained a determinedly stiff upper lip and put on a good show until, like Mafeking, they were relieved.[40]

Robbins later conceded that the decision to seize and entrench the Green without simultaneously occupying the large surrounding buildings such as the Shelbourne was widely regarded as an 'act of suicide'.[41] The incomprehensibility of the rebel strategy has created doubts as to whether the Green's occupation was ever intended by the Military Council. Mrs Kathleen Clarke later claimed that it had formed no part of the Council's plans and that when the GPO was informed of it by a dispatch from Mallin he was ordered to evacuate immediately.[42] But the smooth and co-ordinated manner in which the park was cleared, guarded, barricaded and entrenched, without demur on the part of any insurgent, suggests careful advance planning. One eyewitness observed that 'all [the rebels] seem to have been previously instructed as to their duties'.[43] The operation showed a limited understanding of the nature of urban warfare, but in mitigation it should be remembered that Mallin was functioning under the considerable constraint of an unforeseen and acute lack of manpower. Robbins was emphatic that 'there were insufficient men available to seize and secure' the

Shelbourne, but that it had originally been planned to occupy the hotel.[44] Had the Green and surrounding buildings been securely held, they might have fulfilled a more significant military role – as a rebel base which was centrally located, a potential barrier to British military penetration of the city from the south, as well as a communications and transport centre, and a source of fresh water.

During the retreat to the College of Surgeons, the rebels gained a clearer insight into public attitudes towards them. Skinnider claimed later that she found onlookers to be friendly and anxious to advise her if the coast was clear, but Liam Ó Briain encountered abuse from a group of 'hysterical', 'fainting' women.[45] Robbins was attacked outside the college by a crowd, some of whom were armed with crowbars and a hatchet; he had dropped to his knees to fire at the female ringleader when an officer stopped him just in time. Robbins estimated that about 125 men had transferred from the park, of whom roughly 100 belonged to the Citizen Army; most of the rest were Irish Volunteers and Fianna.[46] Although the college was solidly built and made an ideal outpost, it was also cold and uncongenial, its large, draughty rooms abounding with cases filled with the students' specimens, including jars containing human body parts preserved in liquid. The air also reeked with formaldehyde. Mallin's priority now was to secure the building and the main entrance, so front windows were barricaded with desks, park benches and library books, while sentries were posted at every doorway. A lecture hall on the ground floor was converted into a dining room, recreation area and dormitory, and rugs and carpets were brought in for bedding. When food was available, cooking was done in a small kitchen in the caretaker's quarters on the third floor. A sick bay was immediately improvised in an area at the end of a lecture theatre and placed out of bounds to all but the wounded and first aid assistants. Finally, a mortuary chapel was devised using seats from the examination theatre and anatomy room; the dead were laid out on slabs, a tall dark cross was located and a rough altar was constructed from coffin plates.[47]

Mallin made his headquarters in one of the central rooms on the first floor and placed his best marksmen on the roof, assisted by spotters equipped with field-glasses. At least for the early part of the week he continued to operate the barricade nearest the college; it crossed the road to a point where the trees in the park were tall enough to obscure the view of British machine gunners in the Shelbourne and the United Services Club. However, despite their continuing presence on the streets, the rebels were living under a veritable state of siege with withering machine-gun fire coming from a growing number of British positions.

In an attempt to relieve the pressure, Mallin decided to counter-attack and establish a number of outposts. By Easter Thursday, the OC Shelbourne estimated that the rebels held about a dozen premises around the Green, mostly on its western side. Mallin also considered sending parties to set fire to premises in an attempt to force the British to abandon the Shelbourne and the United Services Club. Early on Tuesday evening he dispatched about twenty men to force their way into the Alexandra College past pupils' club. Their presence initially terrified two servant girls till one saw rosary beads on a man's wrist and cried in relief, 'Look! They're Catholics!'[48] During the days that followed they set up sniper posts. Robbins has described how one party of rebels tried to turn their positions into traps for the enemy.

Robert de Coeur and a small party of our men had taken over a number of houses on the west side of the Green, south of York Street. They put into effect a very novel defence measure, one which hitherto we had not adopted in our area. Instead of barricading, as was done in almost every other place, the bottom portion of the house was left as if nothing unusual had taken place. The idea was to invite the opposing forces to regard the house as an easy position to occupy. The stairway had, however, been carefully sawn through, with sufficient left intact to bear only its own weight. However, the exercise was in vain for the British did not attack. The men who had expended so much labour and ingenuity to bait the trap must have been disappointed. Such are the fortunes of war.[49]

But the whole attempt to pressurise the Shelbourne and the United Services Club was completely unrealistic, because the British presence was burgeoning all the time and the soldiers had far superior weaponry. Furthermore, over fifty properties between the College of Surgeons and the Shelbourne would have had to be burnt out or bored through before an assault could have been launched. Yet Mallin's men lacked adequate manpower, sufficient time and all but the most basic equipment.

On Easter Wednesday Mallin, under pressure from Skinnider and Joe Connolly, approved their proposal that they lead a small group to lob a bomb through the Shelbourne's front windows. However, he insisted on a practice run against property in Harcourt Street which was intended to start a fire that would spread to the British-occupied Hotel Russell. Unfortunately their party was spotted and fired on by British snipers who fatally wounded a young Citizen Army member and seriously wounded Skinnider three times in the back and shoulder. When she was carried back to the college Mallin immediately cancelled the proposed bombing raid on the Shelbourne. It was fortunate that he did so because the British OC in the hotel had received prior intelligence from local sympathisers that his position was to be attacked that evening; his men were ready with a maxim gun commanding the main entrance and every soldier was on duty throughout the night. One morale booster for Mallin was the discovery of the OTC's arms cache in the basement of the college – eighty-nine rifles in perfect condition, with bayonets and 24,000 rounds of ammunition.[50]

Mallin now tried to resolve the problems of shortage of food and men. Throughout the week women from the garrison who looked like looters to casual observers had managed to buy or commandeer some supplies, but even so Markievicz later recalled being 'absolutely starved' on Tuesday and Wednesday.[51] By then some of the garrison were 'fainting at their posts for want of nourishment'.[52] Milk and bread carts had long since disappeared from the streets and little that was edible was found in the outposts. A thorough search of the College produced just two eggs and some tea and on Wednesday evening Mallin sent a female dispatch carrier, Chris Caffrey, to Jacob's urgently requesting food and the transfer of any of its Citizen Army members. In response, MacDonagh sent flour, sacks of cakes and some reinforcements who were extremely impressed by Mallin's strict regime. This was a considerable contrast to Jacob's where Douglas Hyde was amazed to hear from a visitor that 'Volunteers were passing in and out of it freely. He says they were dancing inside and taking it by turns to fight. As one goes out in order to go home and sleep he takes off his bandolier, and hands it along with his rifle to another man coming in.'[53] This may have been an exaggeration, but one of the new arrivals, William Oman, noted the quiet atmosphere in the college where reveille was sounded each morning, beds were neatly made and every available man recited the rosary in the evening.[54] This harsher discipline was rooted, no doubt, in Mallin's own experience in the British Army and he displayed a ruthless intolerance of any infraction. He strongly reprimanded several younger men who slashed a portrait of Queen Victoria with their bayonets and threatened to shoot anyone else who damaged a work of art. But not even Mallin's threats were effective in matters of the heart in wartime. One young Volunteer who was on guard duty in an outpost in York Street had been smitten by one of the girls in the College and after locating some hair oil had deserted his post in order to slip over to the headquarters to conduct an assignation. When discovered he was given a mock court-martial by his lieutenant Bob de Coeur and a solemn reminder of the penalty for deserting a post on active service. But Mallin also demanded much from himself. He led by example and demonstrated great bravery during the evacuation from the Green, when he dashed out in the face of machine-gun fire outside the Shelbourne to drag a wounded man to safety. He had a close call but Robbins recalls Mallin's coolness under fire. 'Mallin took off his hat and, speaking in a quiet and even tone, said, "Wasn't that a narrow shave, Robbins?" I agreed that it certainly was. There was a piece taken out of the hat about an inch above the hat-band.'[55] Despite his strategic errors and some organisational shortcomings, he clearly earned the respect and trust of his company.

As the week progressed the constant barrage and a growing expectation of an all-out British attack created considerable emotional strain, sleeplessness and fatigue within the College garrison. During a brief visit from his outpost Liam Ó Briain noticed the grimmer atmosphere. Grenades were located on the main balustrade and other strategic places ready for a British assault while in the sick bay three first aid assistants nursed gravely wounded patients. Men on the roof and at windows were returning fire as best they could against concentrated British shooting from buildings north of the Green in a gun-battle which injured civilians and combatants alike.[56] To J. Smith, a St John's Ambulance volunteer, the situation seemed like 'a dreadful nightmare, which was only made a frightful reality by the dead, dying and wounded which began to stream in. I can never forget the dreadful wounds we had to look after, for as night fell, more and more wounded poured in on every hand; the fighting got fiercer.'[57]

At his home near Leeson Street Bridge half a mile away, Douglas Hyde spent much of Friday afternoon sitting in the garden. Its peace was constantly shattered by the sounds of battle nearby with 'bullets whistling in the air, striking the slates on our house' and as he listened, it seemed evident that the College of Surgeons had become 'the principal storm centre in this part of the city'.[58] It had also become increasingly isolated from other rebel commands, in particular the General Post Office, as the military cordon tightened around O'Connell Street. Another factor hampering the movement of Mallin's dispatch carriers was the active hostility of some civilians. Until Easter Wednesday, Chris Caffrey had operated successfully as a courier disguised as a grieving war widow, draped in black and wearing a red, white and blue emblem. However, some onlookers had become suspicious of her and when angry 'Separation' women barred her entry to the GPO she was forced to fire her revolver into the ground to make them back away. Then on Easter Thursday morning she was spotted leaving the college and shadowed by hostile civilians who denounced her as a spy to a party of British soldiers. She was escorted to Trinity College and decided to bluff her way out. As they passed through the college gates she put the message in her mouth and started chewing. When challenged by a soldier who had seen her action she coolly replied that she was eating a sweet and offered him one from a bag in her pocket. After being searched and then questioned for two hours she was released when no incriminating material was found on her person.[59]

The decline in dispatch-carrying considerably diminished Mallin's appreciation of the overall situation in the city; not that he had ever divulged information to the rank and file, who were fed bland assurances that everything was proceeding smoothly. Increasingly, however, the true position could not be concealed. James Stephens found pieces of burnt paper on the gravel paths near his home and concluded that they 'must have been blown remarkably high to have crossed all the roofs. . . . From my window I saw a red flare that crept to the sky . . . the smoke rose from the ground to the clouds.'[60] Liam Ó Briain remembered that as he looked out 'the fires on the north side of the city seemed to be enormous and widespread. There was a continuous dull roar which I imagined to be artillery.'[61] Those like Stephens who witnessed the artillery bombardment in O'Connell Street at first hand, doubted that the fighting could last much longer. In anticipation of an imminent British assault, the wounded were transferred from the college on Friday to nearby hospitals. Mallin's staff also debated pre-empting a British attack by fighting through the enemy cordon and conducting guerrilla warfare in the Dublin hills. During the discussion Ó Briain heard an animated Markievicz longing for a bayonet or 'some stabbing instrument for action at close quarters', which elicited Mallin's amused but admiring comment: 'You are very blood-thirsty.'[62] Despite the countess's bravura some men had begun to collapse from mental and physical strain and others had contracted pneumonia from exposure to the rain.

The deserted neighbouring streets heightened the all-pervasive sense of eeriness, isolation and claustrophobia inside the college. After Monday, public and private transport had collapsed and from Tuesday the military had closed most bridges to civilian traffic. On Wednesday, bills proclaiming martial law were posted on the railings of St Stephen's Green, warning citizens to remain indoors between the hours of 7.30 p.m. and 5.30 a.m. Increasingly, at all hours, citizens were being hemmed into their own neighbourhoods and confined to their homes and by Friday one Dubliner wrote that 'the streets were as silent as a tomb; firing was so frequent, no-one would venture out except at great risk'.[63] Grand town-houses, offices, clubs and churches rather than shops preponderated around the Green, so at least the members of Mallin's garrison were largely spared the scenes of looting which so distressed their comrades at the GPO and elsewhere. Nonetheless on Wednesday and Thursday some minor outbreaks occurred in Grafton Street, though undoubtedly these were related to the deepening food crisis. On Sunday, a Red Cross driver reported about a thousand people gathered at a bakery in Ballsbridge almost 2 miles east of the Green.[64]

Throughout Friday night and Saturday morning there was heavy firing in and around the college, but it then tapered off for reasons which were not yet known to the garrison. It had not yet learnt of Pearse's surrender or Connolly's subsequent confirmation that it applied to the men 'under my command in the Moore Street District, and for the men in the Stephen's Green Command'.[65] Gradually, however, a highly confused version of recent events trickled through to the Green, where Robbins first heard rumours from civilians who shouted up to his post from the pavement below. The result was to renew speculation of a possible breakout to conduct guerrilla warfare in the countryside.[66]

On Sunday morning an uneasy college garrison tried to conduct business as usual, whether on sentry duty, on the roof, at the windows, in the kitchen or in the sick bay, but by mid-morning the British authorities had already begun the process of conveying Pearse's surrender to every rebel stronghold. The news was brought to the college by Lowe's staff captain, Major de Courcy Wheeler, and Pearse's messenger, Nurse Elizabeth O'Farrell, after Wheeler had first arranged for troops in Trinity College to be ready to escort Mallin's followers to Richmond Barracks. When their car reached the top of Grafton Street O'Farrell continued on foot and under the protection of a white flag to the college and bullets were still ricocheting around the Green as she approached the building. When she was eventually admitted at the York Street entrance Mallin was asleep and Markievicz was first to see the surrender order. When he was awakened the commandant said nothing to O'Farrell who then retraced her steps to the car, where Wheeler was annoyed that she had not got Mallin to indicate whether he intended to surrender.[67]

Mallin now convened a half-hour officers' conference at around 11.00 a.m. At this many favoured escape from the city and the formation of a flying column. But Mallin was greatly influenced by Connolly's endorsement of the surrender and, like the good staff officer that he was, was determined to obey the order from his superior. He now summoned the entire company to the college lecture hall where Robbins was struck by 'the atmosphere of awful gloom that had settled over the place. . . . Men and women who had been gay and light-hearted were now crying.'[68] Mallin confirmed that a surrender order had come from Pearse and Connolly and that as soldiers they had to obey. One person present remembered how pale and slight Mallin appeared and how he had to repeat the surrender order three times.[69] He predicted that he and other senior officers (though not Markievicz) would be executed, and had started to pay tribute to their courage when he broke down. As murmurs of dissent developed Markievicz moved through the ranks repeating 'I trust Connolly, I trust Connolly' despite her own private reservations; Skinnider had overheard her urging Mallin to fight on.[70] Ó Briain, however, confessed that 'a certain feeling of relief came over me. . . . There was no more need for work and vigilance. We could relax, one was alive.'[71] Mallin had stated that he would not think the less of anyone who slipped away and some left, including a Londoner whose accent enabled him to pose as an Englishman trapped on holiday. Most stayed and a total of 121 insurgents (110 men and 11 women) surrendered.[72]

At noon Mallin ordered that weapons be discarded and a white flag be run up. The OC Shelbourne then shouted for the tricolour, which had flown since Monday, to be lowered and advised Dublin Castle by telephone to dispatch troops to take the surrender. Wheeler now collected the officer in charge of the troop escort and returned to the College of Surgeons, though initially he received no answer at the barricaded main entrance door. After some time a civilian advised him to go to York Street, where he saw a white flag hanging out of the side door. It was now between 12.30 p.m. and 1.00 p.m. and inside most of the garrison were in tears and a restless and impatient Mallin was relieved to learn of Wheeler's arrival. Accompanied by Markievicz, Mallin saluted the British officer, said he wished to surrender and presented him with a walking stick as a memento. Markievicz was dressed in her now familiar green puttees, riding breeches, tunic, slouch hat with ostrich feather and a Sam Browne officer's ammunition belt. When she was asked to disarm, she kissed her revolver before handing it over. This simple, defiant but calculated gesture was to become one of the most celebrated of the entire Rising. When the military escort arrived the pent-up emotion of the assembled men threatened to erupt. Joe Connolly, whose brother Sean had been killed at the City Hall, reached for his automatic but was overpowered before he could fire a shot at Wheeler. Unperturbed and accompanied by Mallin and Markievicz, Wheeler inspected the garrison, ascertained that it had been disarmed and examined the arms cache. He later claimed that the college was in 'an indescribable state of confusion and destruction – furniture, books, etc., being piled up in barricades – food, clothes, arms, mineral water, surgical dressings were mixed up and lying about in all directions. . . . The portrait of Queen Victoria torn.'[73] However, the hostage Lawrence Kettle had been impressed by the rebels' respect for property and said afterwards that they 'even took care not to drop ash on the carpet'.[74] Some of the college staff reported little or no damage when they took possession after the Rising.[75]

Wheeler now ordered Mallin to assemble his men at the front of the building. where a generally hostile crowd had gathered. He offered to let Markievicz travel by car for her personal protection, but she declined and insisted that, as second in command, she should share the fate of the men. So she and Mallin marched at the head of the company between a double line of British troops, one of whom whispered to Ó Briain in a pure Dublin accent: 'Why in the name . . . didn't yiz wait till the war'd be over? We'd ha' been all with yiz. I fired over your heads the whole week.'[76] Many onlookers were far less sympathetic and when the prisoners were escorted along York Street and Stephen's Green West there was 'a great demonstration by the crowd, which surged in on all sides'.[77] The mood became steadily more threatening and after some attacks on the prisoners soldiers threatened to open fire, though later in the march some troops were heard muttering that they were 'goin' to biyenet 'em [the rebels] like the rest [sic]'.[78] When the insurgents eventually reached the apparent sanctuary of the lower Castle yard, at about 1.45 p.m., they passed a freshly dug pit which some of them feared contained quicklime graves prepared for their interment.[79]

After a short delay they proceeded via the Ship Street gate to Richmond Barracks, Inchicore, where Robbins remembered the crowds cheering, waving their hats and Union Jacks and applauding the men of the Staffordshire Regiment as they marched in. There were also cries of 'Shoot the traitors' and 'Bayonet the bastards' and Robbins had no doubt that 'were the British army to have withdrawn at that moment, there would have been no need for court-martials [sic] or prisons as the mob would have relieved them of such niceties'.[80] Markievicz later claimed that as they walked along she discussed with Mallin whether they would be shot or hanged; indeed, shortly before leaving the college, she had made her will which was smuggled out in the lining of Skinnider's coat when she was transferred to hospital. Whether or not this was merely bravura on the countess's part, it was her exploits above everyone else's in the garrison which had most caught the public imagination. There were few places where she had not allegedly been sighted during Easter Week, either lying dead on the steps of the City Hall, dressed in men's clothing, or arrested at bayonet point in George's Street. The many alleged reports on her activities derive to some extent from the fact that Markievicz had been very active throughout Easter Week in an actual fighting capacity. It was widely believed at the time and has been authoritatively asserted since that on several occasions she shot at and may have killed members of the Crown forces, though in fact no definite corroboration has ever been established.[81]

Even after Mallin's garrison at the college had surrendered, the sound of gunfire continued to be heard near Stephen's Green, but normality gradually returned. On Monday morning the last British troops in the Shelbourne transferred to Trinity College and by Tuesday the barricade near the hotel entrance had been removed, along with a dead horse which had lain close by all week. But the Green remained closed, and elsewhere in the city lurid rumours were circulating about the rebels who had been there. One Dubliner recorded in her diary:

> I believe . . . it was pitiable to see the number of dead lying in the park, also on top of the spike railings, etc., where they have been shot by the military on top of the different clubs and houses in the vicinity. It is stated not one of the rebels escaped and all are buried in the park, which will have the effect of closing this beautiful place.[82]

If such a grotesquely distorted account was widely accepted it was bound to colour popular responses to the Rising.

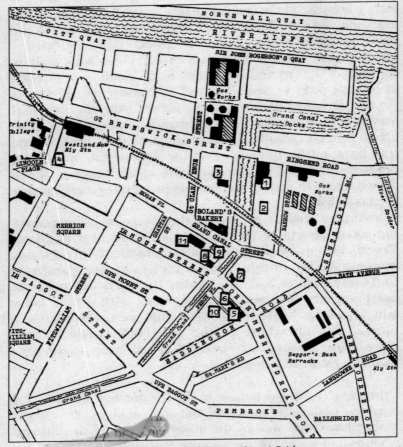

Boland's Bakery and Mount Street Bridge

1. Flour mills
2. Locomotive works
3. Former distillery
4. Oriel House
5. No. 25
6. Parochial Hall

7. School
8. Clanwilliam House
9. Roberts' Yard
10. Percy Lane
11. Sir Patrick Dun's Hospital

4

BOLAND'S BAKERY

The story of the 3rd Dublin Battalion is often associated with Eamon de Valera and Boland's flour mills at the Grand Canal docks. In fact it was the firm's bakery some distance away in Grand Canal Street that was seized on Easter Monday to become the base of operations. The mills were occupied, but de Valera never set foot there during the entire week. Eamon de Valera was a mathematics teacher in his mid-thirties at the start of a career that was to make him the most influential and controversial politician of twentieth-century Ireland. Having enrolled in the Irish Volunteers at its inception he had risen rapidly because of his high intelligence, commanding physical presence and meticulous organisational ability. Although de Valera did not become a member of the IRB until later, Pearse had appointed him battalion commandant in March 1915 after receiving assurances from de Valera that in the event of a Rising he would obey his superiors' orders.

During the week before the Rising de Valera had been virtually resident at battalion headquarters in Great Brunswick Street, a building whose store of weapons and ammunition was under permanent armed guard.[1] The battalion was based in the area from Ringsend in the south-east of the city to College Green in the centre. Its members had maintained constant surveillance on the nearby Central Police Station, the headquarters of the Dublin Metropolitan Police, whose famous or notorious 'G' detective division would certainly participate in any last-minute government swoop against the Irish Volunteers.

De Valera and most of his officers had been geared for action on Easter Sunday and had only reluctantly complied with the Military Council's order to obey MacNeill's countermand. When he consulted his staff that evening they reported a general despondency over the leadership split and Simon Donnelly, an officer in C Company, noted the commandant's 'keen disappointment' when he estimated that only 35 to 40 of its 120 men would respond to another mobilisation.[2]

At 9.30 a.m. on Easter Monday de Valera told his company captains that they were going into action at noon and ordered them to prepare their men within two hours. The main point of concentration was about a mile away in Earlsfort Terrace, outside University College, although some men left directly from headquarters to seize Westland Row station. The turn-out was dismal. By 11.30 a.m. only thirty-four men of C Company were present and since its captain was also missing, Donnelly was promoted on the spot to take his place. Neither was the captain of A Company there and only eighteen of his men arrived; only fourteen of the Ringsend Volunteers turned out and seven of them deserted on the first day along with a large supply of food. The eighty men from B Company comprised over half the total who mobilised and even though others trickled in during the week only 173 Volunteers are listed as having served in the Boland's area. De Valera had hoped for a minimum of 500 men and Captain Joseph O'Connor of A company had estimated that between 800 and 1,000 Volunteers would be required to hold every designated target.[3]

At 11.50 a.m. the 3rd Battalion moved off and at Upper Mount Street fourteen of Donnelly's men under Lieutenant Michael Malone headed along the canal to Mount Street to occupy a number of important outposts in that vicinity. The main body continued to Boland's bakery in Grand Canal Street. This was situated one and a quarter miles south-east of the GPO in a generally poor district on the edge of the Liffey docks. The company's flour mills occupied a stone building at the corner of Ringsend Road and the Grand Canal at the point where the roadway (Great Brunswick Street and Ringsend

Road) crossed a narrow bridge on its way through various suburbs to join the main road to Kingstown. There was a large gasworks on the opposite (city) side of the bridge. For his headquarters de Valera chose the bakery, which was positioned between the mills and the outposts he set up to cover Mount Street Bridge in the adjoining middle-class area. The bakery was a good choice as it consisted of a group of low-lying sheds hidden from the British by higher buildings which could also be used by Volunteer snipers. The zone of the coming action was crossed by the railway line from Kingstown harbour 7 miles away (Dun Laoghaire), from where British forces could be expected to come on the scene by road and rail.

When the Volunteers entered the bakery they ordered the staff to leave. Some believed that they were involved in a routine Volunteer manoeuvre and were reluctant to comply until they were threatened with rifles. An exception was made for bakers who volunteered to remain until a batch of bread in the ovens was finished.[4] Believing that the British might counter-attack before Boland's had been put in a state of defence, Donnelly established four small defence groups. Meanwhile the Volunteers fortified and loopholed the building and manned the low-lying walls. As well as being de Valera's headquarters, the bakery provided a canteen and sleeping quarters and his personal quarters were located in the adjoining dispensary. With his sword drawn, he had led the occupation of the dispensary on Easter Monday but it was empty except for Mrs Healy, the doctor's wife. She was given five minutes to pack up and leave but instead became hysterical and ran upstairs to her bed. De Valera then discovered other pressing responsibilities and left Lieutenant O'Byrne to resolve the problem. At that moment Dr Healy returned and also declined to leave. George Lyons, an officer in B Company, wrote:

The doctor asked what would happen if his property was destroyed. 'The Irish Republic', said O'Byrne, 'will compensate you when it is established.' The doctor proceeded solemnly to take an inventory of all the appurtenances. This done, he asked for a receipt for all the articles. 'I will give you no receipt for anything as I am taking nothing from you,' said O'Byrne. 'We are only in temporary custody here and may be elsewhere tomorrow.'[5]

Although Healy eventually agreed to depart with his wife he deposited an inventory with O'Byrne, though strangely he overlooked six gold sovereigns which the Volunteers found lying loose on the premises. These were retrieved by him after the Rising.

Captain McMahon of B Company also cleared, barricaded and locked Westland Row station and so ensured that any British reinforcements landing at Kingstown would have to march to Dublin. He then sabotaged part of the line and entrenched his men about 300 yards away from the station. O'Connor's company had already stopped and emptied a train and captured a British army officer who was detained in the bakery for the duration of the Rising.[6] The railway was of enormous importance because it ran through de Valera's command area and if it had fallen to the British the Volunteers' base would have been cut in two. To prevent this de Valera assigned its defence to McMahon and O'Connor, two of his best officers, whose men operated both singly and in small groups to snipe and fight running battles. Their first encounter occurred on Monday near Bath Avenue when McMahon and seven of his men repelled soldiers from Beggar's Bush Barracks and killed a sergeant-major.[7] The line was carried on nine stone archways between Westland Row and Ringsend and their walls protected Volunteer marksmen attacking British soldiers on Great Brunswick Street and Grand Canal Street as well as in the square of Beggar's Bush Barracks.

The 3rd Battalion also occupied the railway's locomotive works in Barrow Street, the managers' houses on Grand Canal Street Bridge and the Dock Milling Company's houses. The gasworks on the city side of the canal was briefly seized and vital pieces of equipment removed which resulted in darkness across much of the city. The Volunteers also took over the dock bank from Brunswick Street to the bakery. Guinness's store on the bank was occupied briefly on Tuesday night, but was vacated on Wednesday morning after being heavily attacked. Two Volunteers were placed in a large disused distillery near the gasworks. A barricade of overturned vans was also erected close to the headquarters at Grand Canal Street Bridge. Finally, outposts were also established in private houses on Northumberland and Lansdowne Roads.

Because of the inadequate turn-out de Valera was compelled to abandon plans to seize other positions, while many of those taken were seriously undermanned. His resources were stretched even further by his decision not to bring along the Cumann na mBan partly because of his notorious diffidence in his relations with women but also from a desire to spare them the horrors of urban warfare at close quarters.[8] He did not send the promised courier to the local Cumann who had mobilised in Merrion Square; some went home but others made their way to Jacob's where they were taken in by MacDonagh. The women could have given medical aid in the dispensary or worked in the kitchens of the bakery but instead Boland's operated with only one Red Cross man and doctor in chief, Lieutenant O'Byrne, who was eventually forced to send the seriously wounded to the regular hospitals. Volunteers also had to cook the meals and one man was also assigned full time to care for thirty bakery horses until their food ran out and they were put into the streets.[9]

The weaponry of de Valera's garrison was pathetically inadequate. O'Connor estimated that there were not more than fifty rifles of varying manufacture and ammunition of a different make which meant that even when fighting was taking place the men had to stop to change the bullets they were using. Furthermore the 3rd Battalion had been supplied with hand-made grenades which could not be employed because they were so heavy and unreliable that the officers concluded that they were more dangerous to the Volunteers than the enemy. Their shotguns were just as unstable, though it was discovered that if some were inserted into a metal rainpipe and the triggers pulled by a string the loud explosion at least seemed to intimidate the enemy.[10]

De Valera had also planned originally to seize the railway station and landing area at Kingstown to repel British reinforcements but the few Volunteers who turned out there made their way to Boland's. However, at midnight on Easter Monday he ordered an unenthusiastic Donnelly to lead a party to attack any enemy movements on the road through Blackrock and Ballsbridge to the capital. Donnelly recorded that;

> I didn't altogether like the job as I knew it was rather ticklish and the men fairly nervy, however, orders were orders and we were just about to start off when the Commandant changed his mind, much to the relief of those going on the expedition.[11]

Nevertheless, there was a last line of defence in place in outposts captured by Lieutenant Malone's party in Northumberland Road and at Mount Street Bridge, over which British reinforcements from Kingstown were likely to travel. The large houses of Northumberland Road epitomised prosperous middle- and upper-class Dublin and its residents were mainly Unionist and politically moderate Roman Catholics. About two-thirds along it was intersected by Haddington Road, at which point Northumberland Road turned slightly left and then ran straight on to the bridge, after which it became Lower Mount Street. Malone, a 28-year-old carpenter with the reputation of being a crack rifleman, ordered his section commander, George Reynolds, and four Volunteers to seize Clanwilliam House, a three-storey house at the corner of Lower Mount Street, which faced across the bridge and dominated the route as far as the bend at Haddington Road. Other buildings taken over on Northumberland Road were a parochial hall and a school, although the latter was evacuated on Monday night. Malone located himself in No. 25, the corner house at Haddington Road from which he could see the front gate of Beggar's Bush Barracks. It also provided the first sight of soldiers arriving from Kingstown and who, once they passed, headed towards the bridge, the parochial hall and Clanwilliam House. In this compressed area the British would be hit from front and rear as well as by Volunteers at the Grand Canal Street Bridge, on the railway embankment at the dock, and by snipers perched high on the large water tanks on the roof of the locomotive works.

The Mount Street Bridge garrison was soon in action against the Dublin battalion of the Volunteer Training Corps. This was a reserve military organisation consisting mostly of professional gentlemen, many of them past their prime and dubbed by wags the 'Gorgeous Wrecks' because of their armlets inscribed '*Georgius Rex*'. They were returning to their base in Beggar's Bush Barracks from manoeuvres in the Dublin hills and the subsequent events are often depicted as a massacre of ordinary citizens who were unaware of and uninvolved in the insurrection. Even defenders of the action often describe it as an unfortunate mistake in which the Volunteer Training Corps were mistaken for British infantry. However, not only did the corps know that the Rising had begun but, by the time of the shootings, it was an active participant. It had received news of the insurrection during lunch at its field day from a cyclist whose business had been seized, and Lord Moloney, the head of the corps, had ordered it to return to base. He had also telephoned Under-Secretary Nathan at Dublin Castle to offer his men's services and it was admitted afterwards that 'It was not then anticipated that they would be attacked on the way back but it is clear they came back with the intention of assisting the military authorities and that the latter were aware of their purpose'.[12] When the corps started to return at 3.15 p.m. locals warned its commander, Major Harris, that the GPO and Stephen's Green had been seized though Beggar's Bush Barracks had not yet fallen. He split his men into two sections and led the first down Shelbourne Road where he halted when he learnt that rebels had seized houses in the Haddington Road area. Harris then dispatched a motor-bike rider to the barracks but the commanding officer had closed that gate and said that the men would have to make their way, eight at a time, to the barracks walls. Harris led the first group but it lost a corporal, fatally wounded, though most managed to scramble to safety up ladders and ropes. From inside they heard Malone's men shooting at the other half of the column which had marched into Northumberland Road. Seven soldiers were wounded, four of whom subsequently died, while the remainder fled to shelter in nearby houses. After hiding until dark they escaped, disguised in civilian clothes and women's garments, leaving behind their uniforms and equipment.

Malone's men now barricaded doors and high windows with bicycles and furniture though they lacked the tools to loophole walls. Malone, in No. 25, now dismissed two young Volunteers whom he considered too young to die, but kept their rifles for himself and his solitary comrade, James Grace. As night came on his men waited and watched or snatched some sleep, while in Boland's men were withdrawn into the bakery where they built shell-proof 'caves' out of flour bags. At dawn on Tuesday Malone cut the electric tram wires and briefly illuminated the entire district as the wires fell sparkling to the ground. The residents of Clanwilliam House who had originally decided to stay were so unnerved that they left the house to Reynolds and his men. One Volunteer had deserted Reynolds during the night and another messenger failed to return and so he urgently requested reinforcements from Boland's. In reply, Simon Donnelly managed to squeeze out four Volunteers, including the brothers Tom and James Walsh.[13] During Tuesday a trickle of Volunteers arrived at Boland's, some of whom were bakery employees who produced bread for the local population until near the end of the week. Although enemy fire then made production and distribution too dangerous the consideration shown helped win hearts. So also did de Valera's concern for civilian safety, as when he dashed through gunfire to Grand Canal Street Bridge and shouted at spectators to clear off the roads.[14] By now British snipers were surrounding Boland's and, with Volunteer casualties rising, an attack from Westland Row and Lansdowne Road was anticipated. Excited and nervous Volunteers manned the trenches though they handled with remarkable clumsiness their American shotguns which had a tendency to go off on their own. Some were also rushed along the railway where members of the Royal Irish Rifles who had slipped out through the rear gate of Beggar's Bush Barracks took up position on the line at the level crossing. Here a short but fierce encounter forced the troops to retreat, during which they came under attack from concealed positions on Shelbourne Road.

During the afternoon de Valera selected a detachment to relieve the pressure on Mallin and the Citizen Army in Stephen's Green. According to George Lyons:

> De Valera carefully inspected us and commanded us to to cast off our knapsacks and packs for the sake of greater mobility, warning us we would have tough work to do. As we got the word to go one of the men rushed back through the gates with the extraordinary complaint that he 'had no hat'. 'Here's a hat, —— you! cried de Valera pitching the man his own headgear. The fellow clapped it on his head and rejoined the rank.[15]

However, the operation was countermanded when it was learnt that the Citizen Army had abandoned the Green.

The garrison's morale was high partly because de Valera's officers deliberately shielded their men from unpalatable reality. Donnelly was concerned that his young men would be unsettled by the less promising rumours and stipulated that outsiders with information should report directly to him.[16] O'Connor even encouraged the dissemination of optimistic reports that the ports had been seized and the rest of the country had risen, even though he was fairly certain that the Rising was confined to Dublin alone. Indeed by Tuesday evening O'Connor was convinced that the Rising was in trouble because he had learnt that the *Daily Mail* was on sale in the city. This meant that the port was indeed open and that 'if the British were able to get in their newspapers there was certainly nothing to prevent their landing troops'.[17]

In the early hours of Wednesday morning O'Connor's fears were confirmed when he learnt that enormous British reinforcements were arriving at Kingstown. Shortly afterwards, Malone in Northumberland Road was told by scouts that thousands of Sherwood Foresters were marching towards the city. One column which travelled through Blackrock and Donnybrook reached Dublin completely unscathed, but another 2,000 took the main road through Blackrock and Ballsbridge towards Mount Street Bridge, where Malone and his garrison were waiting. Their commander, Brigadier Maconchy, fully expected to encounter opposition on the way into Dublin because on arrival he had been briefed by an officer from Irish Command who warned him that the route from Ballsbridge into Dublin was strongly held by rebels and 'the houses and points held were detailed to me'. He also received warnings from local inhabitants along the route. Maconchy was not overly concerned about encountering opposition, since that, after all, was the reason he and his men had been brought to Ireland. He was more worried that he was expected to attack and carry houses 'three stories high, occupied by riflemen behind sandbags, without artillery and bombs'. His heavy weaponry had been delayed in Liverpool and his men were equipped with only rifles and bayonets. However, during the march to Dublin, Maconchy managed to acquire officers and 500 grenades from a bombing school and he was also joined by soldiers on leave. At Ballsbridge he commandeered the Town Hall for his Brigade Headquarters and established telephonic communications with Irish Command which had transferred to the Royal Hospital at Kilmainham.[18]

Shortly after midday the Sherwood Foresters entered Northumberland Road, preceded by a line of flankers with fixed bayonets moving carefully in single file along both sides of the street. Malone, in No. 25, allowed the advance guard to pass before he and Grace opened fire, scattering soldiers in all directions. The troops were rallied by their officers and began to return fire with rifles and machine guns, but they also came under long-range attack from Clanwilliam House, 300 yards away at the bridge. When they realised they had stumbled into a deadly trap they scattered in search of cover, but regrouped to assault No. 25 with showers of hand grenades. By 5 p.m. Malone and Grace stood dazed as the house shook and glass and woodwork shattered all around them. One grenade thrown through a back window ignited a pile of ammunition and wrecked the room which they had just vacated. Both men now recognised that the end was near and fixed bayonets for a last stand at the head of the stairs, but were separated when a storming party broke into the house. Malone was driven to the top of the building where he was cut down by a volley of rifle fire, but Grace managed to hide in the basement as troops searched for him and he then escaped into the back garden under the cover of shrubbery and dense clouds of smoke. He eventually made his way into an outhouse in Haddington Road where the owner promised to deliver a note to his family, only to return with a party of soldiers who arrested him.[19]

With one point of resistance eliminated, the Sherwoods now concentrated their attention on Clanwilliam House. Here repeated charges down Northumberland Road disintegrated in the face of devastatingly rapid and precise fire which caused officers to fall with their swords flashing in the sunlight. Supporting fire also came from the parochial hall which the British had not identified as rebel-held, and from the wall of W. & A. Robert's builders' yard on the city side of the canal which ran a few hundred feet from Clanwilliam Place to Grand Canal Street Bridge. This wall was manned by four Volunteers, three of whom were posted on a low roof and the other at Grand Canal corner to repel troops attempting to advance along the canal bank. Tom Walsh, one of the defenders inside Clanwilliam House, was impressed by the courage of the soldiers who stepped forward to take the places of their fallen comrades, creating the impression of a giant khaki-coloured caterpillar.[20] Knapsacks and guns lay scattered among the dead and dying while the wounded, some of whom had tripped over their fallen comrades, lay still on the ground and waited for an opportunity to dash for cover. One local resident, Mrs Ismena Rohde, who watched the slaughter wrote that 'The poor fellows fell in rows without being able to return a shot.

It was ghastly for those who saw it.'[21] Another observer suddenly saw a trooper fall and;

> a woman came out into the open with what looked like a blue enamel jug. She ran down the canal bank into the firing zone and disappeared from view. Then a poor girl ran out on to the bridge while yet the bullets from rifles and revolvers were flying thickly from both sides. She put up both her hands, and almost instantly the firing ceased. Again the woman turned up, and she and the girl picked up the soldier, others then going out from the crowd to help bring him in. He was taken into Sir Patrick Dun's Hospital.
>
> It was a throbbing incident that brought tears to the eyes, and the crowd cheered the little heroine. Several more soldiers were hit, and again the little girl ran out and brought them in time after time. I saw about eight soldiers taken into that hospital wounded, and I helped one in myself along with others of the crowd. The man I helped with was reached by a little girl before we got him in, and she pushed an apron down his trousers to staunch the blood. He was shot in the small of the back and in the thigh. He was a Sherwood Forester, and the little girl was crying over him.[22]

Maconchy, who was angry that he was expected to take fortified houses without the assistance of heavy guns, was becoming alarmed at his heavy casualties. He now ordered Colonel Oates, one of his two senior officers, to detach a company in order to attempt to turn the position at the bridgehead from the direction of Beggar's Bush Barracks. Oates's men had hardly set off before General Lowe, who had taken over command of the army in Dublin, overrode Maconchy and insisted that a frontal assault be pressed home. To Lowe, who was not on the spot, it must have appeared absurd that large numbers of troops upon whom he was relying to crush the rebellion and who were part of an army that under Field-Marshal Kitchener was being moulded into a war-winning instrument, should seek to evade direct battle with a small number of untrained and badly armed Irish amateurs. In addition to professional pride, Lowe probably believed that he was requiring no more of the Sherwoods than Haig was asking of the British Expeditionary Force every day in France when he ordered frontal attacks on well-entrenched Germans. Although the bulk of Oates's men returned, a section actually reached Beggar's Bush where they were detained by the Officer Commanding to assist in the defence of the barracks. Not knowing what had happened, Maconchy had the men posted missing.

He now convened a conference and told his other senior officer, Colonel Fane, that his men were to storm Clanwilliam House, after which Oates's troops would pass through to Trinity College. When Fane attacked he was assisted by the bombing school officers but the Sherwoods suffered heavy casualties, including Fane himself, though he continued in command. The co-ordinated rifle fire of the Volunteers was deadly and even when troops managed to get close the defenders switched to emptying their revolvers. Reynolds also put a coat on a dressmaker's model and placed it at a window where it was riddled with bullets, drawing considerable pressure away from the human occupants. When a small settee caught fire Jim Walsh grabbed a soda-water siphon to extinguish the flames, took a swig from it and was handing it to his brother when it was smashed by a bullet. As the ceilings and walls shook, plaster fell on a grand piano creating weird background music and parts of a chandelier descended on the smouldering chairs which were giving off choking fumes.[23]

Maconchy had become very concerned about the situation. He later wrote;

I then returned to Ballsbridge (not a very nice walk) to the telephone and asked Irish Command if the situation was sufficiently serious to demand the taking of the position 'at all costs' saying that I could take it with another battalion but that we should lose heavily. The reply was to 'come through at all costs'.[24]

At 4.40 p.m. Maconchy summoned Oates and revealed the terrible pounding taken by Fane, most of whose officers were now wounded. After Oates was ordered to storm the enemy positions 'at all costs', he sent for his officers and, under Maconchy's silent gaze, outlined their mission. The 2/8 Battalion now formed up at intervals across Northumberland Road and, at a signal from Maconchy, Oates led his men forward. The school was taken by 7.30 p.m. and discovered to be empty; but an initial attempt to storm Clanwilliam House cost the life of the officer in charge. Oates now called up a reserve battalion. For the Sherwoods it was now a point of honour to avenge their fallen comrades; Clanwilliam House had to be taken. To minimise casualties, which had already reached alarming proportions, the tactics were switched from frontal attack to concentrated sniping. Soldiers fired from concealed positions in houses which they had seized by the canal, along whose banks troops wriggled, partly protected by iron railings and their stone bases. 'The soldiers crawled on their faces under cover of this stone, and seeming, in the distance, like a long yellow boa-constrictor creeping under cover of the wall.'25 From a distance, Volunteers watched the snake-like progress with fascination and opened fire whenever a knapsack appeared or someone rose with their rifle aimed. 'About 200 yards off, the stone parapet has a break of about three feet at a gate. Several soldiers were caught by the oblique rifle fire of the marksmen in Clanwilliam House while creeping past this exposed spot, which proved a veritable death trap.'26

Nevertheless, throughout the evening soldiers worked their way ever closer to houses on the same side of the canal as Clanwilliam House and from which they poured devastating gunfire.

Clanwilliam House had now become a perfect inferno. The glass, sashes, window frames and side shutters had been carried away by rifle fire. The curtains and hangings were torn to ribbons; pictures from the walls, glass mirrors, chandeliers, lay on the floor shattered into pieces, the plaster had fallen from the ceiling and almost every square foot of the walls inside was studded with bullets. The repeated ping of a bullet as it pierced through the woodwork and struck the strings of an upright piano could be heard, or the bell-like sound as it struck the hollow electric posts in the street. Any article of furniture drawn towards the window for cover was immediately carried away in splinters, whenever exposed, and the water pipes had burst, threatening to flood the house. The staircase facing the fanlight of the hall door and the landing windows were also cut into splinters and threatened every moment to collapse under foot. The passage by the stairway from the upper rooms could only be taken by pressing close to the wall, when running up or down, to escape the leaden hail from the windows. The smoke filling the room and the sulphurous smell of burnt powder made breathing difficult; and the wild cries of assault outside, combined with the unceasing rattle of the musketry, made an incredible din. Incendiary bullets seem to have entered the house; some of the beds and the sofa upholstering went on fire and frequently had to be extinguished and the floor carpentry was smouldering in several places.[27]

As sheets of fire lit up the sky in the drawing room on the first floor, Reynolds stood behind three Volunteers, directing their fire, while another three fought on upstairs. Suddenly Patrick Doyle, the company musketry instructor, was killed and Richard Murphy, a tailor who was supposed to have been married in Easter Week, was shot dead, though eerily he remained in a kneeling position clutching his rifle as if aiming to fire.

The time had now come to evacuate Clanwilliam House. But Reynolds could not resist one last shot and it cost him his life when he took a bullet in the hip. The remaining defenders knelt and said a prayer for him and took a final look at Murphy and Doyle. Then, as the building collapsed in flames around them, the four survivors fled, scrambling over barricades and out through a small window. There they flung themselves over the wall of the adjoining house and ran down a lane at the back. When the return fire ceased, soldiers rushed through the front garden gate. One of them carried a bucketful of hand grenades which he lobbed into the building, one rebounding and wounding an officer. With Volunteer resistance broken and the slaughter finally ended, the Sherwoods erupted in cheering, singing and hysterical relief that their ordeal was over, although intermittent sniping continued for some hours. The defenders' flight was not without attendant dangers. Jimmy Doyle, who did not know the neighbourhood well, made his way into Lower Mount Street where he was seized by local people. However, before they could hand him over to the soldiers he was rescued by other residents and taken to safety. The Walsh brothers and Willie Ronan went to the rear of Clanwilliam House and into a laneway. They then crossed several garden walls, moving carefully as wounded soldiers were also being carried through them to Sir Patrick Dun's Hospital. When the enemy had cleared they entered a house with an open door where they asked a young girl to provide them with coats to cover their uniforms. She then told her mother that there were Volunteers in the house and was ordered to put them out before they were all shot. As Tom Walsh laconically records: 'We did not trouble them but continued over the walls.'[28]

The four Volunteers who evacuated the parochial hall by the rear were captured in Percy Lane by angry soldiers who were comforting masses of wounded comrades. When one of the Sherwoods searched Joe Clarke and discovered a revolver he put him against a door with his hands above his head. Clarke sensed that he was about to be shot dead and ducked just before the trigger was pulled, the bullet whizzing just above his head and through the door, narrowly missing a doctor who was attending a wounded man. The doctor quickly intervened to prevent another shot being fired and Clarke was hustled away, his hands tied behind his back. When the scorched shell of Clanwilliam House was searched later for human remains only a leg was found. At No. 25 soldiers had interred Malone's body in the garden, burying him in his uniform, his head and shoulders covered with a canvas cloth. A fortnight afterwards his remains were transferred to Glasnevin Cemetery. When all was over, five Volunteers of C Company were dead, while British losses amounted to 4 officers killed and 14 wounded, and 216 other ranks either killed or wounded.[29]

This carnage took place amid sedate Victorian houses: urban warfare had suddenly arisen in Dublin, something unprecedented in a city of the United Kingdom. Ordinary lives found themselves interrupted by extraordinary events. Louisa Nolan gave a drink of water to the wounded lying on Northumberland Road. In Percy Place Miss Scully and her maid, sitting in a bullet-riddled room, were arrested by soldiers who thought firing was coming from her house. A woman neighbour was shot in the hand – while watching the action through binoculars. And there was the old man, caught in the open, who tried to make a run for his house only to be cut down in a hail of bullets.

The heavy casualties suffered by the Sherwoods were due in large part to the high motivation of the Volunteers and especially Malone who was an inspired commander, a born leader, courageous and endowed with indomitable will-power. Undoubtedly, though, the Sherwoods contributed to the slaughter by having the advance guard move down Northumberland Road without checking houses for rebel occupation, while the main body of troops followed too close behind. Once the gap between them was closed and they merged into what was, in effect, one large mass the advance guard's reconnaissance function had been terminated.

Malone understood the importance of his mission and its likely consequences because at the battalion's Good Friday staff conference it had been agreed that Mount Street Bridge garrison would stay to the very end. Malone had told O'Connor;

Well, Joe, it's pretty close to hand. I know you'll come through, but I won't.[30]

Malone himself had taken the most advanced and dangerous position in No. 25 and his dismissal of two very young Volunteers demonstrated wisdom as well as humanity because he had to be certain that nobody under his command would buckle under heavy attack. The desertion of two Volunteers on Monday night and Tuesday morning from Clanwilliam House shed the remaining weak links and left him only with men who were totally committed, a group loyalty strengthened by family bonds in the case of the Walsh brothers. Time and again during the battle the garrison proved itself determined, patient and disciplined and its co-ordinated, accurate and well-timed rifle fire demonstrated teamwork of a very high quality. And its members refrained from going for the kill at the first sight, waiting until they received their orders.

The choice of outposts was also excellent and it created between No. 25, Northumberland Road and Clanwilliam House a rectangular killing zone. Troops could be seen well in advance, particularly as Malone's men were equipped with powerful field-glasses, while the side windows of No. 25 gave an oblique view of Northumberland Road for a considerable distance. In addition the landing of the Sherwoods at Kingstown had been observed by Irish Volunteer scouts as was their march northwards. Furthermore the Volunteers had decent weapons. Malone possessed a state-of-the-art, high-powered automatic Mauser pistol with almost smokeless fire while Grace had a serviceable Lee-Enfield rifle and the spare rifles left behind by the two young Volunteers. Malone was also an especially good marksman, as was Patrick Doyle, the company musketry instructor.

The Battle of Mount Street Bridge is often regarded as the heroic episode of the Easter Rising, an encounter in which the Irish defenders, and indeed the British attackers, displayed enormous courage and self-sacrifice. Malone and his small garrison faced impossible odds, yet battled for hour after hour and exacted a terrible price from the Sherwoods. The battle has been described, with forgivable exaggeration, as an Irish Thermopylae, and in the endurance which they displayed in the face of almost certain death, the scale of the casualties which they inflicted relative to their own numbers and the legend which grew around them, the story of Malone's garrison has echoes of the 300 Spartans. And at the end Malone, like Leonidas, lay, obedient to his orders. Even as the fighting took place a legend was being created. One Dubliner, Miss Lilly Stokes, recorded on Wednesday 26 April:

> They took the corner house in Haddington Road after an obstinate fight – they bombed it. They say there were 36 dead men, women and children in it who had all been fighting.[31]

George Lyons, who returned to the bakery on Wednesday evening from an outpost in Grand Canal Street, reported that Clanwilliam House was on fire and recommended sending a party to escort its garrison to safety. De Valera was sceptical but as the sky became illuminated it seemed certain that something terrible had occurred, though the garrison did not learn exactly what until after the Rising. What was undeniable was that British troops had marched along Baggot Street and were beginning to exert pressure on Boland's through Kildare Street and Lincoln Place. A night attack was now anticipated and Volunteers were placed behind trenches which had been dug facing Westland Row and Lansdowne Road. The trenches themselves were left empty and the defenders located behind small embankments from behind which they were ready to cut down soldiers who stepped into the trenches. As they waited, Lyons records that;

> De Valera passed along the lines exhorting the men to remain steady in their positions. He gave thrilling pictures of how we were going to have a glorious victory or a still more glorious death.[32]

The attack, however, never came and that was fortunate because by now many men were so exhausted that they were collapsing on duty.

By Thursday all the outposts of Boland's had fallen and it had also lost touch with the GPO while the British net drew ever tighter. Soldiers had crossed Mount Street Bridge and had occupied excellent sniping positions in many of the high houses in Lower Mount Street. From rear windows they dominated the low-lying bakery. Their continual fire limited movement inside de Valera's headquarters from early morning and reduced Volunteers to crawling along on the ground. While there was a plentiful supply of bread, with ovens and fuel for cooking, the sniping made distribution to the various posts become a serious problem. De Valera attempted to break the developing British stranglehold and instructed Donnelly to take a firing party to a tenement house at the corner of Great Clarence Street and the Grand Canal to dislodge enemy marksmen. Donnelly first dashed across the road with a sledgehammer to smash open the hall door, but it was unlocked and he went hurtling through to end up sprawled on the ground, a mass of bruises. His men then followed and climbed to the top of the house where the first person to put his head through the skylight was fired at by British machine guns. As the party retreated to the upper rooms they were tracked by enemy snipers who seriously wounded one Volunteer and fired on the stretcher party which then carried him across Great Clarence Street.[33]

De Valera had originally hoped to occupy many of the high buildings surrounding Boland's, in particular Oriel House at the corner of Westland Row which would have dominated British movements in Merrion Street and Lincoln Place. He was heard muttering continually to himself 'Oriel House, Oriel House, oh if only we had Oriel House' and repeatedly selected Volunteers to seize it, only time and again for him to decide that the expedition was too risky. He then decided to withdraw men from the former distillery near the headquarters, but while this would concentrate his forces it risked a British occupation of this high building. Instead he decided to lure the enemy into destroying it. He sent Captain Michael Cullen to ascend the distillery tower and simulate semaphore messages to create the impression that it was the Volunteer headquarters.

Cullen soon drew fire from a British naval gun situated on a horse lorry in Percy Place and operated by an officer and half a dozen sailors. The *Helga*, a British naval vessel on the Liffey, also joined in and some of its shells landed in Barrow Street. De Valera gleefully raced up and down the line cheering and shouting 'Hurrah! a rotten shot' but, as Lyons noted, the men did not share his jubilation.

> They were rather curious to watch the effect of the shell-firing which they had never before experienced. Moreover the enemy marksmanship was not to be scoffed at. The shells hit the tower of the Distillery every time and a racket and din was kept up by the explosion and falling masonry. They were small shells, however, but they practically had demolished the tower.[34]

To everyone's astonishment, when the shelling stopped two dazed young Volunteers whose presence in the distillery had been overlooked stumbled out shouting that they couldn't take any more. Cullen who had stayed in the distillery during the bombardment had his nerves shattered and had to be sent to a secure area to convalesce.

Up until Thursday de Valera was completely in command, impressing everyone with his courage, his agility, the keenness of his eyesight and his ability to evade enemy fire. However, he was driving himself to the limit. Since even before Easter Monday he had been operating under enormous strains and Easter Week had seen many setbacks, most of them deriving from the pathetically inadequate size of his battalion. He also believed that he could not rely on his officers to ensure that the garrison functioned efficiently, an attitude which can only have been strengthened by the stunning news which he received on Thursday that Begley, his vice-commandant, had deserted.[35] By now he was a lonely figure unable or unwilling to delegate. He was attempting to do everything himself, almost as if he believed that by sheer force of personality he could overcome his depleted resources. He constantly circulated around the garrison to keep the men alert and issued orders that guards were to shoot dead anyone who failed to identify themselves properly. A number of officers, indeed, were wounded by their own men on Thursday night and de Valera himself was almost shot at the dispensary door when he gave the previous night's password. By Thursday night many men were flat out exhausted on the bakery floor but one truculent Volunteer talked incessantly despite the order that strict silence be maintained. When the man was reprimanded by an officer, Peadar Macken, he went berserk and shot Macken through the heart, only to be cut down himself by a sentry.

George Lyons recalls:

When Friday dawned it bore the burden of many rumours of the gloomy night before. A new terror crept amongst us in the feeling that one's immediate comrade might go mad, or what was even worse, that you might go mad yourself. Each man eyed his companion with suspicious glances and a most uncomfortable uneasiness prevailed.[36]

Pressure was increasing steadily as British marksmen inched ever closer. The garrison believed that the enemy were dressing their snipers in the blue clothing of military wounded to enable them to infiltrate Sir Patrick Dun's Hospital and that the inordinate number of men with stiff legs was explained by their having stuffed rifles down their trousers. By now concern about de Valera's behaviour was mounting among his officers, as O'Connor, who was appointed vice-commandant after Begley's defection, hinted obliquely. 'At no time up to Thursday did I receive any order or hold any discussion with the Commandant that was not perfectly clear with precise instructions as to what he wanted done.'[37] Donnelly noted his 'very worn and tired-out appearance',[38] but de Valera obdurately rejected pleas to rest until he was finally persuaded to retire to his quarters in the dispensary. Donnelly then placed a guard there with instructions that he divert all messages to him and at the same time he overrode de Valera's orders and withdrew men from the trenches to get some sleep. Lyons noticed that the officers were 'turning more and more to the imperturbable Donnelly for guidance and advice. It began to be rumoured that the strain was telling severely upon de Valera and that he might not again appear in the field.'[39] The commandant, however, would not be contained and reappeared within a few hours, displaying the same behavioural patterns which had aroused such concern in the first place. Indeed Lyons states that at one point he came very close to being removed from command.

De Valera's staff officers were especially concerned at the extent to which on Easter Friday his fixity of purpose appeared to have disintegrated completely. He was oscillating wildly, issuing a series of dramatic orders only to countermand them soon afterwards. In early morning he decided to transfer the headquarters to the granary on Grand Canal Quay, but the advance party under Donnelly realised its isolated position and returned to the bakery.[40] He then organised a party to 'raise Hell for Leather' on Merrion Square, but then cancelled the mission and instructed the men instead to pack up in readiness for a retreat to the Dublin mountains, a project which he had mentioned as a possibility to O'Connor earlier in the week. De Valera then sent a courier across the Canal Basin to order the commandant in Boland's Mills to fire the building and evacuate to the bakery. The officer was appalled at the destruction of an enormous quantity of potential food and disregarded the message as well as taking the courier prisoner when he attempted to carry out the assignment. De Valera next turned his attention to Westland Row railway station and ordered Lieutenant Sean Quinn to set it on fire. Although he lacked incendiary materials, Quinn finally managed to start a blaze of sorts but de Valera had, in the meantime, been persuaded by two horrified officers that he was also jeopardising Westland Row church. He then sent Lyons to stop Quinn who reacted with a 'hurricane of expletives', but did manage to extinguish the flames.[41]

Despite some piercing criticisms, Lyons respected de Valera's charisma and knowledge. But he remained concerned about him after a bizarre encounter on Friday when the commandant's appearance seemed utterly incongruous as he stood hatless, his scarlet flannel puttees in glaring contrast to his green Volunteer uniform.

I ventured to suggest that he might seek more rest, as the men were rather anxious about officers overworking themselves. He eyed me suspiciously. 'Do you think that I am going insane because I am wearing these?' he queried, as he pointed to the scarlet flannel puttees. 'Sure,' he added, 'this is where I show my sanity.' I walked away rather abashed and depressed. Everyone seemed to be thinking in terms of sanity and insanity.[42]

Late on Friday night de Valera mystified Donnelly by ordering a withdrawal from the bakery to the railway line. Donnelly reluctantly obeyed his superior's order, which resulted in panic when the men reached the higher elevation and witnessed the fires in the city. Soon afterwards de Valera countermanded his instruction and told Donnelly to reoccupy the bakery, a risky enterprise since the British might have occupied the evacuated headquarters in the meantime. Fortunately scouts reported that the enemy had not realised that the Volunteers had temporarily abandoned the bakery.[43]

By Friday night the situation of the Boland's garrison seemed desperate especially when soldiers were reported crossing the loop line from Amiens Street station. Lyons urged de Valera to destroy the bridges spanning Westland Row and Great Clarence Street but the battalion possessed neither dynamite nor effective hand grenades. 'There was nothing for it but to await the advance of troops along the line. Night closed in and we set ourselves in the trenches once again to meet the onslaught that never was delivered.'[44] De Valera's command was probably saved by the fact that Saturday proved to be remarkably uneventful at Boland's. There was only intermittent sniping, though the silence across the city seemed to indicate that some significant event had occurred.

Early on Sunday morning as Donnelly conducted a weapons inspection he was called to the rear of Boland's where Nurse O'Farrell had arrived with an urgent message for de Valera. The commandant was shaving but quickly came to meet the emissary from Pearse, who had brought the news of surrender. O'Farrell recorded later that de Valera, who did not know her, appeared to regard the whole thing as a hoax and refused to accept the order until it had been countersigned by MacDonagh, his immediate superior. When O'Farrell left to go to Jacob's de Valera began to consult his staff and instituted a council of officers, some of whom knew O'Farrell and so confirmed the authenticity of her message. With the British deadline for surrendering drawing closer de Valera warned them that they could be shot out of hand if found with weapons in their possession. However, de Valera had lost his grip on these men days before and the overwhelming opinion was that the struggle should continue. His own vice-commandant O'Connor told him that they had come out as soldiers and should carry on as such.

De Valera now ordered O'Connor to bring the men in from their positions and said that he would inform the British that they had orders to surrender. The ensuing situation in Boland's was remarkably tense because as O'Connor brought in the men from his own A Company one was shot in the throat while O'Connor himself was grazed on the side of the head by a bullet. The garrison was in a foul mood when it was finally assembled in the bakery and officers were accused of engineering a betrayal behind the men's backs. Then tempers cooled somewhat when they learnt that the surrender order had come from Pearse. Lyons says that 'De Valera suddenly rose with tears in his eyes and declared: "I obeyed the orders of my superiors in coming to this fight. I will obey the orders of my superiors to surrender and I charge you all to observe the same discipline." '[45]

Accompanied by Lieutenant O'Byrne with a white flag, he then departed to make contact with the British to elicit details of the surrender process. Initially his appeal to loyalty made little impression and Lieutenant Sean Guilfoyle began to form a 'spartan' band to conduct a heroic last stand. This course was abandoned only when it was pointed out that in that event no mercy would be shown to de Valera in British custody. One exception to the general despair was Volunteer Joe MacDermott, who had radiated optimism throughout the entire week and now gloriously misinterpreted Pearse's dispatch. He ran up and down the lines shouting, 'By Heavens we have beaten the Hell out of them and Pearse has ordered an Unconditional Surrender.' When de Valera returned all but one intransigent lined up behind him and marched out into Great Clarence Street. Nobody was prepared to carry the white flag and it was handed to Lieutenant O'Byrne, the Red Cross officer.[46] Whatever the reaction in other places the local population around Boland's was friendly and sympathetic and the Volunteers received an ovation in Grand Canal Street and Hogan Place where women unsuccessfully begged them to take refuge in the houses and men offered to hide the weapons. De Valera was consumed with regret, saying to himself: 'Ah men, men, if only you had come out to help us, even with knives, you would not behold us like this.'[47] In Grattan Street there was a reception party of British officers and soldiers with grenades in each hand and de Valera brought the column to a halt. His men then flung their rifles down very violently, raised their hands and marched into Lower Mount Street through lines of bayonets. The Volunteers saluted their commandant, some shouted 'God save you, sir' and others ran forward to clasp his hand causing de Valera to break down in tears.

5

JACOB'S FACTORY AND THE SOUTH DUBLIN UNION

MacDonagh's 2nd Battalion had assembled at Stephen's Green West at 11.30 a.m. but did not depart until Michael Mallin's Citizen Army contingent arrived to occupy the park. MacDonagh's second in command was Major John MacBride who over fifteen years before had been the leader of the Irish Brigade which had fought alongside the Boers against the British army in South Africa. His celebrity had been increased further by his subsequent marriage to Maud Gonne, the most famous beauty of her day. Their incompatible temperaments and lifestyles ensured that their relationship was short-lived and disastrous and they separated in 1905 amidst Gonne's accusations of cruelty, infidelity and drunkenness. The scandal seriously damaged MacBride's reputation and obloquy was heaped on him. Yeats, a defeated rival for Maud Gonne's hand, wrote of him in Easter 1916 as;

> This other man I had dreamed
> A drunken, vainglorious lout.
> He had done most bitter wrong
> To some who are near my heart.

In Ireland MacBride sank into financial hardship, unemployment and alcohol addiction. He finally secured a job with Dublin Corporation as a water bailiff and remained politically active as a member of the IRB, to whose Supreme

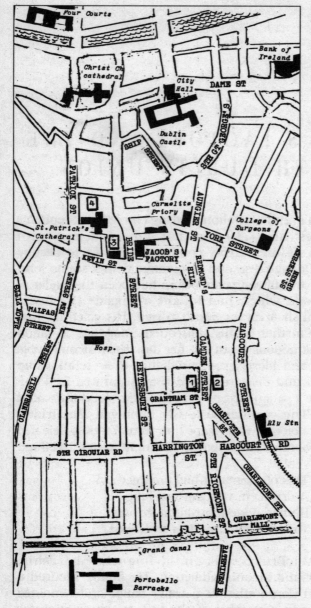

Jacob's Biscuit Factory Area
1. Byrne's stores
2. Delahunt's stores
3. Kevin Street police barracks
4. St Patrick's Park

Council he was elected in 1911. However, he was soon eased out in a purge which led to his replacement by Sean MacDermott. That he had been best man at Tom Clarke's wedding availed him nothing. Despite this reversal MacBride remained on good terms with the new leaders who excluded him from their revolutionary planning because they did not trust him to keep a secret. But they were mindful that one day MacBride's military knowledge and reputation might be of value. On Easter Monday morning MacDermott sent a messenger to MacBride's office, knowing that he often went there during holidays to work on the daily inspection of ships which had arrived in the port of Dublin overnight.[1] MacBride in fact was not there to receive his orders and only fortuitously encountered MacDonagh at the last moment in the city centre, where he was invited to join the Jacob's garrison. Now just past fifty years of age, he had been suddenly presented with an opportunity, perhaps the last, to redeem a decade and a half of drift, failure and dissipation and he grabbed it. Throughout the Rising MacBride cut a distinctive and rather incongruous figure, dressed in civilian clothes of navy-blue suit and grey hat with a malacca walking-cane on his arm.

The main body of Volunteers then marched the short distance to Bishop Street to occupy Jacob's biscuit factory, one of the city's few large employers. This huge building stood more or less on a line between Dublin Castle a quarter of a mile to the north and two army barracks, Wellington and Portobello, three-quarters of a mile to the south. Situated close to a warren of narrow streets, it was an impressive sight, tall and impregnable, with its two immense towers providing a panoramic view of much of the city. Nearby was the large medieval St Patrick's Cathedral where Church of Ireland people from the comfortable suburbs came on Sunday to hear some of the finest church music in the country. Alongside the cathedral, through the beneficence of the Guinness family, slums of the most wretched kind had recently been replaced with St Patrick's Park, working-class flats, public baths and a daily free cup of cocoa and bun for every child. Poverty was the norm in this area where MacDonagh's Volunteers were to make their stand. Jacob's was strategically important because snipers with binoculars and scientific range-finders could command Portobello Bridge, Portobello Barracks, the roof of Ship Street Barracks, Dublin Castle and much of Stephen's Green, all anticipated to be locations of major British military activity.

While one of the main factory gates was smashed open with a sledge-hammer another group of about forty Volunteers occupied three premises in Malpas Street and a house opposite Kevin Street police barracks. There they encountered hostility from the inhabitants of Blackpitts who sang pro-British tunes and threw stones, their opposition culminating in one man being shot and bayoneted fatally when he attempted to disarm a Volunteer. MacDonagh's men at Jacob's were also verbally and physically abused by a large crowd of residents, many of whom were soldiers' wives. Many of these 'Separation Women' who were the worse for drink and emboldened by the Volunteers' reluctance to retaliate, screamed abuse and attempted to seize their rifles. One even tried to incinerate the garrison by throwing paraffin over one of the factory gates and desisted only when a shot was fired over her head.[2] The hostility persisted until the evening when the outposts in Malpas Street were abandoned and the men, who were withdrawn to Jacob's along with four captured policemen, were punched and kicked as they entered the factory. Peadar Kearney, the composer of 'The Soldier's Song', was one of a group who seized a malthouse in Fumbally Lane. When an innocent-looking policeman wandered up to inquire 'What is going on here?', he was taken captive – one of ten policemen captured there and marched later to Jacob's where they spent the week peeling potatoes in the cookhouse. After a short time the malthouse was evacuated and the Volunteers erected barricades in Blackpitts and New Street.[3]

The Jacob's garrison eventually consisted of 178 men, most of them Irish Volunteers but with a sprinkling of Citizen Army members and a few Fianna boy scouts as well as some women cooks from the Cumann na mBan. As

MacDonagh and MacBride established a command post upstairs, the rank and file fortified the building, smashing windows and barricading them with sackfuls of flour, loopholing the walls and placing biscuit tins on the pavement to give warning of a night attack. However, to the men's disappointment and frustration almost the entire military action at Jacob's took place in the first hour when a tentative approach by about thirty British troops down Camden Street was ambushed by Volunteers at the junction of Bishop Street and Redmond's Hill; an officer and six men were wounded.[4] MacDonagh's men assumed that this was a precursor to a full-scale British assault, but Jacob's was of no great military or political importance to the British. Furthermore, because of its fortress-like impregnability and its location in a warren of tenement streets, a frontal assault would have involved the diversion of considerable manpower, while artillery would have inflicted devastation on civilians and property. Instead, General Lowe, the commander of the British forces, decided to contain its garrison and wear it down psychologically by low-intensity pressure until he was ready to deal with it in his own time. That pressure involved sleep deprivation and unnerving the insurgents by sniping and having armoured cars speed noisily past the factory at night-time, a shrewd and effective tactic which had a cumulative effect on the defenders. One Volunteer recalled that 'the ear-splitting crash of all sorts of arms gave the impression that the building was being attacked front and rear. All this meant that nerves were as taut as a violin at pitch, in addition to which physical exhaustion and lack of sleep had the men in such a condition that rows of houses marching solemnly away was a usual occurrence.'[5] Lowe's refusal to take the bait robbed MacDonagh of the initiative which he never regained and he was reduced to sending out small groups to reconnoitre or conduct ambushes. At 2 a.m. on Easter Tuesday morning he sent a group of about fifteen Volunteers to Byrne's stores at the corner of Grantham Street and another half-dozen to occupy Delahunt's directly opposite to serve as outposts which would guard the Portobello approaches to Jacob's.

Shortly afterwards other outposts were established in Camden Street but nearer the factory. These were to come under attack the following day when fourteen soldiers acting as an advance guard for a much larger party moved down Charlotte Street, surrounded Byrne's and began firing repeated volleys into the building. They also attacked Delahunt's and forced an entry but captured only the rifle, shotgun and pistol left behind by the fleeing defenders. By that time all of Jacob's outposts had fallen.

Inside Jacob's effective leadership gradually passed from MacDonagh to the dynamic and decisive MacBride. Throughout Easter Week MacDonagh oozed supreme confidence during his tours of inspection and certainly looked the part in the full uniform, cloak and cap of an Irish Volunteer commandant, but this shy, sensitive academic lacked ruthlessness and drive and the pressures of command were to find him out. His lack-lustre approach established a lax regime at Jacob's where the men endured long periods of inactivity and boredom. In addition his man-management was poor and his attempts to assert himself and act decisively caused only exasperation or resentment. On one occasion he awakened a group of Volunteers who had just bedded down and ordered them to take food supplies to the College of Surgeons and return with rifles. When they had completed their mission they were complimented by MacDonagh but he then asked the officer in charge what had happened to the bayonets?

The officer replied that he had heard nothing about them. MacDonagh then said that there were bayonets in the College of Surgeons to fit the rifles and that they would have to be brought over. He then told the officer that as the men present knew the way he had better take them back and get them! That was nearly the last straw.[6]

On another occasion when Mallin requested the transfer of Citizen Army members from Jacob's to the College of Surgeons, MacDonagh told one of them, William Oman,

'I'm not letting you go. I am keeping you beside myself.'
Then he asked me what I thought of that arrangement.
'Well,' I said, 'you are in command, sir.' However, just as
the party was about to depart, he changed his mind and
released me to go with them.[7]

For many defenders their presence in Jacob's was an eerie
and, at times, a surreal experience. The size of the building
(especially in relation to the small number of defenders), the
gloom and the creaking floorboards were extremely
oppressive and some incidents had an almost hallucinatory
quality. One man woke to the sight of an escort of armed
Volunteers escorting a lady dressed in widow's weeds,
blindfolded and wearing the emblem of the Royal Dublin
Fusiliers. She was not, in fact, an illusion but a woman
dispatch carrier who had passed in disguise through British
lines carrying the message from Mallin in the College of
Surgeons.[8] Another problem for MacDonagh's men,
surprisingly, was the absence of proper food since the
superabundance of rich cake soon induced nausea and a
craving for ordinary plain bread. The announcement on one
occasion that roast beef and vegetables were to be served
resulted in fevered excitement which evaporated when a
meal of a cubic inch of beef and one potato arrived. After
this repast one Volunteer, commencing a siesta under a long
table, accidentally discharged his shotgun with a
tremendous explosion which sent another man's plate flying
through the air, narrowly missing taking his brains with it.[9]
On Easter Thursday MacDonagh seized the opportunity for
some action when de Valera in Boland's requested arms and
ammunition and told him that he was under pressure from
British soldiers in Merrion Square. MacDonagh set off with
fifteen cyclists on a relief mission travelling by the south side
of Stephen's Green and Leeson Street before dismounting at
Fitzwilliam Street near Merrion Square. There they shot a
lone sentry outside a house in the square and fought a brief
encounter with soldiers inside, but broke off when they
decided they would be unable to force their way through to

Boland's. On the return journey they rode in open formation along the dangerous west side of the Green and one cyclist, John O'Grady, was wounded at York Street. He reached Jacob's supported by riders on each side holding him up, but he collapsed shortly afterwards and died.[10]

In addition to unsatisfactory military activity the sense of isolation at Jacob's depressed many of the garrison. The Volunteers had only a fragmentary knowledge of events in the rest of the city, especially since MacDonagh did not communicate information from the dispatch carriers to the rank and file. In the absence of hard news rumours swirled through the factory. One of them recalled:

We heard that German troops had landed at Wexford and were striking inland in thousands, routing British garrisons as they drove towards Dublin in support of the Rising; it was said that the Volunteers were fighting bitterly along the coastline to Cork where the city was supposed to be out like Dublin; British troops were being rushed from the Curragh camp and reinforcements were pouring into Dublin along the Naas road; Dublin Castle was on fire; the British were using explosive bullets and shooting prisoners; buildings all over the city were being burned indiscriminately; Dublin was almost in ruins. Each rumour was more fantastic than the last, one contradicted the other. Everyone was confused, nobody knew the true state of affairs.[11]

What was certainly real and visible were the fires which later gripped the city centre. On Easter Friday one of the cooks in Jacob's, Maire Nic Shiubhlaigh, ascended one of the towers and gazed on the inferno.

Over in the north the GPO was blazing fiercely; it seemed as though the flames had spread the length of O'Connell Street. There were huge columns of smoke. Around us, in the turret, the Volunteers were still keeping up a steady fire on British outposts nearby. In the distance the crackle of gunfire was accompanied by sudden little flashes. All around, through the darkness, bombed out buildings burned. From where we stood, the whole city seemed to be on fire. The noise of artillery, machine-gun and rifle fire was deafening.[12]

By then the defenders knew in their hearts that the end was in sight, though they avoided using the word 'surrender' and concentrated instead on preparations for a last stand in which they intended to inflict massive casualties on the British attackers. On Saturday, while Pearse was arranging surrender elsewhere, the Volunteers in Jacob's were actually strengthening their defences and firing on British troops in the area.

However, on Sunday 30 April MacDonagh's world fell apart with dramatic speed. Nurse Elizabeth O'Farrell was being conveyed by the British to the various commands with Pearse's surrender order and in the course of the morning she arrived at Jacob's. There she was blindfolded and taken to MacDonagh, whereupon the blindfold was removed. She gave him the order and also told of the evacuation of the GPO and subsequent events in Moore Street. MacDonagh replied that he would not take orders from a prisoner and that as the next in seniority to Pearse he would not reply to the surrender until he had conferred with General Lowe and his own officers in Jacob's.[13] The factory was also visited by two priests, Fathers Augustine and Aloysius, who had been mediating between the two sides. They had met Lowe who had intimated that, unless he was able to make contact with MacDonagh, he would demolish Jacob's; a defiant MacBride opposed capitulation and MacDonagh reiterated that Pearse's status as a prisoner invalidated any surrender order. Instead, MacDonagh now donned the mantle of *de facto* Commander-in-Chief and declared that he would negotiate only with the General Officer Commanding the British forces. Detached from reality, he talked like a man holding all the cards. He claimed that his garrison was well supplied and the course of the war was about to change to Ireland's advantage; if Jacob's could only hold out Ireland would be guaranteed representation at a peace conference. With time running short, Augustine and Aloysius returned to Lowe who offered to meet MacDonagh at St Patrick's Park at lunchtime. MacDonagh accepted the offer and during their subsequent discussions, which began on the footpath and concluded in the general's car, Lowe began the painful process of reconnecting MacDonagh to the real world. He described the general situation and the hurricane that was about to engulf Jacob's, and when he emerged MacDonagh informed Augustine and Aloysius that he had decided to advise surrender. He agreed a truce until 3 p.m. to enable him to return to the factory and also to deliberate with Ceannt at the South Dublin Union.[14] Lowe's warning had not been an empty threat. The war diary of the North Stafford Regiment records that it had been ordered at 1 p.m. 'to move to Dublin Castle and made preparations for attack on rebels in Jacob's biscuit factory who had not surrendered'.

MacDonagh's men knew that he had gone to meet Lowe, and Maire Nic Shiubhlaigh remembered them waiting apprehensively for his return. Their agony was made worse by 'the almost uncanny silence which had hung over Dublin since the last shell was fired during the bombardment of the GPO', which 'made everyone uncertain. Everybody waited for MacDonagh to come back.'[15] On his return, the commandant hurried upstairs to headquarters where a lengthy officers' meeting ratified his recommendation to surrender but a shattered MacDonagh was either unwilling or unable to tell the men and women personally. Instead he summoned Maire Nic Shiubhlaigh, who recalled:

When I went in, he was standing behind his desk, beside Major MacBride. He said, very simply, 'We are going to surrender.' He seemed the same business-like person we had always known, until he spoke; his voice was quiet, and he seemed very disillusioned. He said, 'I want you to thank all the girls for what they have done. Tell them I am issuing an order that they are to go home. I'll see that you are all safely conducted out of the building.' I started to protest, but he turned away. One could never imagine him looking so sad.[16]

The rank and file were informed of the surrender by an officer, Tom Hunter, who wept as he made his way downstairs. There he drew his sword and smashed the blade in two before breaking the news to the men. The decision and its maladroit delivery caused uproar as Volunteers shouted, 'Don't give in, . . we can't give in now!'; others collapsed in disbelief or hurled their rifles through the air, while one man smashed the butt of a gun against a wall. Many suspected that a deal had been done behind their backs and an ugly mood developed as the garrison verged on anarchy. They moved upstairs to confront MacDonagh, who, listless and careworn, stood on a table and announced that the surrender would take place at noon. He disowned personal responsibility for a surrender not of his making; he was only carrying out the orders of Pearse. Before he broke into tears, he concluded sadly, 'We have to give in. Those of you who are in civilian clothes, go home. Those in uniform stay on. You cannot leave if you are in uniform.' He said:

> We are about to surrender but we have succeeded in establishing the Irish Republic according to international law by holding out for a week. Although I have assurances from his reverence that nobody will be shot, I know I will be shot, but you men will be treated as prisoners.[17]

Far from restoring discipline this lack-lustre valediction incited a mood of virtual mutiny and Hunter emotionally contradicted his commanding officer by shouting, 'All I say is, any of you who go home now ought to be ashamed of yourselves! Stand your ground like men!' Others shouted: 'We won't be shot like dogs' to which MacDonagh replied, hardly reassuringly, that 'They might shoot some of us. They can't shoot all of us.'[18] Father Augustine then made a speech which mixed praise and comfort with a stark warning.

> Not one amongst you will be shot. The stand you have made this week has gone round the world and the enemy dare not shoot; but let me impress on you all, that

the man who fires another shot in this building will incur a terrible responsibility.[19]

At this point MacDonagh, who could bear no more, left the room. In his absence some, including Peadar Kearney, argued for a mass breakout, while others denounced them as deserters.[20] Discipline threatened to disintegrate completely until MacBride entered the room, still immaculately groomed, the epitome of sartorial elegance in a spotless serge suit and puffing on a cheroot. His presence and a serenity based on his reconciliation to capture and death, contrasted dramatically with MacDonagh's dishevelled, unwashed, unshaven appearance and clear indications of the most intense emotional strain. MacBride told them that;

Liberty is a priceless thing and anyone of you that sees a chance, take it. I'd do so myself, but my liberty days are over. Good luck boys. Many of you may live to fight some other day. Take my advice, never allow yourselves to be cooped up inside the walls of a building again.[21]

Kearney and many others now slipped away, procured fresh clothes at the Carmelite priory and decided to take their chances in the streets. Others delayed their decision until the garrison eventually marched out of the factory and then simply melted into the surrounding crowds during the half-mile march to the surrender point.[22]

With a special permit to travel through the British line and in a car provided by Lowe, MacDonagh, Augustine and Aloysius drove to the South Dublin Union where Ceannt agreed to surrender. But as the three men left they were shot at by a drunken British soldier who was immediately arrested by an officer.[23] When MacDonagh met Lowe again at St Patrick's Park at 3 p.m. on Sunday afternoon he announced his intention to surrender. MacDonagh then visited the South Dublin Union to arrange the details of the surrender but had great difficulty persuading the garrison at Marrowbone Lane to capitulate. When he arrived there at about 4 p.m. one

Volunteer said that MacDonagh 'was hatless and unarmed and looked old, weary and ill and something in his general appearance told me the worst had happened'.[24] After considerable discussion he finally secured the garrison's very reluctant agreement to surrender and returned to Jacob's, where the men had assembled in the basement ready for the evacuation. Then, as Father Aloysius recalled:

> We heard a loud crash and sounds that seemed like bombs exploding. One of the Volunteers came and told us that a crowd of looters were breaking into the office at Bishop Street. Father Monahan and myself went through the factory – with difficulty, owing to the fact that a water main had burst or been broken and was flooding the offices. We found a window had been broken and the looters were getting out to the street again. We mounted to the window and addressed the people, pointing out the scandalous conduct of those who were responsible for the looting. We asked the people to withdraw to their homes and allow the work of peace to go on. They listened to our appeal and withdrew. Before doing so, several gave up the articles they had pilfered – which included rounds of ammunition, revolvers and articles of clothing.[25]

MacDonagh's surrender at St Patrick's Park at 3.15 p.m. was a dismal affair. The pace of events had taken an enormous physical and emotional toll and now the sudden collapse of his hopes, the certainty of British retribution, the chaos of the final hours and the looting all coalesced in his mind. His emotional control had always been tenuous and it now disintegrated into psychic collapse as the looters' rampage was transmuted in his mind into a murderous assault by British soldiers. Major de Courcy Wheeler, the British officer who took the surrender, listened, bemused, as MacDonagh raged that, 'although his men had laid down their arms in order to surrender the soldiers had opened fire on them, were throwing bombs . . . and that the military had broken into the factory and were killing his men and that he had seen one of our soldiers taking up a position in the factory and was using his bayonet'. Wheeler knew this was impossible since there were no troops in that location, but MacDonagh was impervious to contradiction and only when the two men drove back with Augustine and Aloysius and Nurse O'Farrell did the two priests confirm that the disturbances had been caused by the looters.[26]

THE SOUTH DUBLIN UNION

Ceannt's 4th Battalion assembled at Emerald Square, Dolphin's Barn, at about 11 a.m. Among the leading officers present was the muscular vice-commandant Cathal Brugha, the embodiment of unreconstructed militarism who 'knew nothing of fear and had little sympathy for anyone who did. He spoke little of his political views, but one gathered he regarded the gun as the only effective sound in Irish politics. If one could not or would not take a gun one simply did not exist as far as he was concerned.'[27] Another was Con Colbert, a small stocky man who had once been the Chief Scout of the Fianna movement. Colbert did not smoke or drink and his ascetic lifestyle was derived from his study of Irish history. 'All his lectures centred around the subject of "Why we failed." His answer to this question was always 'Drink and want of discipline and loose talk."'[28] At this moment he dreaded a leak of information and a last-minute pre-emptive government swoop, and had ordered that Wellington Barracks be watched for unusual military activity. To Colbert's relief all was normal and at 11.30 a.m. the 4th Battalion proceeded unhindered to its targets, the South Dublin Union and three important outposts at Watkins's Brewery (Ardee Street), Jameson's Distillery (Marrowbone Lane) and Roe's Distillery in Mount Brown.

The South Dublin Union was entered at the front and rear. The main party of thirty men led by Ceannt and Brugha had travelled along the canal bank to Rialto Bridge at the back of the complex. There they cut the telephone wires and went through a small door where they took the keys from the

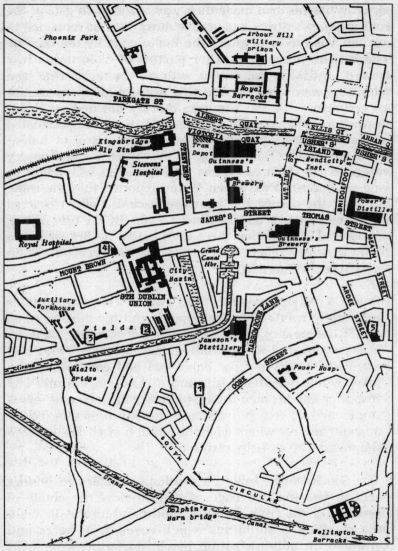

South Dublin Union Area

1. Emerald Square
2. Rear Gate, SDUnion
3. Sheds
4. Roe's Malt House
5. Watkins's Brewery

porter. While his men made their way to the main gate at the front in James's Street half a mile away, Ceannt remained to post ten Volunteers to guard the Rialto gate. By the time he reached the main gate other parties of Volunteers had arrived. Initially the Union officials believed that the Volunteers were simply conducting practice manoeuvres, but the seriousness of the situation quickly dawned on them. Meanwhile, other parties had reached the three designated outposts.[29] Colbert had dispatched a scout patrol of half-a-dozen men under Tom Young to the Ardee Street Brewery with orders to shoot to kill any British soldiers who might be lying in ambush. Even when Young reported that the route was clear the obsessively security-conscious Colbert ordered him to return and scour the district again. By the time Young had assured himself that there were indeed no British troops in the district Colbert had seized the brewery but when Young reported there he;

found a Police Inspector and two or three constables apparently waiting for the Captain and his men to come out of the brewery, with the intention of arresting them for breaking in and for wounding the caretaker (who had attempted to prevent the entry and had got a taste of a pike, which surprised him more than hurt him). The Inspector and his men thought to place my men and myself under arrest, too, but he very quickly remembered an appointment elsewhere when he found himself looking into the muzzles of six hefty revolvers.[30]

The South Dublin Union, a poorhouse situated in James's Street at the western edge of Dublin, was the abode of thousands of the city's destitute, infirm and insane. It was a large complex of buildings which covered 50 acres and contained an administration block, dormitories for over 3,000 inmates, residences for officials and nurses, churches, hospitals, sheds, workshops and fields. At the main entrance in James's Street there was a block of houses running parallel with the road and facing inwards. To the right of the entrance was the South Dublin Rural District Council Office and immediately over it was the boardroom. The remainder of the block was laid out in wards. At the end of the row was the paint shop and running at right angles was the night nurses' home with a Protestant church opposite its entrance and the inmates' dining hall slightly to the right. It was more like a small town and its southern wall followed a full half-mile of the Grand Canal.

Ceannt now led a group into the nursing home while others made for the boardroom; it was their last contact until Easter Thursday. The Union decided not to evacuate the inmates and instead transferred them to buildings draped with Red Cross flags. Initially some inhabitants couldn't comprehend the radical alteration to their lives; one nun who answered her door to an armed Volunteer inquired if he had come to read the gas meters? In the days that followed, both the Volunteers and the British tried hard to minimise the inconvenience and danger to non-combatants and permitted free access for provisions. Even so some perished in the gun battles which raged around them during Easter Week.

Ceannt never had more than sixty-five men to defend such a large area, but even with such an inadequate garrison he ensured that the British had to battle for every foot. Unlike Pearse, Plunkett and MacDonagh, the taciturn Ceannt was a man of action and in the fighting at the South Dublin Union he fully displayed his qualities of energy, resilience, inspiration and physical courage. To his amusement he now heard the sounds of a military band wafting through the air from the nearby Richmond Barracks and remarked, 'They do not know yet', but a sudden silence indicated that the news of the Rising had just reached its garrison. Ceannt knew that a British attack on the Union was inevitable because of its size and strategic importance. It was the largest outlying group of buildings in the west of the city and was close to Kingsbridge railway station, the terminus of the line to Cork and the south. Across the Liffey lay the Royal Barracks, while on a low rise to the north stood the Royal Hospital, Kilmainham, the residence of the British Commander-in-

Chief, with the South Dublin Union in sight of its windows.

The dramatic challenge which this occupation offered to the British army was symbolised by the large tricolour flag which Ceannt had placed at the top of the west wing and which came under fire all day from a machine gun on the roof of the Royal Hospital. The Volunteers hurried to ready their defences. The main gate, windows and passages were barricaded and some buildings were evacuated, including the night nurses' home which became Ceannt's headquarters.

Soon after the occupation the Volunteers attacked a column of soldiers passing into the city by James's Street and shortly afterwards a party of 200 men of the Royal Irish Rifles was scattered at point-blank range. Thereafter the fighting rarely ceased. Ceannt's force was stretched dangerously thin. There were only fourteen Volunteers in buildings and sheds, which dotted the large fields near the canal, and on the canal wall itself, where they were exposed to sniper fire from the other side and, more distantly, from the Royal Hospital. Despite covering fire from the main Union buildings it was impossible to maintain satisfactory communications because of the small size of the Volunteer garrison. Also the mattresses barricading the shed windows offered minimal protection to the crouching defenders.

On Monday British troops entered at the Rialto side by forcing a small door, and 500 yards along others broke through despite sniper fire from Jameson's Distillery. Other soldiers climbing the wall were fired on from the sheds and one soldier, perched on a telegraph pole, was fatally wounded.[31] Under sustained firing and considerably outnumbered, the Volunteers retreated to a hospital, only to be captured after a soldier broke through a door with a lawn-mower. Very quickly Ceannt's men became concentrated in the main group of buildings at the James's Street entrance where Ceannt was almost captured when reconnoitring the Protestant infirmary. A fleeing Volunteer suddenly appeared, chased by troops, and both he and Ceannt ran into a blind alley. Having failed to force a wooden gate, they stood with their weapons at the ready for a last stand but the troops had broken off their pursuit. Ceannt then made it to the safety of the Catholic hospital through a gate opened by a nun.[32] Other inhabitants became actively involved in the struggle. For instance, Ceannt instructed his orderly, Peadar Doyle, to requisition a group of inmates to carry boxes of ammunition into the night nurses' home. Doyle felt uncomfortable at such coercion and preferred instead to set a price for the job, which was completed enthusiastically in less than ten minutes.[33] But not everyone's involvement was as profitable and harmless. During fighting in the hospital in the main complex a nurse, Margaretta Keogh, who was checking patients on the ground floor, was killed instantly by two concealed soldiers covering the open doorway who opened fire immediately they saw her white uniform. During a follow-up search in the hospital an inmate was shot dead in the kitchen. Later, soldiers, hearing noises, climbed up to the window of a room in which eight inmates were clustered around a fireplace and hurled a grenade. The devastating explosion killed one man outright and severely injured most of the rest.[34]

To the participants the combat in the main complex was similar to a walk through a shooting gallery. Nervous and frightened defenders and attackers moved cautiously and quietly along many endless, intersecting corridors and past innumerable hiding places, never knowing if they might be shot at point-blank range. Often only a wall separated the two sides, and the slightest sound produced a fusillade of bullets from men whose edginess was increased by their unfamiliarity with the battle-ground. For these tired and stressed men the daytime was bad enough, but night-fighting at close quarters which often became almost hand-to-hand was a terrifying experience. The more shrewd removed their boots before creeping along the corridors and put their ears to the thin partitions to listen for voices or even breathing. Some fired first and asked questions later, while others wilted and opted out entirely. One British soldier hid in the carpenter's shop until he saw the body of a soldier being placed on a hearse by Union officials, whereupon he surreptitiously slid into an empty coffin beside the corpse and, after an eerie journey out of the battleground, emerged to the consternation of civilian onlookers.[35] The battle's uncompromising nature can be gauged from the fact that as early as Monday evening Ceannt's offer to the military at Rialto, via a female official, of an hour's truce to remove the wounded and bury the dead was rejected out of hand: 'We shall give you no terms, you have killed our major' was the reply.[36]

Volunteer morale in the South Dublin Union was high, sustained in large part by the leadership of Ceannt and Brugha who time and again risked their own lives and survived. Brugha, especially, for much of the week seemed to possess a charmed life, as bullets whizzed past leaving him unscathed. He was constantly active, moving panther-like to check sentries' alertness and watching for enemy activity. The Volunteers were also heartened by civilian encouragement in the form of small parcels of cooked food which were frequently thrown over the walls along with supportive messages.[37] On Wednesday the military appeared to have withdrawn completely and the Volunteers were able to stroll around the interior courtyard, but the lull was only temporary as the British built up their reserves for a massive attack. By Thursday Sherwood Foresters had arrived from England and they were supplemented by troops from the Curragh, Belfast and Athlone, and also by some members of the RIC. The Union garrison had just had lunch when there was a call of 'Enemy attack – to your guns' at about 3 p.m. when the British launched a co-ordinated offensive against the night nurses' home with a terrific bombardment by machine guns and grenades. Peadar Doyle, Ceannt's orderly, was dispatched to warn the men in the front offices that they were surrounded on all sides. As he made his way he discovered that barricades had been removed from one door which, perhaps by coincidence, a party of British soldiers was just then approaching. When the troops noticed Doyle they swiftly retreated but had they entered they would have split the Union garrison. Doyle became convinced that inmates had been responsible for initiating this near-disaster.[38] Hundreds of troops now fanned out from the Rialto side under heavy attack from Volunteers in Jameson's Distillery. Firing continuously, the soldiers moved in sections on the night nurses' home, where Volunteers returning fire shot some of them dead. Inside, holes had been bored in the walls to allow continuous movement to a barricade in the interior, from behind which Volunteers could fire, assisted by others on the stairs and landing. The British were unable to force the front hall door in the face of fanatical resistance, in the course of which Ceannt dashed into the open and cut one attacker down. They then resorted to boring from an adjoining building and finally broke through by blowing in the gable end with high explosive. Even then the soldiers who broke through at five o'clock were confronted by the barricade of barbed wire entanglements and their demand for surrender was answered by volleys of shots. For the next five hours there was incessant firing, deafening noise and exploding grenades, one of which caused frightful injuries to Brugha. He now lay in a room with little or no plaster left on the walls and every piece of furniture wrecked.

Brugha's deputy, William Cosgrave, now assumed command, because Ceannt at this stage was fighting in the region of the paint shop nearby. Cosgrave ordered an evacuation of the night nurses' home and a retreat in the direction of the paint shop from where he hoped to link up with Volunteers in the boardroom. However, British forces fought desperately to drive a wedge between the insurgents by attacking both the paint shop and the night nurses' home. During the attack Brugha's voice could be heard shouting, 'Come on, you curs, till I get one shot before I die. I am only a wounded man. Eamonn Ceannt, come here and sing God Save Ireland before I die.' When Ceannt broke through to the men in the paint shop he learnt that it was Brugha shouting and he decided to lead his men back into the night nurses' home. He knew that Brugha would not have spoken as he had unless he was still free and Ceannt was determined to save him if he possibly could. On arrival in the yard of the night nurses' home he discovered his vice-commandant sitting with his back against the outer wall and his 'Peter the

Painter' revolver to his shoulder, watching for the first enemy to appear. In a poignant scene involving two men who hitherto had been the epitome of unremitting belligerence, an emotional Ceannt went down on one knee and embraced Brugha for about a minute as they conversed quietly in Irish. Then he rose, regained control, and ordered that Brugha be taken to the rear. But he could not be treated there because of the all-pervasive gunfire and bursting hand grenades which continued until the British were driven back by 8 p.m. All that his protectors could do was to staunch the blood and keep moving from place to place and though he was perfectly conscious, Brugha seemed to be sinking fast. Although his wounds were finally dressed he became delirious on Friday morning and was removed to the Union hospital by a Carmelite nun and a Union official with a Red Cross flag. It was discovered that he had twenty-five wounds, five of them dangerous, nine serious and eleven slight. His left hip and legs were particularly badly affected; after the surrender Brugha was treated for months in Dublin Castle's hospital and made a remarkable recovery but he never fully recovered the use of his limbs.[39]

On Friday evening, at 7 p.m., a party of soldiers approaching in the dark from the convent side fired on some of their own men who were attacking the front of the night nurses' home, causing a retreat and giving the Volunteers a respite. There was comparative quiet for the rest of the night. Because of the collapse of the dispatch system the last news which Ceannt received was on Friday and it was not reassuring. The provinces were quiet and the British were conducting a systematic artillery bombardment in the centre of Dublin. There were no further attacks on Saturday and by dawn on Sunday the garrison had not yet heard of the general surrender ordered by Pearse. News of this finally reached the South Dublin Union that morning when MacDonagh arrived from Jacob's to meet Ceannt. Ceannt then summoned his entire garrison and informed them of Headquarters' decision. Some men suggested escape while there was still time, but Peadar Doyle spoke strongly in favour of a complete surrender saying that men who had fought together throughout the week ought to stand together at the end. Although this was agreed several men did break away. The garrison was then paraded in the square at the Union and marched to the main gate.[40]

Ceannt's men were proud of their performance and very heartened by their reception from the local civilian population. Instead of vituperation, Peadar Doyle recalls that they were 'met with marked enthusiasm by a great crowd of people. All along the route to St Patrick's we were greeted with great jubilation, particularly in the poorer districts.'[41]

THE OUTPOSTS OF THE SOUTH DUBLIN UNION

On the first day of the Rising a disappointingly small garrison occupied Marrowbone Lane, where its commander, Captain Seamus Murphy, adopted the Beau Geste defence of putting caps and hats on brush handles and positioning them at the windows.[42] He knew that Marrowbone Lane had to be prevented from falling quickly as it was integral to the defence of the South Dublin Union. Its distillery commanded a laneway called 'The Back of the Pipes' and Fairbrother's Field which bordered Guinness's building as well as covering both sides of the canal along the back of the Union as far as Dolphin's Barn Bridge. There was also direct contact until Wednesday between Marrowbone Lane and the South Dublin Union. This was maintained by runners, one of whom carried Murphy's messages written on the inside of his collar.[43]

Unlike the South Dublin Union, the fighting at Marrowbone Lane was initially light and sporadic. British troops, slow to recognise the rebellion's seriousness, exposed themselves to sniper fire and suffered losses on the north bank of the canal at Rialto Bridge. The Howth rifles, however, were almost as dangerous to the Volunteers, as Robert Holland recorded.

It was a bad weapon for street fighting. Flame about three feet long came out through the top of the barrel when it was fired and a shower of soot and smoke came back in one's face. After three shots were fired from it, it would have to be thrown away to let it get cool and the concussion [*sic*] of it was so severe that it drove me back along the floor several feet.[44]

On Tuesday morning the Union's protective screen was weakened by the mysterious disappearance from Roe's Distillery of Captain Tommy McCarthy and the subsequent abandonment of the post by the entire garrison.[45] That afternoon there was a fierce two-hour gun battle as the fighting in the Marrowbone Lane area intensified. British troops suffered serious losses, including one soldier who had braved everything to get very close before being shot dead. He lay dead among roaming army horses, one of them dragging the body of a lancer whose foot had been caught in the stirrup.[46] Eventually the troops were withdrawn from Cork Street, Fairbrother's Field and the Rialto Bridge end as well as from the Canal Basin side and Guinness's Brewery. The weapons shortage of the Volunteers was alleviated somewhat by the acquisition of the dead soldiers' rifles. As darkness fell Holland's brother Walter, who had been scouting the area, came to the distillery and told him that there were many dead soldiers in Fairbrother's Field.

We crawled into Fairbrother's Field and made very slow progress and the time seemed very long before we picked out the first dead soldier. I cut off his web equipment and one of the others took his rifle. In this manner we stripped quite a lot of dead soldiers. In all we got five rifles.[47]

They crawled back in complete silence, handed over their cache and returned for another five rifles, again without making a sound. After his return from no man's land, Holland himself witnessed the lethal consequences of making one false move or sound. He reported to Jack Saul who;

told me that whilst I was away he thought he heard someone digging at the Canal double gate right under us.

He knew I had crossed the wall to the left of us but he could not account for this noise. I listened and heard this noise, like chains rattling. Something very hard was being moved about. Saul shouted out 'Halt' but the movement still went on. I shouted 'Halt or I fire!' and we both shouted that we had it covered. We then decided to fire at the gate. Both of us fired and then a lot of confusion and noise ensued. A few minutes later Sergeant Kerrigan came up and shouted that someone in our wing had shot and killed 'Mock' Keogh's horse. The horse had been rambling around the yard, nibbling the grass and throwing the collar up around his head.[48]

During the night of Easter Tuesday/Wednesday, Colbert evacuated the Ardee Street Brewery which had proved too large for his small garrison and anyway appeared to contributing nothing to the overall effort. He now transferred to Marrowbone Lane where he soon became *de facto* commandant.[49] By Wednesday, both sides were fully locked, logistically and emotionally, into the struggle. The Volunteers had been roused by the wound inflicted on Mick Liston, the best shot in the entire 4th Battalion, who had been grazed in the head while positioned in the crow's-nest at the top of the building. To his comrades Liston was a heroic figure and, although he was soon back in action, they wanted retribution. Robert Holland recalled that;

We all had a great affection for him, and his wounding brought the first bit of bitterness in us. We all set our teeth to get revenge. Mick was no sooner up in position when he was down again with another head wound, this time more serious. As he passed me I saw blood running down his face. He said he was all right but I got a chilly feeling in my stomach. He was about twenty years of age. Our hearts sank . . . as they brought him down.[50]

As the battle raged, Holland became puzzled by the increasing intensity and accuracy of British sniper fire, which poured in a continuous stream of bullets from all sides and forced the evacuation of the crow's-nest. On the previous day he had noticed a woman leaning out of a window at the gable end of a house opposite and now, as he scanned the roofs of James's Street Christian Brothers' School and the houses in Basin Street and Basin Lane, he saw her again.

She had a hat, blouse and apron on her and I got suspicious. I told Mick O'Callaghan that I was going to have a shot at her. He said 'No.' I said it was a queer place for a woman to be and that it was queer she should have a hat on her, as she must have seen the bullets flying around but took no notice of them. I made up my mind. She was only 35 or 40 yards away from me and I fired at her. She sagged half way out of the window. The hat and small little shawl fell off her and I saw what I took to be a woman was a man in his shirt sleeves.[51]

Holland also spotted the tops of rifle barrels behind the tree trunks under the window. By now supersniper Liston was back in action and had the honour of eliminating the crouching British snipers. His comrades gazed expectantly as he left the room and crept upstairs.

We had to wait about ten minutes. A few shots came from the hidden soldiers, but the soldiers did not show themselves. After another few minutes, another fusillade was fired at us, during which one of them made a mistake and showed himself. Liston potted him. The soldiers then broke cover and ran along the wall towards the South Dublin Union and Rialto Bridge. They had to run about three-quarters of a mile, during which they were under our fire. There were twelve in all and every one of them was hit. From that time on we were very careful and kept a look-out for snipers.[52]

By now Liston felt invincible and when he identified a British sniper sitting on a branch about 200 yards away on the

Dolphin's Barn side of the canal, one shot left the soldier hanging out of the tree for the remainder of the day. These small victories sent morale among the Marrowbone Lane garrison sky-high. Holland noted:

> We had no one killed and only two wounded and these were back in the fight again. If all the garrisons were like ours, and we had no doubt that they were, we were doing very well indeed. We must win and none of us thought otherwise. Failure was the last thing that I or the rest of us thought of. After reading and thinking over our history of the short, quick battles, we could not lose now. We were more than two days and a half fighting and that was longer than four previous rebellions put together.[53]

At dawn on Thursday British troops surrounded the garrison, digging trenches on both sides of the canal and also in Fairbrother's Field. Holland said that 'We settled down to a "battle royal". . . . Some of the soldiers broke and made a run for cover to the outer boundary wall of the Distillery which brings them nearer to us.'[54] Con Colbert marshalled about twenty men and instructed them in the use of grenades, which they threw over the wall when they heard voices outside the Canal gate.

> We heard some screeching and shouting outside and a lot of moaning. As a result, the soldiers at the outside of the wall ran away from it and they were fired on by a volley from the Distillery. I saw Con Colbert smile as he sent us back into the building again, saying 'that stops that attack for the present'. When I got up on top again the soldiers had become scarce but I could see a lot of bodies all around outside the wall and up as far as Dolphin's Barn Bridge.[55]

As night fell the firing eased off and the Volunteers took it in turns to snatch a few hours' sleep, but like so many others in Dublin they watched the bright red glow over the city. Morale remained incredibly high and a quiet euphoria suffused the garrison, particularly as the breakdown of communications meant that everything was seen through the prism of their own isolated and enclosed circumstances. Robert Holland felt:

> We are winning and nothing else matters. We will surely get that help. The Germans could not be far from Dublin now and the country Volunteers are showing the way. They have beaten the British in Athlone, Limerick and Galway days ago and they have only to hammer the troops in the Curragh camp. We have eliminated all the troops that landed at Kingstown and we are only mopping up the crowd that came down from Belfast. All this is what we were told by the odd stragglers that came in and we readily believed it all as we know that the soldiers we have killed belonged to a varied lot of regiments. We have seen their cap and collar badges. Some of these we have in our possession. The Notts, the Derbyshires, the West Kents, the Berks, the Wiltshires, the Royal Irish Rifles, the Dublin Fusiliers, the 4th and 5th Hussars, 17th Lancers, South Irish Horse, Inniskilling Fusiliers and Liverpool Rifles, and several others, so we thought there could not be many more left. We knew that Germany was beating England in France and so a few more days wouldn't matter. We carry on with our spirits getting higher.[56]

Nevertheless it was not all jubilation. Holland's brother Watty brought news that crowds were attacking and looting Volunteers' homes which had also been raided by soldiers and policemen, one of whom had told their mother that they would manure Marrowbone Lane with rebel bodies.

When Friday morning broke the weather was summer-like, warm and dry, and the defenders' morale was high. There was only intermittent British sniping and the garrison believed it was dug in for a long stay. Holland says that 'Colbert all the time seemed to think that we must win and said to me that we must come in at the peace negotiations when the war had finished. But there was no mention of any of us surrendering at any time.'[57] The men relaxed and some even spent time exploring the distillery building. But at 4 a.m. large numbers of soldiers appeared on Rialto Bridge with field kitchens as far as could be seen and Holland expected an attempt to rout all the rebel commands. The British came under attack from both the Union and Marrowbone Lane and the fighting continued till darkness when it eventually died down. On Saturday morning all the troops had been withdrawn out of range, though Colbert still expected a mass attack. Instead, except for a few shots, Saturday was uneventful and the enemy was not seen at all on Sunday. By now Holland estimated that there were over 100 Volunteers and 40 women in Marrowbone Lane where spirits remained high. In a mood of almost religious euphoria, Colbert addressed the garrison. He told them that there was good news from all quarters and was greeted with cries of 'Yes' when he asked if they were ready to fight to the last men even if the enemy tried to starve them out. Captain Murphy then concluded with a quotation from the Bible, 'Greater love no man hath than to lay down his life for his friend.'[58] Preparations were even under way for an evening *ceilidhe* in the main hall.

Then the mood abruptly changed. The garrison was visited by MacDonagh who had already been to the South Dublin Union. After delivering the bad news of Pearse's surrender order MacDonagh left in tears. According to Holland:

A rumour went around that a truce was being called. Captain Murphy, Lieutenant Harry Murray and Con Colbert seemed to be excited and a lot of the older men of the garrison were talking together. When Con Colbert broke away from them I approached him and asked him what the excitement was and had anything serious happened. He said – 'Bobby, I do not know what to say or think, but if what I think comes true our cause is postponed to a future generation. We are to surrender unconditionally and I cannot forecast what that will mean. We must have been let down very badly as we have not had the support of our people that we had expected.'

Colbert's disappointment and confusion was felt by many others as news spread through the distillery.[59]

About 6.30 p.m. Ceannt, a British officer and a priest with a white sheet on a flag-pole entered the front gate. Ceannt shook hands with Colbert and two other officers and the group conversed for a few minutes after which Colbert saluted Ceannt. Ceannt and his two companions then withdrew to the front gate while Colbert returned to his men.[60] Holland recorded:

I asked him what was the news and he said that all was over. When I heard this I felt kind of sick in my stomach, putting it mildly, and everyone else felt the same, I'm sure. It came as a shock. Colbert could hardly speak as he stood in the yard for a moment or two. He was completely stunned. The tears rolled down his cheeks. I glanced at Captain Murphy and he had turned a sickly yellow. Harry Murray bowed his head. Then Colbert pulled out his whistle and blew it. He gave a general order to those around him to bring down all the garrison to the yard. When all came down he told us to 'fall in' in double file.

Colbert, inconsolable and disorientated by the course and speed of events, told Holland that Headquarters had ordered a ceasefire and that Ceannt and his men were already outside the distillery. As he did so one Volunteer dropped his shotgun which discharged and wounded another man in the leg.

Colbert then announced that we were surrendering unconditionally and that anyone wishing to go or escape could do so. We were all in a state of bewilderment but I have a distinct recollection of Jim McGrath saying 'Toor-a-loo, boys, I'm off.' He crossed the wall. Some others broke also. Then Colbert reformed us up, numbered us off and we 'sloped arms' and we marched out of the Distillery through the front entrance with Colbert at our head.[61]

A large crowd had gathered outside and Ceannt remarked bitterly, 'Where were you men when you were wanted?' The column now set off with the South Dublin Union garrison at the front, followed by an ambulance containing some wounded Volunteers. Then came the Marrowbone Lane contingent. They marched in military fashion by Marrowbone Lane, Cork Street, Patrick Street and Bride Street. The journey was not entirely without its lighter side as Holland recalls:

> When we were almost at the Coombe Maternity Hospital, two drunken men insisted on falling in with us. They were ejected from our ranks several times on the route but eventually must have got into the ranks in my rear, for about two months later I saw these two men taking their exercise in Knutsford Prison.[62]

Nevertheless there were many unpleasant incidents. As they marched into Bride Street soldiers with fixed bayonets were formed two deep on each side of the road while machine guns were also trained on the prisoners. There a British officer ordered them to lay down their weapons which were then collected and thrown into a lorry. A few shots were discharged inside the vehicle because Volunteers had forgotten to extract cartridges. After a meticulous search of every man the column was marched back to Patrick Street, then on to James's Street, Mount Brown and Kilmainham. For most of the journey there were few people on the streets but when they arrived at Kilmainham Cross about 8 p.m. in the gathering dusk an angry, jeering crowd had assembled and Holland remembered men, women and children cursing loudly.[63]

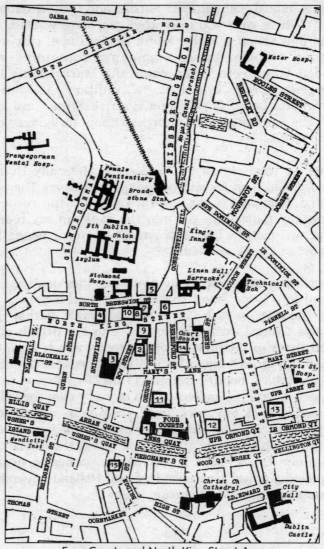

Four Courts and North King Street Area

1 Four Courts Hotel   6 Monks's Bakery   11 The Bridewell
2 Father Mathew Hall   7 Clarke's Dairy   12 Charles Street
3 Jameson's Distillery   8 'Reilly's Fort'   13 Strand Street
4 Red Cow Lane   9 Blanchardstown Mills   14 Malt house
5 Moore's coach factory   10 St John's Convent   15 Brazen Head

6

THE FOUR COURTS

According to General Maxwell the fighting around the Four Courts was, with the exception of that at Mount Street Bridge, 'by far the worst that occurred in the whole of Dublin'.[1] In the narrow surrounding streets Ned Daly's 1st Battalion engaged soldiers in what one writer has described as a 'miniature Stalingrad'.[2] The Volunteers were drawn from the area north of the Liffey which stretched from Phoenix Park to O'Connell Street and contained some of the poorest parts of the capital. In the period before the Rising they had trained regularly at battalion headquarters in Parnell Street or the Gaelic hall in Blackhall Place, where they had received instruction from former British soldiers in street-fighting techniques. By Easter 1916 Daly's officers had identified buildings to be occupied, vantage points for sharp-shooters, manholes covering subterranean wires and properties which contained food, bedding, clothing and medical supplies.[3]

Fewer than a third of his men were present in Blackhall Place at 11.30 a.m. on Easter Monday to be addressed by Daly, a frail and spare 25-year-old smartly turned out in his Volunteer uniform. He came from a family steeped in republicanism; his father had taken part in the 1867 Fenian Rising and his sister Kathleen was married to Tom Clarke. Daly had risen rapidly in the Volunteers from private to commandant and, though many regarded him as rather withdrawn and taciturn, he was to provide highly effective and humane leadership throughout Easter Week. In his speech Daly surprised many of the 300 assembled members by announcing that they were going into action and that the Irish Republic would be proclaimed at noon. Nevertheless only two men withdrew as the rest cheered loudly.[4]

The Four Courts area was both extensive and of great strategic significance. It stretched from the Mendicity Institution and the Liffey quays in the south, initially as far north as the Cabra and North Circular Roads, east towards the Bolton Street approach to North King Street, and west to North Brunswick Street as far as Red Cow Lane. While some units departed to seize outposts, the main column marched on the Four Courts, Dublin's seat of justice, a massive eighteenth-century edifice facing the Liffey. Behind it lay an area of minor streets crossed by the narrow though more substantial North King Street. To the north-west, behind the parallel North Brunswick Street, the area was dominated by hospitals and grim nineteenth-century institutions, including two asylums, a female prison and the poorhouse of the North Dublin Union. On rising ground half a mile due north lay Broadstone station, the terminus of the line from Galway and Athlone, an important British military base.

Daly's column arrived to find the Four Courts virtually deserted and guarded by a solitary policeman because court sittings had been suspended for the Easter vacation. After some hesitation the constable obeyed an order to open the gate and handed over the keys while the caretaker who was located in the basement was allowed to leave. Volunteers were soon systematically radiating through the complex as others cut telegraph and telephone wires on the roof or occupied the adjoining Four Courts Hotel and houses in nearby streets. Simultaneously a group of sixty-five Volunteers had marched from Blackhall Place to North Brunswick Street and halted in front of St John's Convent. After an enthusiastic reception from the nuns, Daly established his battalion headquarters in a room in the entrance hall but transferred next day to the Father Mathew Hall, a building in Church Street which belonged to the local Capuchin Priory. Its central location was to give him greater control over his command area; as well, it could serve as a prison and a first aid station. It was not until Easter Friday, and only in the face of mounting British pressure, that Daly again moved his headquarters to the Four Courts where the largest concentration of his Volunteers were based during the Rising.[5]

One of Daly's most important outposts was the Mendicity Institution, which was seized at noon by about a dozen men led by Sean Heuston. This building occupied a commanding position on the quays and its occupation was intended to prevent or at least delay a military advance from the Royal Barracks against the Four Courts or the Post Office in O'Connell Street. The Mendicity's glory days had been almost 150 years before, when, with windows inlaid with mother-of-pearl, it was probably the most splendidly furnished house in Ireland. After a subsequent conversion to a centre for the relief of the city's destitute it had gone into steady decline; its inner fittings had been removed and its beautiful garden had become a barren courtyard. By 1916 it had become 'the daily haunt of the very poorest of the poor'.[6] When Heuston's unit arrived at the Mendicity as the midday angelus sounded they forced open the front door, ordered out the occupants and began to fortify the building.

The 1st Battalion was soon in action because of the sudden arrival of about fifty lancers from Marlborough Barracks, who were escorting five lorry-loads of ammunition along Ormond Quay to the Magazine Fort in Phoenix Park. They had been allowed to pass Liberty Hall and the top of O'Connell Street unchallenged, and the Citizen Army garrison in the City Hall on the other side of the river had left them to be dealt with by the insurgents in the Four Courts. When Daly's men opened fire, a local shopkeeper, John Clarke, noted in his diary that 'Soldiers got dazed, horses reared, plunged, seeing their danger, they [the soldiers] turned into Charles Street. . . . All this time, the air was ringing with Volunteers' shots from the Courts. Soldiers did not fire a shot.'[7]

The lancers had only five rounds per man and most, if not all, of their weapons appear to have been unloaded. As they loaded their rifles the soldiers cut loose some of their terrified horses, overturned the munitions lorries to form a barricade or else ran for cover wherever it could be found. Others charged wildly up Church Street but were forced back by firing from the rear of the Four Courts. With their escape route closed they remained cooped up in a relatively secure side road for a further three and a half days before they could be relieved. Nevertheless the conditions which they had to endure were harrowing, particularly as 'the horses, after a few days, became maddened by hunger and several were destroyed by the soldiers. At length they were let loose and ran wild about the locality, the clattering sound of their hoofs occasionally raising a false alarm amongst the midnight watchers at the barricades.'[8] The victorious rebels celebrated by placing a captured lance outside one of their outposts, surmounting it with a tricolour and firing a volley of revolver shots.

Heuston's Volunteers in the Mendicity were also in action within half an hour against a considerable force of British troops who had come from the direction of the Royal Barracks on their way to strengthen the defences of Dublin Castle. They were marching four-deep along the north side of the River Liffey when several volleys from the Mendicity scattered them panic-stricken. As they crouched behind the quay wall or dashed into houses in the side streets or hid in abandoned tramcars, Lieutenant Nielson was killed and at least nine other ranks were wounded.[9]

The sudden engagement with the lancers and the sound of battle from the Mendicity galvanised the men in the Four Courts to work feverishly to make their position secure. They were vulnerable to attack from all sides. To the north, Broadstone station was soon in military hands, in the west there was the large Royal Barracks a short distance up the quay and to the south army units could push across the river from Dublin Castle. The Four Courts complex was soon heavily fortified, with its gates closed and the smashed windows barricaded with furniture and sandbags. Volunteers were posted at the various entrances, snipers were stationed on the roof where a tricolour had been unfurled, and the Lord Chancellor's office was converted into a first aid post furnished with beds commandeered from neighbouring hotels. The Four Courts was to prove a secure base from which Volunteers could be dispatched to the various outposts and in the final stages it became Daly's headquarters and a relatively safe haven for retreating rebels.[10] Meanwhile, Volunteers had blocked the bridge at Church Street, positioned units on the North Circular and Cabra Roads, and erected barricades in North King Street and North Brunswick Street. The materials for these obstructions had come from local business premises such as a coach factory, a builder's yard, a foundry, a large bakery and a distillery, as well as furniture from private houses, bricks from a building site and vehicles wherever they could be commandeered. The barricades were often ramshackle but they proved cumulatively effective in an area 'penetrated by infinite passages and alleys and more nearly resembling a rabbit warren than a battle field. In such mean and compact streets the barricade system of the rebels was indeed formidable.'[11]

Many of the 1st Battalion's outposts were in business premises such as 'Reilly's Fort', a public house at the corner of North King Street and Church Street, Moore's coach works, Monks's bakery and Clarke's dairy in North Brunswick Street. These provided an open field of vision north towards Broadstone station which as yet Daly had made no attempt to seize because of the unexpectedly low turn-out. The takeover of these outposts had often been achieved only in the face of reluctance or outright hostility. A 70-year-old man was shot through the eye during an argument and a doctor at Richmond Hospital, Joe O'Carroll, who advised residents not to co-operate, had a pistol put to his head. Later on Monday O'Carroll clashed again with rebels when he objected to their plan to take over a balcony at the Richmond but this time the Volunteers backed down and agreed to respect the hospital as neutral ground.[12] The Four Courts area was also thoroughly combed for supplies; weapons were commandeered from a gunsmith and provisions were appropriated from local hotels, shops and stores. Blanchardstown Mills was taken over for its large stocks of flour, meal and cereals. Although Monks's bakery was also seized, staff maintained production throughout the week. After the surrender, an astonished John Clarke watched;

> All day Sunday, the military taking motor lorries loaded with ammunitions and food from the Courts. . . . [the soldiers] can't understand why the Volunteers gave in as they had enough to last a month. . . . Patsy and I saw sacks of flour, all kinds . . . even to bars of soap. . . . It was a wonderful feat.[13]

During the early part of the week reinforcements arrived at the Four Courts, including Volunteers who had initially gone to work on Easter Monday. Some were sent by Connolly from the Post Office and women were dispatched by the Central Branch of the Cumann na mBan. Most saw little immediate action and when Clarke reconnoitred the neighbourhood on Easter Monday afternoon he discovered that 'It was safe at this time to move about as there were neither police nor soldiers to be seen'. Nevertheless, in the early evening, 'the firing from all parts became terrific. One would think half of Dublin should be down. We went to bed and slept as best we could.'[14] By then the throngs of holidaymakers who arrived back in the Four Courts area on Monday evening were in an anxious and confused state and they had to negotiate a way through the barricades to reach their homes. At some they were initially allowed through individually or in small groups but later as their numbers grew they were escorted in a convoy system through each of the obstructions.[15]

A mood of nervous anticipation descended on Daly's men. Paddy Holohan, who was stationed on a roof in North Brunswick Street, remembered how it seemed to him that 'every chimney pot was a soldier and I was shooting at them during the night. The nerves of everyone were at their tensest awaiting the expected attack.'[16] The tension was heightened by the darkness into which the area had been plunged and guards at the barricades had to challenge anyone who approached them. At 1.00 a.m. on Tuesday

Volunteers wounded several members of a military party travelling along Usher's Quay and collected the weapons which were abandoned when the soldiers fled. From Tuesday morning until Thursday there was a series of minor engagements. Daly's northern outposts on the Cabra and North Circular Roads were extremely vulnerable because of their remoteness from the rest of the battalion and their proximity to military headquarters in Phoenix Park. On Tuesday afternoon soldiers from Marlborough Barracks launched a heavy attack with artillery and machine guns, driving some defenders to flee towards Glasnevin cemetery. This British operation resulted in the establishment of a military cordon along the northern side of the city.[17] Daly retaliated by dispatching fifteen men to reconnoitre and, if possible, occupy Broadstone station. Before they set out, the Volunteers were blessed in front of St John's Convent by a priest, while the sisters recited prayers for their safe return. However, after a cautious approach, the men found that the enemy was firmly entrenched at the station and after a brief fire-fight they were ordered to retreat.[18] No further attempt was made to capture the Broadstone, although Holohan's units in the North Brunswick Street outposts kept up a sustained barrage against its military occupants. Volunteer snipers also operated briefly from the North Dublin Union, but left after protests that they were endangering inmates' lives. Instead, the Union became a sanctuary for local inhabitants, a growing number of whom sought shelter behind its massive walls, where they were joined by the entire male ward evacuated from Richmond Hospital. Nevertheless the Union was not quite an impregnable fortress and on Easter Friday evening two civilians who were sightseeing on the high tower were shot dead by military snipers. Heuston's unit in the Mendicity was by far the most exposed in Daly's command, although Tuesday began quietly and the post was sent a dozen reinforcements by Connolly in the Post Office. During Tuesday and Wednesday it came under intense and ultimately overwhelming military pressure from a sustained sniper attack, which tailed off only towards nightfall. During the night the garrison of twenty-six men remained on the alert with never less than half on guard in the hall, on the stairs and on the first floor.[19]

Daly's battalion captured many prisoners, especially in the early days. A group of soldiers was taken at noon on Easter Monday while on their way to Fairyhouse race-course. Among others arrested along the quays was the poet peer Lord Dunsany, in uniform as a British officer. His car was ambushed at the Church Street barricade.[20] The Bridewell police barracks situated close to the rear of the Four Courts was captured on Easter Wednesday and twenty-five policemen were discovered hiding in the coal cellars, almost overcome with hunger and fatigue. They were taken to the Four Courts where a Cumann na mBan member, Brighid Thornton, was initially exhilarated by the sight of men 'wearing these capes and helmets with chinstraps and spikes on top. They looked to me like Germans and my first thought was that the Germans had arrived at last. But of course they were just policemen . . . and they did not know what to do with them.'[21] Daly's men also took the isolated Linenhall Barracks in Yarnhall Street which housed the Army Pay Department. It was surrounded and twice unsuccessfully fired before the outer wall was breached by gelignite on Wednesday morning and a gate was smashed open with sledge-hammers. The thirty-two beleaguered and unarmed clerks then emerged under a white flag accompanied by a single policeman and were escorted to Father Mathew Hall where they were put to work filling sandbags for rebel barricades.[22] Daly's prisoners appear to have been humanely treated. Some were released, while at the Four Courts British officers were given separate accommodation as well as receiving meals and bedding. One prisoner, Captain Brereton, praised his captors as 'not out for massacre, burning or loot. They were out for war, observing all the rules of war and fighting men. . . . They fought like gentlemen. . . . They treated the prisoners with the utmost courtesy and consideration.'[23] On Easter Friday, when the fighting became intense, the prisoners were transferred to safer locations and Daly even struck up a relationship with a British officer to whom he frankly confided the acute and irreversible deterioration in his strategic position.[24]

After they seized the Linenhall Barracks the Volunteers bombed the complex to prevent its reoccupation. But a fire started and spread with alarming speed to threaten adjacent tenements and houses. By Easter Thursday afternoon, the conflagration had enveloped a local wholesale druggist's and detonated a huge store of inflammable chemicals. The conflagration was;

> like a rearing furnace, really spectacular. Barrels of oil were projected high in the air and exploded with a loud report. A stifling smoke cloud shrouded the district. On Thursday night, it was as bright as day. A pin could be picked up by the glare overspreading the surrounding streets. By Friday, it had subsided, though occasionally the dying flames flickered before it finally extinguished.[25]

On Wednesday morning, the Volunteers also attempted to burn down the Medical Mission in Charles Street close to the side of the Four Courts, where lancers had taken refuge on Monday, but Volunteers who dashed across to set it on fire were driven back.[26] At midnight snipers in the Four Courts foiled an attempt by an ambulance crew to recover the body of a lancer officer.[27]

On Wednesday morning the military net began to close in rapidly around the Mendicity. A large detachment of soldiers had taken up position in surrounding streets and houses and ordered the occupants to leave. An all-out assault was clearly imminent. Heuston dispatched two Volunteers to tell Connolly of his desperate position, but they were unable to break through the cordon which was also tightening around the Post Office. By now Heuston estimated that he was surrounded by 300 to 400 troops. The British attack began with rifle and machine-gun fire and as combat developed the shooting was frequently at close quarters, sometimes as close as 20 feet. At about noon the British tried a new tactic by sending soldiers creeping along the quay until they reached a wall in front of the Mendicity, from behind which they hurled hand grenades into the building. Although Heuston's men tried to reply by catching the bombs and throwing them back, at least two Volunteers were left seriously wounded. Gradually, as one of the defenders later wrote, 'The small garrison had reached the end of its endurance. We were weary, without food and short of ammunition. We were hopelessly outnumbered and trapped.'[28] As he faced the certainty of being shortly overrun Heuston consulted his men and decided that the condition of the wounded and the safety of his entire garrison necessitated surrender. Although a number of men dissented, the order to that effect was obeyed and the Mendicity became the first rebel garrison of the Easter Rising to capitulate.[29]

Daly initiated one attempt to disrupt British pressure when he ordered a number of Volunteers to destroy a footbridge at Jameson's Distillery in Smithfield if the British attempted to get access. The defenders had a large canister bomb which they took to the roof of the distillery counting house, lit its fuse and dropped it on the roof of the footbridge. One of them, Liam Archer, recalled:

It hopped off the roof of the bridge and landed in the road below. Nothing happened. Then John O'Connor went into Bow Lane, lay down in the road and pumped some rounds of rifle ammunition into the bomb from a short distance. Again nothing happened. This experience left us feeling that these bombs were not much use.[30]

Throughout the week, the Four Courts sustained a steady, if indiscriminate, barrage along both sides of the river. A St John's Ambulance Brigade member recalled:

The North side of the quays, just over Capel Street Bridge, had always to be rushed at as high a speed as possible, it being constantly swept by fire from the Four Courts. While not saying we were deliberately fired at, the fact remains we cannot recall a single journey on which we did not get a bullet through somewhere.[31]

None the less, shopkeeper John Clarke's growing sympathy and respect for the rebels were substantially increased by an incident which he himself witnessed on the quays. At noon on Tuesday, he writes:

A soldier was passing through (Charles) Street. As he was passing Cooney's . . . one of the soldiers who are here attempted to detain him. Unlucky, a sergeant shouted to let him go. The moment he stepped on the bridge the Volunteers from the Courts pinked him again. One of the priests [Fr Begley] was on the spot. By simply raising his hand, the Volunteers allowed the wounded man to be removed.[32]

As the week went on, normal civilian life around the Four Courts disintegrated as transport and mail services collapsed, shops shut, newspapers became unavailable and the absence of gas forced residents to rely on candles. But looting was successfully discouraged by Daly's battalion and the Volunteers also arranged for bread to be issued to queues of local inhabitants, and conveyed supplies to local institutions such as St John's Convent. Movement in the area became increasingly dangerous as two early casualties in Father Mathew Hall discovered after they had been 'fired on and wounded on refusing to halt their motor car when called on by the Volunteers'.[33] Residents in North King Street were progressively evacuated, especially after the fire at the Linenhall Barracks. Some sought refuge at the municipal technical school in Bolton Street, but most fled to the North Dublin Union which eventually housed 400 refugees, most of them women and children.[34] John Clarke, who lived on the fringe of Daly's command area, did not vacate his home but became increasingly apprehensive after Easter Wednesday when, on a stroll, he was warned by a fellow shopkeeper on Ormond Quay that he was 'walking into death'. Shortly afterwards two men were wounded nearby and a young man was shot inside the porch which Clarke and his friend had just vacated. They carried him to Jervis Street Hospital and 'the moment the doctor saw him, he ordered a priest'. That night the danger of breaking the curfew, which extended from 7.30 p.m. to 5 a.m., was brought home forcefully to Clarke.

> In early or dark hours, it seems there was a poor man walking through . . . Charles Street and the soldiers in the Medical Mission [who had been attacked on Wednesday morning] shot him dead. There he lay on the street outside Doyle's until Friday evening, when four brave fellows walked up carrying a white flag and stretcher.

Next day, Clarke roamed the neighbouring streets for a last time and was standing in Strand Street when heavy firing commenced. 'The earth shook. I lost all nerve. How was I to get home? I darted out on the quays, got in safely and shook hands with myself. Not out since.'[35] Mounting casualties had begun to stretch the resources of local hospitals. By Easter Friday morning there were about thirty bodies in Jervis Street Hospital, which was also treating many civilians who had been wounded while searching for food.[36] Before the street-fighting became intense, Volunteers passed freely in and out of Richmond Hospital with their most severely injured, but less serious cases were treated at their own first aid station in Father Mathew Hall. There several doctors from the Richmond helped out as well as a dozen women of the Cumann na mBan, who, at great personal risk, also prepared and delivered meals to the barricades and outposts.[37]

As in other garrisons, morale at the Four Courts was temporarily sustained by rumours that the Germans had landed and that Cork and Limerick were up and marching on the capital. But by Wednesday, it was evident that the British military net was beginning to close in. Outposts came under sustained sniper fire from soldiers on the roofs of Jervis Street Hospital, Christ Church Cathedral and Power's Distillery, although the Malt House garrison in Beresford Street used a powerful field-glass to locate and eliminate the machine gunners at the hospital. Daly attempted to relieve the pressure on Wednesday night by igniting four houses which dominated Church Street and threatened his barricade at the Church Street Bridge. The resulting flames actually engulfed seven houses and three other buildings before stopping just short of the historic Brazen Head Hotel. On Thursday morning, the Volunteers repelled an advance by twenty soldiers along Usher's Quay. But the scale of the British assault from across the river intensified and the Volunteers retreated from the bridge soon afterwards. The Four Courts garrison became increasingly vulnerable and one Volunteer was shot dead at a window in the Public Record Office in the west wing. Two priests who then tried to reach the victim had to crawl under the continuing fusillade.[38]

With the likelihood of an all-out military assault growing by the hour, Daly prepared on Wednesday and Thursday for a last stand. He strengthened barricades and augmented the garrisons of strategically placed outposts. In North King, North Brunswick and Church Streets glass was removed from shop windows and the frontages blocked with corrugated iron. Volunteers were also positioned at upstairs windows behind bags of meal and sawdust and every movement was carefully scrutinised. The first significant British manoeuvre occurred on Thursday evening when General Lowe ordered the Sherwood Foresters to move out of Dublin Castle and occupy Capel Street and Parnell Street. As they moved towards the quays there was 'heavy fire from the Four Courts. Bullets struck the parapets and tramlines and ricocheted sparks.'[39] After securing a city map from a newspaper office the soldiers erected barricades along both sides of Capel Street and completed a wedge which had been driven between Daly's command and the headquarters in the Post Office. Daly was so concerned at his growing isolation that he summoned an officers' conference at midnight on an open space in front of 'Reilly's Fort'.[40] Illuminated by the glow from the Linenhall Barracks, the leaders of the 1st Battalion discussed whether to send a party to attempt to force a way through to the Post Office. But the intense light from the flames rendered such an operation foolhardy, as the men would have been an easy target for enemy snipers.[41]

That the tide of battle was running irreversibly against the rebels became clear on Friday when the arrival of the first British armoured cars in Charles Street began the last phase of the Four Courts occupation. Their immediate task was to rescue the trapped lancers and remove the body of the commander, Lieutenant Sheppard, from Collier's dispensary, opposite the Medical Mission. By the time the British assault was launched in the afternoon it had been reinforced by the South Staffordshires operating from their base in Trinity College. The soldiers had begun placing a cordon around the Four Courts which passed from Bridgefoot Street and Queen Street in the west, along North King Street to Bolton Street and Capel Street on the east side. But the British mistakenly thought that North King Street and North Brunswick Street lay outside the rebel area, an error which was to lead subsequently to very heavy fighting.[42]

Lieutenant-Colonel Taylor, the South Staffs OC, said later that the North King Street operations were 'conducted under circumstances of the greatest difficulty and danger for the troops engaged who were subjected to severe fire not only from behind several rebel barricades but [in some sections] from practically every house'.[43] His company's official history described how;

the successful storming of a barricade achieved no more than to drive its defenders into the houses, and having emerged by back doors, they were able to repeat their resistance further along the street. [Their strength was because] they reinforced or were reinforced by sniping posts in the houses of the street. [They] delayed the troops and made them a steady target. [The snipers were mostly] isolated riflemen, shooting from sandbagged windows. . . . They had so situated themselves as to be able to inflict maximum casualties on the English troops with minimum loss to themselves.[44]

Frontal attacks risked a repetition of the battle at Mount Street Bridge where the Sherwoods had suffered so grievously and so it was decided to employ armoured cars containing up to twenty men to approach rebel strongholds at speed. Half the party would suddenly erupt from the vehicle and, under covering fire from those inside, they would storm the nearest buildings and take up positions at top windows. Meanwhile the rest would be dropped at the corner opposite, where they repeated the same procedure.[45]

The immediate prelude to the fighting in North King Street was sudden and dramatic when, at daybreak on Friday, an armoured car of the South Staffordshires accelerated along Bolton Street and screeched to a halt outside the municipal technical school. After the building was stormed it served as the headquarters of the commanding officer, Lieutenant-Colonel Taylor. A barricade was then put across the street, snipers were positioned on the roof and residents were questioned to gather intelligence about the numbers and dispositions of the Volunteers. Taylor's men quickly captured corner houses at the junction of North King Street and Bolton Street which became a useful first base of operations on the fringes of the rebel stronghold. It was over the next 150 yards that the real battle was to be fought, as troops attempted to push through North King Street and on to Church Street. A ferocious fight occurred at the first rebel barricade outside 27 North King Street. Although this house was manned by only a few Volunteers they received supporting fire from successive barricades behind them, as well as outposts such as 'Reilly's Fort'.[46] One account describes how;

Whilst advancing in the darkness the military fired into practically every house in the line of advance, and the few terrified inhabitants who had had the temerity to remain throughout the terrible night took refuge in the cellars or by lying flat, face downwards on the floor, sought to escape the continuous fusillades, whilst the flying bullets shattered everything around. In storming the houses several soldiers were shot down. During the conflict a soldier bursting in a door accidentally killed a comrade beside him through the premature explosion of the gun.[47]

Repeated British assaults were hurled back and, as night fell, the attack ground to a standstill amidst steadily mounting casualties. Nevertheless, soldiers had succeeded in occupying houses which commanded the first barricade and by daybreak on Friday its defenders had decided on a retreat to avoid certain annihilation. Troops could now advance under cover towards Church Street by boring through the successive terraced houses which ran along the south side of North King Street. As a result Volunteers and soldiers on opposite sides of lower North King Street were soon firing at each other at almost point-blank range across the narrow roadway. The defenders crouched in the shadows or beneath splintering window-sills whose protective bags of meal had been sliced to pieces. In this small area the fighting was of concentrated ferocity. The pressure on the combatants was increased by the intense and all-pervasive noise from gunfire, shouted commands, the screech of armoured cars and the crash of artillery shells. The darkness was also pierced by the flash of rifles and machine guns and the glow of burning buildings as nervous combatants were only too aware that, unseen but close by, were probably men seeking to kill them. Two Volunteers from 'Reilly's Fort' learnt this when, armed with hand grenades, they crept to a disused house in Beresford Street to launch an attack on passing armoured cars. As one of them carefully opened an upstairs window and lit a match to ignite a grenade the momentary gleam drew the attention of a British sniper, whose bullet passed clean through the Volunteer's hat. The battle was frenzied and nationalists were convinced that British soldiers went berserk and massacred fifteen civilians between 6.00 p.m. on Friday and 10.00 a.m. on Saturday.[48] General Maxwell later dismissed some of the allegations as stemming from local sympathy for the rebels or bogus compensation claims. He did, though, accept that;

possibly, some unfortunate incidents which we should regret now may have occurred. . . . It is even possible that under the horrors of this attack some of [the troops] 'saw red'; that is an unfortunate consequence of a rebellion of this kind. It was allowed to come into being among these people and could not be suppressed by velvet glove methods.[49]

But nationalist Ireland was in no doubt that the deaths in North King Street were the result of a massacre by soldiers.

On Friday evening Daly transferred his headquarters, arms and ammunition to the Four Courts because Father Mathew Hall had become increasingly threatened by the British advance as well as being congested with wounded. The Army Pay Corps prisoners were escorted to the Bridewell, 'under heavy fire, the bullets spattering the walls around the party who stumbled in the dark over obstacles strewn between the barricades'.[50] Inside they were taken to three large cells on the ground floor where they were well treated. Those who had served on the Western Front even regaled their guards with a running commentary on how to distinguish between the different sounds of shotguns, rifles and machine guns. At one point they faced great danger when a large water main burst and threatened to drown them, but the leak was repaired. Even then a heavy artillery bombardment was under way. Presumably unaware that the Bridewell station was in rebel hands, the Chief Secretary is recorded as having notified its occupants by telephone on Friday morning that the military were about to shell the Four Courts and advising them to take shelter in the cellars. Meanwhile, the twenty-four policemen from Bridewell station, held since Wednesday, were released.[51]

The British capture of the first barricade in North King Street had cost them thirteen dead and wounded. Further heavy casualties were suffered as soldiers reduced more rebel barricades and outposts and by daybreak on Saturday troops held strong positions on both sides of lower North King Street. At 6.30 a.m. Lowe was informed that the cordon around the Four Courts had been completed. By 9 a.m. the Volunteers had abandoned a barricade in Beresford Street and also 'Reilly's Fort' and were retreating on a broad line south into Church Street and in the general direction of the Four Courts. Nonetheless, intense fighting persisted in this area because the insurgents were still active in the upper part of North King Street and attacking troops who were advancing up Church Street. Furthermore, strong outposts in North Brunswick Street, such as Monks's bakery, Clarke's dairy and Moore's coach works, lay outside the military cordon. By the time the last volley was fired, late on Saturday afternoon, the operation had cost the South Staffordshires sixteen men killed and thirty-one wounded. Treating the wounded Volunteers had exhausted the supplies of drugs and dressings in Father Mathew Hall and the option of transferring them to the Richmond Hospital had ceased once the military cordon on North King Street had closed. A British officer later claimed that 'the men in the Four Courts had been nearly off their heads with strain' and certainly the records describe symptoms such as 'shock and fatigue', 'shock and fainting fits' and 'shock and loss of nerve later in night'.[52] One Volunteer went mad and had to be handcuffed to a bed.[53]

By 4.00 p.m. on Saturday most of the Volunteers who had fought in the North King Street area had retreated to the Four Courts. Although Daly now concluded that his situation was hopeless, an officers' conference decided to launch a counter-attack on Saturday evening in a desperate bid to regain lost positions. It was also hoped to re-establish contact with the headquarters staff which was mistakenly believed to be still inside the Post Office. However, one officer drew attention to the strange stillness which had descended on the city. He thought this indicated that the British had suspended their military operations.[54] Gradually rumours of a surrender filtered through and a sombre mood descended on the Four Courts. Brighid Thornton recorded that Volunteers;

began to look out the back to see if there was an avenue of escape. And some of them gave me addresses and said: 'when you get out, if we're taken prisoner, will you call my mother?' I had a whole list of names. And then someone gave me a gun and said: 'will you keep that for me?'[55]

Confirmation came from Pearse's emissary, Nurse O'Farrell, who was brought to Daly, and;

gave him the order and told him of the Headquarters' surrender. He was very much cut up about it, but accepted his orders as a soldier should. He walked back with us to the side entrance and by this time the news had got about of the surrender. Several officers of the Republican Army were down at the railings waiting for us.[56]

News now spread rapidly throughout the building and Volunteers began handing up their arms through railings at Chancery Place to troops standing outside. Inside, as Brighid Thornton noted, 'It was a terrible, shattering, chaotic moment. They [the Volunteers] cried and they wept and they protested and they did their best to destroy their guns. I could see them hacking away at them. But there was no escape for them.'[57] Some men wanted to fight on, but Daly warned them that, like him, they had to obey their Commander-in-Chief. Whatever his own disappointment, Daly had already accepted his impossible military position and must surely have been relieved that the end had come without much greater loss of life. He had been particularly anxious to prevent casualties among the Cumann na mBan.[58]

When British soldiers arrived, one young Volunteer, Sean Harling, recalled that;

The officer who took the surrender seemed to be a very decent sort of fellow. . . . I was just standing at the end of the line and he came along and he looks at me, you know, and he gives me a clip on the ear and tells me to get the hell home. I was very annoyed at not being arrested but that's what happened and I watched the others being taken off as prisoners.[59]

Daly led the column as it marched, under guard, along the quays and through almost deserted streets. Just before 8 p.m. on Easter Saturday it reached O'Connell Street. There a British general asked who was the leader and Daly proudly replied, 'I am. At all events, I was.' As Piaras Beaslai wrote, it was 'a remark which, he must have known, would be his death warrant'.[60] After British officers had recorded their names and addresses, Daly's men were marched to the grassy plot inside the railings at the front of the Rotunda Hospital where they remained overnight in the open.

Incredibly, even when the main column left for Richmond Barracks on Sunday morning, one of Daly's units had not yet surrendered. Still holding out were sixty Volunteers in North Brunswick Street, who had lost contact with the Four Courts after the closure of the military cordon in North King Street on Saturday morning. They conducted a fierce gun battle until late Saturday afternoon when news of the surrender was brought by Father Albert, a Capuchin priest. But their young commanding officer, Paddy Holohan, was not prepared to countenance unofficial instructions and told Albert that he and his men would hold till the end. He remained intransigent even when the British broke off the attack and an officer under a white flag confirmed that Pearse had indeed surrendered. Holohan was adamant that he would only capitulate to a direct order from his Commander-in-Chief, so an overnight truce was arranged. But the truce seems to have been honoured more in the breach; because Volunteers claimed that the British manoeuvred to gain territorial advantage while Lieutenant Taylor insisted that for some hours rebels continued firing, wounding his men and preventing the removal of wounded soldiers. Early on Sunday morning Father Columbus, another Capuchin priest, travelled to Arbour Hill Barracks where Pearse wrote, signed and dated an order of surrender. This was presented to Holohan at 9.30 a.m. and shortly afterwards the final surrender from the 1st Battalion took place outside Monks's bakery. It occurred under the gaze of the sisters from St John's Convent, one of whom stuffed a Volunteer's revolver up her sleeve. After

Holohan briefly addressed his men they proceeded to Richmond Barracks and the last resistance inside Daly's command had come to an end.[61]

For the next ten days the South Staffordshire Regiment combed the Four Courts area and claimed to have found pistols, shotguns and dum-dum bullets. Even so, a number of rebels evaded capture. They included all the insurgent casualties in the Father Mathew Hall, who were evacuated on Saturday evening during the truce. The seriously wounded were carried on stretchers to Richmond Hospital, while those with minor injuries were smuggled into safe houses. By 11.30 p.m. on Saturday evening the hall was deserted, apart from the Cumann na mBan members who had helped organise the evacuation and destroy incriminating papers. The women were allowed by Father Augustine to sleep overnight in a small room in the church. On Sunday they attended early mass and then slipped away with some Volunteers who were also in the congregation. Their escape was made easier by the crowds which had gathered outside the church searching for relatives.[62]

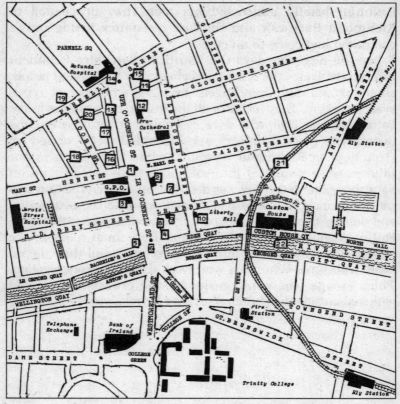

The General Post Office and O'Connell (Sackville) Street Area

1. Nelson Pillar	12. Gresham Hotel
2. Imperial Hotel	13. YMCA
3. Metropole Hotel	14. Parnell monument
4. Hopkins & Hopkins	15. Tom Clarke's shop
5. Kelly's Gunpowder Store	16. Henry Place
6. O'Connell monument	17. Moore Lane
7. Sackville Place	18. Sampson's Lane
8. Dublin Bread Co.	19. Williams & Woods
9. Wynn's Hotel	20. Sackville Lane
10. Abbey Theatre	21. Loopline (elevated)
11. Findlater's Place	22. The *Helga*

7

THE GENERAL POST OFFICE

On Easter Monday morning only about 150 men assembled at Liberty Hall for duty with the Headquarters Battalion which was to occupy the General Post Office. About forty were members of the Citizen Army but because of MacNeill's countermand many Irish Volunteers had not mobilised. The Volunteers were drawn from the four city battalions and about seventy-five men from the Kimmage garrison which consisted of Irishmen who had fled conscription in Britain or were on the run in Ireland. The Headquarters Battalion was to be led to the Post Office by Connolly in his capacity as Commandant-General of the Dublin Division of the army. Just before the column set out he made his famous remark to a Transport Union colleague that the Rising had no chance and that they were all going out to be slaughtered. But one should be sceptical at taking this statement literally since Connolly had been under great physical and mental strain and was no doubt distracted by the manifold tasks which he had to accomplish that morning. Before departure Pearse was approached by a woman, identified by the historian Ruth Dudley Edwards as his sister Mary Brigid, who pleaded unsuccessfully for him to return home and to leave all such nonsense behind.[1] As the Headquarters Battalion readied itself a Post Office employee in overalls set off to disconnect the telegraph and telephone wires in streets adjacent to the Post Office.[2]

Connolly led the column which set off at about 11.50 a.m. with Pearse at or near the head of the line; as Plunkett joined the column he unsheathed a sword cane and threw away the sheath. In deference to age and ill-health, Clarke and MacDermott had travelled ahead by motor car and were waiting at the Prince's Street corner of the GPO. Winifred Carney, Connolly's devoted political secretary, was the only woman who made the journey. One officer present has described how 'As the order "By the left, quick march" was given a rousing cheer rang out from the rather imposing crowd who had by then gathered in front of Liberty Hall. We moved off at a brisk pace, swung left into Lower Abbey Street and headed up towards O'Connell Street. We had, for good or ill, set out on a great adventure.'[3] To keep the column as inconspicuous as possible only a single cab full of ammunition and explosives was brought initially. Furthermore the route chosen avoided the main thoroughfares until the last moments, marching along Eden Quay and turning into Lower Abbey Street before wheeling right on O'Connell Street. From there it advanced northwards and as it passed the Metropole Hotel British officers on the pavement outside grinned and chortled. When it reached the Post Office at noon the order was given, 'Left Wheel! – The GPO! – Charge!'[4] and the main entrance was invaded while a specially selected squad entered at the side in Henry Street and raced to occupy the roof. Downstairs public customers and staff were hustled out while a number of British soldiers who had been in the Post Office on private business were taken captive. The garrison then set about fortifying the building, which had the advantages of being situated in Dublin's main street, containing a vital telegraph office and providing roof snipers with a commanding view of the surrounding area.

From the start it was understood that Connolly was, in the words of Pearse, 'the guiding brain of our resistance'. It was not that Connolly cut an impressive military figure; many thought him a glaring contrast to the magnificently attired Plunkett with his immaculate uniform, riding boots, spurs and pince-nez. Slightly pot-bellied with bandy legs and an unkempt moustache, Connolly appeared a drab figure, but from the moment he entered the Post Office nobody doubted that, while Pearse was titular Commander-in-Chief, it was Connolly who was in charge of military operations. Furthermore it was Connolly's performance during Easter Week as leader of the republican forces which established indisputably that he was a born leader of men. It was a role for which, in a sense, he had been preparing himself for years as he discarded his earlier persona of trade union organiser and agitator and adopted that of military boss and theorist. By 1916 he was no longer referred to as Mr Connolly and instead was routinely addressed as Commandant, a position of authority reinforced by his cultivation of an aura of charismatic remoteness.

Since its opening in 1819 the Post Office had been the most impressive structure in O'Connell Street, a thoroughfare which had originally provided residences for Dublin's aristocracy and its professional class but in the nineteenth century had become predominantly commercial in character. In 1916 it was lined with shops, offices, restaurants, a cinema and a number of large hotels such as the Gresham, Imperial and Metropole. Just beside the GPO was the Coliseum, a 3,000-seat theatre which, ironically, had opened on Easter Monday 1915; by Easter Saturday 1916 it was to be a smouldering ruin, never to be rebuilt. The Post Office was situated on the western side of Lower O'Connell Street which ran from Henry Street to O'Connell Bridge where a right turn took one westwards along the Liffey quays and past the Four Courts. The other important buildings in this section were the Hotel Metropole, Eason's stationers and the picture house. On the opposite side Lower O'Connell Street ran from North Earl Street to the bridge where a left turn took one down Eden Quay to Butt Bridge and Liberty Hall. Its most prominent buildings were the Dublin Bread Company, which was actually a large restaurant, the Imperial Hotel and Clery's department store.

The GPO was well over 200 feet wide and 150 long, and its three storeys stood 50 feet high to the top of its cornice. Dick Humphries, a nephew of The O'Rahilly and one who fought there with the Volunteers, noted that 'The building seems immense. The number of separate rooms in the place is unbelievable.'[5] While its interior was functional, it was one of the major edifices of Dublin's eighteenth- and early nineteenth-century classical architecture, built from mountain granite, except for a portico of Portland stone. This portico was 50 feet long and included a pediment surmounted by three statues of Hibernia, Fidelity and Mercury and a tympanum decorated with the royal coat of arms. Above the cornice was a balustrade which ran round the entire building and completed its elegant exterior. The heart of the recently renovated building was the main sorting hall which extended to Henry Street and around which ran a block of offices whose windows looked out on to the street. This hall was separated by a door and a glass partition from the public office at the front. On the upper floors were a telegraphic office and a restaurant for post office staff. Windows were now knocked out, barricaded with furniture and guarded by Volunteers. The door and glass partition were also smashed and screens were used to create a hospital, an armoury and a kit store stocked with boots, trousers, shirts and overcoats. The sorting tables were employed as beds and a secluded corner was soon set aside for Father Flanagan of the nearby Pro-Cathedral to hear confessions. Upstairs the restaurant was converted into a commissariat whose waiters were captured British soldiers.

Meanwhile a squad led by Volunteer Michael Staines ascended to the telegraph room whose female operators had already fled. There they opened fire with their revolvers on seven armed British soldiers who suddenly appeared from their guard room on the same landing. When their sergeant was grazed on his forehead the troops put up their hands and Staines was astonished to discover that they didn't have a round of ammunition between them. The shock and humiliation appear to have unhinged the officer who adamantly refused to go to hospital because he was on duty till six o'clock that evening! Even after he was transferred to Jervis Street Hospital he came back to display increasingly delusional behaviour. When a priest in O'Connell Street was attempting to disperse a crowd the sergeant concluded that an outraged populace clamouring for his release was being obstructed and screamed that 'I'm no religion no more! [sic] Look at the people of Dublin coming to rescue me and the priest is pushing them back!' A Scottish lady in charge of the telegraph office refused to leave: the garrison suspected her of trying to transmit information to the military authorities but after they refused to let her send telegrams about deaths before the Rising, she gave up and left the building.[6]

Within half an hour of the occupation a tricolour had been run up at the Henry Street corner and a green banner with the inscription IRISH REPUBLIC was hoisted on the Prince's Street side. Then at 12.45 p.m. Tom Clarke locked the doors and handed the Proclamation of the Irish Republic to Pearse who, accompanied by an armed guard, went outside. Standing on the step he read out the Proclamation and announced the establishment of a Provisional Government, of which he was President and Commander-in-Chief. This was a document that in time was to prove momentous: 'In the name of God and the dead generations . . . Ireland, through us . . . strikes for her freedom.' The right to freedom was fundamental; long usurpation by a foreign people could not extinguish it. Six times in the past 300 years the Irish people had asserted that right in arms. 'Having organised her manhood . . . she strikes in full confidence of victory.' The Republic it now proclaimed guaranteed religious and civil liberty to all its citizens; 'cherishing all the children of the nation equally', it disregarded the differences 'carefully fostered by an alien government which have divided a minority from the majority'. The signatories invoked the blessing of the Most High God on the cause of the Republic and prayed that no one who served that cause would dishonour it by 'cowardice, inhumanity and rapine'. In this supreme hour the Irish nation must by valour, discipline and readiness to sacrifice for the common good 'prove itself worthy of the august destiny to which it is called'. Clarke, the prison veteran who had dedicated his life to reaching this day, headed the seven who had put their name to this

Proclamation. MacDermott, Pearse, Connolly, MacDonagh, Ceannt and Plunkett followed.

The Proclamation was the paced composition of an orator such as Pearse, who probably wrote most of it. The sometimes overblown language and inflated sentiments only reflected the passion behind it. If it was stronger in rhetoric than historical and other realities of a deeply divided country, its understanding of 'the nation' was inclusive and generous. The dogmatic claim that through this group of revolutionaries Ireland was summoned to her flag sprang from a conviction that they spoke from the country's deepest self and that freedom was essential for Ireland's well-being as a nation. For this, in the wider political spectrum, they would be classed as 'extremists'.[7]

There was a distinctly muted response from the crowd and only a few cheers before Pearse withdrew inside, after which hundreds of copies of the Proclamation were posted up around the city centre or taken to other garrisons. The Provisional Government was also keen to announce its Rising to the world and hoped to by-pass British censorship by sending three Volunteers, including an ex-British army signaller, to occupy the Atlantic School of Wireless in Reiss's Chambers at the junction of Lower Abbey Street and O'Connell Street. They managed to reassemble its transmitter which had been dismantled as a wartime precaution and their messages were picked up in parts of Europe and on ships which brought the news to America. But this remained unknown to them and the leadership in the Post Office because it proved impossible to get the receiver working before Reiss's was burnt out on Easter Wednesday.[8]

Two small but crucially important garrisons were also established early on Monday in Kelly's gunpowder store on the corner of Bachelor's Walk and Lower O'Connell Street, and in Hopkins & Hopkins, a closed and shuttered jewellery shop on the opposite corner.[9] These two positions fronted O'Connell Bridge and the Liffey quays and looked down towards College Green and Trinity College from where British action against the GPO could be expected to come. Kelly's was commanded by Peadar Bracken and Hopkins by Seamus Robinson, both Kimmage men. The Kimmage men were based in a mill on Count Plunkett's estate where they manufactured pikes, bayonets and most of the buckshot which was used during the Rising. After they mobilised early on Easter Monday they famously commandeered a tram to O'Connell Bridge and then walked down Eden Quay to Liberty Hall. There Peadar Bracken, who had been in hiding in Kimmage since firing the shots at Tullamore in March 1916, was promoted to captain by Pearse and given typed orders to occupy two important positions at the southern end of O'Connell Street.[10] As Robinson's party attempted to force a way into Hopkins a party of lancers, escorting an ammunition train, came along Eden Quay, having got so far only because the guards protecting the ammunition stocks in Liberty Hall were only permitted to respond to a British attack. Even at O'Connell Street, where they sneered at the Volunteers, they did not grasp what was occurring, and they moved on, to be cut down shortly afterwards at the Four Courts. Hopkins was finally entered through a hall door in Eden Quay and after the building was fortified the garrison commenced tunnelling through adjacent premises. On the other side of the street Bracken had barricaded the ground floor of Kelly's and placed men at windows on the first storey, protected by large piles of books and ledgers. One Volunteer made bombs by filling kettles and saucepans with the shop's store of gunpowder and when the entire block down to Middle Abbey Street had been tunnelled every vessel was filled with water in case the supply was cut off by the British.

Half an hour after Pearse had read the Proclamation the Post Office garrison was in action in what is often described inaccurately as the 'Charge of the Lancers' down O'Connell Street. The cavalry had in fact been dispatched from Marlborough Barracks to investigate reported disturbances in O'Connell Street and were simply trotting down from the northern end, completely unaware of the danger ahead. When they reached Nelson's Pillar the waiting Volunteers in the Post Office opened fire, killing three soldiers and fatally wounding another. One horse was also killed and its putrefying body lay in O'Connell Street till the end of the Rising. About the same time, across the city, Volunteer Liam Ó Briain encountered Eoin MacNeill cycling along the Rathgar Road with his son and Sean Fitzgibbon of the Volunteer Headquarters Staff. After adjourning to a nearby house, MacNeill said he was investigating rumours of Volunteer movements, though he still believed that only harmless route marches were planned. Fitzgibbon went off to gather more information, then returned and threw himself on the sofa, shouting, 'They have started.' Although actual fighting had not yet commenced, Fitzgibbon knew that the Volunteer movements which he had seen meant hostilities were about to commence. MacNeill still could not bring himself to accept Fitzgibbon's analysis, but Ó Briain now made a cycle tour and witnessed the Citizen Army in action at Portobello Bridge. After that Ó Briain returned to MacNeill who was stunned by the news and raged at Pearse and his co-conspirators. 'I have been fooled, tricked and betrayed.' Then;

He sat down and stared at the floor for five minutes, not saying a word. I'd never seen a man so deep in thought. Then he lifted his head: 'I'll go home and put on my Volunteer uniform and I'll go out.' 'You'll go out,' I said, greatly surprised, 'after all that's happened?' 'I will,' he said quietly. 'People are fighting and dying. I will go with them.' Those words went through me like a knife.[11]

But although MacNeill went home he stayed there, apparently shattered by the turn of events.

When order was finally restored in the Post Office after the attack on the lancers, Tom Clarke and Diarmuid Lynch discovered reports in the RIC's pigeon-holes on the Irish Volunteers' strength and activities and 'chuckled at the fact that all their spying was in vain, and that neither they nor their superiors realised the imminence of the climax'.[12] Clarke and MacDermott were now in their element; both men were physically and emotionally revived after the strain of recent days which had seemed to age the younger man considerably. A delighted Lynch saw them sitting on the edge of the mails platform, beaming satisfaction and expressing their congratulations amidst the frenetic activity in the central postal hall. It was;

> full of uniformed Volunteers, boxes of ammunition, revolvers and automatic pistols lying on tables and chairs, knapsacks, blankets and tents. The middle of the hall had been allocated for use by the leadership, some of whom like Pearse and Clarke chatted while a sombre and tired Connolly was dictating notes to his secretary Miss Kearney [*sic*] who was typing furiously by his side. Plunkett and The O'Rahilly, who had just returned from a tour of inspecting the building's defences, were in jovial mood and laughing heartily.[13]

Outside, a few angry soldiers' wives attempted to force their way in but friends in the crowd dragged them away. In the late afternoon the munitions stores in Liberty Hall which were being guarded by Frank Thornton of the Citizen Army were transferred under armed guard to the GPO in fifteen commandeered lorries and cabs, the last of which trundled into O'Connell Street just as the angelus bell rang. Thornton also brought to the Post Office a considerable number of late-comers who had arrived at Liberty Hall after the departure of those who had mobilised in the morning. Liberty Hall was now left empty, except for a caretaker and another civilian, but Thornton had left the building barricaded and with a Starry Plough flag flying and he, for one, was not surprised when the British later in the week bombarded it in the belief that it was occupied.[14]

During Monday reinforcements trickled into the Post Office. These included the Hibernian Rifles (an organisation of Irish-American exiles), a group of older republicans who had been waiting for the call in a house in Parnell Square and individual Volunteers who made their way to O'Connell Street. Most reinforcements who came to the Post Office were made welcome, including two foreign sailors, a Finn and a Swede, who explained in halting English that they belonged to small nationalities and hated England. However, the line had to be drawn somewhere, as it was by a surprisingly tolerant Connolly. One Volunteer recalled:

> Whilst I was talking to Connolly he was approached by a man who was somewhat under the influence of drink. This man said that he wanted to join the garrison and Connolly asked him why. 'Because', the man said, 'I want to fight for Ireland.' 'Are you sure you want to fight for Ireland?' Connolly asked him. 'I am certain,' said the man. 'Well, then,' said Connolly, 'will you go home now, have a good sleep, and when you are sober come back and tell me that you still want to fight for Ireland and I'll give you a rifle.'[15]

The reinforcements eventually doubled the strength of the Headquarters garrison. As well, Winifred Carney was now joined by other women from the Cumann na mBan and the Citizen Army who arrived in the late afternoon and were assigned by Connolly to the nursing and kitchen staff or were appointed as dispatch carriers.

One development on Monday which distressed many of the insurgents in O'Connell Street was the looting and sporadic arson by civilians from the nearby tenements. Sean T. O'Kelly who was sent out to deal with it was unable to cope and was rebuked by an angry Connolly. 'Shooting over their heads is useless. Unless a few of them are shot you won't stop them. I'll have to send someone over there who'll deal with these looters.'[16] Clearly, however, Connolly never did get round to act in such a ruthless manner. In Kelly's Peadar Bracken held up several looters with his rifle and forced them to abandon their booty. One of his men, Joe Good, threatened to open fire and forced a group to place their jars of sweets on the pavement, but when he turned his head momentarily both the looters and the jars had disappeared. Good was later offered a new motor-bike by a young boy who complained bitterly that he couldn't get the bloody thing started. Good, a 21-year-old Londoner, was the son of Irish parents and had joined the Gaelic League and then the Irish Volunteers before fleeing to Ireland in February 1916 to escape conscription. His enchanting memoirs are a major source for any study of the Easter Rising.[17] On the other side of O'Connell Street, Brennan-Whitmore, who commanded the North Earl Street garrison, was followed into the first house he occupied by a crowd of looters whom he then had to eject.[18] Ultimately all attempts either to intimidate or reason with the looters proved futile and the insurgents were forced to settle for an uneasy truce with them.

During Monday afternoon and evening more outposts were established close to the GPO, in houses in Henry Street and the block opposite the Post Office. At the same time barricades were being erected which were;

> models of ingenuity. In a carpet and linoleum warehouse, the linoleum and carpets were arranged so that the unwary pursuer could be buried under an avalanche. Another barricade stretched across Upper Abbey Street was made with the entire stock of a bicycle warehouse: thousands of bicycles, piled eight or ten feet high, jammed into each other. Fire had little effect on it. To cross it on foot was impossible. The most delightful of all was a barricade of clocks. At last I saw a use for those horrible marble clocks, like the ones inside the entrance to a bank. I had seen them in many homes, rarely keeping the correct time.[19]

On Monday evening The O'Rahilly persuaded MacDermott and Clarke to authorise the release of Bulmer Hobson who was still under arrest by the Military Council. Sean T. O'Kelly went to the house where;

> Martin Conlon quickly appeared and I was shown into the parlour. There I found Mr Bulmer Hobson seated in an armchair with a book in his hand. Opposite to him sat Maurice Collins but instead of a book Maurice held a gun. I announced I had an order for the release of Bulmer

Hobson and immediately relief was visible on all faces. Maurice Collins expressed his pleasure and relief. Hobson made no comment.[20]

O'Kelly claimed, improbably, that when they left Hobson agreed to come to the GPO but only after he went home for his rifle. Any such promise, if given, can only have been intended to ensure a safe getaway. Instead Hobson remained at home until Tuesday morning when he went to stay with MacNeill at Rathfarnham, where he found the agitated Chief of Staff still gripped by a compulsion to join the Rising. On Easter Wednesday MacNeill donned his Volunteer uniform, and was dissuaded only when Hobson protested that he would put those Volunteers who had obeyed his countermand in an impossible position.[21]

On Easter Tuesday, 25 April, Dick Humphries noted that 'The sun rose at 4 a.m. on a beautiful summer like day with a slight breeze coming in through the GPO's many glassless windows. O'Connell Street was eerie, silent, empty of people and with its cobbles snow-white with sheets of paper. Not a living thing is in sight. Even the birds shun the district.'[22] Some Dubliners still found it difficult to grasp the upheaval which had occurred. A group of postmen gathered outside Hopkins and debated whether to enter the Post Office but departed when a fellow worker reported that he had been threatened with a bayonet and warned that there would be no mail deliveries for some time to come. In the early morning Connolly ordered that barbed wire be placed across O'Connell Street to keep out civilians and the overhead tram wires were to be blown down and used as well. Inside the Post Office a calmer regime now existed, with breakfast being served in the restaurant, guards on security duty and the hospital (which was filled with beds from the Metropole Hotel) fully functioning under Jim Ryan, a UCD medical student. All the ammunition, rifles and revolvers were now stored in one central department in the general sorting office and another room had been allocated for the grenades.

During the morning lull Volunteers commandeered a car and went to Parnell Square, the headquarters of Redmond's National Volunteers, where they appropriated the armoury of rifles and ammunition.[23] More rifles were brought in from dumps across the city by members of the Cumann na mBan to be graded by the Quartermaster, Jim O'Neill of the Citizen Army, and dispatched to various parts of the building. O'Neill also issued bombs (tin cans filled with explosive, each with a long fuse covered with red sulphur), and his instructions were short and to the point. 'Strike a match, touch the fuse, count three, throw the bomb and the job is done.' Although there were large supplies of bombs in the Post Office, additional stocks were being continually manufactured and shotgun cartridges were filled with buckshot. Fire extinguishers were also distributed throughout the building, and in the yards outside men filled sandbags. Basic telephonic communications had been installed throughout the GPO, including a line to the roof to enable Connolly to contact the sniper posts. Large rolls of newsprint were seized in a printing store in Lower Abbey Street and trundled across O'Connell Street to reinforce the defences of the Post Office. Cumann dispatch-carriers were in contact with other garrisons and provided Headquarters with reports of the progress of the Rising in the rest of the city.

The mood of the Post Office garrison was relaxed and in the yard younger Volunteers passed the time doing trick-riding on the bicycles of the telegraph boys.[24] But discipline was strict, especially in the matter of alcohol. When looters pillaged a public house in Henry Street, alongside the GPO, and a woman staggered across to offer bottles of stout she was rebuffed by all but one Volunteer. However, just as he put a bottle to his lips an officer appeared, smashed it to pieces and warned that the next man found taking drink would be shot without warning.[25] The high morale of the garrison on Easter Tuesday was reflected in the public utterances, bulletins and published statements of the Provisional Government. At 9.30 a.m. a statement by Pearse claimed that there had been 'heavy and continuous fighting' in which the British had suffered far heavier losses, that the whole of the city centre was in the hands of the Republic and that the people of Dublin were overwhelmingly on its side. The same message was propagated in the first and only issue of *Irish War News*, a four-page paper costing a penny. In the afternoon Pearse stood on top of a table in O'Connell Street and in his dual capacity of President and Commander-in-Chief read a manifesto to the citizens of Dublin which asserted that republican forces were holding the line everywhere and that the country was rising in support, and which then outlined ways in which the civilian population could assist the revolution.

Nevertheless despite the insurgents' euphoria and optimism the initiative was passing inexorably from the rebels to the British army. The Military Council's original plan had been to sandwich the enemy forces in the city between the garrisons in the centre and forces moving on Dublin from the countryside but that had failed. By Tuesday, despite Pearse's claim that 'the country is rising' a nationwide revolt had not materialised and Connolly hurriedly began to fashion a new strategy to take account of that disappointing development. He now set about preparing for a siege in which British soldiers, no longer liable to attack from the rear, would launch a frontal attack on the Post Office. Connolly obviously assumed that the attack would be conducted by the infantry because, as a revolutionary socialist, he believed that the capitalist class would never permit widespread destruction of its property by an artillery bombardment. Accordingly the dispositions which he now made in response to the changing military realities envisaged close, even hand-to-hand, fighting. He decided to garrison buildings in the immediate vicinity of the Post Office which commanded those routes along which British soldiers might attack. The block opposite the Post Office containing the Imperial Hotel and Clery's department store was occupied at about noon. Its garrison, consisting of seven Citizen Army men and one woman as well as Volunteers from the 2nd Battalion, was commanded by Frank Thornton; for Connolly it was spectacular revenge for his union's defeat in 1913 at the hands of William Martin Murphy, the hotel's owner. It was Connolly who ordered Thornton to fly the Starry Plough, the flag of the Citizen Army, over the building, which was to be a charred ruin when Murphy eventually regained possession. Connolly had told Thornton that 'The British must not occupy these buildings'. Shortly after the Imperial was occupied the British attempted to shell the Post Office from an 18-pounder located at the Parnell monument but the gun crew was sniped at so effectively while trying to get the gun into position that they were all badly wounded or killed. British reinforcements managed to load and fire the gun but the shell missed the GPO and hit the YMCA in Upper O'Connell Street which was occupied by British troops. They assumed that they were under rebel attack and immediately evacuated the YMCA, whereupon they came under attack and suffered heavy casualties.[26]

Another strategically vital location which was occupied was the Metropole Hotel next to the Post Office.[27] Indeed its whole block of buildings from Prince's Street to Mansfield's boot shop at the corner of Middle Abbey Street guarded the eastern side of O'Connell Street and commanded three lines of approach to the GPO via Middle Abbey Street, Lower Abbey Street and Sackville Place. To secure sufficient men to occupy the hotel in strength, Connolly dispatched couriers to Fairview to order units of the Irish Volunteers and Citizen Army there under the command of Captain Frank Henderson to withdraw to the GPO. Sixty-six insurgents and half a dozen British prisoners in full khaki then marched into the city centre where, as they crossed in single file to the Post Office, they came under fire from the garrison in the Imperial Hotel. In the ensuing gun battle some of Henderson's men were wounded and the shooting stopped only when Connolly dashed out into O'Connell Street, shouting and waving his hands over his head. As they assembled outside the GPO a chagrined Connolly apologised, 'It's all a mistake.' In the Post Office the Fairview men were addressed by Pearse in what had been the new public office at the entrance. There one of Henderson's men noticed a pile of saddlery and sabres collected from the lancers on Monday. This was 30-year-old Oscar Traynor, a future commandant of the Dublin Brigade of the IRA and an Irish government minister.

Connolly now divided them into three groups, sending Henderson and twenty men to occupy outposts in Henry Street, another twenty to reinforce the Imperial garrison and the remainder under Traynor to occupy the Metropole Hotel and adjoining premises.[28] Traynor was now promoted to lieutenant and commanding officer by Connolly over the head of Captain Poole of the Citizen Army, a turbulent character whom Traynor sensed, correctly, was trouble. When Traynor raised his invidious position with an irritated Connolly, Poole shouted, 'Did I say that I would not obey you?' Poole was now spoiling for a fight and not necessarily with the British. No sooner were they through the swing doors of the Metropole than he picked on Harry Boland, a Volunteer who had joined up with Henderson's men in Fairview, and whom Poole accused of being a deserter. Poole continued to rant, ignoring Traynor's exasperated explanation that a deserter would hardly be on duty with them, and then raised a rifle butt at the hapless Boland. Traynor managed to separate them and got Poole out of the way by ordering him to verify that the guests had vacated their apartments. However, a triumphant Poole was soon back with a civilian captive whom he had discovered in the smoke-room and in a surreal scene he charged the man with being a British officer and a spy. As he explained to an incredulous Traynor, the man had given himself away by stepping off with his left foot when ordered to quick march; irrefutable proof of military training! But Traynor soon established that he was simply a teacher from Portora School in Enniskillen and he was quickly escorted from the premises. That little matter settled, they went to work to fortify the hotel, boring through on the first floor into Eason's next door and on to Mansfield's corner; every available receptacle, from bath to jug, was filled with water. They discovered that the hotel was a gastronomic paradise, stuffed with food, biscuits and rich cake as well as cigars and cigarettes, though the drinks cabinets remained untouched except for a particularly expensive brand of tonic water. The Metropole garrison saw very little action during Easter Week since the British shrank from taking the hotel by storm, preferring to shell it instead. Darkness fell on Tuesday night after a day of comparative quiet and most of the garrison in the Post Office managed to get a good night's sleep.

Whereas Monday and Tuesday had been devoted to occupation, fortification and preparation, the situation in O'Connell Street on Wednesday was dominated by a military activity whose tempo increased relentlessly thereafter. Shooting began early when the Imperial garrison hoisted the Starry Plough of the Citizen Army and British snipers retaliated. Movement in and out of the building now became very dangerous and to minimise the risks a cord was tied across O'Connell Street to enable messages to be sent across to the Post Office in cans. Then at 8 a.m. the garrison in Hopkins heard explosions. The men initially believed that they were being shelled but when a Volunteer raised an improvised periscope, a mirror attached to a broom handle, he was shocked to see a British naval vessel, the *Helga*, attacking Liberty Hall. Peadar Bracken in Kelly's shot at its crew on the deck, forcing them to take cover, and he continued firing when the ship pulled up at the Custom House and they dashed for cover. The shelling from the *Helga* was ineffective because of the angle of fire but heavy guns near Trinity College soon scored direct hits on Liberty Hall and reduced the deserted building to a charred ruin.[29]

The British were not yet able to target the Post Office, but as the morning went on its roof snipers were in action against troop movements at Amiens Street station, Parnell Street and Findlater's Place. The British increased pressure on O'Connell Street from across the Liffey and Hopkins came under heavy but ineffective machine-gun fire for half an hour from the tower of Tara Street fire station. From both Hopkins and Kelly's troops could be seen marching into Trinity, out of shotgun range. Only Peadar Bracken had a rifle and just before noon he spotted British soldiers about 300 yards away, standing in the open in D'Olier Street. The troops were confident that they were out of range and were preparing to fire across the river. However, Bracken had a surprise for them.

One exposed himself a little at a side door whom I pointed out to my comrades. I told them not to move a trigger until he came outside and to leave him to me. He came out on the path and I dropped him. Another showed up and I allowed him to pull in the casualty. In a few seconds he reached out with his rifle to 'fish in' the rifle on the path. While doing so he exposed his arm and side and I let him have one which caused his cap to bound out on the street.[30]

But British machine guns on top of Trinity College were soon sweeping O'Connell Street and turning it into a 'no man's land'. In the afternoon intermittent sniper duels also developed between Volunteers on the roof of the GPO, and British marksmen at the Custom House, Westmoreland Street and the Rotunda. Inside the Post Office the defences were made as bullet-proof as possible by a wall of notebooks 7 feet high and sacks of water-drenched coal. Then, according to Dick Humphries, at;

About 2 a.m. a gigantic boom shakes the edifice to its foundations and everyone looks up with startled eyes. From all sides come questioning words. Some say that a bomb has exploded in a lower room. Others that it is a dynamite explosion but a second and third in quick succession prove the correctness of those who proclaim it heavy artillery. The detonations are truly tremendous and were we not absolutely certain that the gun was situated on the opposite side of the river, one could have sworn that it must be in Abbey Street.[31]

The big guns at Trinity College had begun to shell 'Kelly's Fort', as it had been nicknamed, displacing plaster everywhere and starting a blaze on the top floor. Bracken failed to eliminate the gunners crouching behind the weapons' shields and at about 2.30 p.m. he was ordered by Connolly to evacuate his garrison to the Post Office and three hours later Hopkins was also abandoned along with the Dublin Bread Company whose fragile tower was too thin to withstand even sniper bullets. The Hopkins garrison was now ordered to reinforce Traynor's men in the Metropole block which stretched from Middle Abbey Street to Prince's Street. On late Wednesday afternoon this block was extended to Eason's in Middle Abbey Street, an extension which achieved Connolly's goal of dominating Sackville Place, the Lower Abbey Street approach and the whole of Lower O'Connell Street. A British frontal attack on the Post Office now risked suffering formidable casualties but when Connolly inspected the work he rather ungraciously remarked, 'I wouldn't like to be getting through that hole if the enemy was following me with bayonets.' However, he had the good grace to smile broadly when Traynor retorted that the tunnelling had been carried out in accordance with his own lectures on the subject. Traynor recorded:

Although at this time heavy firing was taking place, Connolly insisted on walking out into Abbey Street and giving me instructions as to where I should place a barricade. While he was giving these instructions he was standing at the edge of the path and the bullets were actually striking the pavement around us. I pointed this out to him and said that I thought it was a grave risk to be taking, and that these instructions could be given inside. He came back to Eason's with me, absolutely unperturbed, and while we were standing in the portico of Eason's a shell struck a building opposite – I think it was the Catholic Boys' Home – and a gaping hole appeared in the front of the building. Connolly jokingly remarked 'They don't appear to be satisfied with firing bullets at us, they are firing shells at us now.'[32]

Late on Wednesday night the British fired shrapnel shells into O'Connell Street, some of which hit the Metropole Hotel and collapsed its chimney stack. Traynor noted their impact.

The amazing thing was that instead of bullets coming in, it was molten lead, actually molten, which streamed about on the ground when it fell. I was told that the shell was filled with molten wax, the bullets were embedded in wax, and the velocity of the shell through the barrel and then through the air caused the mold [sic] to melt. As the first of these shells hit the building the Volunteers informed me of the fact. I rushed up to the third floor, which had been hit, and found an oldish Volunteer crawling about on his hands and knees gathering up the stuff as it hardened. I asked him what he was doing, and what he intended to do with the stuff. He answered 'Souvenirs'. That was all he said.[33]

The Imperial Hotel was also attacked by a machine gun on Tara Street fire station and another at Trinity College sent up clouds of mortar from the front of the Dublin Bread Company. They, in turn, were attacked by roof snipers on the Post Office. Towards six o'clock the fighting subsided and quiet reigned for a few hours but inside the Post Office the men could scarcely relax in comfort. Dick Humphries noticed that;

When an off-duty turn arrives we hunt around for a reasonably quiet place where we might snatch a short sleep. But despite its huge size the GPO seems to possess no amenities of this kind. At the best most us can do is to bed down under a table or desk with a top cover thrown over us in lieu of the normal sheet or blanket. Needless to say, no one gets much sleep. The short intervals of silence outside are even more ominous in their eerie intensity than the shots, explosions, strange whistling sounds, odd bursts of patriotic songs which punctuate the night.[34]

At dusk Joe Sweeney on top of the GPO saw a British armoured vehicle moving slowly down O'Connell Street. After locating a slit at the front through binoculars he shot and brought it to a halt. He and the rest of his unit kept firing to prevent its being evacuated by its occupants, but another vehicle came along and towed it away. Even more satisfying for the garrison was the news brought in by dispatch carriers of the Battle of Mount Street Bridge and the large casualties inflicted on the British reinforcements there. It was a good way to end what must, on balance, have appeared to the garrison to have been a good day. Michael Staines recalled that 'Wednesday night was immensely calm. Scarcely a sound was to be heard outside the garrison. It was indeed the calm before the storm.'[35]

By now the expectations of the Post Office garrison had begun to change when it became clear that the country had not risen in support of the Rising and that British reinforcements were pouring into Ireland. Pearse, however, continued to radiate supreme optimism and assured a sceptical Desmond Fitzgerald that a German submarine would soon appear in Dublin Bay. Among his men, however, there was a growing conviction that their struggle would culminate in a massed British infantry assault and even hand-to-hand fighting in the building. A heroic last stand such as that at the Little Big Horn or Rorke's Drift would be a fitting end to their Rising and would echo through the ages. Jim Ryan, the GPO's Medical Officer, recalled:

In spite of that optimism we all seemed to take it for granted we would finally be crushed. By common consent it was to be a fight to a finish. It was thought that the enemy would rush our position with superior forces and would take it with enormous losses. None of us expected mercy but we felt we would sell our lives dearly. There was no feeling of despondency. The atmosphere was one of subdued excitement and determination – desperation maybe – for we appreciated only too well the odds against us. We talked confidently of holding out for two or three weeks, of being able to make enough noise to draw the attention of the world to this small nation. We would hold our post until the last man's rifle was silenced.[36]

These expectations as to how the Rising would end were not confined to the rank and file alone. Whatever the personal inclinations of individuals such as Pearse and Plunkett, the words and actions of the collective leadership during Easter Week do not endorse the blood sacrifice theory that they had carefully planned to survive the Rising and end their lives in front of British firing squads to redeem the nation and inspire it to future freedom. The leaders did not talk and act like men who intended to die in such a manner. Tom Clarke, for instance, clearly did not expect to survive the Post Office. Jim Ryan has recorded that;

> On Wednesday Tom Clarke came to the hospital and sitting down quietly beside me began to talk. . . . I was now Red Cross and so he said I might possibly be spared by the enemy in the final bayonet charge which was evidently expected by him as well as by the rest of us. If therefore I should survive he hoped I now understood and would make known the motives of those who signed the Proclamation.[37]

Clarke later took Desmond Fitzgerald out to a yard and pointed to a concrete shelter into which he wanted him to herd all the women when the final moments came. He held out little hope for Fitzgerald and thought he would perish in the final British assault or be executed soon after.[38] The actions of some of the Provisional Government also are hardly consistent with that of men who were bent on the preservation of their persons at all costs for future execution. Connolly, for example, risked death on a number of occasions. He might well have been killed on Easter Tuesday night when he dashed out of the Post Office to stop the garrison in the Imperial firing on Frank Henderson's men. His two subsequent wounds inflicted by British snipers came as he exposed himself to them in the open air and they could as easily have been fatal. Similarly Ceannt in the South Dublin Union participated in some of the most concentrated fighting of the Rising; his deputy Cathal Brugha had a miraculous survival from his numerous bullet wounds.

On Easter Thursday, 27 April, the Post Office garrison

awakened early to another glorious cloudless day. Although heavy firing could be heard in the distance morale was still high and as yet the full weight of the British counter-attack had not been brought to bear. Ryan's hospital staff had not been busy and had treated only three or four men for minor wounds. But everyone sensed that this day would be different because 'Overwhelming and modernly equipped enemy cordons had been tightened around the GPO and its adjacent outposts'.[39] The British were now concentrated in strength in College Street, Trinity College, the Custom House, Liberty Hall and Amiens Street, and from Parnell Street to Findlater's Place. At the same time The O'Rahilly was supervising teams strengthening the window barricades. In the subsequent defence of the GPO, its roof snipers played a crucially important role, being responsible for locating enemy machine-gun posts and snipers and putting them out of action. They also had to monitor and counteract British troop movements in the surrounding streets which usually consisted of sudden dashes, allowing only a second or two to react. A measure of their importance was the fact of Pearse's frequent visits to the roof, though he also wanted to see the St Enda's boys who were positioned there.

Shortly after dawn British machine-gun fire from Abbey Street was countered from the Post Office and adjoining outposts, and the fight was fully on. One defender recalled that;

Every machine gun within range began to pour in a fierce fire upon the area and every soldier, including the British snipers, joined in with rapid rifle fire. The torrent of bullets on and around our Field Headquarters could only be compared to a violent hailstorm.[40]

The British tried repeatedly to advance from the junction of Marlborough and Abbey Streets, but Traynor's men and especially Harry Boland were outstanding in repelling them, even when their rifles became over-heated and had to be cooled by oil extracted from tins of sardines. Towards noon a tremendous explosion startled the Post Office garrison who saw an incendiary ignite the offices of the *Freeman's Journal* in Prince's Street. Intensive bombardment of outposts such as Hopkins, the Dublin Bread Company and the Imperial had resumed and heavy sniping was also directed against the GPO where a shell also damaged the figures over the porch, though a direct hit had still not been registered on the building. In the Imperial an incident took place which might have come from a Hollywood disaster epic. Some of Frank Thornton's men were resting in an annexe at the back of the hotel when a large overhead tank was hit by a shell and sent down a huge cascade of water, washing the men out of it and along the main passage.[41]

During Thursday Connolly inspected the Metropole and allocated an additional twenty men to its garrison. Shells did hit the hotel whose ceiling collapsed, sending bricks tumbling down the chimney and acrid yellow flames leaping in through the window. In the midst of it two men disdainfully reclined on mattresses beneath a window, calmly smoking their pipes. The hurricane was unremitting and Traynor ordered his men to descend two storeys, except for a young Cockney member of the Citizen Army called Neale. He had ruined his shoes and stockings on Easter Monday and replaced them in the Metropole with a guest's boots and a pair of girl's stockings which he pulled up to his knees. He now made a bizarre spectacle acting as lookout during the bombardment, sitting right out on the parapet on the top floor and scanning O'Connell Street with a pair of field-glasses.[42] But lighter moments like this did not alter the seriousness of the situation. When a man came up to the GPO and asked to be allowed to join, Joe Good of the Kimmage garrison overheard Connolly tell him, 'Go home while you can, man, we thank you. Too late now, man; it's a hopeless case.'[43]

About 3 p.m. a report of an imminent British attack on the Post Office from the north-west side brought every available man scurrying from the eastern to the western windows. As they braced themselves a false alarm that an armoured car was driving up Henry Street caused many Volunteers, dangerously, to stand up and look out the windows. Shortly afterwards the shooting ceased abruptly. During the subsequent lull Pearse made a morale-boosting speech in which he claimed that all the principal targets had been taken and the Linenhall Barracks captured and set on fire, the country was still rising and a large band of Volunteers was marching from Dundalk to Dublin. In addition they had successfully held out as a republic for three full days and under international law were entitled to send a delegation to the peace conference which would immediately follow the end of the war. When he finished the men's spirits had revived and a deafening cheer spread throughout the entire building.

The first serious casualty among the GPO garrison occurred on Thursday when a Volunteer was wounded in the neck by a bullet which came out under his eye. Much more serious in its implications was the injury to Connolly's leg inflicted by a British sniper. This was, in fact, his second wound. He had already received a flesh wound in the arm but had managed to conceal it from the garrison by having Ryan treat him behind a folding screen and swearing him to secrecy.[44] This wound, which was much more grim and could not be hidden, happened as Connolly returned from establishing two outposts in Liffey Street, though he managed to drag himself to Prince's Street where he was collected by a stretcher party. In the GPO Connolly was treated by a captured British army doctor and chloroform had to be used as anaesthetic. Thereafter Connolly survived on frequent injections of morphine and for the rest of Thursday was removed from the action.

Connolly's incapacitation led to The O'Rahilly assuming the most prominent military role in the Post Office but, in terms of overall control, it also led to the growing assertiveness of Clarke and MacDermott. Pearse, who was unable to sleep throughout the Rising, was clearly suffering the effects of sleep deprivation. As was obvious to the whole garrison, Plunkett was seriously ill after the operation on his glandular neck though accounts which depict him lying helplessly and ineffectually for the entire Rising are wide of the mark. There are enough sightings of Plunkett in the GPO, animated and in good humour, to confirm that he enjoyed periods of remission. His emotional health, however, can only be guessed at; on Easter Thursday as fires swept the east side of O'Connell Street he was exulting that 'It's the first time this has happened since Moscow! The first time a capital city has burned since 1812!'[45] Although both Clarke and MacDermott were in civilian clothing their increasingly open authority was accepted without question by the garrison. Those Volunteers who were members of the IRB knew the importance of the pair, an importance now publicly proclaimed by their membership of the Provisional Government and the respect and deference displayed to them in the GPO by Pearse, Connolly and Plunkett. Although neither Clarke nor MacDermott had any formal military rank they now intervened to issue promotions, gave instructions on the movement of munitions and prisoners and commanded Volunteer parties who fought the fires which swept the Post Office on Friday.

At 3.45 p.m. British howitzers began dropping shrapnel shells over the roof of the GPO where three men were also wounded by British snipers. Their unit was then hastily evacuated and tumbled down into the telegraph room through safety manholes – spaces torn in the slates from which a rope stretched down to the floor inside. Dick Humphries watched as 'Some of the men in their hurry fail to catch the rope altogether and take the eighteen foot drop as though it were an everyday occurrence. The wounded are lowered safely by means of two ropes.'[46] The bombardment continued for two and a half hours but the shells failed to inflict any serious damage to the Post Office. British snipers on top of the Gresham Hotel poured bullets through the windows of the Post Office where the defenders crouched as low as possible. On the roof Humphries and his comrades determined to eliminate this threat. 'We allow them to continue firing until, mystified at our silence, they grow bolder, and incautiously show themselves over the top of the parapet. Immediately a single volley rings out. There is no

The inscrutable Tom Clarke, veteran revolutionary and the driving force behind the Easter Rising.

Anticipating his future? Patrick Pearse, eight years old.

James Connolly, founder of the Irish Citizen Army, signatory to the Proclamation and Commandant of the Irish forces in Dublin during the Rising.

Members of the Citizen Army on guard on the roof of their headquarters at Liberty Hall, Dublin.

Countess Markievicz (centre, second row), surrounded by boys and young men of the Fianna. Chief scout Con Colbert, executed after the Rising, is second to the right of her.

A well-equipped section of Ceannt's 4th Battalion of the Irish Volunteers in September 1915.

Eoin MacNeill, President of the Irish Volunteers.

An imaginative recreation of the signing of the Proclamation at Liberty Hall on Easter Sunday, 1916. The members of the Provisional Government (from left to right) are Plunkett, Pearse, Clarke, Ceannt, MacDermott, Connolly, and MacDonagh.

General Sir John Grenfall Maxwell, who was appointed Commander-in-Chief of the British Army in Ireland during the Rising.

General Maxwell and his staff pose for a group photograph after the Rising.

Brigadier-General W.H.M. Lowe, who directed British army operations in Dublin during the Rising.

The main entrance gates to Upper Yard, Dublin Castle. The circle indicates the point where the first fatality of the Rising, Constable O'Brien, was shot.

British soldiers manning a barricade.

An apparently posed photograph of British soldiers at an improvised barricade of beer barrels on the Dublin quays.

British troops on guard against a possible rebel attack at the corner of Parnell Street and Moore Street.

A civilian motor-car is stopped and searched by British soldiers at a military cordon.

An armoured car with mounted machine gun. This type of vehicle became familiar to the city's population during the Rising.

An armoured car of the type used by the British army to get to close quarters with houses occupied by the rebels. Like others it was constructed out of disused boilers by tradesmen at Guinness's.

This watercolour by Walter Paget is an imaginative recreation of the scenes inside the General Post Office during the final stages of its occupation. Pearse, Clarke and Plunkett hover over the wounded Connolly. Members of the garrison confirmed that it gave an accurate impression of the situation.

Brigadier-General Lowe (centre) and Major de Courcy Wheeler receive Pearse's surrender. The figure standing beside Pearse, almost completely hidden, is Nurse Elizabeth O'Farrell.

British troops inspect the ruined interior of the General Post Office at the end of the Rising.

Firemen removing a red-hot safe from the ruins after the Rising.

The exterior of the gutted General Post Office.

Rounding up the rebels. A Volunteer prisoner is escorted by British soldiers to Dublin Castle.

Rebel suspects who were detained at Richmond Barracks after the Rising.

Rebel prisoners after the Rising being permitted to meet with their families and friends.

O'Connell Street on Easter Monday, 24 April 1916.

O'Connell Street as it appeared on the Monday after the collapse of the Rising.

The structural damage inflicted on the east side of O'Connell Street by British incendiary and artillery shells.

The devastation wreaked on O'Connell Street and Eden Quay.

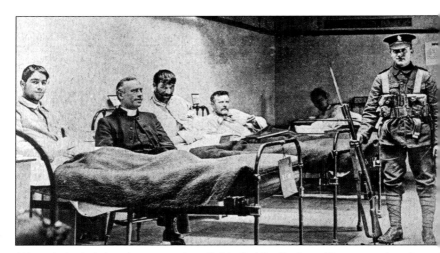

Wounded rebels in a temporary hospital in Dublin Castle, with an armed sentry or guard and a priest in attendance.

Business as usual after the collapse of the Rising. A newsvendor stands among the ruins.

more sniping that evening from the Gresham.'[47] The British were clearly increasing the pressure, especially at the rear of the GPO, and Connolly transferred men to Henry Street and Liffey Street to guard the approaches. Also by now the dispatch system had completely collapsed and this strongly reinforced the Post Office garrison's increasing isolation; they were now on their own and as they listened to the big guns they realised that the other garrisons were similarly isolated. On Thursday evening a rumour swept the building that a British gas attack was imminent and the defenders were issued with cans whose liquid was to be dipped in handkerchiefs and placed over their mouths. When the false alarm was over the tins of magic fluid were stored in a corner, close to a thirsty Dublin raconteur nicknamed 'The Cuban'. When he imbibed the contents of one he developed pains all over his body and was rushed to the Post Office hospital, though he recovered and returned to duty.[48]

At 7.30 p.m., after the battle had subsided, the reinforcements were transferred back to their positions in the eastern rooms. There Dick Humphries spent a nerve-shattering evening after the British launched intense sniper attacks at the roof of the GPO and a tremendous bombardment of the Metropole block, and also dropped incendiary shells on the Imperial Hotel. A fire-storm now developed along the opposite side of O'Connell Street and soon Hopkins, the Dublin Bread Company and indeed the entire block as far as Lower Abbey Street were well ablaze. The fires gradually worked their way round the corner and soon ignited Wynn's Hotel, the Royal Hibernian Academy and nearby houses, their progression helped by flames travelling along the barricades.

Humphries saw that;

Hopkins is just beginning to blaze, while somewhere down in Abbey Street smoke is rising into the still evening air. Not realising that this is the commencement of the large conflagration which is to devastate O'Connell Street we watch the leaping flames while gradually night darkens over the city. On returning to our post after tea we are appalled at the stupendous increase that the fire has made. The interior of our room is as bright as day with the lurid glow of the flames. Reiss's jewellery shop is a mass of leaping, scarlet tongues of light.[49]

Spectators could often watch the fires develop gradually from the first impact of the incendiary shell but at other times they grew at stupendous speed. One spectacular detonation occurred at Hoyte's, the City of Dublin Drug Hall, a pharmaceutical chemist's, glass and oil warehouse in Lower O'Connell Street, four doors from the Imperial. Here an incendiary created a fire-storm of tremendous terror and beauty, graphically described by Humphries.

Suddenly some oil works near Abbey Street is singed by the conflagration, and immediately a solid sheet of blinding death white flame rushes hundreds of feet into the air with a thunderous explosion which shakes the walls. It is followed by a heavy bombardment as hundreds of drums of oil explode. The intense light compels one to close the eyes. Even here the heat is so terrible that it strikes one like a solid thing as blast and scorching air come in through the glassless windows. Millions of sparks are floating in masses for hundreds of yards around O'Connell Street and as a precaution we are ordered to drench the barricades with water again. The whole thing seems too terrible to be real. Crimson-tinged men moved around dazedly. Above it all the sharp crack of rifle fire predominates, while the deadly rattle of the machine gun sounds like the coughing laughter of jeering spirits.[50]

From a different vantage point in the Metropole Charles Saurin was also staggered by the sight.

When Hoyte's first caught fire it was a terrific spectacle, as it burst into one huge flame the moment it was hit. It was a roaring inferno in less than a minute. Stored as it was with chemicals of all sorts and with oils and colours it spouted rockets and stars of every hue and was the most wonderful fireworks show I ever saw.[51]

To one Volunteer the noise of the inferno was 'like the song of a great dynamo'.[52] In the Metropole Saurin dashed through the front rooms from second floor to the top pulling down all inflammables and cutting away curtains and blinds. As the fire spread to Clery's and the Imperial Hotel Traynor's men sent urgent but unavailing semaphore warnings and soon the huge plate-glass windows of Clery's were running molten from the tremendous heat.[53]

The fires had now reached such terrifying proportions that Humphries felt that he was;

situated in the midst of a circle of flame. Inside the central telegraph room which runs along the entire length of the GPO the men stand silently at their posts, black and bronze statues against the terrible glow of the sky. Unawed and undaunted, their gaze ever-fixed on the glistening cobbles and the shadowed lanes whence all attacks must be directed, they wait expectantly. Now and again the flames beat upwards in a flash of light that reveals every detail behind the barriers. Then they subside as suddenly and lines of black shadow, rays of darkness, as it were, creep over us. Fortunately the wind is blowing seawards, the myriads of blazing fragments are carried away from the GPO. Glowing sparks however now begin to shower down with a pattering sound like soft rain and threaten to set everything on fire.[54]

Michael Staines wrote:

The heat from the burning block opposite the GPO was beyond belief. Despite the great width of O'Connell Street the sacks, etc. in the windows began to scorch and show signs of smouldering. Batches of men had to be hastily formed to continually drench the window fortifications with water. Dense volumes of acrid smoke, myriads of sparks and splinters of falling debris were being blown to the GPO by a strong north-east wind. Lurid flames leapt skywards and the spectacle in the gathering darkness could only be likened to Dante's Inferno. The intensity of the heat grew steadily worse and the water being poured from buckets and hoses was converted into steam as it touched the fortifications. There had to be a withdrawal from the front of the building of all save those who were combating the risk of a conflagration in the Post Office itself. Our struggle with this new danger seemed to go on for interminable hours. The men were soot-stained, steam-scalded and fire-scorched, sweating, weary and parched.[55]

In the Imperial Frank Thornton was determined to hold out as long as possible but he knew that the end was near. The hotel had been riddled with gunfire from the dome of the Custom House, Amiens Street station tower, the Bank of Ireland, Trinity College and the YMCA in O'Connell Street. This had been followed by the explosion in Hoyte's when many barrels of methylated spirits and turps had been blown into the sky and exploded when they landed on the roof of the Imperial. Quite a few of Thornton's men had been wounded as a result of this 'cauldron of flames' and he now started to concentrate his men in one area.[56] At last the terrific heat in O'Connell Street died down, the smoke lessened and, although the fires smouldered for days, the immediate danger had passed. The rest of the night was peaceful as the big guns were silent and, except for an occasional sniper shot, the riflemen and machine gunners appeared to have gone to sleep. At about 12.30 a.m. Patrick and Willie Pearse and The O'Rahilly appeared satisfied after a tour of the Post Office defences.

In the light of day on Easter Friday, 28 April, the Post Office garrison could witness for itself the spectacular impact of the British blitzkrieg on the eastern side of O'Connell Street. Humphries saw that

On the opposite side of O'Connell Street nothing is left of the buildings except the bare walls. Clouds of grey smoke are racing in around everywhere and it is difficult to see as far as the Bridge. Occasionally some side wall or roof falls in with a terrific bang. The heat is stupefying, a heavy odour of burning cloth permeates the air.[57]

Sean MacEntee was stunned:

Directly opposite me was the Imperial Hotel, or what had been the Imperial Hotel, for only the facade of the building remained The rest, windows, floor and roof had become a prey to the fire, so that now without any substantial background, with its gaping window-sockets and the flames that licked around them, the facade itself was like a huge stage-set prepared for some spectacular drama. There was no sign of the enemy.[58]

Thursday night's hurricane of fire and the fact that British infantry were not massing for an assault on the Post Office meant that a last stand was now very unlikely. The British were not prepared to conduct their operations in the way the enemy desired, particularly as the troops who encircled the GPO were the Sherwoods who had suffered so grievously at Mount Street Bridge. Having lost so many men in a frontal attack against a fortified building containing a small number of opponents, they were not prepared to risk an even more bloody repetition in O'Connell Street. Instead, frustratingly and maddeningly for the Post Office garrison, there were only fleeting and distant glimpses of soldiers dashing across the street or else snipers wriggling across rooftops.

It seemed certain now that the British intended to devastate the western side of O'Connell Street. Aodogán O'Rahilly has speculated convincingly that the rebel leadership must have convened to determine its response. That such meetings took place during Easter Week is not in doubt because Eamon Dore, Sean MacDermott's bodyguard, saw one in progress on Easter Wednesday in a room at the

front of the Post Office with Clarke presiding and
MacDermott apparently acting as secretary.[59] A crisis session
would almost certainly have been held in the early hours of
Friday morning and in addition to Clarke, MacDermott,
Pearse, Connolly and Plunkett, The O'Rahilly probably
attended also and perhaps Willie Pearse. Almost certainly it
was now conditionally agreed that if the British attempted to
annihilate them by shelling or to engulf them in flames they
would not stay to be incinerated in a Gaelic Masada but
would depart. When the British strategy of blasting and
burning the rebels out was confirmed on Friday the
continued resistance from the Post Office and the fire-fighting
efforts within it can be understood only as holding operations
to allow outposts to congregate in the Headquarters and an
orderly evacuation to proceed. One major step to prepare for
a British bombardment commenced at 1 a.m. when
MacDermott ordered Diarmuid Lynch to transfer munitions
from the upper floor to a basement room which extended
under the Henry Street sidewalk. As this got under way
galloping hooves in O'Connell Street sparked fears of a
cavalry charge though, in fact, they were from terrified,
riderless horses which had been released from their stables in
Prince's Street. Snipers in the Metropole fired at the beasts
and one Volunteer swung a billy-can packed with bolts, nuts
and gelignite above his head to gain impetus until the handle
parted company with the can which flew across the room
and hit a wall. Luckily it did not explode.[60]

At daybreak the weather was fine and the guns were silent
but many Volunteers in the GPO sensed that the end was
near, even though only the inner circle knew for certain. To
Sean MacEntee it seemed that, 'The air was heavy with
premonition, and the brooding calm forebode a storm'.[61]
True enough at daybreak the British launched a
bombardment of incendiary shells and continuous bursts of
machine-gun fire raked O'Connell Street. Having discovered a
winning formula on the previous day their tactics for Easter
Friday were simply more of the same. Initially the shrapnel

shells which hit the Metropole inflicted only minor damage to the roof but large numbers of British troops assembled around the Abbey Theatre a short distance away. Traynor warned his men to expect a frontal attack up Sackville Place and those in Mansfield's boot shop attacked the soldiers constantly; they, in turn, were fired on from a new British position at the junction of Westmoreland Street and D'Olier Street. Then shells finally set the top of the Metropole on fire and the hoses and water-filled baths proved useless to combat its spread.[62]

Inside the GPO where the commissariat still functioned and those not on duty took breakfast, MacDermott instructed the medical officer, Jim Ryan, to prepare the sixteen wounded Volunteers for removal to Jervis Street Hospital.[63] Connolly, apparently cheerful, had insisted on becoming actively involved again and moved among the garrison on his bed, which was on castors. A message which he had dictated to Winifred Carney was read out by The O'Rahilly, declaring that other garrisons were holding out and urged, 'Courage boys – we are winning!' However, the preliminaries to evacuation were already under way. Just before daybreak MacDermott had ordered Diarmuid Lynch to withdraw the outposts in Henry Street and Middle Abbey Street to the Post Office, though a post in Liffey Street was overlooked and remained in place until after the surrender.[64]

As the men in the Post Office continued strengthening the defences Connolly sat up joking and laughing as his bed was wheeled among the garrison. He now issued a manifesto to the insurgents which he had dictated in the morning to Winifred Carney. It was delivered eloquently by The O'Rahilly who stood beside Connolly as he spoke. Joe Good thought that message was the most amazing thing he had witnessed in the entire week. 'It was an extraordinary communique considering the situation we were in and what lay before us.'[65] Certainly the overall picture of the state of the rebellion was a distorted one, though that is hardly unique in the annals of military history. Connolly claimed that the various outposts were still defeating enemy attempts to dislodge them.

Outside the capital he stated that men everywhere were rallying in large numbers to the cause. But, of course, the manifesto's primary purpose was as a morale booster and as a means of thanking those who had fought in Easter Week and of paying tribute to their courage. In particular, Connolly was thanking the Post Office garrison and there was more than a grain of truth when he referred to the impact of their resistance on enemy commanders.

> The British Army, whose exploits we are for ever having dinned into our ears, which boasts of having stormed the Dardanelles and the German lines on the Marne, behind their artillery and machine-guns are afraid to advance to the attack or storm any positions held by our forces. The slaughter they suffered in the first few days has totally unnerved them and they dare not attempt again an infantry attack on our positions.

About midday a British machine gunner opened fire on the Post Office, snipers and howitzers in the gardens behind the Rotunda Hospital sent in shells and incendiaries which set fire to a corner of the GPO roof. The evacuation process commenced with about thirty women being assembled around noon in the main hall to be told by Pearse that they were to leave. He was shaken and confused by their angry and tearful reaction and MacDermott, who limped forward, appeared to countermand his order. However, Pearse reasserted control and the women were ushered into Henry Street during a brief lull in the fighting. The only females now left in the Post Office were Winifred Carney and a small number of nurses. About 1 p.m. as the fires spread and parts of the roof fell in Pearse ordered the rooftop snipers to abandon their posts. They now descended to the next floor, though Joe Sweeney and another Volunteer could not resist returning to re-engage the British snipers and stayed there until Willie Pearse chased them down. About 3 p.m. Clarke, MacDermott, Diarmuid Lynch and a Volunteer, Sean MacGarry, had a final meal with Father Flanagan who was soon to lead out the wounded. For a last supper the mood was remarkably cheerful and MacGarry joked to Flanagan that even if they were damned for eating meat on Friday they were still going to chance it.[66]

Soon afterwards the final British assault commenced. In the Imperial Thornton's garrison had stuck to their instructions until only six men remained on the first-floor landing as the British worked their way to the rear of Marlborough Street. Only when the ceiling fell in did Thornton order a retreat and when he and his men failed to reach the GPO they made their way to a building at the corner of Gloucester Street where they remained until the surrender.[67] Inside the Post Office the first fires had been quickly brought under control, but about 3 p.m. a shell inflicted serious damage over the portico. Having at last got their range, the British intensified the bombardment and serious fires broke out around the building where every hose, fire extinguisher and bucket of water was employed against them. On the ground floor Volunteers continued to pile up higher breastworks and Diarmuid Lynch organised squads in the yard to fill mail sacks with debris to reinforce the defences. Soon the flames had eaten their way through the roof of the cupola and about 3.30 p.m. a hail of incendiary bullets came from the direction of the Gresham Hotel. Dick Humphries watched, astonished, as the walls where the bullets lodged apparently flashed into flames, though, finding no hold, they soon died out. On the roof the fires had taken a grip on the portico and burnt through to the interior. Humphries wrote:

> Someone discovers that the roof is on fire and immediately commences a perfect babel of shouting, order-giving and talking. The two main lines of hose are quickly brought to the spot and two streams of water are thrown against the lower part of the roof. Lines of buckets are also organised and after a quarter of an hour's hard work the outbreak seems to be practically under control. Suddenly another part of the roof is set on fire by the incendiary bullets and

half the available water supply has to be turned upon it. Heavy firing in the meantime is going on in all directions, and adds to the confusion. Pearse and J Plunkett are holding a short conversation in the doorway. They both appear very excited. Finally a large number of men are selected for extinguishing work and the remainder are ordered to be at the windows. Everyone seems to consider it his duty to give orders at the top of his voice. The noise is terrific. The fire is gaining ground like lightning.

Humphries also discovered that an astonishing situation had developed in the telegraph room.

It presents a most extraordinary spectacle. In one part the fire has eaten right through the roofs and slates of mortar are commencing to fall on the floor. The two hoses are brought to bear on the spot. They are held six feet above the ground (to enable a better head of water to be obtained) by lines of men. Here and there the water spurts out through small holes in the rubber, drenching the men completely. In one place a huge leak from a faulty connection runs down the uniform of an officer. In a few seconds he is wet to the skin but stands as unconcernedly as though on parade. Further above a line of buckets extending down to the second floor is working with incredible rapidity. After a few minutes, however, we see that all is useless. The fire is gaining ground in all directions. Huge masses of the roof commence to fall inwards with terrific noise. The floor on which the men are working threatens to give way with each blow. Clouds of smoke from the burning debris writhe around the corridors and passages. It gets into our eyes and noses and compels fits of coughing. The floors are covered to a depth of three inches with grimy water.[68]

Amid tumultuous scenes at the top of the building men attempted to extinguish the fires. Among them was Plunkett's brother Jack. Originally when he had seen the holes where the shells had gone through the portico and little specks of smoke appearing, the situation seemed harmless enough. Then he heard the cries of 'Fire' and they discovered that the low pressure was preventing the hoses from bringing water to roof level. The garrison should have prepared for this because the canteen boiler on the top floor had been running short of water. Jack Plunkett and the others were ordered down from the roof to the top floor where smoke was filtering into the telegraph instrument room at the front of the building. Heavy boxes were thrown frantically in efforts to break the glass of the roof-lights and allow fire extinguishers to be directed out on to the roof, though one bounced off and landed on the head of Jack Plunkett's neighbour. The irony was that there was plenty of water but it could not reach the top of the building, so although the floor was deep in water the roof was blazing away. Jack Plunkett's hair caught fire from a falling spark and pieces of timber fell on his head though his heavy felt hat saved him from serious injury. Eventually he and the others gave up and soon the only fire-fighters left were a few men on the ground floor using pitifully inadequate hoses. The sacks of water-drenched coal now caught fire and the atmosphere became one of fire, smoke, burning timber, and cascades of melted glass and molten lead. Another problem was the British sniper who was working the roof of the burnt-out Imperial and targeting the fire-fighters in the Post Office. Jack Plunkett was ordered back on to an undamaged part of the roof where, despite the dark and smoke, he eventually located the soldier. From behind a chimney stack he fired and the sniper fell so hard that his rifle snapped in two on impact with the ground.[69]

Sean MacEntee was one of the fire-fighters and he found himself in the middle of a nightmare:

When the water from the fire-hoses impinged on the glass of the canopy, it appeared to explode into hundreds of gleaming stars which reflected lurid rays of flame. Often a jet of water from the hoses, as it flowed across the glass, would seem to sweep the fire before it. And if the mass of water was large, it would go billowing back and forward from end to end of the transparent ceiling; so that the flames went oscillating to and fro on the crystal above us.[70]

MacDermott and Patrick Pearse were actively involved in the efforts to keep the fires at bay until the wounded had gone and the evacuation proper could get under way. MacDermott supervised Volunteers sweeping up inflammable materials and rubbish while Pearse, who supervised the fire-fighters, stopped occasionally to peer outside through a loophole. MacEntee observed that Pearse;

seldom spoke except when a spark or a fall of burning matter from the roof set some of our defences ablaze. Then he would direct his men in extinguishing the fire. He appeared cool and unmoved. Now and then an orderly would report to him on the progress of the fire, although indeed the progress was only too apparent. From my position at the window I could see the advance of the flames. I was fascinated by the long snaking tongues of fire that went curling and writhing above the glass canopy of the central hall, and I watched them like a boy at his first fireworks display.[71]

Eventually the situation became untenable as the intense heat melted the glass overhead and every man was ordered to assemble in the general sorting office at the rear. There at about 6 p.m. the wounded and their Volunteer escort were readied for evacuation, except for Connolly who utterly refused to leave. They were led out by Father Flanagan and accompanied by most of the remaining nurses who had taken farewell messages before they departed. Tom Clarke had told one, 'If you see my wife, tell her the men fought . . . ' but then broke down and turned away.[72] Only three women now remained: Connolly's secretary, Winifred Carney, and two nurses, Elizabeth O'Farrell and Julia Grenan.

Diarmuid Lynch records that by 7 p.m. the flames had spread along both sides of the roof.

Myriads of live sparks fell through the open shaft to the immediate vicinity of the Henry Street basement room in which the stocks of gelignite, powder and bombs had been placed for safety; a possible explosion of these just then might have had serious consequences, not alone in casualties but in blocking the intended exit for retreat.[73]

MacDermott now summoned a hose which was immediately grabbed by The O'Rahilly who sprayed the sparks coming down the elevator and air shafts, through the doorways and indeed every other aperture. Diarmuid Lynch led twenty men to transfer the munitions as far away as possible along an underground passage and around three wings of the building to a cellar in the yard outside at the Prince's Street end. He had previously explored this route and discovered a large tube protruding midway along and he now posted Volunteers with lighted candles there and in other unlit places. He also ordered the carriers to cover their bombs with water-soaked cloths but despite these precautions, one petrified Volunteer set his grenades on the stairs and walked away.[74] Meanwhile the rest of the garrison was drawn up in ranks and, as orderlies passed along distributing a ration of biscuits to each man, Pearse selected an advance guard of twenty-five men led by The O'Rahilly. They were to secure possession of a new headquarters at the factory of Williams & Woods in Parnell Street. These premises were full of foodstuffs and close enough to British lines to make shelling them a risky enterprise and O'Rahilly's men were to hold them until the leadership arrived.

As darkness fell the top of the Metropole block became a blazing mass and several of the roofs now fell in. Traynor who had seen the Post Office on fire assumed the Headquarters had been abandoned and decided to evacuate his own garrison. As he considered one Volunteer's proposal that they descend down a manhole and make their way through the sewer system to the Four Courts MacDermott suddenly remembered the Metropole garrison, and sent Traynor an order to retreat to the GPO. His men now dashed across Prince's Street, through the big doors across the yard and into the sorting office where they lined up with the assembled garrison of about 300 men. Barely 30 yards away a wall of flame extended to the very roof, loose ammunition exploded like machine-gun fire and bombs detonated. Amidst this Wagnerian denouement men with rifles slung or at the slope were filing to the side door, singing and then plunging in small groups into Henry Street. One grinning Volunteer even insouciantly plonked a German *pickelhaube* on his head as he departed. Just as the Metropole men were about to leave they lost Neale, their Cockney look-out. He was wounded when either a carelessly discharged shotgun or a stray British sniper bullet exploded an ammunition pouch like shrapnel in all directions. Neale, whose lower torso was ripped to shreds, swayed and gasped to his neighbour, 'Can't you stand away and let a fellow lie down.' He was set down on a pile of mail sacks where he told Traynor, 'I'm dying, comrade'; an accurate prognosis because he expired the following day.[75]

Pearse now made his final speech of the Rising to the assembled garrison. He paid tribute to 'the gallantry of the soldiers of Irish Freedom who have during the past four days been writing with fire the most glorious chapter in the later history of Ireland'. When he finished the men spontaneously erupted into singing 'The Soldier's Song'. Shortly afterwards The O'Rahilly left. The evacuation began about 8 p.m. and took place from the Henry Street side entrance. 'Shells were screaming and exploding with periodic regularity, the ear was assailed with the roar of machine-guns in full action; the incessant pattering and zipping of bullets; the crash of falling beams and tumbling masonry and a circle of blazing fires menaced them.'[76] The garrison departed in batches, crossed into Henry Place and around into Moore Lane, Connolly's stretcher being shielded from sniper fire by the devoted Winifred Carney. Pearse stood by the door until the last contingent had passed safely through and then went back into the blazing building to conduct a hasty search through the rooms and apartments for anybody left behind. After what seemed an interminable interval he returned, 'begrimed with soot and dust, his face and eyes swollen with the heat', and passed out into Henry Street.[77] The occupation of the GPO was over. Pearse believed, and subsequent accounts assert, that he was the last person to leave the doomed headquarters but he had missed Diarmuid Lynch and Harry Boland. They were still underground making the ammunition safe, totally unaware of events overhead. When they re-emerged they were astonished to see the hall totally deserted and so it was Lynch who had the distinction of being the last person to depart the Post Office.[78]

The side entrance led into Henry Street which directly faced Henry Place, which in turn led into Moore Street and Parnell Street, and the evacuees were warned that British snipers were operating in Capel Street which overlooked Henry Street. The O'Rahilly had led his men out and, after a momentary pause, he shouted, 'Left turn. Quick march' and they set off at a marching pace towards a barricade near the junction of Moore Street and Henry Street which was manned by British soldiers. Sean MacEntee who was in the party was struck by the tranquillity until they reached Moore Street. 'All was quiet and still. It might have been a lake shore at the fall of evening.'[79] But that changed with deadly suddenness when they turned into Moore Street and the column split into two sections which moved slowly in single file on opposite pavements. They then came under heavy fire from the barricade at the top of the street and most dived for cover wherever it could be found, mostly in doorways about 6 inches deep. MacEntee, however, charged up the street with men falling away wounded as they went, until about half-way he stopped, alone and disorientated, without a clue where Williams & Woods was situated. As he debated with himself what to do he saw about a dozen comrades in an entry on the other side but as he crossed over to them he was shot at by a soldier in a house nearby. MacEntee returned fire with his shotgun but he made it to the safety of the entry and then accompanied the group of Volunteers when it set off down the lane in search of a route to the rear of Williams & Woods.

The O'Rahilly had already fallen wounded at the corner of Sampson's Lane. Aodogán O'Rahilly estimates that his father had covered 180 yards towards the British barricade and was only 30 yards away when he was cut down, possibly by a machine gunner. Although he had been wounded twice The O'Rahilly was able to cross Moore Street to shelter out of sight of the British snipers, an indication, Aodogan believes, that the injuries themselves were not lethal. The loss of blood, however, was catastrophic and with no medical assistance available The O'Rahilly knew his inevitable fate. He still had time to compose a last message to his wife Nancy, which ended, 'I got more than one bullet I think. Tons and Tons of love dearie to you & the boys and to Nell and Anna. It was a good fight anyhow. Please deliver this to Nannie O'Rahilly, 40 Herbert Park Dublin. Good-bye Darling.' The knowledge of the anxiety which his participation in the Rising had inflicted on his wife and four children had weighed heavily on The O'Rahilly. But he had always believed that revolution was inevitable at some point and because his arming of the Irish Volunteers had made the Easter Rising possible he could never have walked away. In words which Yeats placed in his mouth, 'Because I helped to wind the clock, I come to hear it strike.' As his son Aodogán has written, if his father had 'chickened out' he would never have been able to look himself in the face again. Instead he became the most famous of the nine members of the Post Office garrison who were killed in action.[80]

Joe Good's own party, which left the Post Office after The O'Rahilly's, arrived in Henry Place to be met by a scene of complete confusion. In this dark, narrow lane Volunteers were being wounded by fire from a whitewashed house by comrades who had mistaken them for British soldiers, some of whom indeed were dashing past windows having just been released from their captivity in the GPO. Other Volunteers were injured by men who attempted to batter down doors with rifles whose safety catches had been left off. Good asked one man where he could get a grenade to throw into the whitewashed house but the man simply pointed at the GPO and said, 'In there.'[81] All this time Connolly was lying on his back on a stretcher in the middle of Henry Place shouting to the men around him before he was eventually lifted into a house through a small window.

Oscar Traynor's party had followed Good's out of the GPO and as they dashed across the roadway he heard the whizz of ricocheting bullets. A tin of cocoa dropped out of his haversack and, against all logic, Traynor turned back to pick it up. A colleague who was following him remarked that it was a dangerous thing to do and then said 'But maybe it saved you from another bullet'. 'As far as I was concerned I did it without thought, and of course it is possible that I might have run into one of the many bullets which were flying around had I not turned back'.[82] In Henry Place, as Traynor stood appalled at the dead and wounded, Tom Clarke appeared with a revolver in his hand having just fired his only shots of the Rising. He had attempted, unsuccessfully, to blow the lock off a gate to get through a building to save his men exposing themselves to British fire.[83] When Clarke called for volunteers to cross this dangerous position and break into houses in Parnell Street, Traynor was among those who followed, some being wounded before they reached the end of the lane jutting on to Moore Street.

Joe Good who was now accompanying members of the Provisional Government was under machine-gun fire from the Rotunda Hospital and Moore Lane and cover had become essential, especially for the large number of wounded. Volunteers started to force their way into houses in Moore Street, many of which had been locked by their terrified residents. The lock of one door was blasted off, fatally wounding a young girl who was crouching behind it. As the mother cried 'My child. Oh my child,' an agitated MacDermott shouted for the name of the man responsible, but the woman insisted that it had been an appalling accident. As they talked Joe Good noticed a piece of skull, about the size of half an orange, lying on the floor and he surreptitiously slipped it into his pocket.[84] Meanwhile Connolly was being manhandled up the stairs but the house was so cramped that he had to be lifted almost perpendicularly over the banister. Despite his agony Connolly never complained, though like all the wounded he had a dreadful thirst and spoke of how he longed for a cup of tea. When Nurse O'Farrell asked him how he felt, Connolly replied, 'Bad. The soldier who wounded me did a good day's work for the British government.' Shortly afterwards they were joined by other members of the Provisional Government and some mattresses were procured for Connolly and many of the other seventeen men who had been wounded in the retreat from the Post Office. O'Farrell and others spent the night treating them amid 'the roar of burning buildings, machine guns playing on the houses, and, at intervals, what seemed to be hand grenades'.[85]

The house was very crowded but the pressure diminished as men moved into others in the block after holes had been made in the walls. As the Volunteers bored from house to house Connolly was carried in a stretcher. British dispositions and intentions were unknown and in case soldiers were boring from the opposite direction the men prepared for hand-to-hand fighting by carrying daggers, hunting knives, rifles, pistols and home-made bombs. As almost sixty men crawled through holes in darkness one man, carrying a large unsheathed knife, accidentally stabbed the backside of the man in front and was angrily warned to put it back in the sheath which he had unfortunately lost. Luckily he saw a number of hams hanging on a wall and stuck the knife into the smallest which he now carried along.[86] The occupied houses were darkened to prevent sniper fire and during the night some men slept, though none of the leaders did so. Others discussed quietly what the next day might bring. Outside, the shelling, machine-gun fire and bombing continued and in the middle of the night everyone jumped at a massive explosion when the munitions dump in the GPO finally detonated.[87]

Clarke now ordered Traynor to lead a tunnelling party through to the end of Moore Street, a weary and frustrating mission which lasted throughout the night. Traynor led the way through each hole that was bored and was the first to witness many distressing sights. In one house he encountered a woman, an old white-bearded man and two young children crouching in a corner, terrified by the apparition covered from head to foot in plaster and brick dust. In another house Traynor crawled out into the street to drag a semi-conscious and delirious Volunteer into the hallway where he successfully bandaged the most gruesome wound he had yet seen – a whole calf of the man's leg appeared to have been blown away. Then Traynor, who thought that by now he had seen it all, looked through a hole and saw a very large dog staring into his eyes.

It was hard to know if the dog was looking scared or fierce. Some of the men thought it would be safer to shoot it. I thought I would have a try at coaxing it, but all my approaches were met by the same stony stare. I decided to take a chance and go through the hole. I approached very gingerly, and eventually put my hand on his head. At this he seemed to come out of a trance and immediately became friendly. He was probably there on his own for the best part of the week with an inferno raging round him.'[88]

At one point Traynor, who knew the area well, was summoned back by Pearse. As the two men scrutinised a large map of Dublin, Traynor indicated where they were, where they had been and the locations of the British army. He also showed Pearse the shortest route to Williams & Woods and warned that to get through to the factory they would have to overcome a heavily fortified barricade and some houses at the top of Moore Street which were occupied by British soldiers. By the time Traynor left to resume tunnelling, Pearse must have had strong doubts about the feasibility of battling on. When Traynor's men finished early on Saturday morning Diarmuid Lynch asked for volunteers for a bayonet charge against the barricade at the end of Moore Street and both Traynor and Harry Boland stepped forward. Traynor remarked, 'Well, this looks like the end for us', but the indomitable Boland simply replied that, 'The only thing that is wrong about this order is that it should have been given a long time ago.'[89] In all, between twenty and thirty men were recruited for this deadly mission and were waiting, ironically in a slaughter-house, eating a tin of pears when a man rushed in and told them that the operation had been cancelled.

As O'Farrell cooked breakfast for Traynor's exhausted tunnelling party the wounded men were carried through the holes to 16 Moore Street where Connolly was put to bed in a back room. During the morning a group of mainly female civilians who attempted to leave Moore Street were shot at by British soldiers. Joe Good was convinced that the British had played a lethal trick by calling on the women to advance before opening fire which left at least one man riddled with bullets and lying on a white sheet, attached to a sweeping brush.[90] Jim Ryan, the Post Office Medical Officer, confirmed that this and similar incidents were witnessed by Pearse and were largely instrumental in bringing about the decision to surrender.[91] The process which led to surrender began when Pearse, Connolly, Clarke, MacDermott and Plunkett held a lengthy 'council of war' in the company of Willie Pearse, three wounded Volunteers, a badly injured British army sergeant and the three women, O'Farrell, Grenan and Carney. As the leaders debated the soldier called out for Pearse to shift him, which he did gently before returning to Connolly's bedside. By the end of the conference it had been decided to seek terms from the British, to prevent 'further slaughter of the civil population and to save the lives of as many as possible of our followers'. A minute by Pearse recorded that the decision had been taken by majority vote and, though the identity of the dissenter or dissenters is unknown, the irreconcilable Clarke was almost certainly opposed. If it was only he who rejected capitulation then there is an exquisite symmetry to the Rising, because less than a week before, at Liberty Hall, Clarke had stood alone and argued for action that day; perhaps on Easter Saturday he stood alone again. Certainly after O'Farrell had left Joe Good noticed that Connolly, Pearse and Plunkett were 'talking quietly and occasionally laughing, like men who had made a decision and were passing the time' but that a silent Clarke was literally standing alone at a window.[92] Almost twenty years earlier he had been given a second chance to rebuild his life and resume his political career and he had done so with extraordinary single-mindedness. Now the project to which he had dedicated his every moment since release from prison was collapsing all around him and, if he could be certain of anything, it was that he would not be offered another opportunity.

At about 12.45 p.m. Nurse O'Farrell, with something like a white handkerchief tied to a piece of stick, was led to a doorway by MacDermott. After a sustained burst of firing when the improvised flag was waved she stepped outside and walked very slowly up Moore Street. Julia Grenan watched, terrified for her friend's safety, but Connolly reassured her. 'Don't be crying for your friend. They won't shoot her. They may blindfold her and bring her across their lines to wherever the Commandant is, so she may be away for some time. But they won't shoot her.'[93] O'Farrell took a verbal message to the Commander of the British Forces from Pearse stating that he wanted to discuss surrender terms. On her way to the military barrier at the top of Moore Street she saw The O'Rahilly's hat and revolver lying on the ground and prayed that he had managed to take cover in a nearby house. The British officer in charge initially ordered her back to extricate the other women but then changed his mind and dispatched her to a house in Parnell Street. There a hostile officer accused her of being a spy and ordered that the Red Cross be removed from her arm and apron. She was then moved, by an amazing coincidence, to Tom Clarke's shop, where, after a lengthy wait General Lowe arrived. He listened to her courteously and then drove her back to the top of Moore Street where he instructed her to tell Pearse that unconditional surrender was required within half an hour. Lowe then confirmed the message in writing. It was now about 2.25 p.m.[94]

On her return journey O'Farrell passed Sackville Lane and was horrified to see that The O'Rahilly's body lay about 4 yards up the lane, the feet lying against the side entrance of a shop and his head on the kerbstone. When she delivered

Lowe's ultimatum there was another leadership conference after which O'Farrell was sent back with a note which attempted to bargain. But Lowe was immovable and reiterated his demand for unconditional surrender from Pearse. If Pearse did not return with O'Farrell within half an hour followed by Connolly he would recommence hostilities. The members of the Provisional Government then held a short war council and Pearse decided to accompany O'Farrell to meet Lowe. Before he left Pearse took a sad, silent farewell while a weeping Winifred Carney knelt at Connolly's bedside and asked 'Was there no other way?' Connolly quietly reassured her that he was not prepared to see his brave boys burnt to death.

Lowe now received Pearse at the top of Moore Street and proposed that Nurse O'Farrell should remain with his officers to convey Pearse's surrender order to the other rebel garrisons. Lowe promised that once O'Farrell had completed the task she would be set free with a safe convoy pass. O'Farrell later wrote that

> Pearse turned to me and said: 'Will you agree to this?' I said 'Yes, if you wish it.' He said: 'I do wish it.' Pearse then shook hands with me, but spoke no word. After this he was taken away in a motor car down O'Connell Street, accompanied by Gen. Lowe's son and another officer inside, and an armed guard outside. He was preceded in another car by Gen. Lowe and Capt. [sic] Wheeler. I saw him no more. There were several officers standing round as Com. Pearse was driven off, one of whom remarked, 'It would be interesting to know how many marks that fellow has in his pocket.'[95]

Pearse was driven to Military Headquarters at Parkgate where he met Maxwell and then signed an instrument of surrender. This stated:

> In order to prevent the further slaughter of Dublin citizens, and in the hope of saving the lives of our followers now surrounded and hopelessly outnumbered, the members of

the Provisional Government at Headquarters have agreed to an unconditional surrender, and the Commandants of the various districts in the City and Country will order their commands to lay down arms.

During Pearse's absence, Jim Ryan, the Medical Officer in the GPO, was in Moore Street preparing Connolly for his departure to Dublin Castle. Ryan inquired what terms the British would issue and Connolly replied that, while the Provisional Government would be executed, senior Volunteer officers and the rank and file would be allowed to go home.[96] Connolly now sat up in bed and shaved himself while Carney held the mirror, combed his hair, washed him, re-dressed his wounds and made his uniform as presentable as possible. Four very smart Volunteers then arrived to take him away. When he reached the Castle Hospital Connolly was brought Pearse's document and endorsed it for the men under his command in the Moore Street district and the Stephen's Green Area. After Connolly left, Ryan asked Sean MacDermott what terms, he believed, Pearse and Connolly had agreed to and was told;

That the signatories would be shot and the rest of us set free, he thought. I found it hard to believe this at first but later Tom Clarke and Joseph Plunkett used practically the same words when I asked them. Is one to conclude then that these men had agreed amongst themselves before Pearse went to the Castle that they should offer their own lives in an attempt to save those of their followers?[97]

This is a fascinating piece of speculation which puts the blood sacrifice theory into an entirely new light; not a strategy carefully thought out in advance, but a gambit hastily concocted as the Rising disintegrated, probably at the war council around Connolly's bedside on Saturday morning. And one designed not to redeem Ireland but to perform the eminently practical task of saving the lives of their men.

The surrender orders of both Pearse and Connolly were

brought to Nurse O'Farrell who took them to Moore Street. Breaking the news to the rank and file was a matter of enormous sensitivity. The leadership conferences around Connolly's bedside had been very dignified; no bystander heard a voice raised, despite the emotional pain which the participants must have felt as their dreams faded. It was not certain that the men would show the same discipline and lack of recrimination, especially after the grim experiences of the previous twenty-four hours which they had endured in the belief that the struggle would continue. Yielding now then, in a sense, would be an admission that all the sacrifices they had made since the evacuation of the Post Office had been for nothing. They were already emotionally drained. Jack Plunkett remembered how 'That last morning in Moore Street was dreadful. The absence of activity made it horribly depressing. The lack of news and food and sleep.'[98] At this moment the remaining members of the Provisional Government, despite their differences, had to display a collective solidarity, a rock-like unity in the face of whatever dissension the news of surrender would provoke among the rank and file. After the cancellation of the bayonet charge Oscar Traynor had returned to one of the houses in Moore Street to sleep on a bare floor until he was awakened with the news of surrender. He and many of his comrades were dumbfounded because they had always understood that surrender would mean a lengthy prison sentence at least. Some of them reacted by destroying their weapons, though others argued that because they had fought for a week, they were entitled to prisoner-of-war treatment. Oscar Traynor has recorded how Sean MacDermott tried to reassure them that the latter was indeed the case.

As we were leaving the houses to line up in Moore Street I met Sean MacDermott, whom I had met on many occasions, and I said to him, more in sorrow than anger 'Is this what we were brought out for? To spend the rest of our lives in English dungeons.' His reply to that was to wave a piece of paper, about 3" by 6" [3 inches by 6 inches], which he held in his hand, and which had about half-a-dozen lines of typescript on it, and in addition what I thought were two signatures. 'No! No!,' he said, 'We are surrendering as prisoners of war.' I often wondered what significance the paper had. But though I discussed this incident on many later occasions with my comrades of the fight, we could never arrive at a satisfactory solution as to what it could have been.[99]

Joe Good wrote that 'something close to mutiny'[100] erupted in and around Moore Street, especially among his Kimmage comrades who had fled conscription and now feared being shot as deserters or shipped to the Western Front. As a mood to fight on developed among the rank and file the leaders stepped forward, one after the other, to support their agreed policy. Clarke spoke first and was followed by Plunkett who dragged himself forward to plead unsuccessfully for unity. It was MacDermott who, standing precariously and, for a polio victim, dangerously, on the lid of a dustbin, managed to quell the mounting disaffection. He urged them to look outside at the dead civilians lying in the streets and imagine how many more there would be if the Rising had been prolonged. He also pointed out the even more terrible destruction which could be inflicted on their city. 'You've all seen what happened to the Post Office!' Their duty now was to survive and endure, spend at most some years in jail and then renew the struggle. 'We, who will be shot, will die happy – knowing that there are still plenty of you around who will finish the job.'[101]

The surrender began with the wounded, rebel and army, being carried out into Moore Street where the Volunteers formed up amidst a scene of carnage memorably described by Joe Good.

A number of the dead were lying around: civilians, soldiers and Volunteers. One of the civilian casualties was squatting against a wall with a white bundle; his head was slit open like a pomegranate. A Volunteer was lying at the corner of Moore Lane, a dead Tommie beside him. I'll never forget that little Volunteer. I looked at him. He was very dead. They had played a machine-gun on him. Pieces of wool, his undergarments, protruded through his uniform, making a scarecrow character of a man.[102]

After Pearse's surrender order was read out the Volunteers were marched up Moore Lane and Henry Place, then into Henry Street and then round to Nelson's Pillar. Willie Pearse was at the head of the column carrying a white flag while the leaders, with Winifred Carney and Julia Grenan, followed towards the rear. At the Gresham Hotel the Volunteers laid down their arms and equipment and the Ambulance Corps members were ordered to take off their Red Crosses. Grenan recalled that;

> Two officers came down and one said to the other, 'There's Tom Clarke.' One of them called Mr Clarke out of line and several other officers came to have a look at him.' Another officer looking at Sean MacDermott said, 'You have cripples in your army,' and Sean replied, 'You have your place, sir, and I have mine, and you had better mind your place, sir.'[103]

The column then marched up O'Connell Street and was crowded uncomfortably into a grassy area in front of the Rotunda Hospital. There during the bitterly cold night MacDermott and Plunkett in particular suffered terribly, even though Winifred Carney gave them Connolly's coat and hers to wrap around themselves. British sentries monitored every move and a Volunteer who started chewing an Oxo cube was taken out and thoroughly re-searched. On Sunday morning detectives arrived to identify the ringleaders, though MacDermott was assured that because of the leniency displayed to the police during the Rising they would speak in the leaders' favour.

> Later on a detective came up with a military officer, and brought away Tom Clarke under an armed guard. He returned after some time and told us they had searched

him and taken away all he had, and that the record of his whole life had been read out to him. His life in prison, his conduct there, his life in the U.S., even to the cut of clothes he wore there; his life from his return to Ireland up to the present day. 'Everything, they have everything,' he said.[104]

At about 9 a.m. the prisoners were assembled to commence the transfer to Richmond Barracks. As they marched down O'Connell Street they passed the GPO and the Metropole Hotel and Oscar Traynor 'was very proud as I looked at the spot where the Metropole and the other buildings had been, because all that was left of that fine six storied building was a lone gable end at the corner of Prince's Street'.[105] The marchers were taken through Westmoreland Street, College Green, Dame Street, Lord Edward Street, High Street, Thomas Street, James's Street and on to Richmond Barracks. Far behind came Sean MacDermott who had explained to the officer in charge that he was unable to march in step and was allowed to walk alone in the rear under escort. He arrived three-quarters of an hour late, completely exhausted from the night's exposure and the rigours of the journey. Plunkett had fainted on arrival and had to be carried in through the prison gates.[106]

Any evaluation of the performance of the rebel leadership in O'Connell Street during Easter Week must emphasise the contribution of James Connolly. For years before 1916 he had been unswervingly committed to revolution, writing, speaking and lecturing in favour of a Rising and, through his Citizen Army, preparing for one. The Citizen Army was entirely his creation, its men and officers had been vetted by him and its structure had been decided by him. He exercised ruthlessly autocratic control over the organisation through a leadership style which stressed distance and authority. He demanded from his followers efficiency, sobriety, seriousness, ideological commitment and absolute obedience to higher authority. At times Connolly could be positively brutal even to his inner circle; he once unjustifiably accused Michael Mallin of being under the influence of alcohol. However, it is a measure of the respect and indeed fear which he inspired that his absolute integrity, moral ascendancy and leadership position were never challenged.

Connolly's achievements before the Rising had been impressive because, while the Irish Volunteers numerically dwarfed the minuscule Citizen Army, in almost every other respect Connolly had created a superior organisation. It was committed ideologically to the single, unambiguous goal of revolution, an objective clearly understood and supported by its membership; Connolly had once questioned every single man and recorded whether he was willing to fight. Furthermore the Citizen Army's training and lectures were both directed towards preparing the men for urban warfare. Its unity of purpose and its discipline were in stark contrast to the Irish Volunteers, an organisation riven with ideological disputes and faction-fighting, and whose indecisive Chief of Staff was being continually and successfully subverted by a determined minority.

In the light of these facts, the Military Council's eagerness, at the start of 1916, to have Connolly on its side then is understandable. More surprising and impressive are the ease and effectiveness of the subsequent military collaboration between this one-man band and a group of similarly strong-willed men. Behind the stern, humourless, prickly, stubborn exterior there was a greater flexibility in Connolly than is often realised and this ability to bend according to the circumstances was also displayed during Easter Week. Ratifying his selection as Commandant-General of the Dublin forces must have been one of the easiest decisions which the Military Council had had to make. There simply was no rival. That he justified their faith during Easter Week is amply demonstrated by the many tributes paid to him then and subsequently by the Post Office garrison. By his insistence from the start of the Rising that the only army he now recognised was the Army of the Irish Republic, Connolly ensured an amicable working relationship in the Headquarters area between his own Citizen Army and the

Irish Volunteers. These two organisations had had past differences but any lingering hostility was greatly assuaged by the admiration felt by many Volunteers for the professionalism, dedication, bravery and ruthlessness of the members of the Citizen Army. Furthermore Connolly's only criterion was military effectiveness and he was prepared to promote Irish Volunteers such as Traynor over Citizen Army officers such as Poole in the Metropole.

As a leader Connolly emerges as an authoritative and inspirational figure who displayed bravery, decisiveness, enormous energy and resilience. Furthermore, he was aware of the importance of showing a greater ease and warmth in order to establish a rapport with the rank and file. He had never been known for a lively sense of fun, but tried his best in the Post Office to soften his habitually brusque manner with some rather wooden attempts at humour. His courage, however, was never in doubt and indeed it led directly to his fearsome wound. It can be argued that as Commandant-General he should never have placed himself in such danger and risked removal from active command at such a crucial time. However, historians will debate eternally and inconclusively the wisdom of military leaders sharing the same dangers as the rank and file. Some great generals always insisted on doing so, including Alexander the Great whose many wounds were incurred by leading from the front, a leadership style which, in part, explains the Macedonian army's fanatical loyalty to him. Furthermore by 1916 it was the prosecution of the European War by commanders safely ensconced in châteaux far away from the front lines whose dangers and horrors they never shared and barely understood, which had become the source of so much resentment.

In terms of his reading of the overall strategic situation, Connolly emerges quite impressively. He had grasped quickly on Easter Tuesday the implications of the failure of the country to rise in support of the Dublin forces and he had reacted flexibly to that disappointment. He had remodelled his strategy, redeploying his forces in the city and strengthening the defences around the Post Office in readiness for an anticipated British assault. It is often argued, correctly, that Connolly was found out by his insistence that the British capitalist class would never permit an urban insurrection to be suppressed by an artillery bombardment which would cause widespread devastation to property. However, if Connolly was blinded by Marxist theory it must also be remembered that many other people of very different ideological persuasions had also reached the same conclusion. Indeed, to almost everyone before Easter 1916 it would have seemed inconceivable that any British government would approve the levelling of much of the centre of one of the largest cities in the whole of the United Kingdom. If Connolly had miscalculated then so had almost everyone else. Furthermore Connolly was prepared to admit his miscalculation and act accordingly. Above all it was the men under his command who mattered most to him. While he certainly expected them to be prepared to die for their cause, he never swerved from the belief that the least they deserved was a fighting chance. Once the British had revealed their strategy as one of blasting and burning the rebels into defeat, Connolly was not prepared to let his men simply stay to be physically annihilated from a distance without having any chance of retaliating effectively.

8

A CITY AT WAR

In 1916 Dublin may well have been the Irish capital, but in some respects it wore the appearance of genteel decline. The northern city of Belfast was an industrial power-house at its zenith whereas Dublin reflected a past when it prided itself as the second city of the British Empire. Like an aristocrat fallen on hard times, it still maintained a façade of grandeur as the seat of the viceroy and the centre of British rule in Ireland. The Castle 'season' of receptions and balls and the Royal Dublin Society's horse show were the social highlights of the year. With only light industry, Dublin's functions were primarily administrative, commercial, professional and cultural.

Lack of development had left the city's eighteenth-century heritage of spacious streets and classical public buildings largely unchanged. Despite its social problems, Dublin was considered a beautiful city. Defined on the north and south sides respectively by the Royal and Grand Canals, it was bisected east to west by the River Liffey with its quays, seven city bridges and two outstanding edifices, the Custom House and the Four Courts. The street pattern related to two main axes, one north–south from O'Connell Street via College Green and Grafton Street to St Stephen's Green, the other east–west from College Green to the oldest part of the city round the cathedrals and the Castle. College Green, with the Bank of Ireland and Trinity College, was the banking and business centre, Grafton Street the fashionable shopping area. St Stephen's Green, the largest of the five Georgian squares, was now a public park with ornamental lake. North of the river,

O'Connell Street was a broad boulevard whose principal features were the colonnaded General Post Office and the 134-foot Nelson Pillar erected in 1809 and the first such monument to the British victor at Trafalgar. At either end of the street stood Daniel O'Connell 'the Liberator' and the Parnell monolith, with its challenging inscription on behalf of a subject people: 'No man has a right to fix the boundary to the march of a nation.' They symbolised the advance of constitutional nationalism; there was no inkling yet that their tradition, too, with Home Rule now in sight, was in the end to be swept aside by the events about to unfold at the General Post Office.

At the end of the Liffey quays on the western edge of the city lay the Phoenix Park, popularly claimed to be the largest urban park in Europe. Within its wide terrain were located the Vice-regal Lodge (the residence of the Lord Lieutenant where visiting royalty stayed) and the lodge of the Chief Secretary; near the main gates were the headquarters of the British army in Ireland and of the Royal Irish Constabulary. Among its monuments was the towering obelisk to the Duke of Wellington, while the Peninsular War hero, Field Marshal Gough, was a lone bronze horseman on the main avenue which traversed the park for 2 miles. More distant prospects could reveal some of the herd of deer, a reminder that this began in the seventeenth century as a royal deer park. Long a favourite resort of Dubliners with its playing fields, band performances and zoological gardens, Phoenix Park, laid out in the grand manner, was also an expression of the imperial state. On the other side of the Liffey, across from the Park, was the Royal Hospital, Kilmainham, opened in 1784 as a home for old soldiers and now as well the residence of the British Commander-in-Chief. A short distance from its entrance was the gaol soon to acquire a grim significance in the story of Easter 1916.

For many years now the middle classes had been gradually migrating from the centre to new Victorian suburbs beyond the canals. Here in their leafy avenues the still dominant Unionist business and professional elite and the rising Catholic middle class enjoyed cleaner air away from the deteriorating central areas. While Merrion and Fitzwilliam Squares remained socially prestigious, on the north side the Georgian streets were in decline, with houses often becoming overcrowded tenements. The poor family living in one room under a beautiful plasterwork ceiling became a stock image of the Dublin slum. But that was only one aspect of the widespread poverty. In run-down dwellings, congeries of back lanes and insanitary courts 100,000 people – a third of the city's population – lived in conditions that were common in cities at the time, but present in Dublin to an extreme degree. Squalor, malnutrition and rampant disease helped to produce the highest death rate in the British Isles. Dublin was also unusual in that the slums were often adjacent to the principal streets. A few minutes' walk from the hotels and shops of O'Connell Street, for example, deprivation mingled with prostitution in the extensive red-light district. The lowest classes were inured to long-term unemployment or a precarious existence as casual labourers, dockers, coal-heavers and in other occupations on low wages and bad working conditions. But the passive acceptance of their lot was changing. Liberty Hall, the headquarters of the Irish Transport and General Workers Union, was becoming the focus of increasing labour militancy.

For a century after the abortive Emmet Rising of 1803, a rebellion against the Act of Union, Dublin had been a politically quiescent city. Nineteenth-century violence was concentrated overwhelmingly in the countryside but in the years before the First World War the city experienced serious political, social and economic tensions. There was a major and bitter industrial dispute in 1913 between the Irish Transport and General Workers Union led by Connolly's boss Jim Larkin and the Dublin United Tramways Company of William Martin Murphy, whose business empire also included newspapers, the Imperial Hotel and a department store. It was a violent and protracted struggle which began when Murphy locked out the tramwaymen and retaliated against the subsequent wave of sympathetic strikes by employing strike-breakers. Murphy's trams were stoned and the police were involved in frequent confrontations with Larkin's pickets. On 1 September 1913 Larkin attempted to make a speech in O'Connell Street from the balcony of the Imperial Hotel. Scuffling broke out and the police panicked, baton-charging even the crowds which were coming from mass in the nearby Pro-Cathedral. In the subsequent rioting which lasted until the following day two men were killed and 200 policemen injured along with a far greater number of civilians. The labour dispute dragged on through the winter and into 1914 before the union's resistance collapsed. Nevertheless Murphy's apparently complete victory engendered a resentment in the Dublin slums which surfaced again during the Rising when tenement dwellers took spectacular revenge on those businesses which had supported him. There was another bloody episode on Sunday 26 July 1914, at Bachelor's Walk by the River Liffey. Troops of the King's Own Scottish Borderers who had been called out in an abortive attempt to frustrate an Irish Volunteer gun-running operation at Howth, just outside Dublin, were confronted by an angry crowd. Eventually the soldiers opened fire and wounded thirty-eight people, one of whom later died.

In 1916 Dublin was a city involved in a great war. Many of its citizens were fighting and dying in places as far apart as the Western Front in France and Suvla Bay in Turkey in battles which dominated conversation, political debates and newspapers. Its streets and hospitals contained many disabled and convalescent soldiers and troops on leave mingled with civilians, refugees and recruiting officers. The Defence of the Realm Act had given the government unprecedented powers to regulate social and economic life and sometimes the ruthless face of modern warfare came uncomfortably close, as when hundreds of bodies were washed up on the southern coast of Ireland from the torpedoed liner *Lusitania*. However, in many respects, Dublin was strangely detached from the conflict, hardly burdened by the disciplines of total war. Its geographical remoteness removed the fear of falling to the enemy that was ever-present in Paris and Petrograd and it did not even suffer the Zeppelin raids made on British cities. Nor were Ireland's coastal towns bombarded by German warships or even afflicted by the sound of the great guns in France as were those on the south coast of England. Furthermore, while partial conscription had been introduced into Great Britain in 1915, Ireland continued to rely, with diminishing results, on voluntary recruiting. As a result it had become a refuge to those in Britain fleeing compulsory military service.

During 1915 and 1916 Britain abandoned 'business as usual' and mobilised politically, socially, economically and psychologically for total war. This transformation entailed the sacrifice of many peacetime pleasures and modes of behaviour. By contrast Ireland became a magnet for those seeking rest and recreation and for the first time it experienced the greater traffic of people between the two islands. Soldiers from every part of the Empire came on leave and prosperous English couples on motoring tours stayed in Dublin's two finest hotels, the Shelbourne and the Royal Hibernian, and frequented theatres such as the Abbey and the Gaiety. Horse-racing continued with meetings which attracted hordes of punters and bookmakers from Britain who had at their disposal public houses which took a relaxed attitude to opening hours. Soldiers who were based in the city's nine functioning barracks regarded Dublin as an easy posting where they could walk the streets in complete safety, where officers frequented the city's high-class brothels and the rank and file availed themselves of prostitutes in one of the largest red-light districts in Europe. Officers also enjoyed weekend sojourns in the big houses of the Anglo-Irish ascendancy where they socialised, hunted and relaxed. Visitors from Britain travelled to Ireland in complete safety from Holyhead and Liverpool, despite rumours of a German submarine in the Irish Sea. There were no fatalities until October 1918 when the RMS *Leinster* was sunk just out of Kingstown.

On Easter Monday 1916, Dublin's transformation from normality of a kind to deadly urban warfare took the citizens totally by surprise. For some hours the city existed in a limbo of unreality. At Stephen's Green, for instance, civilians complained about the disruption caused by 'practice' Citizen Army manoeuvres and threatened to call the 'polis', while one young lady whose British officer boyfriend was arrested insisted that she would wait till the performance was over.[1] At Lansdowne railway station, an amused Volunteer officer, George Lyons, watched the reaction of British officers to the start of the Rising and the premature termination of their Easter leave:

I turned my attention to some khaki specks I perceived in the motley throng on the departure platform. 'Military men advance to the edge of the platform,' I shouted. I had to repeat the order several times before I could command any attention. There were four British officers in the crowd. They instinctively sought each other and grouped together and looked our way. This was just what I wanted. 'Gentlemen,' I cried, 'you will stand to attention. My men have you covered.' They consulted for a moment, trying to look indifferent and feigning to take the matter as a joke. 'What's the trouble?' enquired one tall cavalry officer, who seemed to be looked upon as a senior. 'No trouble yet,' I answered as I ordered six of my men to keep them covered with their rifles. 'We are in earnest today, however, and there will be heaps of trouble if you break ground without orders,' I added. Some of their fine indifference seemed to fade away and to be replaced by perplexion and doubt. 'You will hand over your arms, gentlemen,' I next ordered. 'Oh, we have no arms whatsoever,' declared the senior officer referred to. 'We will take your word as soldiers for that and we will punish you as soldiers if you have lied. Consider yourself prisoners of war,' I added as I perceived a detachment of my men advancing from the main entrance behind them. These men marched the British officers down to one of the rail offices where they were provided for.[2]

An officer in de Valera's 3rd Battalion recalled that at Boland's bakery the insurgents;

started to clear out the staff, but some of them were reluctant to leave until they were shown the business end of our guns – as they were under the impression that we were just on manoeuvres and had carried the joke a bit far. However, our businesslike attitude very soon made them make up their minds.[3]

Many Volunteers had been caught out by the speed of events, including Peadar Healy, a ticket collector at Broadstone railway station. He had reported for work but as packed trains departed for Fairyhouse race-course rifle fire started. Healy immediately hurried off and entered the combat zone in Church Street near the Four Courts, dressed in his railway uniform with his ticket-punching machine strapped over his shoulder and a Howth rifle in his hand.[4] Even though news spread quickly by word of mouth or by telephone some Dubliners remained ignorant. They included Christina Doyle who had gone with her family to Fairyhouse races and though rumours of rioting in the city centre had circulated there, they were still unaware when their car entered O'Connell Street. Doyle's mother became indignant when she saw the dead lancer horse lying near the Post Office and began berating Dublin Corporation for permitting the animal to lie unattended. Her anger increased when she spotted one of her apprentices walking about armed with a rifle and she warned him that his father would learn of this outrageous behaviour![5] At the GPO a judge whose car had been stopped threatened to summon a policeman but reversed at speed when a Volunteer produced a revolver and warned him that if he did not comply he would be shot.[6]

Many Volunteers who were mobilised on Easter Monday had received only a few hours' notice and assumed that they were going on practice manoeuvres. They only learnt the truth at the last moment, though some commandants did give them the opportunity to withdraw. Only 2 of Ned Daly's 300 members of the 1st Dublin Battalion backed out and the others cheered, though it is impossible to know how many had private reservations but remained through a reluctance to desert their comrades.[7] Other Volunteers had been absent from home when their mobilisation orders arrived on Monday morning. Liam Ó Briain, a private in the 1st Dublin Battalion, had spent the previous day in the midlands delivering MacNeill's countermanding orders. But when he returned to Dublin and saw Volunteers firing at Portobello Bridge he hurried to join his company in North King Street and on the way was persuaded at Stephen's Green to join Mallin's Citizen Army garrison instead.[8]

The pace of developments also disorientated army reinforcements who had been rushed to Ireland from England. Most of them were young recruits who were untrained for urban warfare and had never fired a service bullet. Their emergency mobilisation orders arrived at teatime on Easter Monday with departure fixed for the early morning hours. This precipitated a frantic search for those who were spending their Easter leave in pubs, cinemas and even on honeymoon. Even after the trains departed most of them still had no idea of their destination and assumed only that a critical situation had developed on the Western Front. During the journey north from St Albans some learned the truth from newspaper posters or the dock authorities at Liverpool, where officers raced into the city centre to scour shops and hotels for guidebooks with maps of Dublin. The soldiers were also travelling with few weapons, no bombs and only fifty rounds of ammunition each; their superb Lewis guns were left stranded on Liverpool docks and although large supplies of munitions were rushed to Kingstown they arrived only after the men had disembarked. On the transport ships the men were packed like cattle and for a while an erroneous warning that rebels had taken Kingstown prompted fears among the officers that they would have to fight their way ashore. Astonishingly, even at this stage many of the troops were still unaware of their destination and one stunned Irish recruit only realised it as they sailed into Dublin Bay. Others assumed that they were in France and disembarked shouting 'merci' while one remarked to his comrade, 'I say, Bill, they've picked up our language pretty quick.'[9]

The battle which raged in the streets of Dublin during Easter Week 1916 was a revelatory experience for combatants who learnt much about the realities of urban warfare and the demands it imposed on a person's physical, mental and emotional resources. Many discovered qualities which they had never suspected they possessed, and in some cases wished they didn't. Members of the Irish Volunteers and Citizen Army at least had an advantage over their opponents in that they had had classes in street-fighting. But from the first hours they realised the limited value of these lessons and that in urban warfare the expected rarely happened while the unanticipated frequently did. Joe Good became aware of this uncomfortable fact when he began fortifying occupied premises and knocking holes in walls to facilitate movement between them.

> Theoretically, in house-to-house fighting, one bores from house to house, stepping from one room into the next. It does not work out that way, it's a Lewis Carroll looking-glass experience. One bores a hole at a convenient height, and when the hole is enlarged one prepares to step through – only to find oneself at the ceiling-level of the next apartment, and looking down on a dining table. Worse again, after laborious work one gazes down into the well of a staircase and a hall, the stairs perhaps twelve feet distant below one. Sometimes one unexpectedly breaks through such apartments – one may conjecture with humour on what difficulties all of this would present to your pursuers.[10]

Sometimes, frustratingly, little or no military action ensued. At Stephen's Green and then at the College of Surgeons Liam Ó Briain spent most of his time observing and boring holes and did not fire a shot until Easter Friday.[11] For others, however, the first sight of blood, the first shot or the first killing came quickly, and often the steadying hand of a senior officer was required to see them through the experience. At the Four Courts shortly after noon on Easter Monday as Daly's 1st Battalion occupied houses and business premises at the junction of North Brunswick Street and Church Street a cavalry party appeared escorting munitions lorries. The lancers charged at eight Volunteers who had never fired a shot in anger and Daly took command personally, calming their nerves until he ordered them to fire. A volley from their Howth rifles then fatally wounded the leading officer and sent the others fleeing panic-stricken into North King Street, their horses' hooves knocking sparks off the cobblestones.[12]

The physical act of firing was part of the blooding process in which men became attuned to their weapons. It was often a disconcerting experience, because the Howth rifle favoured by Volunteers was an unstable weapon. Tom Walsh learnt this at a window in Clanwilliam House during the battle of Mount Street Bridge.

> I fired for the first time from my Howth gun, and for that matter from any other rifle! I do not know what happened to me or for how long I was unconscious. In the excitement I did not heed the lectures and did not hold the weapon correctly. The result was the butt hit me under the chin and knocked me out. When I came to I discovered that a large piece of the granite window sill had gone. . . . I had received a good lesson, and for the remainder of the scrap I remembered it was a Howth rifle I had to deal with.[13]

After the first shots many were relieved, proud but dangerously exhilarated men. The jubilation on Easter Monday of the Volunteers who had attacked the lancers in O'Connell Street was so intense that many suffered a physical reaction. There was a chaotic and dangerous scene inside the Post Office as rebels who were temporarily unable fully to control their movements accidentally discharged their rifles all over the place.[14] Some men revelled in the drama and excitement of the Rising from the very start, but many others needed to go through a painful process of adaptation before accepting the reality of their involvement. One was young Matt Walton whose confrontation with a howling mob at Jacob's Factory left him distinctly queasy:

There was a big, very big tall woman with something very heavy in her hand and she came across and lifted up her hand to make a bang at me. One of the Volunteers upstairs saw this and fired and I just remember seeing her face and head disappear as she went down like a sack. That was my baptism of fire and I remember my knees going out from under me. I would have sold my mother and father and the Pope just to get out of that bloody place.

However, as in many cases, Walton's discomfort quickly passed: 'You recover after a few minutes.'[15]

Fighting on the other side was a British officer, Lieutenant Jameson of the Leinster Regiment.[16] He had been rushed to the city from the Curragh military camp and in a series of letters to his family he vividly described his odyssey through its streets. Initially Jameson blanched and lost his appetite at the first sight of death as three dead Volunteers were washed down by nurses in the Castle Hospital. Soon afterwards he inflicted his first fatality in O'Connell Street. 'I shot my first man at the top of O'Connell's statue. I felt horrid and as if I wanted to go and apologise and help him!' However, like Matt Walton, Jameson quickly perked up. 'I very soon got over that and was very annoyed when I missed anybody.' Soon he was thoroughly enjoying the Rising, relishing the challenge of command and the excitement of battle. Nevertheless, others were swiftly overwhelmed and crumbled, seeking only escape from the conflict. Some who deserted were senior Volunteer officers such as Captain McCarthy at Roe's distillery near the South Dublin Union, and P. Begley, de Valera's vice-commandant at Boland's.[17]

Others endured longer but eventually cracked, including two battalion commanders, Thomas MacDonagh and Eamon de Valera. A Volunteer unit at Boland's bakery was also badly affected. Its members had been stationed along a low-level, elevated railway line where the members had been shielded from the city's skyline. They endured easily enough until Easter Friday, but were then transferred and suddenly witnessed the inferno raging in the city centre. Captain Simon Donnelly described how

It unnerved a great number of the men. One officer particularly, his nerves completely shattered, lost his head and fired at a Volunteer who was standing near me, inflicting a slight wound. Luckily the revolver used was of small calibre, otherwise the result would have been fatal.[18]

Another case occurred in the malthouse of Guinness's Brewery where a British soldier, Sergeant Robert Flood of the Royal Dublin Fusiliers, broke down. Flood's unit had been guarding this dark, creaky, rambling edifice and his fevered imagination ran completely out of control. His paranoia focused on Lieutenant Lucas who had taken over command for the evening and who, tragically, opened a window in direct contravention of a standing order. When Flood then saw Lucas smile at John Rice, a civilian night-watchman, he became convinced that the enemy had infiltrated the complex and were about to launch an attack. He arrested Lucas and Rice, and had them put them up against a wall and shot dead by a firing squad. He then finished matters off by arresting another officer, Lieutenant Worswick, whom he considered was acting suspiciously, as well as another night-watchman. When Worswick resisted he and the civilian were also shot dead. Flood then turned himself in and after the Rising was tried by a court-martial in which, incredibly, he was found not guilty of murder and released.

Lieutenant Jameson's young recruits were also nervous of the darkness and in constant dread and they required his constant attention. On one occasion he led them fighting down Dame Lane to establish a line of communication to Trinity College. He was glad when he returned with twenty of the unit and finally managed to get them bedded down for the night, only for panic to start soon afterwards.

At 4 o'clock in the morning they all got an attack of funk – swore they had seen about '20 men stealing by', loosed off any amount of ammunition at nothing and then ran away and collected in a quivering bunch at the end of the street. I had to go and get 'em all back to their places with

12 more of my men to give them confidence and had to report the sergeant next morning for deserting his post. He got it very hot![19]

Like many officers on both sides, Jameson also fretted at his subordinates' youth and inexperience. On the Irish side, for instance, when Matt Connolly of the Citizen Army fought at the City Hall he was only fifteen years old – the same age as Volunteer Matt Walton at Jacob's. Fianna scouts who acted as dispatch carriers were frequently even younger. One incredulous rebel encountered a cheery 11-year-old with a great head of curls, a cap with a gaping hole and a large cross in his hands among the flames and bullets of O'Connell Street on Easter Friday.[20] Twelve-year-old Tommy Keenan fetched food and medicine for Mallin's garrison in the College of Surgeons, his tiny size deceiving British soldiers who never suspected that the smiling schoolboy was wearing a green Fianna shirt under his jacket. Keenan survived the Rising, unlike 15-year-old John Healy, an apprentice plumber who was shot dead carrying dispatches in the Phibsborough area. Many commandants dreaded the responsibility of caring for such young lives and ordered the youngsters to leave. Michael Malone, for example, sent away two young Volunteers before the battle of Mount Street Bridge.[21] Others exerted pressure on them to go home. De Valera assembled everyone under eighteen at Boland's bakery on Easter Tuesday morning and persuaded all but Richard Pearl to leave. Pearl insisted on staying to the end.[22] Sometimes ruses were employed to remove them from the danger. Little Tommy Keenan was induced to return home from the College of Surgeons in order to reassure his anxious family of his safety. Other parents endured agonies of uncertainty, such as Frances Downey, who had three members of her family involved in the Rising. She recorded on Easter Wednesday:

I have been awake since 5 o'clock listening to the heavy firing. Every gun that goes off might as well be going through me for I think to myself, 'that one might have killed

Hugh or Frank or Paddy'. Poor Paddy, he is only a kid of sixteen. But he is a real man to go out and fight like this.[23]

Some sought to pluck their sons from danger, though their interventions usually failed. Mrs Pearl's journey to Boland's ended with Richard's rebuff that 'This is no place for a woman.' Tommy Keenan was locked in a room on his return and Matt Walton, who on Easter Monday morning had looked in vain for a dentist, returned home to discover that his parents had taken the valves from his bicycle to prevent him going off to join the fighting. However, youth was not to be denied. Keenan escaped through a window to report back to the College of Surgeons, while Walton, after convincing his parents that he had to go to work or he would be sacked, went straight to Jacob's Factory.[24] One group of Fianna who were sent home on Easter Monday afternoon simply tried their luck at the GPO and were allowed in to join its garrison. In the Rising, age was relative because many adult combatants were not much older than those sent home: at the Mendicity Institution, apart from a 40-year-old man, all the Volunteers were aged between eighteen and twenty-five while their commander Sean Heuston was only twenty-five.

The fighting in Dublin at Easter 1916 was multi-faceted. It included rifle fire from and into occupied houses and large buildings as well as ambushes and pitched battles. Grenades and bombs were thrown from roofs. Snipers operated from windows, barricades, church spires and clock towers and were, in turn, hunted down by individual marksmen or groups. Sometimes the combat was at close quarters, almost hand-to-hand. At the Mendicity, the British concentrated rifle and machine-gun fire on Heuston's Volunteers and crept along the quayside to the wall in front from where they hurled grenades which the rebels attempted to catch and throw back. Both sides also engaged in incendiary warfare. While Volunteer attempts were crude, the British made sophisticated use of shells fired from howitzers. Furthermore, while the insurgents were restricted to pistols, shotguns and rifles, the military possessed machine guns and artillery, with big guns used on land and also by the vessel *Helga*, on the River Liffey. The British also made increasing use of armoured motor-cars which had been fitted out by engineers at Guinness's, who welded engine boilers on to lorries, equipped to carry up to fifteen troops. These vehicles had dummy holes painted on them to deceive the snipers who peppered the vehicles whenever they appeared on the streets. They worked to a set pattern, advancing up a street to the house to be stormed, inching as close as possible to the front door. The attacking party would then emerge from inside with crowbars and sledge-hammers and while the rest of the party engaged the surrounding enemy they smashed down the door and occupied the house. The car would then return for a second party and this *modus operandi* continued until the whole street had been brought under control.

In the scale of military operations Dublin 1916 was not Flanders, the GPO was not Verdun and the Mendicity was not the Somme. Furthermore, the casualty figures for Easter Week were dwarfed by those of a single day on the Western Front. Nevertheless, the intensity of combat which was endured by participants should not be lightly dismissed, especially since most had little or no previous military experience when they were pitched suddenly into battle without any gradual acclimatisation. Certainly the sights and sounds of Dublin were etched in the memory of Lieutenant Jameson:

> Nobody had any idea how serious matters were. However, we started fighting on Tuesday at midday and never stopped until midday Saturday! It was a very ghastly affair – so many civilians and women and children shot. Everybody who had been in France seemed to think the Dublin fighting was a far worse thing to be in![25]

He vividly recalled the strains of an armoured car operation in rebel-held Capel Street on Easter Thursday:

> I was right in front with the driver when the car stopped and had quite a job in making the men get out. When they

did they all lost their head and shouted. However, they eventually bashed in the house and bullets were whizzing at us all the time from the barricade in Little Mary Street and the house at the end.[26]

To survive in this battleground men required various qualities. Vigilance and extreme caution dramatically reduced the odds against being shot dead. It was vital for combatants never to offer themselves as a target by standing at a window, putting a head through a skylight or even showing a shadow. They had to move and speak as quietly as possible. As well they always had to be cautious and on guard against traps set by the enemy. Frank Robbins, the Citizen Army officer at the College of Surgeons, was almost the victim of a lethal mistake on Easter Wednesday when he led the occupation of a club for former pupils of Alexandra College. His unit had been warned that a ringing telephone was always to be regarded as a British ruse, yet a captain lifted the receiver. When his pronounced Dublin male accent in such a location was heard by a British officer the building was raked with machine-gun fire. Robbins and his men only just managed to evade the bullets by hurling themselves on the floor.[27] The careful handling of weapons was important. On both sides there were many narrow misses but also fatalities from discharges when men used rifle butts to smash in doors and windows. Others were dangerously lax when they worked to clear a bullet jammed in their weapon and caused an accidental shooting. Volunteer Liam Archer was at a barricade in the Four Courts area when a comrade pointed out the stupidity of standing with the barrel lodged in his toecap; when Archer jerked the weapon away he literally shot himself in the foot.[28] Some of the casual handling of bombs and grenades was hair-raising, especially with the primitive concoctions which had been manufactured at Liberty Hall. These cocoa-tins, filled with explosive, had a string attached which had to be set on fire, pulled and then thrown quickly as far as possible. In the Metropole Hotel a terrified Charles Saurin witnessed one bomber play with his lethal hoard. 'He put his complement of bombs in a row at his feet with the sulphur-tipped fuses pointing upwards. He was continually lighting his pipe and throwing the ignited matches amongst the bombs, greatly to my terror, for every second I expected to see one catch on a fuse and eventually send himself and myself through the roof.'[29] Circumspection and a cool head were crucially important at night-time when darkness frayed men's nerves and, as Matt Connolly discovered in the City Hall, played tricks with the imagination.

Prowling about the dark, deserted rooms imagination exaggerated things. For instance, I entered one room and was startled to see an armed man confronting me. I immediately challenged, and receiving no reply, fired. The crash of breaking glass brought me to my senses. I had fired at my own reflection in a wardrobe mirror.[30]

Those combatants who were able to focus completely on the battle, control their emotions and filter out extraneous concerns had a tremendous advantage over their opponents. This proved difficult for many, especially those worried about their families and relations, at home or fighting elsewhere in the city. The Rising indeed was to some extent a family enterprise. The Pearse brothers, for instance, fought in the GPO as did the Connollys, father and son. The brothers Sean and Matt Connolly were at the City Hall together and the Walsh brothers both fought at Mount Street Bridge. In a poignant variation of this phenomenon there were families with some members serving in the Volunteers and some in the British army. The O'Reillys, for instance, had four sons, two of whom, Richard and John, fought with the rebels at the South Dublin Union where Richard was killed on Easter Tuesday. The other two brothers had joined the British army and one of them had been killed fighting in France.[31] Sometimes, however, those family members in the British army were not as far away as the Western Front, as Volunteer Joe Sweeney discovered on Easter Saturday when his unit had surrendered and the men were being processed by their captors.

Officers with notebooks then came along and took down our names. A funny incident happened there. One of the officers just looked at one of our fellows and without asking him anything wrote down his name and then walked off. After he had gone a certain distance, somebody asked this fellow, 'Does that officer know you?' 'That's my brother,' he said.[32]

Home weighed heavily on many insurgents, especially those who had not taken proper leave on Easter Monday morning. Dispatch carriers did sometimes bring news, but it could be chilling. At the South Dublin Union Frank Holland learnt that soldiers and police had raided houses in the Inchicore area and threatened his parents that they would manure the lanes with their son's body. He was also told that a mob of hostile neighbours had gone on the rampage wrecking and looting another Volunteer's house.[33]

Physical and mental stamina helped lessen the pressures caused by sleeping fitfully on floors, tables, roofs or pavements and in fields. By the end of Easter Week many combatants ached for the joys of a bath, a wash, a shave or a change of the clothing in which they slept. Those who spent extended periods in cramped tenement houses often suffered from claustrophobia, longing for fresh air and the sight of open blue skies, or else discovered that they had opened a new battlefront against the multitudes of fleas. Men in the open were often drenched and risked contracting severe chills and even pneumonia. The treatment of the ill and wounded was frequently rudimentary. At the City Hall, Dr Kathleen Lynn's facilities for the Citizen Army garrison amounted to a small room for a dispensary, a supply of tablets, some nurses and a treatment room. At the GPO the medical officer was James Ryan, a student who had four assistants and a dozen Cumann na mBan. His hospital consisted of two rooms used as a first-aid post and a recovery station which had been equipped with beds. Ryan treated his most famous patient, James Connolly, without a choice of anaesthetic and had to use chloroform. Thereafter, Connolly only survived with frequent injections of morphine. At Stephen's Green and the College of Surgeons Nora O'Daly stitched the wounded without any anaesthetic, though to her delight she discovered that she could indeed work miracles:

> Mr. Partridge had received a wound on the top of his head which I dressed and bandaged. He told me the next morning that since the bandage was put on he was free from a headache which he had suffered from for years.[34]

In the Four Courts area Father Mathew Hall doubled as Ned Daly's headquarters and a hospital in which thirty-two patients were treated during Easter Week, the overwhelming majority of whom were Volunteers. Minor injuries treated included a sprained ankle and broken fingers but others had been shot in the ear, arm, hip, face, thigh, stomach, or lungs. One Volunteer had been seriously wounded when the grenade he was about to throw exploded in his hand. A Volunteer wounded in the hip and leg bled to death and another died after being shot in the temple; these deaths occurred despite the services of the Red Cross and three doctors from the nearby Richmond Hospital. Others were suffering from shock and one had gone 'religiously mad'.[35] Physical and emotional resources were drained by lack of sleep; many men got little or none during Easter Week. Ultimately men ached physically or longed only to surrender themselves to their overwhelming fatigue. At the City Hall Matt Connolly stayed awake for three days and struggled on even after his fellow guards had curled up on the ground snoring. Nevertheless, he finally succumbed just before the British offensive which captured the building:

> I lay down flat in the valley gutter and remained quiet. Some form of helplessness came over me and I felt unable to move. I tried to fight off a drowsy feeling, but failed and passed into a sound sleep. A hand gripped the shoulder of my coat and a voice shouted, 'Get up!' My eyes opened to see a revolver pointed at me. It was in the hand of a British

officer who wore a white arm band on which was a red cross. It was now daylight.[36]

In the Post Office Pearse stayed on his feet for the entire week and even a sleeping draught had no effect on him. Sleeplessness made many men more dangerous to themselves and their comrades than the enemy as they became prone to misjudgements, hallucinations and sudden reactions when startled. They also suffered from a loss of a sense of time, a disorientating condition which was exacerbated by an absence of watches and the disabling of many clocks which occurred during sniper battles. Many combatants and civilians lost track of the day of the week and even whether it was day or night.

The psychological moorings of many combatants were also loosened by hunger. Neither side fought the Easter Rising on a full stomach and most men existed on a monotonous, inadequate and inappropriate diet. For instance, during the entire week Liam Ó Briain consumed only a small cake of home-made bread on Easter Monday and a meal which he shared with his unit the following day and which consisted of a big pot of tea, plenty of bread and butter and ten boiled eggs. After that he received nothing except for a little boiled rice on Easter Friday evening.[37] The GPO garrison had ample supplies, but Desmond Fitzgerald, in charge of the commissariat, doled out only small measures and often seemed, to many, to be preparing for a medieval siege.[38] At Boland's bakery there were plenty of food, ovens and fuels for cooking, but distribution to the various posts was difficult because of the continuous fire from British sniper nests in the high surrounding buildings. The British commissary arrangements broke down under the strain of thousands of soldiers flooding into the city: many of these had to exist half-starved on a diet of bully beef and biscuits.

Luck often decided who lived and who died. Some men seemed to have charmed lives and survived impossible odds while others perished simply because they were in the wrong place at the wrong time. Cathal Brugha survived multiple gunshot wounds at the South Dublin Union. Another

Volunteer in O'Connell Street demonstrated an amazing ability to dodge the bullets after he;

> appeared at the door of Clery's, the big drapery establishment opposite the GPO. It was the headquarters of the Citizen Army and they had their flag, the Plough and the Stars on top of it. But this fellow came out with a mattress wrapped around him and he ran like the blazes. But when he got to the middle of the street he tripped and fell. We all thought he was a goner because the fire was so desperate. But he discarded the mattress then and ran like the hammers of hell for the GPO and got in safely. I found out afterwards that it was Gearoid O'Sullivan, who later became Adjutant-General of the Free State Army.[39]

And yet close by, poignantly, another insurgent who had endured everything in the Metropole and reached the GPO as the evacuation was under way was fatally injured when a large haversack of ammunition exploded. He even lingered on till after the surrender when he died in the Castle Hospital from a severe loss of blood.[40]

Courage was important and there were many acts of astonishing heroism performed during the Rising. But the bravery of the hot-headed and impulsive was a dubious commodity to possess. Self-discipline and prudence saved the life of Volunteer Joe Good in O'Connell Street on Easter Wednesday, when he was ordered to leave the GPO and reoccupy a vacated building. Good had serious reservations about the operation which initially entailed erecting a barricade across Abbey Street:

> The method was simple enough. Baskets on wheels were loaded and packed tight with newspapers and journals; those were to be run out one after another from a shop to form a barricade across the road – and I was to push out the first hamper. Fortunately, there was an inclined plane leading from the shop into Abbey Street. It was cut to bits by machine-gun fire. We shut and barricaded the door, withdrawing towards the GPO.[41]

A similar caution was displayed by many British soldiers, who fought under the additional disadvantage of an inadequate knowledge of the city's topography and were very aware that any hasty movement could take them straight into a death trap. These considerations clearly influenced the troops who were dispatched from Marlborough Barracks in a major operation to search and clear the suburbs on the North Circular Road. A local resident, Austin Clarke, sunbathing in his front garden, observed their nervousness as they warily advanced behind a field gun which was being trundled along by men crouching low behind its shield. Their cautious tactics consisted of firing shells at a barricade a quarter of a mile away while Volunteers retreated by skipping over back garden walls and fleeing along a railway embankment. Finally and seemingly in slow motion the troops crept gingerly forward through flower beds and then over walls, and to Clarke;

> the twenty minutes of advance seemed as slow as an hour. At last, the entire regiment seemed to have vanished. Suddenly there was volley after volley. Then a detachment of the infantry charged past the broken barricade. In a few moments the empty houses had been captured. The Battle of the North Circular Road was over.[42]

People with good faculties prospered during the Rising. Sharp hearing enabled men to hear an enemy creeping up a staircase or the whizzing of a shell. They could also distinguish between the bark of a shotgun, the loud explosion of the Howth rifle or the sharp crack of the Lee Enfield British standard rifle. Clear eyesight and a steady hand made some men crack shots. Michael Mallin, who had served in the British army, proved himself to be such during an early-morning tour of the College of Surgeons when Liam Ó Briain saw that he was carrying his long 'Peter the Painter' revolver in his hand:

> He motioned me aside, stood in front of the glassless window, took aim and fired. An answering shot seemed to whisk by his head. He took aim deliberately again and fired.

'Got him,' he said. I looked at him enquiringly. 'A sniper who had come across the Green to the railings opposite,' he said, in his usual quiet tone of voice and went off.[43]

But many combatants on both sides proved to be abysmal marksmen. This is hardly surprising in view of their lack of training and consequently there is a striking contrast between the vast expenditure of ammunition during the Rising and the relatively small number of casualties which were inflicted. There were a few exceptions such as at Mount Street Bridge but even there, as one Volunteer marksman admitted, 'A lot of their losses were their own fault. They made sitting ducks for amateur riflemen.'[44]

Many British artillerymen were also incompetent, though the potential consequences of their mistakes were correspondingly greater. One team almost demolished Under-Secretary Nathan's lodge in Phoenix Park by landing a shell in the garden. Two 18-pounder guns outside Trinity College had no directors or ranging instruments of any kind and were placed in the charge of newly recruited gunners who had never before fired a round. Another gunner, James Glen, who had taken refuge in the university, had no experience of such big weapons but only narrowly missed the honour of demolishing a famous landmark in O'Connell Street. A Brigadier-General;

> told me that a lot of coming and going had been reported between the GPO and Clery's across the street, most of it under the shelter of Nelson's Pillar. He was considering whether it was a good plan to demolish the Pillar, using artillery, and he asked me whether I had any good ideas as to the size of gun and the number of rounds that would be needed. This was beyond my limited knowledge of ballistics, but it was plain to anyone that, even if it could be done, there were two serious flaws; the pillar could only be cut through at a level above the base portion, and the resulting debris would provide even better cover than before the operation. And so the Pillar lived to fall another day.[45]

High morale was most important and the rebel leadership used every available technique to sustain it. Volunteers engaged in defiant singing of patriotic tunes such as 'A Soldier's Song' and 'The Bold Fenian Men', communal cheering and the reading out loud of the Proclamation and 'War News'. In the Post Office Pearse read the men encouraging dispatches from his 'generals'. The sight of a flag flying over a garrison headquarters also inspired many insurgents though, surprisingly, no common pattern had been approved by the Military Council. A tricolour and an Irish Republic bannerette flew at the GPO, a tricolour at the Four Courts; a green flag with harp was raised at Marrowbone Lane; a tricolour seems to have flown at the South Dublin Union and the City Hall as it certainly did at Jacob's and the College of Surgeons and also at the Imperial Hotel, where it was joined on Easter Wednesday by the Plough and the Stars. A green flag with harp was hoisted at Boland's.[46] The British devoted an inordinate amount of time and ammunition trying to blast the flags off their poles and the failure of such attempts heartened many rebels such as Joe Sweeney in O'Connell Street:

Friday dawned on a desolate sight opposite us. All that remained of Clery's and the Imperial Hotel was the front wall of the building on the top of which to Connolly's great delight the flag of the Citizen Army still floated proudly.[47]

Rebel morale was also temporarily sustained by the welter of rumours which swirled through the city. These purported to reveal that Verdun had fallen to the Germans, that Zeppelins were raiding London and that the German North Sea Fleet was trying to effect a landing in England. The whole of Ireland was supposedly up in arms with insurgents marching on Dublin, Derry was in flames and Dublin Bay full of German submarines. Dick Humphries on his way to the GPO on Easter Monday encountered an excited old lady who informed him that a 'corpse' of Germans had just landed in Phoenix Park ('whether from warships or Zeppelins is not stated').[48] Some Volunteer commandants were exponents of a 'good news' philosophy and filtered out any adverse reports. At Stephen's Green Mallin addressed his garrison on Easter Monday and gave it the encouraging news that the Rising was proceeding successfully, not just in Dublin but throughout the entire country. But Desmond Fitzgerald in the GPO refused to let men live in a fool's paradise and when he discovered Volunteers at mealtime telling the Cumann na mBan women that the Germans had landed he tried without success to kill such fantasies.[49]

The infectious humour of individual Volunteers was often effective in lightening the mood on even the most sombre occasion. Dublin had many natural comedians and, time and again during Easter Week, men and women were reduced to helpless laughter and rolling about on the ground because of the antics of their extrovert comrades. There were indeed many tears shed during the Rising but at least some of them were tears of joy. There was delight among the Post Office garrison when Tom Kilgallon returned from the waxworks next door dressed in an exhibit's postman's trousers, puttees, a magnificent fur-lined blue coat with very high collar and an Australian hat. Even Connolly, never a barrel of laughs, rather awkwardly entered into the spirit by circulating through the building and repeating a joke he had been told: 'Well, boys it's all over. We just bagged three of their generals,' pausing for effect before remarking 'We captured them in the waxworks.'[50] Lieutenant Jameson of the Leinster Regiment demonstrated his sense of the ridiculous on Easter Wednesday as he worked the roofs of the Tivoli and the adjoining houses. He and his men had been forced to remove the slates and smash holes because of the absence of skylights but Jameson's corpulence produced comic difficulties as he attempted to squeeze through.

It's a horrible thing being so fat! When I got the slates off I was too fat to get thro' the beam, so I got my burberry off and tried again – still too fat. Then I tried with my Sam Browne off – still too fat, so I had to take my tunic off, and just managed to squeeze through with the help of my sergeant who shoved! They were sniping at us from over the river all the time but they were rotten shots and hit nobody! However it cheered us up lots, cos all the men and myself were roaring with laughter![51]

Some people used laughter as a release mechanism, as Joe Good did with a group of young Volunteers who had become terrified by the fires sweeping O'Connell Street.

It was awe-inspiring. The red glare of the burning buildings opposite lighted the rooms. It was no wonder that the lads were depressed, at that height and looking at an inferno all day long, and now night falling without darkness. There were twelve of them, mostly young boys and they lay there quietly at their posts, not talking to each other. I spoke to them one by one and concluded by asking them, 'Do you think you are going to die?' Each of them answered 'I suppose so, Sir.' I told them all to fall in, in the corridor outside the room. One of our flags was flying at our corner of the Post Office. I got them in line facing and gave the 'Present Arms.' Then I said, 'Lads, you have done that in accordance with tradition. You're now free to go back and die – but I'm damned if I'm going to do so.' There was a roar of laughter from the young fellows; they had been left too long looking at that holocaust. I took care not to look at it at all.[52]

Some Volunteers, however, through a combination of temperament and environment found it very difficult to remain cheerful and genial. Liam Ó Briain, indeed, contracted a depression which afflicted him intermittently for the rest of his life, an illness triggered by physical and mental strain as well as a tendency to meditate on his personal responsibility for the destruction and suffering which he witnessed. In addition Ó Briain had the misfortune to be teamed for the duration of the Rising, not with a Dublin wag but an elderly, deranged obsessive from Tralee called Sullivan. Sullivan had jumped the railings at Stephen's Green along with Ó Briain, but while the latter was fighting the British army and Empire, Sullivan had set his ambitions much higher. He sought to become the nemesis of an academic who had offended him in the dim and distant past but whose villainy was now about to be avenged. Sullivan's malice infected everyone around him as became very clear to Ó Briain.

> The men were all in very good heart but Sullivan was beginning to worry us. The inaction was getting on his nerves. Had it come to real fighting he would probably have been the best and coolest of us. As it was, he began and kept up for the next three days an extraordinary muttering of hate against his fellow-Traleeman, Doctor Denis Coffey, president of University College, Dublin, demanding to know why we did not go over there and kill him. He usually accompanied his demand with an odd, malevolent glance at me, as if he suspected me of being contaminated by contact with Doctor Coffey in U.C.D. I became more and more convinced as the days went by that he might be demented and violent and, with so many weapons lying about, dangerous. I was prepared to shoot him if it really became necessary.[53]

Cunning and a willingness to adopt unorthodox methods were also useful attributes. At Boland's bakery, for instance, de Valera had insufficient men to occupy a distillery which dominated the area. Nevertheless he not only managed to eliminate the threat it posed to his position but tricked the British into doing it for him by arranging for them to destroy the building. His ruse entailed flying a green flag at the distillery to convince the enemy that it was rebel-occupied, an impression which he reinforced by flashing misleading messages which the British could intercept. As a result of a severe artillery bombardment the building was badly damaged.[54] Cunning allied with patience was another effective combination in the sniper duels of Easter Week. Some snipers were very daring, deliberately presenting themselves as targets to draw fire to enable their comrades to eliminate the enemy sniper nest. Often the sniper battles developed into a protracted battle of wits, a duel between two individuals or groups battling to outwit each other. Sometimes these contests became distinctly personal. On Easter Monday a Volunteer unit which included Cormac Turner occupied Hopkins & Hopkins, the jeweller's shop on the corner of O'Connell Street at the bridge. Next day, as Turner came back from delivering a message to the Post Office he was targeted by a British sniper operating from McBirney's, a general store at Aston's Quay on the southern side of the bridge and diagonally opposite to Hopkins. Instead of downing Turner, the sniper shot dead a civilian passer-by and a young girl. Although he subsequently stopped when night fell he resumed on Wednesday morning, concentrating initially and unsuccessfully on Hopkins before turning his attention to large crowds of civilians which had gathered at the O'Connell monument. These fled across the bridge but not before a blind man had been wounded and also a St John's Ambulance member who tried to help him. Until then Turner's unit had been unable to locate the sniper's exact position and was also hindered by girls standing at the windows of McBirney's. While they had only one rifle and a limited supply of ammunition Turner was determined to deal with the sniper once and for all. By using a pair of binoculars which had been discovered in Hopkins, Turner was able to pinpoint the enemy marksman at a top window and his unit now co-ordinated its stalking operation with the garrison located in Kelly's gunpowder store on the opposite corner of O'Connell Street. While one Volunteer in Hopkins waited with the single rifle Turner scoured McBirney's with the binoculars and when the sniper reappeared Turner directed his man's aim and then cried, 'Fire.' Simultaneous volleys from Hopkins and Kelly's terminated the sniper's career.[55]

The military conduct of the Rising is often compared favourably with subsequent and more squalid conflicts and depicted as a clean, chivalrous fight – civilised warfare at its best. Even Under-Secretary Nathan conceded that 'Undoubtedly many of the rebels behaved in a manner to which exception would not have been taken had they been belligerents'.[56] For its part, the Military Council was very conscious of the historical scrutiny to which its rebellion would be subjected and was anxious to avoid accusations of barbarism. It had, for instance, ordered that at the start of the insurrection unarmed soldiers who were promenading should not be fired on and that captured military and police personnel should be treated as prisoners of war. Many of these captives were seized on Easter Monday in parks, on the streets, in railway stations, hotels and business premises. One British officer was on a train which was stopped while passing Boland's and was taken there for the duration of the Rising. Others were taken when their cars were stopped at barricades such as Lord Dunsany and Captain Lindsay, two high-ranking officers from the Inniskilling Fusiliers who were ambushed by Daly's Volunteers from the Four Courts. Dunsany and Lindsay had been on leave in Londonderry when they heard of the Rising on Easter Tuesday and hurried to Dublin where they were assigned to Amiens Street. But they were not provided with directions through an unfamiliar city and were fired on when they stopped near the Four Courts. Both Dunsany and Lindsay were wounded along with their chauffeur and all three were taken prisoner.[57]

Policemen were opportunistically seized in the vicinity of rebel garrisons, while off-duty colleagues were often recognised on the streets or in shops or pubs. Others on plain-clothes assignments were captured during the week after the unarmed Dublin Metropolitan Police were withdrawn from the streets entirely on Easter Monday. More soldiers and police were seized later when their barracks were surrounded. At the isolated Linenhall Barracks thirty-two unarmed clerks of the Army Pay Department resisted Daly for four days and managed to douse two fires, but capitulated when gelignite was employed against them and the barracks door was smashed open with sledge-hammers. The Volunteers then successfully attacked the Bridewell and captured in the cellars a group of policemen who were transferred to Daly's headquarters in Father Mathew Hall.[58] But an attempt to capture forty policemen pinned down in Moore Street barracks failed.

In most cases prisoners were treated reasonably well. On Easter Tuesday Daly even released a policeman and fourteen soldiers who were stripped of their uniforms and weapons and provided with safe-conduct passes. Later he sent the Bridewell policemen rather incongruously under the charge of two bespectacled and rather small Volunteers to Richmond Hospital to be handed over to doctor Sir Thomas Myles with the message that he could not afford to keep them.[59] The wounded Lord Dunsany was also sent to recuperate in Jervis Street Hospital and was full of praise for his captors. 'The man who took me prisoner, looking at the hole in my face made by one of the bullets, a ricochet, made a remark that people often consider funny, but it was quite simply said and sincerely meant: he said, "I am sorry."'[60] Dunsany returned the compliment at the end of the Rising by lending some Volunteers a razor to shave off moustaches and beards to evade military policemen checking the wounded.[61] Daly used the captured army pay clerks in his headquarters, Father Mathew Hall, to fill sandbags. British officers in the GPO were guarded in a room at the top of the building and ordinary soldiers served in the Volunteer commissariat.

But Nathan also accused the insurgents of conduct in which 'the lapses from fair conduct were both numerous and grave' and 'made hideous by cold-blooded murder and arson'.[62] One of his most serious allegations was that, whatever the Military Council may have stipulated, many unarmed soldiers were shot on sight and wounded or killed. There are many verified accounts of such incidents.[63] Peter Ennis, an unarmed private in the Scots Guards, was killed on the canal bank on Easter Monday morning by de Valera's Volunteers, who were then believed to have climbed on to the roof of Sir Patrick Dun's Hospital to fire on convalescent soldiers. Doctors intending to examine Ennis were warned that anyone approaching him was being shot at. Eventually a civilian rescued the body under fire and doctors were able to confirm that he had been shot though the heart and died instantly. At about the same time Captain Humphries, a British officer returning from furlough, was fatally wounded by a shot through the head in Westmoreland Street. At Stephen's Green a captured policeman was released on Easter Tuesday but shot in the back as he walked away. He lay on the ground critically wounded for five hours before he was rescued. A motley crew of vacationing Irish, Australian and South African soldiers came under fire in O'Connell Street and took refuge in Trinity College. Others who received sanctuary in private houses in some cases managed to reach nearby barracks disguised in clerical or female clothing. Outside Dublin, Lieutenant Dunville of the Grenadier Guards, in uniform but unarmed, had his car stopped at Castlebellingham by Volunteers from Dundalk. He and three captive policemen were placed against railings and guarded with rifles and revolvers for about five minutes before, without warning, fire was opened on them. Dunville was shot in the chest and though he recovered in hospital one of the policemen was killed. Nevertheless it should be acknowledged that some British soldiers during the Rising displayed a great disregard for their own safety. On Easter Wednesday, a priest in Parnell Street in the city centre noticed 'soldiers home on leave, standing about hallways with their friends. Though in khaki, and well within the danger zone, they did not seem to fear being shot at by the Volunteers.'[64] It should also be pointed out that members of the Royal Army Medical Corps wore khaki with only a small badge on the arm to distinguish them from the regular army. Since the badge was almost impossible to see at even fifty yards it is hardly surprising that many of those wearing it became targets of Volunteer snipers during the Rising.

Some prisoners of the Volunteers had frightening experiences. At Boland's, a terrified detective who was accused of spying was paraded from post to post by a delighted de Valera, but he was not physically harmed.[65] Soldiers in the GPO were put up against a wall on Easter Friday and mistakenly feared the worst was about to happen. Later that day, in a most controversial incident, one of them,

Lieutenant Chalmers, alleged that they were locked in the basement to 'die like rats' but were then taken out at the time of evacuation to be offered a choice of leading the way and being shot at or staying to be shelled and incinerated. Chalmers said that they decided to take their chances outside where the dead body of one who took a chance was later seen in Moore Street. However, Chalmers' allegations were strongly contested by Diarmuid Lynch, the senior officer at whose court-martial Chalmers testified. Lynch had been in charge of the Post Office prisoners and was ever after indignant at what he regarded as Chalmers' dishonourable behaviour. He was adamant that, far from the prisoners being deliberately placed in danger, everything was done to protect them. The transfer to the basement of which Chalmers complained had been made because the room at the top of the building where they had been lodged was endangered by fire. Even then it was only a temporary measure prior to evacuation. Lynch despised Chalmers for failing to acknowledge this 'honourable act' and regarded him as scared witless and incapable of rendering any coherent account of the final hours in the GPO. Lynch's assertions are substantially corroborated by Volunteer Joe Good who, near the end, discussed the prisoners with The O'Rahilly and suggested that they be let go to take their chances. The O'Rahilly initially misinterpreted this as using them for cover and was so incensed that Good thought he was about to be struck before The O'Rahilly recognised his true intention and apologised. Good says that The O'Rahilly let them go, but most likely this means that they were informed that they were to be released. Certainly they were still in the GPO when The O'Rahilly left with his advance party at 8.10 p.m. on Easter Friday. They were still under Lynch's command then and he categorically states that twenty minutes later the prisoners were given the choice of staying with the insurgents or advancing towards the British lines. All of them decided to take the second option except three members of Irish regiments, two of whom actually enthusiastically threw in their lot with the rebels.[66]

There were no independent witnesses to these events but Lynch's arguments are persuasive, especially since his whole body of writing on the Easter Rising displays an assiduous, even relentless, concern for accuracy and putting the record straight. In addition it is impossible to believe that the members of the Provisional Government, so concerned with how their rebellion would appear to future generations, would ever have approved an action which would besmirch their historical reputation.

A further allegation made by Nathan was that insurgents used dum-dum ammunition – split-nosed, soft-nosed and flat-nosed bullets which inflicted terrible wounds. His claims were supported by post-mortems on Volunteer Training Corps members killed on Easter Monday near Beggar's Bush Barracks. While these accusations have often been dismissed as British propaganda it is beyond doubt that dum-dum bullets were employed. A bag of such ammunition was left behind by a Volunteer unit in a house in Lansdowne Road. Also, after the surrender Volunteer Patrick Rankin dropped his dum-dum bullets at his feet while standing at Nelson's Pillar. He then suddenly realised that the inspecting British officer was looking at the bullets lying on the ground.

I stared at him but never answered for fear he would call me a coward. None of my comrades spoke up for me. The officer eventually moved on while his aides were filling their pockets with small arms etc, for souvenirs. I was saying my prayers as never before as he moved away.[67]

Many British soldiers had decided early in the Rising that the rebels were employing dishonourable tactics. The reinforcements which were rushed to Kingstown on Easter Tuesday quickly concluded that the enemy was operating with the connivance of at least part of the civilian population. When Brigadier Maconchy of the Sherwoods was given a glass of water by an old lady, fire was opened from surrounding houses and garden walls the moment she returned to her cottage.[68] At Trinity College the Provost's daughter, Miss Mahaffy, was regaled by officers with stories of alleged 'dirty tricks' used against them. They told her that a trap had been set in Middle Gardiner Street where Volunteer snipers had been positioned on a roof:

Our soldiers wondered greatly at seeing the civilians in the street suddenly all lie down, faces downwards on the pavements but at this moment bombs began hurtling down. The throwers had evidently instructed their sympathising friends what to do when this crucial moment came. Here also for the first time the aged beldames from the tenements brought hot cups of tea to the tired soldier boys; which proved to be poisoned and from the results of which three soldiers died.[69]

The poisoning seems apocryphal and whether this is an embellished account of a real incident is impossible to establish. What is not in doubt is that such stories circulated on the military grapevine and strengthened a belief that the friendliness of many civilians was a mask for treachery. Lieutenant Jameson believed that he had seen the rules of warfare violated.

The brutes always took either a woman or child with them whenever they crossed the street so it was hard to get a shot at them, but we got a good few. They had a house with a small Red Cross flag hung out and I told my men not to fire at it. But one of my men fired just as a Red Cross ambulance drew up there; and I asked him what he fired at. He said he saw a man firing behind the van. I was just beginning to curse him hard when about 15 armed rebels ran out of the Red Cross house round the corner. We blazed away like fury but only winged a couple as they had only a few feet to cross.[70]

Mrs Norway, wife of the Secretary of the Post Office, was told by her army contacts that troops had been tricked by Volunteers who pretended to capitulate behind a white flag. When officers stepped forward to take the surrender they were allegedly gunned down by snipers hidden in nearby houses. An order was then issued that white flags were not to be recognised and rebels who surrendered did so at their own risk.[71]

The civilian population of Dublin suffered more deaths and casualties than the British and Irish combatants combined. The Provisional Government had not intended such widespread civilian suffering and, while it never seems to have considered the radical step of calling for the city's evacuation, it was very concerned for the inhabitants' welfare and sought to minimise the inconvenience and dangers that they would have to endure. The leaders of the Rising were mindful of previous rebellions which had degenerated into undisciplined, drunken rampages and the Proclamation declared 'that no one who serves that cause will dishonour it by cowardice, inhumanity or rapine'. They forbade their followers to consume alcohol; stocks located in private houses were to be immediately destroyed, taps in pubs were to be opened and bottles were to be poured down the sink. Commandant Daly's first action in the Four Courts was to order that every bottle of spirits and every barrel of beer be put in the sewers. Nevertheless not every Volunteer desired a teetotal rebellion. Just before the Rising started Peadar Kearney, the composer of 'The Soldier's Song', encountered a fellow Volunteer who;

> announced that he was going over to the Grafton Bar to get a plebeian pint. He was immediately reminded that an order had been issued that any Volunteer found taking intoxicating liquor was liable to be shot. The incorrigible one simply grinned and said, 'The way things are looking you'll be all shot, order or no order before the night is out.' He crossed the road and called for the usual.[72]

To win the hearts and minds of civilians it was ordered that residents of houses which were taken over were to be treated courteously, even if they were politically suspect. A judge's house on prosperous Lansdowne Road was seized by a

Volunteer unit shortly after midnight on Easter Monday and his son, Denis Johnston, who later became an important Irish dramatist closely associated with the Gate Theatre in Dublin, marvelled at the rebels' courtesy. He almost forgot that his family were hostages who had been coerced into sharing potentially lethal danger:

> There we were in the middle of the night, with four men in our house, preparing to turn the place into a fortress from which to fight the British Empire, and extremely apologetic about it all. That is the thing that remains most firmly in my memory – how polite and reasonable it all seemed. They were sorry to disturb us, and would do no more damage than was absolutely necessary. And any damage that they were forced to do would all be repaired by the Irish Republic. So we weren't to worry. They would take over the upper part and we could have the rest. And would we please not leave because these were their orders, and it would be dangerous anyway. Meanwhile if we required any food from the shops on the following day, they would be glad to go and get it for us.[73]

There were many such stories. At the Metropole in O'Connell Street, Charles Saurin, a Volunteer officer, gently escorted the manager and his wife from their beloved hotel. He was even thanked when he regretfully declined a request for an escort because he did not want to place them in danger from British snipers. At Mount Street Bridge, George Reynolds displayed extraordinary solicitude in Clanwilliam House when he promised to return it to the owners untouched. He refused to allow his unit to barricade the building, break windows or smash walls to provide an escape route. At the end of the subsequent battle against the Sherwoods one of Reynolds' men ruefully recalled the self-denying ordinance as he stood in the devastated and burning shell and water poured all over him from the shattered pipes.[74]

Even many who were politically hostile to the Rising paid tribute to the behaviour of the insurgents. Denis Johnston's mother described them as 'very nice civil boys'. Diarmuid Coffey heard widespread praise of how they had tried to prevent looting and that in the College of Surgeons the garrison had not left even a drop of cigarette ash on the carpets.[75] And yet many civilians still suffered, killed or injured during the Rising at the hands of Volunteers and soldiers. The elderly were extremely vulnerable because of declining faculties which made them slow to comprehend and react and there were many unfortunate incidents. After Joe Sweeney's unit evacuated the GPO on Easter Friday its members reached a house in Moore Street where they ordered that the door be opened. When the door remained closed they shouted for the occupants to stand away and then blew open the lock – only to find the dead body of an old man lying on the floor.[76] Austin Clarke's sister witnessed the last moments of an old lady:

> One night on her way home she was stopped with several others at Binn's Bridge by a party of British soldiers. An elderly woman went on, although a young sentry called on her several times to stop. Before anyone could rush forward to drag her back he raised his rifle, fired and she fell dead. Afterwards a girl who had known her told my sister that the old woman had been stone deaf for many years.[77]

Senior citizens who ventured out during fighting were often simply too slow to reach cover when the bullets started flying about. Others were cut down when they were mistaken as combatants because they were dressed in green. Civilians who clambered on to roofs to get a better view of the conflict were assumed to be snipers and fired on. Some came too close to the action because, extraordinarily, many Dubliners regarded the Rising as almost a spectacle laid on for their enjoyment and competed for the best view. From the GPO Dick Humphries marvelled at the 'ever-inquisitive crowd' standing in D'Olier Street and at O'Connell Bridge, quite unconcerned, as firing took place between the two sides. 'Indeed, one would think from their appearance that the whole thing was merely a sham battle got up for their amusement.'[78] Across the city during the battle of Mount Street Bridge a British soldier noticed maids coming out of the houses in Northumberland Road to watch the fighting and then throwing their aprons over their heads and running away whenever a bullet came too close. A Dubliner watching the same battle noticed how reluctant spectators were to drag themselves away, despite the danger and the large number of civilian casualties. Even when they fled into neighbouring streets 'they could not resist the temptation to creep back again and join the crowd of stalwarts who shadowed the advancing soldiers'. Later he cycled to near O'Connell Bridge, where he secured 'a ring seat view' of a British attack on a music shop. Observing the crowd of spectators, he discovered why they were acting in such a manner.

Even the booming of the guns of the gunboat *Helga* down the river near the Custom House did not terrify them, and they paid no more attention to the bullets whistling over their heads than if they had been a drove of starlings. Their foolhardiness and disregard of danger was due, I believe to insatiable curiosity plus a good deal of fatalism. Dublin, even in normal times, is an inquisitive city. Any little incident that occurs – the break-down of a car, a fight between husband and wife, a dog fight – collects a crowd of interested onlookers quicker than in any other capital in the world.[79]

Some civilians who felt obliged to risk such danger were members of voluntary organisations such as the St John's Ambulance Brigade. During the battle at Mount Street Bridge a house in Northumberland Road was occupied as a dressing station and during Easter Wednesday afternoon and evening a Red Cross ambulance with a Mrs Chaytor sitting beside the driver drove continuously under heavy fire to remove wounded from it to the hospitals.[80] One British soldier marvelled at the bravery of such people:

No one who saw it will ever forget the spectacle – the blazing house in the background, with the spurts of fire coming from the rifles of the Rebels concealed on the neighbouring housetops and behind the street windows, the answering shots from the troops, and the grandest sight of all – four white-robed Red Cross nurses calmly walking down the centre of the street between the combatants, their leader holding her right hand above her head, demanding that their errand of mercy should be undisturbed. Largely owing to the courage of these devoted women, assisted nobly by loyal inhabitants, the wounded were speedily dragged into the neighbouring houses and received whatever attention was possible on the spot.[81]

In some places such as Mount Street Bridge short, informal truces took place to allow the wounded to be removed from the scene of battle. But elsewhere the firing sometimes continued without interruption. A St John's Ambulance member was shot dead by Volunteers in Baggot Street on Easter Wednesday as he attempted to treat a wounded man, while a driver was hit in the lungs as he carried wounded passengers past the Four Courts. On Easter Thursday W. Smith, a St John's Ambulance man, witnessed the carnage inflicted on civilians who were being ferried from Mount Street Bridge ('a regular death trap for its inhabitants') to Sir Patrick Dun's Hospital. The nurses' home brimmed with wounded who were lying on the floor, in the passages, on sofas and even two in a single bed. Smith watched one old man who had gone out for a loaf of bread die from gunshot wounds and saw the body of a servant girl who had been shot dead at her bedroom window.[82] In a Red Cross hospital in Merrion Square Mrs Augustine Henry, a VAD, was shocked by the ghastly scenes she encountered:

The packing room is turned into an extempore theatre with operating tables. There are about twenty cases upstairs. One boy is shot through the lungs and dying. A woman leading a child has come out crying as we went in. It is awful.[83]

Not every civilian casualty was an accidental victim; some were clearly the intended target even when no fighting was in progress. A large number of such cases occurred at Stephen's Green. Liam Ó Briain attributed civilian casualties there to poor barricade organisation, which allowed cars to filter through, and to the absence of a clear policy for dealing with such vehicles. However, the casual violence of some rebels also demonstrated arrogance, insensitivity and a determination to chasten those deemed insufficiently respectful or obedient. This is hardly surprising, since some clearly lacked discipline and were having the time of their lives. Douglas Hyde noticed that;

> Among these were some who were only infants – one boy seemed about twelve years of age. He was strutting the centre of the road with a large revolver in his small fist. A motor car came by him containing three men, and in the shortest of time he had the car lodged in his barricade, and dismissed its stupefied occupants with a wave of his armed hand.[84]

Some cars had harrowing experiences at Stephen's Green, such as the chauffeur-driven vehicle of Lord Donaghmore on Easter Tuesday afternoon. He later complained bitterly that he and his companions had travelled from Naas without any sign of military or police activity and had been allowed to drive straight into a trap. Only when they were 200 yards from the Green did a pedestrian warn them that every motor was being seized by rebels who were firing indiscriminately on passers-by. When his driver started to reverse a bullet shattered the hood and ricocheted around the interior, wounding all three passengers.[85] In O'Connell Street on Easter Monday, Professor Pope of Trinity College suddenly saw a man in green uniform open the door of the Post Office and fire a revolver at the crowd, fatally wounding a young woman of about seventeen in the left breast.[86] The police files on such incidents are replete with phrases such as 'bayoneted by a rebel as he looked like a policeman', 'shot by a rebel when he refused to go away', 'bayoneted by rebel at New

Street, whilst walking along the thoroughfare', 'shot by rebels for refusing to erect barricades when requested by them to do so', 'shot by rebel, it is said because he refused to join them when requested', and 'shot by rebels for not getting off the streets'.[87] It was also noted that the information on such cases came from people who almost without exception refused to give their names because they were afraid of their businesses being attacked or their lives endangered.

Many Dubliners did not believe that British troops behaved much better during the Easter Rising. One described the Staffordshires as 'demons' and another complained that;

> The English soldiers are showing no mercy. A young lad of fifteen riding on his bicycle was shot stone dead for not answering when challenged crossing Portobello Bridge and a young girl was wounded in the leg. There has been slaughter in the town. The soldiers are shooting anybody and everybody.[88]

Nathan rejected all allegations of slaughter and wrote that;

> considerable numbers of troops were required to cope with the insurgents, and on the whole the troops behaved unexceptionally. There may have been a case here and there where soldiers dealt out a summary justice, but it is remarkable in view of the nature of the struggle that these instances were not the rule. The soldiers found a great majority of the citizens sympathetic to them and a small but violent minority hostile and treacherous. Cakes and drinks were offered them at one house, bullets were fired at them from the next. In every large city are strong elements of lawlessness, and these elements in Dublin responded when the moment was opportune.[89]

His concession that summary justice might have occurred was wise, because some rebels were clearly killed when they posed no danger. A Volunteer who surrendered at the Mendicity was shot dead by a British sniper, despite the fact that his unit had walked into the open behind a white flag.[90] Many other soldiers took no chances, especially after an order issued on Easter Wednesday that they were to fire immediately on any armed man in uniform or in plain clothes whom they believed to be a rebel but who did not surrender.[91] British soldiers clearly shot at civilians, sometimes in the mistaken belief that they were insurgents but in other cases certainly not. When a milkman's cart was stopped by troops on Leeson Street Bridge it was searched despite the driver's pass and when the soldiers discovered ammunition they shot the driver as he attempted to escape.[92] At the Post Office, Joe Sweeney watched a drunk stagger along O'Connell Street and though the man was abusing the rebels he was cut down by British snipers. Volunteers with Red Cross armlets who tried to rescue the victim were also shot at.[93] Early on Easter Wednesday a theatre critic, Joseph Holloway, saw British soldiers firing on anyone crossing O'Connell Street at the Parnell Monument, bringing down a woman at the foot of the statue and a man near the pavement. Both bodies were eventually allowed to be removed by ambulance, the incident, bizarrely, being recorded by a man with a camera.[94] One factor which led to Pearse's decision to surrender on Easter Saturday was the sight of three civilians being shot dead by British snipers, although they were carrying a white flag. Lieutenant Jameson of the Leinsters who had been so indignant at the behaviour of Volunteers was nevertheless delighted in Marlborough Street when;

My corporal saw a civilian walking where a whole lot of Sinn Feiners were so he said he didn't know whether he was a Sinn Feiner or not, but anyhow he oughn't to be there so he'd 'just shoot him in the foot'. So he up with his rifle and fired, and the man hopped down the street on one leg!

Jameson was also prepared to coerce civilians to risk their lives, even those with military passes:

At that time I had three men lying in the street, so I took the passes of the first few civilians who came by, and made them go down Little Mary Street and take the men into the nearest houses to be looked after, and wouldn't give them back their passes till they had done so, 'cos I didn't like to see them wriggling. I thought it was rather a good idea![95]

By Easter Thursday British troops obviously regarded certain areas as free-fire zones in which anybody who had remained was deemed a rebel liable to be shot dead. On Thursday afternoon, for instance, military parties in Amiens Street, Store Street and Beresford Place and from Talbot Street to Gardiner Street ordered everyone off the streets. Those who did not comply were fired on and seriously injured men were taken away in an ambulance.[96] Sometimes in the free-fire zones armoured cars raked entire streets with machine-gun fire, such as occurred in North King Street where fifteen soldiers fired into every house and the few remaining civilians threw themselves on the floor. After the Rising there were allegations that troops of the Staffordshires had massacred civilians in North King Street after a ferocious fire-fight on Easter Saturday. The Staffordshires were accused by local residents of systematic murder which had been committed, not in the heat of battle, but in some cases hours after the danger had passed. The murders were also alleged to have been supervised by officers who left fifteen men dead, most in a small block of ten houses. One resident, Miss Anne Fennel, described the death of a fellow tenant George Ennis who worked as a carriage-maker in a local factory. She claimed that early on Easter Saturday about thirty soldiers and two officers burst into the house, shouting furiously:

I nearly fell on the ground and clasped the officer's hand in terror, but he flung me off. As poor Mrs Ennis saw her husband being led upstairs she clung to him and refused to be parted from him, and said, 'I must go up with my husband.' One of the soldiers pulled her off and put a bayonet to her ear and uttered the foulest language. She said, 'You would not kill a woman, would you?' He shouted, 'Keep quiet, you bloody bitch.' After a long time, it must have been a couple of hours, we heard a noise at the parlour door, and to our horror poor Mr Ennis crawled in. I will never forget. He was dying, bleeding to death, and when the military left the house he had crept down the stairs, to see his wife for the last time. He was covered with blood and his eyes were rolling in his head. He said to his wife, 'O Kate, they have killed me.' She said, 'O my God! for what?' He said, 'For nothing.'[97]

At a subsequent inquest, Lieutenant-Colonel Taylor, the commanding officer, denied all the allegations and stated that 'only those houses were entered by the military which the exigencies of the case rendered actually necessary, and no persons were attacked by the troops other than those who were assisting the rebels, and found with arms in their possession'.[98] The allegations were so serious that the army instituted a court of inquiry which, perhaps surprisingly, was not a whitewash. It made exhaustive efforts to discover what exactly had happened in North King Street but, not unexpectedly, failed to resolve the matter. The inquiry examined, in particular, the deaths of four men in No. 27 but was unable to locate witnesses to their fate. It did turn up a next-door neighbour who said he had spoken to the men through a grating in his cellar. He thought that he later heard some crying, but though he spent all day at the back of his house he heard no shooting. He was also present later when the bodies which were hurriedly buried in a garden on Saturday were dug up and noticed that one had the top of his head blown away and another his throat and chin. The court confessed bluntly that it could 'get no evidence as to how these men were killed'. It was unable to locate any military witness who had been inside the house or seen any soldier entering it, and it noted soldiers' extreme reluctance to come forward. Neither was it helped by the chaotic situation afterwards during which companies had become mixed up, making it hard to trace participants. In addition it was impossible to reconstruct which soldiers had been in any particular house at a given time. The court concluded, tentatively, that the marks in the room where the men were found indicated that if they were shot there one must have been shot lying on the floor with his head against the wall, an unlikely scenario. There were no other bullet marks showing where the others could have been shot. The court praised the Staffordshires ('a quiet and very respectable set of men') whose behaviour had received favourable comments from many civilian witnesses. It concluded that it was 'very unlikely that any persons were shot or killed, unless the men had reason to think that they had been fired on, whether they were mistaken or not'.[99]

The court complimented the women who had given evidence to it, describing them as 'very respectable people who gave their evidence clearly and showed no animosity to the soldiers'. The Staffordshires, however, were less gracious, because 2,000 of them were paraded at their base for the benefit of their accusers in a vain attempt to identify the alleged perpetrators. The account in the regimental history of the women's 20-mile taxi journey is, perhaps, partisan:

> One lady, arrayed in a fur coat evidently looted during the burning of O'Connell Street, wished [for] whiskey before she started, and shouted for it when passing public houses. When passing along the ranks she remarked: 'Sure, I feel just like Queen Victoria reviewing the troops.'[100]

General Maxwell assured Prime Minister Asquith that demands for public inquiries into civilian deaths were manufactured to discredit the military but confessed to his wife that he was 'bothered to death with these cases where soldiers are accused of having murdered innocent civilians in cold blood. I fear there have been some cases of this.'[101] He told Kitchener that 'It must be borne in mind in these cases that there was a lot of house-to-house fighting going on, wild rumours in circulation and owing to darkness, conflagrations, etc, apparently a good deal of "jumpiness".

With young soldiers and under the circumstances I wonder there was not more.'[102]

The most notorious such incident involved the murder of Francis Sheehy-Skeffington, a well-known, loved and somewhat eccentric Dublin character dressed in a knickerbocker suit who was actively involved in every worthy cause such as pacifism, socialism, vegetarianism, alcohol abstinence and votes for women. He had become an object of resentment in military circles because of his opposition to the war which the authorities believed hindered recruiting. In one speech in May 1915 he had blamed the Allies for provoking the war and declared that if there were any power that should be smashed in the conflict it should be England.[103] He had been arrested, gone on hunger strike and been released on health grounds. When the Rising broke out Sheehy-Skeffington was moved by the suffering of the civilian population and on Easter Tuesday he convened a poorly attended public meeting to co-ordinate relief measures. Walking back to his suburban home he was arrested at a British army checkpoint and taken to the nearby Portobello barracks; there his rather outlandish appearance, which included a votes for women badge, convinced Captain J.C. Bowen-Colthurst that a radical subversive had been apprehended. Bowen-Colthurst had already rounded up two completely innocent journalists and he seems to have decided that he was in charge of a group of extremely dangerous men. During the night he took the three prisoners out on a raiding party during which he shot dead an innocent youth. On Easter Wednesday morning he had them taken out into the barrack yard and shot dead by a firing party.

When Bowen-Colthurst submitted a report on the events to his superior officer, Major Rosborough, later on Easter Wednesday he stated that a study of documents found on the three men had led him to conclude that they 'were all very dangerous characters'. He had sent for an armed guard of six men to escort them to a small courtyard close by where he could conduct an interrogation. Unfortunately, he added, he did not have them handcuffed and when they arrived in the yard he discovered that it was a place from which an escape could be easily accomplished. When he realised this, and aware of the risks the prisoners posed, he ordered the guard to fire, shooting them dead.[104]

It might be thought that even this sanitised version would have raised questions. Far from it. As it worked its way up through the system it reached Major-General Sandbach, commanding troops in the Dublin area on 3 May, and he noted that, 'Capt Bowen-Colthurst seems to have carried out his duties with discretion'.[105] On the very same day Bowen-Colthurst was arrested, largely as the result of the indefatigable efforts of another officer in Portobello barracks, Major Sir Francis Vane. His determination to expose the crime led to his professional ruination at the hands of a military establishment which was hardly grief-stricken at Sheehy-Skeffington's death; General Maxwell wrote of 'a certain Sheehy Skeffington, a very poisonous person. But he was shot in a very unceremonious way.'[106] As Bowen-Colthurst's culpability became clear his fellow soldiers in Portobello raced to dissociate themselves from him and his actions. On 16 May Sandbach withdrew his previous commendation saying: 'I never imagined for one moment that the men could actually have been killed by design. But having since read the evidence of Sergt. J Aldridge the act appears to me in quite a different light and if this latter statement is true, then the officer in question used no discretion.' Sergeant Aldridge who had commanded the guard revealed that 'He [the Captain] told the prisoners to stand up against the wall and then ordered the guard to load, present, fire. The prisoners were shot dead.'[107]

Bowen-Colthurst's statement to a court of inquiry at Victoria Barracks in Belfast on 10 May 1916, while obviously self-serving, does plausibly convey the picture of a stressed man who, like others in the city, had been tipped right over the edge. As Portobello Barracks swarmed with terrified women and wounded soldiers he was overwhelmed by fears of an imminent attack by a rebel army marching on Dublin.

I knew of the sedition which had been preached in Ireland for years past and I was credibly informed that unarmed soldiers had been shot down in the streets of Dublin by the rebels; on the Wednesday morning (26th) all this was in my mind; I was very much exhausted and unstrung after a practically sleepless night. I took the gravest view of the situation and I did not think it possible that troops would arrive from England in time to prevent a general massacre. I was convinced that prompt action was necessary to ensure that these men should not escape and further spread disaffection. It was impossible for men to move the prisoners to a more secure place of confinement owing to the armed rebels having possession of the streets all around the barracks; believing that I had the power under martial law, I felt under the circumstances that it was clearly my duty to order these men to be shot.[108]

There was a general consensus in army circles that Colthurst had had a complete breakdown. Maxwell told his wife that 'his history points to madness but he refuses to plead insanity'. Major Vane likewise was in no doubt that he had been 'temporarily insane' at the time of the shootings. There was no high-level attempt to protect or save Bowen-Colthurst; he was as expendable as Sheehy-Skeffington. His superiors regarded his behaviour as indefensible, the actions of a deranged man. But there was a cover-up, an exercise in concealment which was designed to protect the reputation of the British army, whose elite was alarmed at the affair's ramifications. Maxwell regarded it as 'a bad case and [it] excites much interest in army circles'.[109] The fact that Sheehy-Skeffington had been a completely innocent victim was irrelevant and indeed British military intelligence even considered a desperate, ludicrous scheme to smear him as the leader of a Volunteer bombing unit in O'Connell Street. The strategy which was finally adopted was to attempt to bury the scandal as deeply as Sheehy-Skeffington himself. Nevertheless, keeping the case well away from public and press scrutiny did not prove easy. On 16 May Deputy Judge

Advocate Marshall decided that Bowen-Colthurst should be charged with murder, with an alternative charge of manslaughter. To the horror of the legal and military establishment he also concluded that the Army Act forbade a trial by court-martial if the offence was committed in the United Kingdom, even if the accused was on active service at the time. Unless martial law was still in operation when the case was heard Bowen-Colthurst would have to be tried by a civil court. This opened up the alarming and unacceptable prospect of testimony in open court and while the Irish law officers agreed with Marshall's interpretation they warned him that a civil trial with widespread coverage would lead to 'turbulence and disorder'.[110]

The machinery to circumvent such an eventuality cranked into action immediately and the conspiracy went right to the top. The lawyers recognised that the route out of this judicial swamp lay in a new DORA regulation overriding Section 41 of the Army Act and ordering a military tribunal. To facilitate this the Lord Chief Justice of England, Lord Reading, was brought in and he convened a meeting in his office at the Law Courts in London on 18 May 1916. The conference was attended by the English Solicitor-General, the Director of Public Prosecutions, the Irish Attorney-General and Brigadier-General Byrne, Deputy Inspector-General of the RIC. In the course of three hours' deliberations they mulled over the opinions of Marshall and the Irish law officers and concurred that a Special Defence of the Realm regulation should be framed to allow civil offences to be tried by court-martial. Work began immediately and on 22 May 1916 the DPP forwarded the new regulation to Byrne in Dublin with the comment that 'In this case there has been much to do and comparatively short time to do it in, but I hope that everything may be in order'.[111]

All that was required now was to close one final bolthole. It was learnt that the nationalist MP Tim Healy was to call on the Attorney-General in Parliament to examine a provision in the Army Act, ' from which we were somewhat concerned to learn that a trial by court martial would not be a bar to a second trial in a civil court. In the particular case to leave such a contingency even remotely possible was not, in the L[aw] O[fficers'] opinion to be thought of.'[112] Accordingly the new regulation had been framed to exclude the possibility of a civil trial. Bowen-Colthurst was finally convicted of murder and ordered to be confined to a hospital for the criminally insane. After some years he was eventually released and emigrated to Canada where he lived for the rest of his life.

The Rising came as an unexpected and shocking experience to the civilian population of Dublin. One inhabitant, Ismena Rohde, wrote after the Rising that 'That fortnight of shot and shell, fierce fighting all around and death and destruction was like a lifetime. We thought Ireland was the only safe place to live in at present, so remote from battle. And then this storm burst over our heads.'[113] Many were initially confused as to the Rising's character and purpose. Mrs Nellie O'Brien who lived near Trinity College believed at first that it was simply a demonstration against conscription.[114] But the reality of rebellion and urban warfare soon began to make a tangible impact on the fabric of Dublin life, especially as essential services such as transport and gas began to shut down. By Easter Monday afternoon trams had been withdrawn to their depots, taxis had ceased to ply for trade and the number of private cars had declined dramatically. The railway stations closed down or were occupied. The gas system was also closed down by de Valera's battalion at Boland's, which seized the gasworks; it was vital to prevent explosions in any building which was occupied by Volunteers and attacked by the British. The loss of the gas supply had a major impact on domestic and industrial life, except on those firms which had their own supplies. Street lighting was also run on gas and the nights of fearful darkness had begun. Cinemas and theatres also closed.

The first real intimation that the theatre critic and inveterate first-nighter Joseph Holloway had that something serious was happening came on Easter Monday when the matinee performance at the Empire was cancelled and a group of agitated actresses stood on a street corner. The public houses also closed temporarily on Easter Monday, partly on their own initiative and partly because the authorities had instructed plain-clothes policemen to advise owners to shut their doors. One gleeful Dubliner observed the incredulity of thirsty racegoers just back from Fairyhouse: 'They looked up at the windows, in through the keyholes and couldn't believe the evidence of their own senses.'[115]

There was an increasing dearth of accurate information partly caused by the severance of communications between Dublin and the outside world and within the city itself. The telegraph connection to England was broken at 12.20 p.m. on Easter Monday, but the telephone system was left working despite the fact that the Military Council had intended to seize the Telephone Exchange in Crown Alley near Dublin Castle or at least to cut the wires from the Exchange and the Castle. R.M. Fox claimed in his history of the Citizen Army that the plan failed because the Volunteer members of a joint team with the Citizen Army did not appear. Crucially, the twenty female telephone operators remained on duty when the Rising started, sleeping in the cellar and protected by boards from snipers' bullets which entered the switch room. The military did not arrive at Crown Alley until 5 p.m. on Easter Monday, but when they took over the system civilians could only receive calls and not initiate them.[116] The newspapers were also seriously disrupted. Of the Dublin papers, only the Unionist publication the *Irish Times* managed to keep going for the first half of the week, though copies of English papers such as the *Mail* and *Sketch* were brought in and sold for a shilling each. As a result the city swam with all sorts of wild rumours during the Rising. Much of the city's distribution network broke down, including deliveries of bread, milk and coal. Many shops closed along with much of the commercial and administrative system such as post offices, banks, offices, civil service departments and Dublin Corporation. No mail was collected or delivered. Funeral parlours and cemeteries ceased to operate.

Dublin's unarmed police force, the DMP, was also quickly taken off the streets on Easter Monday. News of this spread rapidly and droves of residents emerged from the slum districts on free shopping expeditions in premises whose owners had already locked up and departed. Some of the looting which occurred directly opposite the Post Office shocked the more idealistic or naive rebels. It also embarrassed Pearse, who in his valedictory address of 28 April attributed the phenomenon to 'supporters of the British government and hangers-on of the British army'. Many accounts of the Rising describe the comic and even carnival aspects of the looting. There are numerous stories, including that of the old lady whose swag had been stolen chasing the perpetrator and bawling, 'Stop thief, stop thief. I've been robbed.' In another, a woman in O'Connell Street whose bundle of looted shoes had vanished, raged that the police could not even 'protect the property of a poor old woman'. Thomas Johnson, a trade union leader, saw boys in silk hats mimicking Charlie Chaplin, old ladies in rags sitting on the pavement trying on fancy shoes, a paper-seller with a gold watch on his wrist and young boys with toy guns and helmets in uniforms taken from the fancy goods stores, playing 'shoot the German'.[117]

Much of the looting verged on the pathological and the looters, many of them women and children, displayed an extraordinary rapacity. One onlooker in O'Connell Street on Easter Monday night followed a woman and her small daughter who was pushing a pram. The mother emerged from one shop with an armful of ladies' shoes and deposited them in the pram. They moved on to an already pillaged confectioner's, where she 'slowly and obstinately butted her way through the looters like a Whippet tank at the front', emerging with a large jar of lollipops and boxes of chocolates. There then followed an assault on a clothes shop, which they left with the girl in a red-riding-hood cloak and the woman dressed in a fur coat and large feathered hat. Sated at last, they journeyed to the Pro-Cathedral, sacred ground being regarded as sufficiently safe to hide their booty from thieves.[118] The looters were brazen and, despite the fact that hundreds were arrested, continued like locusts right up to the collapse of the Rising. Both soldiers and rebels fired over their heads and some were shot dead but nothing seemed to deter them. One old biddy waddled past a military checkpoint openly carrying a huge box of soap, receiving only an insult from a soldier that she looked dirty enough to need it all.[119] In Dorset Street on Friday 28 April, a looting expedition broke into a row of shops in full view of soldiers stationed at nearby corners.

Suddenly a shot is heard, then a series of shots striking the bricks and raising a cloud of dust like smoke which makes many onlookers think snipers are firing on the houses. But it is the military sending warning shots to frighten the looters. Suddenly as though one shot has gone through a window and taken effect a panicky rush is seen from one shop door – a full score of women and children with parcels and bundles rush out of the doorway and into the lane leading to the back street and for a few minutes there is no one to be seen in that quarter. But only for a few minutes. In less than ten out they come again one by one, then more openly in couples and threes and start the game again.[120]

One witness to the 'macabre and fearless' looters was reminded of Goya's paintings of the Witches' Sabbath. Another watched from her hotel as a mob in Grafton Street stripped fruit shops:

It was an amazing sight, and nothing daunted these people. Higher up at another shop we were told a woman was hanging out a window dropping down loot to a friend, when she was shot through the head by a sniper, probably our man; the body dropped into the street and the mob cleared. In a few minutes a hand-cart appeared and gathered up the body, and instantly all the mob swarmed back to continue the joyful proceedings![121]

The looters also displayed considerable self-righteousness, taunting the Volunteers that they were only following their example in smashing windows and appropriating the contents. They gleefully set up stalls opposite rebel garrisons, to sell their plunder and even sidled up to offer bargains to the insurgents. And the mobs were extremely vicious, brooking no opposition; a civilian who attempted to remonstrate with them on Easter Tuesday was shot dead. Some looters were also arsonists. They ignited Lawrence's toy shop with fireworks and set off explosions over O'Connell Street from showers of sky rockets, star-bursts, Catherine wheels and Roman candles. Even the old displayed infinite malice, as Volunteer Joe Good discovered when he returned to the GPO from an outpost with a sword he had found:

On my way I found a pavement littered with stiff starch collars the looters had no use for; it's hard to march through a street carpeted with stiff collars, and it was a strain on my dignity as I walked along carrying my shotgun and sword. An old lady, one of the looters still as busy as termites in the streets, perhaps sensed my embarrassment, struck me in the face with a rotten red cabbage. She was about to follow up her attack. If I'd threatened her with my gun, it would not have stopped her. I drew the sword and slashed – intending to clear her head. She fell on her knees – and to my horror something rolled on the pavement. It was her high toque. She begged for mercy and showered silver napkin rings on the pavement from her apron. I marched on – as shaken as she was.[122]

The strain of urban warfare on civilians was intense, often producing fainting fits and hysteria, and harmless occurrences were suddenly interpreted in the most sinister light. Dorothy Stopford, a guest in Nathan's lodge in Phoenix Park, 'Saw a Volunteer clothed all in green with something in his hand, advancing across the field about 300 yards away. Every now and again he knelt down taking cover then got up ran a few paces and dropped down again. I watched petrified for a few moments thinking that at any moment he was going to snipe.' However, with the aid of opera-glasses she could see that the deadly menace was in reality only 'a child in a green frock picking cowslips'. Later when Stopford ventured out she suffered palpitations when, 'To our horror we saw five men come across the road signalling with a white flag. I started to go round and climb in a back way over the fence to the lodge.' Again her glasses saved the day when through them she saw that, 'instead our five Sinn Feiners were aged road makers wielding their tools, spades and picks and talking to a young lady holding a white jersey'.[123] The situation was also ideal for Dublin wags and practical jokers who had a field day, causing panic by shouting supposed warnings of gunfire and chortling at the resulting stampedes.

Those civilians whose houses were occupied by either the rebels or the army were sometimes forced to leave but others stayed, partly because they were too old or infirm to flee. On Easter Monday a unit of Volunteers arrived in Leeson Street to commandeer the home of an aged, bed-ridden judge. His feeble protests that 'You are not my guests' were ignored by insurgents who took over the top floor, leaving him to fend for himself. He managed to survive on supplies brought by a minister every day until the end of the Rising when he was rescued by relatives.[124] However, some senior citizens put up very spirited resistance. One 80-year-old lady who was forced to admit a Volunteer unit on Easter Monday warned it that 'I am an old woman and I can't do anything against four armed men but if you come in I will make it as uncomfortable as I can for you.' She was as good as her word and climbed the stairs frequently to bang her dinner gong and shout, 'As long as you're in my house, I'll take care that you don't get any sleep.' Next day, to their immense relief, the Volunteers were withdrawn.[125]

Dubliners experienced a serious food shortage during Easter Week, with bread especially in short supply. The situation had been created because of the collapse of the distribution system, the closure of many grocery and butcher shops, the commandeering of meat supplies by the military to feed troop reinforcements and seizures by the rebels, and also because of panic hoarding by civilians. The bread crisis worsened when flour and meal sold out early on and greatly diminished home baking. Furthermore, while some bakeries kept going, Boland's, a main supplier, was occupied by the Volunteers. When de Valera's battalion arrived at Boland's on Easter Monday a batch of bread was actually being baked in the ovens and the employees' offer to stay until it was ready was accepted. The loaves were made available to the garrison and local residents but not to the wider population.[126] Because of abnormal demand the prices for eggs, butter and milk doubled and then trebled. Vegetables were virtually impossible to obtain in Dublin during the first part of the week. Then news of the prices available brought in supplies from outlying areas, where, incidentally, gangs of hungry poor were scavenging for cabbages and cauliflowers in the fields of large market gardens.

In the hunt for food many wealthier people who normally had their supplies delivered had to swallow their pride and go foraging.

> It was a novel sight to see well-known clergymen, professional and commercial men passing along, struggling with bunches of cauliflowers, cabbages, meat, biscuits, bread and a hundred and one other articles which in ordinary times would be sent home in receptacles more imposing than a wrapping of old newspapers.[127]

Queues formed very early at those bakeries and shops which continued to function. Some people travelled to suburbs such as Rathmines and Terenure or farther afield to Bray and Kingstown though even in such districts they experienced difficulties. In Rathmines, for instance, a committee of traders and prominent residents was established to deal with the food crisis and though it secured an offer by the authorities to get supplies to the town hall for distribution to shopkeepers these did not arrive until Tuesday 2 May. In Bray stocks gave out and shopkeepers sent a ship to Liverpool for supplies, while one Dublin priest obtained 1,000 loaves in Belfast and brought them to the city on Easter Saturday. On Easter Friday the Local Government Board had been requested to arrange for a supply of food for the poor of the city to be brought to Kingsbridge and the North Wall channelled through depots established by the St Vincent de Paul organisation. By Easter Saturday supplies were being distributed from thirty-one depots.[128]

Certain groups of civilians and organisations were heavily involved in the events of the Rising. Holden Stodart, the Dublin superintendent of the St John's Ambulance Brigade, provided orderlies for the RAMC at Portobello Barracks and the hospital at Dublin Castle, and also established an ambulance service. Brigade volunteers were also allocated a room at the City of Dublin Hospital in Baggot Street from which they ventured out to Northumberland Road to deal with military and civilian casualties from the battle at Mount Street Bridge. It was here that Stodart was shot dead as he accompanied a stretcher party to relieve a wounded soldier. Particularly vulnerable were those St John's volunteers who staffed the motor ambulance service provided by the Irish Automobile Club. This undoubtedly saved many lives during the Rising because without it many wounded would have been unable to reach hospitals, because of either the distance involved or the risks from the fighting. One St John's Ambulance man graphically described the conditions which they endured:

Day by day these cars ran the gauntlet of bullet-swept streets, frequently struck by shots whilst on their journeys to and fro; the dangers always present by day increased a hundred fold by night, when streets shrouded in Cimmerian darkness and encumbered with obstacles had to be negotiated without the aid of lights.

A Brigade officer attached to Dublin Castle Hospital described his own experiences:

The north side of the quays just over Capel Street Bridge had always to be rushed at as high a speed as possible, it being constantly swept by fire from the Four Courts and our wonderful driver just gloried in the pace he got out of the very fast ambulance. On several occasions elsewhere we were very thankful indeed it was so fast, and wonderfully driven. While not saying we were deliberately fired on, the fact remains we cannot recall a single journey on which we did not get a bullet through somewhere. Picture the conditions – no traffic, of course, but glass everywhere around, tram wires coiled in big loops lying about, and once we had to stop, much against our will, at the top of Capel Street and remove yards of telephone wire coiled round our wheels, making progress impossible: houses partly down everywhere, military barricades, etc. all to be noted and remembered in the daytime for it was necessary to remember them when out at night. No street lamp lighting, no houses lighted, no head lamps on the ambulance, nothing but Stygian darkness, so if obstacles were not remembered the consequences might be awkward. Yet our driver never made a mistake; he drove carefully but very skilfully and brought us home safe.[129]

On Easter Saturday evening he was dispatched in an ambulance to Church Street to collect two members of the Staffordshires who had been wounded in the operation to clear North King Street. Because the insurgents were shooting in breach of a cease-fire entered into several hours earlier, they were ordered to transfer with their stretchers to an armoured motor car which proceeded at a snail's pace to Church Street:

The armoured car turned so as to interpose its bulk, as far as possible, between the snipers and ourselves, and we opened the door, threw out the stretchers, and, acting on instructions, jumped out ourselves, lay down in the street and crawled, dragging the stretchers after us, into the house. The shop was small, a wooden counter in front, no plate glass windows, six or seven soldiers (two dead), two RAMC men, five of our squad, and the sergeant in charge of the soldiers all lying down. One of us lifted his head to see where the wounded lay, and was told more forcibly than politely to keep his head down unless we had a spare stretcher. It was not easy, in any case, to load a man on to a stretcher, but lying down yourself in the dark and under fire does not make matters more easy. However, we got the men on the stretchers and loaded into the armoured car safely. Two bearers had very narrow escapes, bullets passing through their clothing; one stretcher handle had a splinter knocked out of the extreme end. Two stretchers loaded take up a great deal of room, and having seen all safely away our Superintendent had to remain behind, the armoured car promising to return later on and take him and the soldiers away. The snipers were very busy when the armoured car went off, several bullets striking the floor a short distance from the bulkhead behind which the soldiers were lying.[130]

The St John's Ambulance Nursing Division set up a temporary hospital in a house in Merrion Square in three hours with beds acquired from neighbouring houses. VADs, doctors and nurses all gave their services and by early evening on Easter Monday an amputation was taking place in an improvised operating theatre. Auxiliary hospitals were also established at Litton Hall in Leeson Park, in the High School in Harcourt Street and in private houses in Fitzwilliam Square and Busby Park Road, Rathgar. St John's Volunteers also helped house women and children refugees, assisted at RAMC dressing stations, carried bales of dressings on stretchers through the firing lines to the various general hospitals, fed the poor and gave first aid to numerous civilians.

Priests were deeply involved in the events of the Rising. Many were hostile to the rebellion either on theological grounds or because they feared its destructive impact on the city and its inhabitants. While the Volunteers were religiously devout, some rejected clerical strictures in uncompromising terms. The subtle and complex relationship between the Church and the rebels is illustrated by an incident at Lansdowne Road station after George Lyons had bagged his brace of British officers.

By some means the front gates leading to the street had been opened and a number of priests from St Andrew's Church were advancing up the sloping passage towards our point of occupation. Shouting through the iron rails which still divided us, I commanded the reverend gentlemen to turn about and depart. They paid no heed whatever to this but continued to advance. 'Reverend Sirs,' I said, 'you must return and those gates must be closed and barricaded. You are endangering your own lives and ours. An enemy force is expected from the street and you will be in the line of cross-fire.' Still the priests approached and some of them, looking extremely excited, tried to climb over the railings onto the platform. 'Retire,' I cried. 'Soldiers, prepare to fire.' Only two of my men raised their guns. Discipline seemed to be on the verge of dissolution. I trembled for the consequences. 'May I speak a word to you,' enquired the priest whom I was personally threatening with my weapon. 'You may give us your blessing, father,' I answered. 'What are you here for?' asked the priest. 'We are out to fight for Ireland, father. We love our country and we are going to die for her,' I cried bringing my rifle butt to the pavement with emphasis. 'Do you refuse me your blessing?' I challenged as I removed my cap, an example which was followed by the men nearest me. 'Wait a moment. Tell me who is in charge here,' demanded the priest. 'I am in charge for the present,' I answered. 'Are you going to start a war here and have all our people killed?' he enquired. 'Every man is fighting for his own country now, father, and we are going to fight for ours. Better that than we should fight for an enemy land,' I answered. 'But,' replied the priest, 'you will have all our people slaughtered and our country made desolate.' 'We hope to set our country free, father.' 'But will you cease fighting, if you see you cannot win or will you fight to the last man? You are morally bound,' he added, 'to yield to superior odds and save useless sacrifice.' 'I will promise you to retire if we cannot hold our ground,' I answered. 'There is no disgrace in defeat.'

Just then one of my men rushed forward and knelt at the feet of the priests and started his confession. The other priests demanded that they be allowed to minister to the spiritual needs of the men. I consented to open the gates and let them pass through the lines on the strict understanding that they would regard us as soldiers under orders from our superiors and that they would not seek to advise the men to go home or otherwise interfere with the military situation. Receiving this information, I caused the gates to be opened and I passed the priests down the line with a small escort.

The incident was witnessed by one of the British officers whom we had captured and he afterwards described it in the public press as a shocking display of 'irreligious savagery'. I presume the same officer was really disappointed to find we are not as priest-ridden as we are supposed to be.[131]

Another futile attempt to dissuade the rebels was made at Jacob's Factory where Father McCabe, the prior of the nearby Carmelite Priory, warned MacDonagh's garrison that the Rising was an insane enterprise. He singularly failed to make any impression during a heated argument in the course of which a Volunteer perched on an upper landing dropped a bag of flour on him. A disconsolate McCabe left the building white as a sheet from head to foot.[132]

Many priests attempted to sustain a semblance of normality by keeping their churches open and celebrating mass. They also offered a refuge to distressed parishioners who had been forced to leave their houses either because these had been seized by the combatants or because of the shooting and fires. Many Dubliners who stayed still prepared for a sudden evacuation by packing their money, life insurance policies, post office savings books and food into pillow cases. Priests, sometimes under fire, entered rebel garrisons such as the GPO, Jacob's and Boland's to hear confession or give the last rites to the dying. Others were attached to hospitals such as Jervis Street, Mercer's and Sir Patrick Dun's where they gave religious comfort to the wounded. They also intervened at great personal risk during fighting to comfort or rescue wounded civilians and belligerents and minister to the dying and the dead. At Mount Street Bridge Father John McMahon of Haddington Road tended British soldiers who had fallen during the attack on Clanwilliam House and here also Father Watters, the president of the Catholic University School in Leeson Street, was fatally wounded. One of the most haunting incidents which involved a priest occurred in O'Connell Street on Easter Wednesday evening. An old man with a walking stick hobbled past Hopkins the jewellers, one of the most dangerous locations in the city, when firing was in progress. As bullets sent sparks shooting around his feet he jumped in the air before embarking on a feeble attempt to cross O'Connell Bridge as bullets whistled around him. He finally collapsed mortally wounded on the spot where his body lay for the rest of the Rising. It was not until Saturday evening after the surrender that the first non-combatant, Father Brendan O'Brien, was allowed to enter O'Connell Street. Accompanied by a military escort O'Brien went up to the body and, as his military escort stood with bare heads, he was finally able to give the last rites to the old man.[133]

Some priests witnessed enough drama during Easter Week to last a dozen lifetimes. Capuchin Father Aloysius, whose church was near North King Street, had been concentrating on a fête at Father Mathew Hall and, though he saw the Pearse brothers cycling past as he went to mass on Easter Monday morning, he believed that they only intended to conduct the cancelled Volunteer manoeuvres. At lunchtime his world changed for ever when he heard rifle fire and soon afterwards a small wounded boy was brought into the friary, followed by a group of frightened children seeking shelter.[134] By 1.30 p.m., as the fête continued, Volunteers had erected barricades in Church Street and Aloysius ordered the participating children to hide under the stage. They were later sent home. On Tuesday morning Aloysius sent priests to the Richmond Hospital, where the wounded were already pouring in, and allocated others to take up residence in Father Mathew Hall which Daly's battalion had appropriated as a hospital. On Friday, as the Staffordshires tightened the net around North King Street and the Cumann na mBan girls tending the wounded became hysterical, Aloysius and a colleague, Father Augustine, became actively involved in the final stages of the Rising. They sent a message to Lieutenant-Colonel Taylor of the Staffordshires that Father Mathew Hall was a hospital, but he replied that he would treat its occupants as rebels and outlaws. The two priests now feared a massacre and approached Taylor themselves in North King Street but he listened to their pleas with a silent, icy contempt before turning and striding away. After an hour's hiatus during which they waited anxiously the priests saw and approached Taylor again and learned that a cease-fire had been arranged. When Volunteers in a nearby house opened fire Taylor threatened severe reprisals until the priests managed to persuade the rebels to stop firing while they made contact with Pearse in the morning and got confirmation of the cease-fire. By accident they had now become intermediaries, but first they hurried back to Father Mathew Hall to evacuate the wounded to the Richmond Hospital.

Easter Saturday was a busy day for Aloysius and Augustine, as they first met Pearse and Connolly at the Castle and then shuttled between rebel garrisons and the British authorities. They helped to arrange the surrender of MacDonagh at Jacob's, Ceannt at the South Dublin Union and Colbert at Marrowbone Lane. Another Capuchin, Father Columbus of Church Street, carried the white flag when Nurse O'Farrell went to see Daly at the Four Courts with the surrender order. Aloysius later had the harrowing experience of being one of the priests who comforted those rebel leaders sentenced to death and also attended their executions. Another priest who was heavily involved in the Rising was

Father John Flanagan of the Catholic Pro-Cathedral, which was situated about 200 yards from the GPO.[135] He had been summoned by Pearse to the Post Office on Easter Monday night and heard confessions from the garrison until 11.30 p.m. Over the next few days as the Cathedral became increasingly isolated and the fighting intensified Flanagan attended several wounded men lying in the streets. On Easter Wednesday morning, as he celebrated mass with a congregation which consisted of a few women, the bombardment of Liberty Hall began. 'The passage of the shells over the church was a rude accompaniment to the Holy Sacrifice.' Later, after a visit to Jervis Street Hospital, he discovered the church and sacristy were full of refugees from neighbouring houses and as night fell the fires which had been smouldering near the Cathedral broke out again.

A steady west wind swept sparks across the church roof. The Brigade, we were told in response to a call, would not be allowed out and further fires might be expected before the week closed. We therefore spent the night preparing for the removal of books, registers and sacred vessels, feeling that if the fire spread along Cathedral Street, nothing would have saved the church. Luckily the wind died down towards daybreak.

Flanagan celebrated Thursday mass to the accompaniment of gunfire and a non-existent congregation because he had closed the church. At 10.30 a.m. his doorbell rang and he was again summoned to the GPO to attend a dying Volunteer. He was not to return to the Cathedral till the end of the week and everything which he had endured hitherto was as nothing compared to the ordeal which lay ahead. Flanagan had now been sucked into the tumultuous final stages of events at the heart of the Rising. His guide took him on a very circuitous route along Marlborough Street, Parnell Street and Moore Street. During the journey Flanagan anointed an old friend who had been shot just beside him and watched as he was lifted on to a handcart and carried to

Jervis Street Hospital where he died two days later. After running across Henry Street he and his guide scrambled through the walls of houses into the Post Office where his ministrations to the wounded and dying kept him busy for the rest of the day.

The last day inside the rebel headquarters was dreadful for Flanagan. 'Friday dawned to the increasing rattle of rifle and machine gun. Early in the day I succeeded in getting through the *Freeman's Journal* office into Middle Abbey Street where I prepared for death a poor bedridden man whose house soon became his funeral pyre.' By Friday evening, Flanagan was haggard and fatigued and watched transfixed as the inferno spread within the building. It was time for him to flee with the Red Cross party, who carried the wounded on blankets as they came under fire from an armoured car and military barricades at the end of Moore Lane and Moore Street. They worked their way through houses, evading the bullets by creeping on their hands and knees beneath the windows. After crossing a roof and climbing up a ladder they got into the bar of the Coliseum Theatre where the withering British gunfire and shrapnel even prevented an attempt to hang out a Red Cross flag. There was a considerable danger that the fires would spread to the Coliseum from the Post Office and so Flanagan's party continued into Prince's Street and then Middle Abbey Street. Here they had to vault a barricade of burning paper as a battle raged between Volunteers in the houses and a military barricade at the dispensary entrance to Jervis Street Hospital. Fortunately their Red Cross flag was visible in the light of the fires from O'Connell Street and firing stopped to allow Flanagan's party to make its way to the corner of Liffey Street. Here it encountered a suspicious British officer, but eventually Flanagan was allowed to come forward and have his identity confirmed by two medical students.

It was within an hour of midnight when the good Nuns and Nurses in the hospital received us all – weary and well-nigh exhausted. Next day, Saturday, the male members of our Red Cross party were marched off to the Castle, the ladies being permitted to return home. The wounded all recovered, and neither they nor anyone concerned are likely to forget the experiences of that terrible night.

Dublin priests had demonstrated immense bravery in the face of considerable danger from gunfire, flames and collapsing buildings. Far from evading these dangers, they often sought them out to help others, risking their lives for wounded civilians, rebels and soldiers. Many were emotionally drained by the blood on pavements, the sight of screaming refugees, the sound of a last dying breath. Priests comforted many people, whether in a church hall, a rebel garrison, a hospital ward or the cell of a condemned man. They also provided shelter and food for those civilians who had been forced out of their houses. They undoubtedly saved lives by rescuing the wounded off the streets and getting them to hospital or, as in the case of Flanagan, Aloysius and Augustine, transferring them from rebel garrisons. The courage, endurance and humanity of priests evoked widespread and, in some cases, grudging admiration. They had risked their lives for and dispensed their services to rebel, soldier and civilian alike. Flanagan, for instance, unhesitatingly answered the requests of the military prisoners in the GPO, including one who had suffered a nervous breakdown.

Amidst the fighting many people sought to continue normal life as best they could, a determination which led to many incongruous incidents. The Dublin Spring Show, a major agricultural event held at Ballsbridge, continued while the battle of Mount Street Bridge raged close by. Mrs Arthur Mitchell who lived in that normally quiet south Dublin suburb finally risked going out briefly on Wednesday to the bottom of her street to see where the firing was coming from.[136] She saw what she thought were dead and wounded bodies lying in the street but found it hard to grasp that a real battle was taking place so near to her home, especially as all around ordinary civilians were behaving as if nothing untoward was occurring. 'Whole families: Father, Mother, swarms of kids, pram with the baby and dog on a string which was a common sight.' The *Irish Times*, which managed to continue publication on 25, 26 and 27 April, also attempted to sustain the illusion of normality by allocating its main coverage for Easter Wednesday to the Dublin Spring Show. Since the schools were already closed for the Easter vacation many young people became spectators of the fighting or played games as firing took place near by or just sat on the pavements relaxing in the sunshine. Mrs Augustine Henry recorded how her friend Nettie went out under crossfire to bring in her terrier or water the plants in her garden 'to the cheery accompaniment of whizzing bullets'.[137] At Trinity College four female students travelled through back streets to sit their French examination. Since no examiners were available these were conducted by the Provost himself, after which he, the party and three professors adjourned for a lunch which was taken as shooting raged outside. Also in the college grounds was Lieutenant Luce, defending his *alma mater*; he was the recipient of a note from Dr Roberts, the Senior Lecturer, who in a truly magnificent gesture of indifference, kindly invited him to conduct a *viva voce* in logic. In view of other pressing engagements Luce regretfully had to decline.[138]

It is generally believed that the reaction of Dubliners to the Rising and the rebels was initially one of virtually unanimous hostility which was only transformed by horror at the subsequent executions. That there was considerable civilian anger is undoubtedly true and more than one insurgent was chased by an angry mob or had his home or business attacked while the Rising was still taking place. Volunteers being marched to prison after the surrender later recounted depressing experiences. When Mallin's column were on the stretch from Dublin Castle to Richmond Barracks, civilians hurled abuse, waved Union Jacks and incited the soldiers to mete out summary justice. To Frank Robbins it seemed that if military protection had been withdrawn there would have been no need for the subsequent courts-martial. Major Wheeler, the British officer who took Mallin's surrender, was so concerned at the hostile crowd which followed the prisoners down Grafton Street that he ran in front and ordered pickets to keep it back at bayonet point.[139]

Patrick Rankin, who had fought in the GPO, remembered the interminable wait at the Rotunda on Sunday, during which a drunken British officer ripped the epaulette from a Volunteer's uniform, seemingly intent on provoking the prisoner and giving him an excuse to shoot the man. The only friendly expression that came Rankin's way during the entire day was from an old lady on her way to church who cried, 'God bless you, boys.' After that he encountered only blind hatred, especially as his column approached Richmond Barracks.

Dublin's worst was let loose, the women being the worst. They looked like a few who were around during the French Revolution. One of my companions answered one of the women and a sergeant broke through our ranks and struck him on the breast with his rifle saying, 'You speak again I will kill you.' The women were allowed to follow the men to the barracks shouting to the soldier, 'Use your rifles on the German so and sos.'[140]

When Ceannt's 4th Battalion arrived at Kilmainham Cross at about 8 p.m. in the gathering dusk an angry, jeering, cursing crowd of men, women and children had assembled. A disillusioned Robert Holland recalled:

F Company, which was mainly made up from Inchicore, heard all their names called out at intervals by the bystanders. They were 'Shoot the Sinn Fein ——s'. My name was called out by some boys and girls I had gone to school with and Peadar Doyle was subjected to some very rude remarks. The British troops saved us from manhandling. This was the first time I ever appreciated the British troops as they undoubtedly saved us from being manhandled that evening and I was very glad as I walked in at the gate of Richmond Barracks. I had played with some of that mob in my childhood days.[141]

But the accepted historical interpretation has to be modified in the light of various factors. First, even as the Rising was taking place, many Dubliners felt some ambivalence towards the rebels. It was an emotion which was captured well by Michael Ceannt, who did not share his brother's republican politics. He witnessed Volunteers occupying railway bridges and private houses in the Phibsborough area on Easter Monday afternoon and wrote that when a commandeered car whizzed past with three young armed rebels 'most of the spectators, including myself, thought it was a terrible mad business'. But their expression also indicated to Ceannt that they were thinking, 'Lord, if we thought they had the least chance wouldn't we all be in it.' In the days which followed he was certain that there was a shift of opinion in favour of the rebels. He felt this was due in large part to a perception that it was an unfair fight because of the overwhelming preponderance of British military power and the army's 'excessive' use of big guns and incendiaries to drive the rebels out.[142]

Secondly, the routes to captivity taken by the defeated rebels must be borne in mind. That taken by Mallin's column on its way to Richmond Barracks, for instance, was approximately 2 miles long and went via Dame Street, High Street, Thomas and James's Streets, the ancient backbone of Dublin. On Thomas Street, incidentally, it passed the spot where Robert Emmet was publicly beheaded in 1803. This was an old working-class area and one can conjecture that some of the most virulent hostility came from the minority Protestant artisan class, who were strongly loyalist; but this was also the kind of district from which the Royal Dublin Fusiliers and other Irish regiments in the British Army drew many of their Catholic recruits. Furthermore, it is hardly surprising that the vituperation heightened as the prisoners approached Richmond Barracks, because soldiers' dependants lived in the areas as well as civilians who were economically dependent on the base. Others might have felt that a display of outrage was expedient to impress the military authorities. But even at the gates of Richmond Barracks some people dared to shout expressions of support; Frank Robbins noted that 'a very small section of those assembled did spread a ray of hope amongst us by raising their voices in support'.[143]

Thirdly, it is indisputable that in some locations the response of the local population was extremely friendly and supportive of the rebels. At the South Dublin Union and Marrrowbone Lane the rebels were heartened by the sympathy they received after the battle was over. Ceannt's men were proud of their performance and pleased at their reception from the local civilian population. Peadar Doyle recalls that they were 'met with marked enthusiasm by a great crowd of people. All along the route we were greeted with great jubilation, particularly in the poorer districts.'[144] Doyle's impression was confirmed by the British officer Major de Courcy Wheeler who had accompanied MacDonagh when he delivered Pearse's surrender order to the South Dublin Union and Marrowbone Lane. As their car made its way through immense crowds in one of the poorest parts of the city, Wheeler felt no hostility from inhabitants who were clearly delighted that the fighting was over. Nevertheless 'it was perfectly plain that all their admiration was for the heroes who had surrendered'.[145] Nor is this a unique example. When de Valera's 3rd Battalion departed from Boland's bakery after the surrender it received an ovation from crowds of civilians who lined the pavements in Grand Canal Street and Hogan Place. Here, women begged Volunteers, unsuccessfully, to take refuge in their houses and men offered to hide their weapons. The sympathetic reception consumed de Valera with regret and he kept repeating to himself, 'Ah men, men, if only you had come out to help us, even with knives, you would not behold us like this.'[146]

A detailed examination of one garrison area indicates clearly that civilian attitudes towards the rebels defy simple generalisation. In the Four Courts there was certainly resentment against Daly's battalion because of the deaths and injuries which occurred, as well as the considerable material destruction and social dislocation. During Easter Week, Richmond Hospital admitted 15 persons dead on arrival and over 200 wounded, while Jervis Street Hospital dealt with 45 fatalities and 550 injured. A member of the Cumann na mBan in the Four Courts recalled the resentment directed at the rebels when, shortly after the surrender, 'some of the Church Street priests came in and lambasted us with abuse all night for doing what we did. They disapproved highly of the Rebellion, of the damage to the city and the people who were killed and whose homes were burned. We took it all,' she writes, 'we didn't say anything.'[147] Likewise, Sean Harling describes how, after the death of a young Volunteer, 'a priest came up from Church Street chapel and he kicked up murder with Holohan. He said it was a bloody shame to have children like that out and insisted that Holohan pull us home.'[148]

Another factor which limited support for the rebels was that many families in the area had relatives serving in the British army. One Volunteer, Liam Archer, recalled:

The people were very hostile and one buxom woman dressed in her holiday attire of snow-white apron and heavy shawl took a flying leap from the pathway when she saw us approaching and landing in the middle of the narrow street beat her broad bosom with her clenched fist and shouted at me, I having a fixed bayonet, 'Put it through me now for the sake of my son who is in France.'[149]

Local dissent is clearly indicated by the prisoner list for Daly's headquarters which records civilians, men and women, who had been detained as spies.

Nevertheless, public attitudes locally were not uniformly hostile in an area which the police had come to regard as increasingly militant in the months before the Rising. Some of the soldiers who fought there noted a strong antipathy towards them and one officer acknowledged that 'crowds of men and women greeted us with raised fists and curses'.[150] One of the lancers attacked on Easter Monday related that they had had to put up with a lot of abuse from women and young people during the journey. Undoubtedly Daly's men received a significant level of sympathy and active support from the neighbourhood. Soon after evading the distressed soldier's mother, Archer captured what he believed was a plain-clothes policeman and as he was marching him up Church Street he was approached by a young lady who wanted to know if Archer was going to shoot his prisoner. When Archer said that he might, the delighted woman said that in that case she was coming with him. Although the captive turned out to be only a police clerk and was quickly released, Archer's female companion joined up with the Cumann na mBan working for the insurgents.[151] On Wednesday evening Dublin Castle was informed by a cleaner living in North Brunswick Street that people in Richmond Hospital were 'signalling to Sinn Feiners the movements of the military, some of whom are in people's gardens. She thinks some of the people are students but there is no doubt that they were giving the Sinn Feiners all the help they can.'[152] All the rebel casualties in the Richmond evaded arrest and this was partly due to assistance from some hospital staff. Archer who had been taken to the Richmond after shooting himself in the foot had been placed in a ward along with other Volunteers. About a week after the Rising ended they received a visit from two policemen who first went to speak to Patrick Daly. As they did so the house surgeon, Michael Bourke, warned Archer that the police were looking for him but that he had told them he had been discharged. The police then asked Bourke about Eamon Martin who was in the ward, having been shot through a lung; Bourke told them that their mission was pointless since Martin was dying.[153] The medical head of the hospital, Sir Thomas Myles, was a nationalist who in August 1914 had captained his own yacht at Kilcoole to smuggle in arms to the Volunteers there. Although he regarded the Rising as rash and cared for the wounded without distinction his sympathies appear to have been with the rebels.

Some members of the religious communities in the Four Courts area also gave active support and encouragement to the insurgents. The nuns in St John's Convent made food for the rebel outposts, provided accommodation and also promptly reported British troop movements to Daly's officers.[154] A number of priests were clearly sympathetic to the rebels even if they had to express their support in a somewhat guarded manner. On one occasion Archer and a Volunteer officer were anxious to block a passage which ran from Church Street to Bow Street and which actually belonged to the adjacent Franciscan church. Archer's officer intended to use seats from the church to block the passage, but some priests became upset and accused him of sacrilege.

> But the superior – I think Fr Dominick – said to them, 'Let us go quietly away and we will not see or know what he does – he has a job to do.' They departed leaving us to our own devices. However, Hegarty thought better of the move and we did not remove the benches.[155]

A letter from Father Augustine of the Capuchins to the mother of Sean Howard, a dead Volunteer, conveys the intensity of his commitment to the Volunteer cause:

> I am just writing you a hurried line to tell you of the brave Catholic death of your dear boy. . . . When he fell at the barricade in Church Street, he told the men who bore him away to tell his mother that he had died for Ireland. . . . He made his confession . . . in a quiet and beautiful way. My heart went out to him. . . . In the [Saturday] evening, immediately after the Truce, he was carried to Richmond Hospital and there he breathed his last, surrounded by most kind and friendly care and amongst some other brave lads who had fought for what they believed and felt to be the cause of Ireland. May God bless you, dear Irish mother of our Irish martyred boy, I feel your dear brave one is praying for you in Heaven.[156]

Holohan's claim that 'after we have been in occupation for a couple of days, they [the public] were impressed by our discipline and friendly attitude and became more favourable' may have some justification. It was certainly true of John Clarke whose admiration for the rebels mounted during the course of Easter Week – long before the executions and apparently without knowledge of the alleged military atrocities in North King Street.[157] Indeed Clarke felt some sympathy, even gratitude, towards the troops whom he described on 30 April as 'now friendly to us. The military on the street was really a protection.' He was also fully aware of the death and destruction that the Rising had caused and, as a small shopkeeper in a deprived area, was acutely sensitive to wage stoppages among the residents. Yet despite all this, once it had become clear that the Rising had collapsed, he wrote disconsolately 'Thus ends the last attempt for poor old Ireland. What noble fellows. The cream of the land. None of your corner-boy class.' That others shared Clarke's sympathies is suggested by an incident which he witnessed on Easter Saturday afternoon just after he had heard of the surrender:

> We ran around to the Four Courts, where we saw an officer of the Volunteers coming up the quays escorted by soldiers. The Volunteer was bareheaded but in uniform. Reaching [the] corner, [the] escort halted and he proceeded along the quays towards Church Street. As he looked back a number of times some thought he was going to be shot. Women screamed. Some men thought as women did.

Although the Volunteer was not in fact shot the responses which Clarke had observed were a portent of possible future reaction should the execution of the leaders occur. Clarke came to admire the general demeanour and overall military performance of the Volunteers in an area which Pat Hally thought well held, well defended and well led. He considered that Daly had displayed fine military skills, concentrating his unexpectedly small force, establishing strong outposts, impeding the movement of British troops from the Royal Barracks, tying them down and delaying their attack and finally marching his garrison into O'Connell Street 'in perfect order'. Also, though there had been extensive damage throughout the area of Daly's command, the Four Courts itself, both in structure and content, survived largely intact. The courts were soon able to resume business and though many documents in the Public Record Office had been tossed about few had been seriously damaged. Only a few bundles of wills were missing, having been thrown on to adjoining streets and taken away as souvenirs by residents in Church Street.

The attitude of the civilian population to the Irish administration was much less ambivalent than it was towards the Volunteers. To many people the fact that Birrell and Friend, the political and military heads, had both been absent in London on Easter Monday seemed to epitomise a regime riddled with incompetence and ignorance. Unionists who had despised Birrell for years now felt fully vindicated. The scornful and contemptuous Miss Mahaffy, daughter of Trinity College's Provost, was vitriolic in her condemnation of 'a vain worthless man, a failure not only in all his various offices but in his profession and every walk of life, except as a talker; we must all despise him'. She also poured her opprobrium on the Lord Lieutenant whom she contrasted with the rebel leadership which had at least had the courage to share the danger of the GPO with its rank and file. She wrote of Wimborne that 'He has cowered in the safety of the Vice-regal Lodge, unconsidered by soldiers and civilians; doubtless the laughing stock of the Sinn Feiners.'[158] Even as Birrell and Friend hurried back to Ireland they can have been in little doubt that their professional life-expectancy had been dramatically reduced. On 3 May 1916 a doleful Birrell telegrammed Nathan, 'Prime Minister thinks you must share my fate' and Nathan resigned that day.[159]

During the Rising Dublin suffered both materially and in human terms. Most of the physical damage was inflicted by the British army through shelling and incendiary bombs. Fire had long been used as a military weapon for encouraging a civilian population to pressurise its rulers to surrender in order to avoid the destruction of a city's wealth, industry and cultural heritage. In more recent times before the Easter Rising the Prussians had employed incendiaries successfully aganst French towns in the war of 1870 and by the outbreak of the First World War most European armies were equipped with shells of thermite and white phosphorous which were fired from howitzers. These incendiaries were intended to produce a major fire in a target zone before the defenders could introduce extinguishing apparatus. On impact the bomb ignited and kindled combustible objects in the surrounding area. The fire would then extend throughout a single building by travelling upwards through unprotected openings such as stairways or else by burning through floors. Concentrations of smoke and volatile vapours could also filter through to the upper chambers and then explode. If the defenders were unable to control this primary fire it could pass to adjoining buildings through an unprotected vertical opening or burn through a combustible interior wall or pass along cornices and roof coverings. Heat radiating from an intense fire was capable of igniting buildings as far as 50 feet away and once a number of secondary fires combined they could produce a conflagration of immense proportions which rendered all available fire-fighting equipment redundant. Most of the fires started in Dublin in 1916 were initiated by the British army, which decided that shells, incendiaries and incendiary bullets were the most effective and (in terms of manpower) cheapest weapon to drive the Volunteers out of the occupied buildings in the O'Connell Street area. It was here that almost all of the fires of the Rising occurred. But the insurgents also employed incendiary warfare although in an amateurish, even primitive form. At the Four Courts one of Daly's Volunteers fashioned a piece of ash into a bow and an arrow to which he attached a petrol-soaked rag and fired at the Medical Mission nearby. British lancers had sought shelter in this building but they were not burnt out because although the arrow passed through a window it failed to ignite the flooring. Since there was nothing available to make more arrows three Volunteers were ordered to dash across, smash in the windows, pile in straw which would be covered with whiskey and set it on fire. However, intense fire from the defenders cut the rebels down before they could carry out the plan.[160]

The rebels also used fire to relieve pressure on themselves. On Easter Wednesday Ned Daly ordered that the Linenhall Barracks, where his men had just captured a large number of men of the Army Pay Corps, be set on fire in order to prevent its reoccupation by the encircling British forces. The blaze was one of the most dramatic of Easter Week and lit up the streets around the Four Courts throughout the night. It became even more spectacular next day when it reached a druggist's in Bolton Street and barrels of oil were tossed in the air and exploded, sending a cloud of choking smoke over the surrounding area. The fire turned night into day and subsided finally only on Easter Friday. Some fires were also started by looters such as at Lawrence's toy shop in O'Connell Street which was set alight by rockets and other fireworks, and the Trueform shoe shop in Linenhall Street.

To many people the fires, from a distance, were very beautiful. Lieutenant Jameson wrote that they 'were the most gorgeous thing I've ever seen'[161] while a civilian wrote that they were 'a wonderful and awful sight'.[162] An observer of the fire at the Dublin Bread Company wrote that;

> The flames kissing the ball on the dome's summit are singularly impressive. Standing high above the lower plane of flame and smoke, it is thrown into relief by a background of clouds. A scene of greater splendour I have never before witnessed, not even in the realms of cinematography. It is only outdone by the avalanche of flame and smoke that crashes to the ground when the dome collapses at 5 o'clock.[163]

To those nearer the epicentre the aesthetic qualities of the conflagration were of secondary importance compared with escaping with their lives. By mid-afternoon on Easter Thursday the flames had reached the houses on Eden Quay where the bedridden were incinerated. Men, women and children emerged from the houses and fled to the sanctuary of the Custom House but other petrified residents stayed. Eventually a soldier crept from Butt Bridge to the burning block and managed to encourage some of the occupants to leave. They included young women who fell on their knees and kissed his hand while another soldier with a megaphone bellowed, 'Come out! Come out!' until they were satisfied that they had done everything they could.[164]

The fires did immense damage to the city centre which to many resembled the Western Front. The Lord Mayor, James Gallagher, called Dublin 'a Louvain by the Liffey'[165] and the *Irish Times* compared O'Connell Street to Ypres. Captain Purcell, the chief fire officer of the Dublin Fire Brigade, estimated that 179 buildings had been fired, and £1 million worth of property and over £750,000 of stock had been destroyed in O'Connell Street where 27,000 square yards had been affected on the east side and 34,000 square yards on the west. The principal buildings affected on the east side were the Imperial Hotel and the Dublin Bread Company. On the west side the GPO, the Hotel Metropole, Eason's, the *Freeman's Journal* office and Bewley's were worst hit. Outside this central area the only large building fired was the Linenhall Barracks. In Abbey Street, Wynn's Hotel and the Royal Hibernian Academy, which contained the work of Ireland's famous artists, were both devastated. Both sides clearly fired at or intimidated the fire brigade if its presence was considered disadvantageous. After the attack on the Magazine Fort on Easter Monday a fire engine was stopped by armed Volunteers, one of whom placed a loaded revolver to the head of the driver and ordered him to return to his station. Eventually the situation in O'Connell Street became so dangerous for his men that Purcell withdrew the service.[166]

To the more refined sections of Dublin society the worst aspect of the inferno was the sheer injustice of the places that had been destroyed and those that had been undamaged. A mortified Mrs Henry was aghast at the sight of O'Connell Street. 'A desolate wreckage. Everything on the right hand side from O'Connell Bridge to past the Pillar is in ruins. The GPO had just been newly done up. The cleanest and best buildings are destroyed. The miles of slums are intact.'[167] On 4 May 1916 Nathan suffered the final insult of a chirpy letter from George Bernard Shaw which inquired:

Why didn't the artillery knock down half Dublin whilst it had the chance? Think of the insanitary areas, the slums, the glorious chance of making a clean sweep of them! Only 179 houses, and probably at least nine of them quite decent ones. I'd have laid at least 17,900 of them flat and made a decent town of it.[168]

There was also human damage and the official figures record that during the Rising 450 people were killed, 2,614 were wounded and 9 were declared missing, almost all in Dublin. Military losses were 116 dead, 368 wounded and 9 missing while 16 policemen were killed and 29 wounded. The figures do not distinguish between Volunteers and civilians for whom the combined figure was 318 dead and 2,217 wounded. However, a roll of honour which was compiled later records 64 rebels as having died out of a grand total of 1,558 insurgents.

The burial system broke down during the Rising as funeral parlours and cemeteries closed down. It often proved impossible to remove bodies from private houses and hospitals and the results were sometimes distressing. One young Volunteer, Gerald Keogh, who had been sent from the Post Office by Pearse to summon fifty Volunteers from Larkfield, was shot dead as he passed Trinity College. The motley crew of defenders brought his body inside where it lay for three days in an empty room. Eventually its physical decay became so unpleasant that the corpse had to be buried in the college grounds. Uncoffined interment was the fate of many who were shot or died naturally, including infants. They were buried in backyards, patches of garden and other out-of-the-way places. After the Rising many were dug up and given a proper burial. The staff of Glasnevin Cemetery worked day and night to bury people by the score and of more than 200 who were buried over 150 had been shot dead.

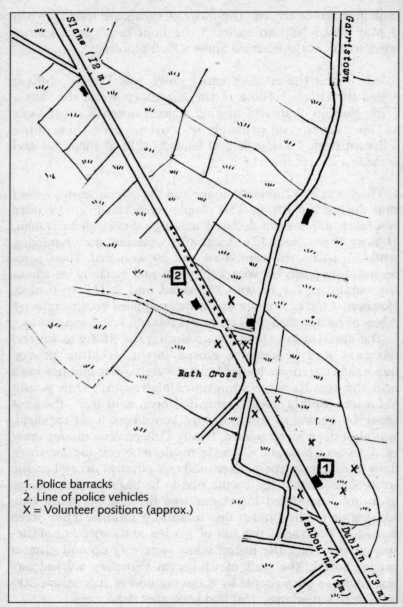

1. Police barracks
2. Line of police vehicles
X = Volunteer positions (approx.)

Battle of Asbourne

9

THE RISING OUTSIDE DUBLIN

Because of the MacNeill countermand and the confusion which it created, the Rising in the provinces never came close to being the nationwide insurrection for which the Military Council had hoped. The Volunteers of Cork, for instance, did not mobilise and the resentment at this inactivity led to their officers resigning *en masse* after the Rising. In Limerick, Commandant Colivet convened a staff meeting on Easter Tuesday and it voted by a majority of ten to six to take no action. The Volunteers of Enniscorthy did rise on Easter Wednesday after receiving an order from Connolly to sever the railway line from Rosslare and prevent British troop reinforcements from reaching Dublin. Although they occupied the town of Enniscorthy the Volunteers lacked the men and weaponry even to capture the police barracks. Instead, there was a desultory exchange of fire between the police station and the rebel headquarters in the Athenaeum Club beside the castle. When news arrived of the surrender in Dublin on Saturday 29 April, the Enniscorthy rebels were visited by a local priest and a group of businessmen who appealed to them to accept the inevitable. But the insurgents would only surrender if they received a direct order from Pearse and so the local British army commander authorised two Volunteer officers to travel to Dublin to meet their leader in Arbour Hill prison. In front of the guard Pearse ordered them to lay down their arms but when the soldier took this order outside to have it inspected by his superior officers, Pearse whispered to them to hide their weapons because 'They will be needed later.' There was some action also in Galway where a thousand Volunteers mobilised on Easter Monday. After some police stations had been raided and captured, a general sense of demoralisation set in. An officers' conference on Easter Thursday rejected a proposal to disband and this decision was confirmed at another conference on the following day. By now they were being pursued by a thousand British troops and when a local priest brought news that the Rising in Dublin was collapsing the officers finally agreed, early on Saturday morning, that continued resistance was impossible.[1]

The only serious encounter outside the capital occurred at Ashbourne to the north of the city. Here the 120 Finglas Volunteers in north County Dublin were organised as a fifth Dublin battalion and led by Thomas Ashe, who had been appointed commandant a few weeks before the Rising. It had achieved an almost complete mobilisation on Easter Sunday but, because of the MacNeill countermand, only about fifty reappeared the following day. Their ranks were further depleted when Connolly summoned twenty men to reinforce the garrisons in the GPO and the Mendicity. At the same time he instructed Ashe to launch diversionary raids in his area to relieve the pressure on the Volunteers in the city as well as capturing arms and disrupting military and police movements. On Easter Tuesday Ashe was reinforced by some Dublin Volunteers who had missed their own company mobilisation and wanted action wherever they could find it. Among the newcomers was Richard Mulcahy, a talented future chief of staff of the I.R.A. whose organisational ability, decisiveness and tact made him an ideal second-in-command to the inspirational but somewhat impractical Ashe.

Ashe's men camped on the Dublin side of Finglas until Easter Tuesday evening, when they set off to carry out the mission which Connolly had allocated to them. Next morning they acquired another half-dozen men led by Paddy Houlihan who had been sent by James Connolly.[2] The column of fifty men descended on Garristown, accompanied by a vanload of bread and provisions and a large wagon full of ammunition and equipment. There it took over the village, forced the police station to surrender and remained until Thursday morning when it advanced about 3 miles south to Newbarn. On Friday, when he learnt troops were preparing to move by rail from Athlone to Dublin, Ashe decided to cut the line at Batterstown about 12 miles away and attack any soldiers who arrived to repair the sabotage. He left one group of Volunteers at Newbarn and set off on a bicycle at 10.30 a.m. with the main body towards the Dublin–Slane road which passes through the village of Ashbourne. Just as they departed one man remembered that while they had forced most police barracks in the area to evacuate, the one at Ashbourne might still be occupied. His suspicions were soon confirmed by scouts who reported the station to be in a state of defence with a barricade under construction across the main road. Ashe determined to capture it and disarm the garrison and dispatched Houlihan at the head of an advance party which dismounted at a cross-roads known locally as Rath Cross.[3]

From there the Volunteers opened fire on a party of about thirty-five policemen situated behind a barricade in front of the barracks. Shortly after the enemy retreated into the station, Ashe and Mulcahy arrived and ordered nine men to cross the fields and take up position at the rear of the building. As they did so three fully armed policemen cycled round the corner of the main road and were confronted by four Volunteers who ordered them to halt and surrender their weapons. The two constables threw down their rifles and bayonets and revolvers, raised their hands and shouted: 'We surrender.' But their officer, Sergeant Brady, who recognised one of his captors, drew his revolver and shouted, 'Golden, I'll get you before I die.' Jerry Golden was armed with a Martini rifle and tried to shoot Brady, but the cartridge jammed in the breach. He then charged with his bayonet but Sergeant Brady took evasive action and the bayonet stuck in a ditch. Brady now grabbed the rifle muzzle and wrestled

Golden down on top of him while trying to draw his own revolver. Fortunately for Golden another Volunteer helped him overpower his opponent but though Brady was made captive, one of the constables had fled during the mêlée.[4]

The men who had been sent behind the police station now signalled that they were ready but Ashe decided to attempt diplomacy first and ordered Houlihan to take Brady with a white flag to the barracks and demand the surrender of its occupants. Houlihan kept a cocked rifle aimed at Brady's spine when he warned the garrison that they would be annihilated if they did not capitulate. The officer in charge shouted his rejection and Houlihan returned to Ashe with Brady, who persuaded the commandant to allow him to return and reason with the policemen in the station. However, when Brady reached the barracks he leapt through a gap in the hedge and made his escape.

Ashe now ordered men to advance down the road until they came near the station and then climbed up on a rock, but when he called on the police to surrender he was fired at. An attack was now ordered, but those at the rear discovered that part of the building had no windows. The shooting at the front was continuous, with the police replying through loopholes in the iron-shuttered windows. Mulcahy ordered that two grenades be thrown against the lower windows, but the first rebounded from the iron shutter and fell on the ground, where it blew a small hole in the wall. The second grenade cracked the wall and also broke the defenders' resistance. When they shouted 'We surrender', the Volunteers ceased firing and the battle was apparently over. But just as Ashe and Mulcahy were about to enter the barrack yard to take the surrender the hooting of motor cars drew their attention to a motorised column of policemen heading towards the cross-roads. The appearance of these reinforcements now encouraged the station garrison to change its mind about capitulation.

The new arrivals had been mobilised at Slane and were hunting across the territory in search of the Volunteers who been raiding police stations. The convoy, which consisted of

fifteen cars and fifty-five policemen led by a Chief Inspector
and a District Inspector, had actually been warned by an old
man during their journey that rebels were in the area.
District Inspector Smith had tried to bring the column to a
halt and ordered one man to speed to the front and stop the
lead cars. But the advance group did not hear his warning
whistle and he did not get ahead until they stumbled into the
battle at Ashbourne.[5] Their arrival was completely
unexpected by Ashe because the attention of two scouts
whom he had posted at the cross-roads had become
concentrated on the events at the police station. The scouts
saw the newcomers only at the last moment but they and a
number of men at the barracks managed to fire some shots
which brought the police column to a halt. Ashe was
somewhat shaken by these developments and since he was at
this stage outnumbered by the enemy he gave the order to
retreat. Before it could be delivered Mulcahy made a decisive
intervention which turned the course of events in the
Volunteers' favour. He realised that the reinforcements were
as taken aback as their opponents and also lacked accurate
information on the Volunteers' positions and strength.

> His plan of attack was to make full use of the morale factor
> by driving home a vigorous assault with all possible force
> from the vicinity of the cross-roads, and giving the enemy
> an impression of superior force on our side by fire from the
> rear.[6]

Mulcahy persuaded Ashe to rescind his order to retreat and
instruct the men at the rear of the barracks to attack the
new arrivals on their left flank. At the same time the
remainder would race to the cross-roads and prevent the
police spreading out to envelop the gullies. Ten of Ashe's men
threw themselves into the rain gullies while others mounted
the bank on the other side and opened fire at the enemy cars
200 yards away, spread out on the Slane side of the cross-
roads. Their concentrated fire was extremely effective. Jerry
Golden saw;

an RIC man step from the leading car with his rifle in his hands and just as he stepped from the running-board Mick Allister, who was lying along the ditch on the other side of the road, stepped out into the middle of the road, raised his rifle and fired. The policeman fell into a cutting in the ditch on our side of the road and lay with his head and shoulders above the bank, with the result that we thought he was firing at us, as his rifle was held in his hands and pointing down the road towards us. But after we had each taken a shot at him and saw that there was no reply from his rifle we concluded he was dead.[7]

For half an hour the police took cover wherever they could find it, such as under the vehicles, until the Volunteers who had been attacking the rear of the station arrived to join in the main attack. Meanwhile Ashe had summoned the men he had left in camp at Newbarn and they split into two groups, one of which was to attack the right flank and the other to block their retreat at the rear. During these manoeuvres one Volunteer who stood on top of a ditch to find out if any policemen were in the fields was shot dead.

It was now nearly one o'clock and a considerable amount of ammunition was being expended in the continual rifle fire. As a group of men led by Mulcahy manoeuvred for position District Inspector Smith shot a Volunteer dead, but the victim's rifle was grabbed by Mulcahy, who shot the police officer through the head. This pressure succeeded in driving the policemen down the road to the crossroads. It was at 4 p.m. that Mulcahy decided to deliver the *coup de grace* by leading half a dozen men in a bayonet charge at the enemy position. This daring stratagem broke the nerve of the defenders, some of whom fled to a labourer's cottage about 50 yards away on the Slane side of the cross-roads. As they huddled together, attempting to force their way in, they were fired on by the pursuing Volunteers. After another ten minutes their resistance crumbled completely and they shouted: 'We surrender.' They then threw away their weapons and marched out with their hands above their heads, some waving white handkerchiefs. Between 4.30 and 5 p.m. Ashe ordered that firing cease.

As the police convoy was rounded up the station garrison also filed out, led by a district inspector who marched up to Ashe and surrendered his revolver. Ashe was puzzled as to why the district inspector's men had not attacked the Volunteers in the rear to relieve the pressure on their besieged comrades. When the District Inspector replied, 'I had already surrendered and would not break my word', Ashe was too gracious to point out that he had already done so or to suggest that, perhaps, he had felt safer remaining in the station. The wounded policemen were now calling for help as the Volunteers moved through the dead and injured. Four died as their injuries were being dressed and an officer died the following day. While there is agreement that only two of the forty-eight Volunteers died in the battle of Ashbourne, the RIC fatalities are disputed. Volunteer Frank Lawless estimated eight to eleven killed and some police drivers, while Jerry Golden believed he counted fifteen.[8] There were some civilians among the casualties. Albert Keep, the chauffeur to the Marchioness of Conyngham, had been commandeered along with his car to convey the police to the scene of the battle where he was fatally wounded. Another vehicle caught up in the shooting was a taxi carrying John Carroll, the son of the chief of the fire brigade at Kingstown. He was killed along with the driver, Jeremiah Hogan.[9]

When all arms, ammunition and equipment had been secured and all the wounded treated, Ashe ordered the remainder to carry the wounded to the cars and directed them to return to Slane. The conclusion of the day's grim events was not without its comic aspect. Ashe paraded those police who had not been wounded and told them that they could march back to their homes, but warned them not to become involved in further military activity. When one constable expressed his anxiety to Paddy Houlihan that they might be at risk during the journey, Houlihan facetiously suggested that he and his colleagues should show the white feather. Somewhat surprisingly, the policeman missed the allusion and when he pressed further Houlihan said that they should place white handkerchiefs on top of their helmets. Even more surprising was the policeman's grateful acceptance of the suggestion and Houlihan's last sight was of white handkerchiefs at head height fading into the distance.[10]

Many myths have grown up around the Battle of Ashbourne, which is often perceived as a daring Volunteer ambush against a much larger enemy force, succeeding through careful planning, tactical superiority and the leadership quality of the rebel commandant. In fact none of these factors was present. The impression of a large enemy force grew out of the victor's oversight in not counting its size and subsequent estimates by participants vary widely. Volunteer Frank Lawless believed that there were 15 police in the barracks, but his estimate of the police reinforcements ranged from 50 to 70 and from 70 to 90. Jerry Golden was convinced that there were 21 in the barracks and at least 108 in the motorised column. In fact the true figure for the reinforcements was 55 and, while they did initially outnumber Ashe's men, the Volunteer reinforcements brought his force to 48. Since the garrison in the barracks played no further part in the battle there was eventually a rough equality between the two sides. Nor did the Volunteers display tactical superiority. Ashe's look-outs performed very poorly and were taken by surprise, creating a potentially disastrous situation. Only the fact that the enemy was equally surprised and confused about the overall situation gave the Finglas men the opportunity to retrieve the situation. Nor was Ashe's crisis leadership particularly impressive. He proved unable to react speedily and flexibly in a fluid situation. Far from his seeking opportunities to seize the initiative, his initial response was to break off the engagement and start a retreat which might have developed into a disaster. The real victor of Ashbourne was undoubtedly Mulcahy, who kept his nerve, recognised the enemy's uncertainty and disorientation, determined to take the battle to them and rallied his commandant and the rank and file. Once he had restored a sense of discipline the greater fighting spirit of the Volunteers did the rest.

10

SUPPRESSION, COURTS-
MARTIAL AND EXECUTIONS

The outbreak of the Rising caught the Irish administration by surprise and it was soon in almost complete disarray. Birrell, the Chief Secretary, and Major-General Sir Lovick Friend, the army GOC, were both in London and Under-Secretary Nathan had been left in charge. The military resources at Nathan's disposal were seriously depleted. Once headquarters, training and administrative staff had been discounted, the Irish garrison consisted of 2,400 troops scattered over nine barracks. But at 12.00 noon on Easter Monday just 400 were available for immediate service against about 1,000 rebels and even Dublin Castle was virtually unguarded. Furthermore, within about an hour, after two policemen were killed, the Chief Commissioner of the Dublin Metropolitan Police withdrew his force of 1,100 unarmed men from the streets. Nevertheless, after the initial shock, the British reacted speedily with a clear, coherent response. Reinforcements were summoned, intelligence was gathered on the enemy's strength and disposition and key positions such as the Magazine Fort and the Vice-regal Lodge in Phoenix Park, Kingsbridge and Broadstone railway stations and the docks were secured. Generally this was done quickly, though the telephone exchange in Crown Alley lay unprotected until 5.00 p.m. on Easter Monday and Trinity College was held by its OTC and army officers on leave until noon the following day.[1]

Protecting Dublin Castle was an immediate priority and troops who were summoned from the Royal, Portobello and Richmond Barracks arrived at 2.00 p.m. By evening its garrison had been augmented by 300 soldiers. These army movements had precipitated clashes with the rebels located in the Four Courts, the Mendicity Institution, the South Dublin Union and at Portobello Bridge and Camden Street. By 5.20 p.m., 1,600 standby troops from the Curragh camp had arrived at Kingsbridge station without having been detected by the rebels. Some of the soldiers proceeded directly to the North Wall to protect the docks and others secured Amiens Street railway station and the Custom House. By then substantial numbers of troops were preparing to converge on the city – 1,100 from Belfast, 100 from Athlone and 500 from Templemore. In addition, before he left England to return by warship, Friend had arranged for about 10,000 troops to transfer to Ireland from camp at St Albans in England.[2]

At 3.45 a.m. on Easter Tuesday Brigadier-General William Lowe arrived at Kingsbridge station with a further 1,000 troops from the Curragh and, in Friend's absence, took command of all available forces. Already that morning soldiers had occupied the Shelbourne Hotel which dominated much of Stephen's Green and soon forced the Volunteers to evacuate the park and transfer to the College of Surgeons. By 5.30 p.m. military headquarters estimated that there were 4,000 troops available and more were arriving all the time. Using these reinforcements Lowe was able to make remarkable progress and by midnight Lieutenant-Colonel Portal had established, without significant losses, a 'protected line' of posts from Kingsbridge station through Dublin Castle and Trinity College to the Custom House. This split the rebel forces in two, giving a safe line of advance to troops, extending operations to either north or south and facilitating communication by dispatch rider: the telephone wires were believed to be tapped. Meanwhile a partial military cordon was placed around the northern side of the city: when completed the following evening, it ran from Parkgate (at the main entrance to Phoenix Park) via the North Circular road to the North Wall on the

Liffey. Wimborne, the Lord Lieutenant, advised Birrell at 1.58 p.m. on 25 April that they would await troops from England before taking decisive action, but would then 'contemplate drastic disarmament' and defeat the rebellion.[3]

On Easter Tuesday reinforcements from England disembarked at Kingstown and on the following day the Sherwoods were blooded in the fierce encounter at Mount Street Bridge. Despite this temporary setback, isolated rebel positions around Dublin Castle continued to be captured. So were others, such at the Mendicity Institution and the City Hall, which had significantly hampered troop movements. Liberty Hall, which had been left barricaded and still apparently occupied by the rebels, was shelled. In general, as Nathan reported to Birrell on Wednesday evening, 'no considerable advance' had been made that day in Dublin but some preparatory steps had been taken for an attack on O'Connell Street.[4] Soon afterwards he advised Asquith that troops were being concentrated for its envelopment. He added that 'house-to-house fighting is necessarily slow' and that troops had to overcome considerable opposition, but he reassured the Prime Minister that he fully appreciated the 'necessity for disposing of the Dublin situation as quickly as possible'.[5]

On Easter Thursday more reinforcements arrived at Kingstown and by then the British military authorities had established a firm grip on the city. Vital strategic locations had been reinforced and the rebel positions and their relative importance had been identified. Troop levels were now vastly superior to the enemy's, despite some diversion of resources to Athlone and Limerick. Friend, who had temporarily resumed command, had decided to construct an inner cordon around the GPO to isolate the nerve centre of the Rising. This objective was successfully achieved by 5.00 p.m. The task of suppressing the Rising, therefore, was not far from completion when, at 2.30 a.m. on Friday morning, Major-General Sir John Grenfell Maxwell arrived in Dublin to assume command. Friend's absence in London at the start of the Rising had been a gaffe and made his replacement inevitable. Maxwell was a Scotsman in his mid-fifties who, because of the patronage of Field Marshal

Kitchener, had enjoyed a steady, if undramatic, rise in the British Army. Much of his career had been spent in Africa, though he had served briefly in Ireland in 1904 as the chief staff officer to the GOC, the Duke of Connaught. Maxwell was a fervent believer in the British Empire and a resolute opponent of any threat to its unity, especially if there was any suspicion of German involvement. During the first two years of the war he had been GOC in Egypt before being eased out in 1916 to make way for General Archibald Murray, a former Chief of the Imperial General Staff. On his recall to England in March 1916 Maxwell had checked into a nursing home for a detailed medical examination because of suspected gallstones. Just as he was passed fit news arrived of the Rising and Maxwell was chosen to replace the discredited Friend. His selection as military ruler of Ireland is often depicted as evidence of a deliberate policy to install a Cromwellian figure who would restore order ruthlessly and govern Ireland with an iron fist. In fact Maxwell owed his appointment to Asquith's desire not to offend Irish sensitivities. The Prime Minister had originally favoured General Sir Ian Hamilton, but Hamilton had been in command at Gallipoli during the ill-fated Dardanelles expedition when many Irish soldiers had been killed at Suvla Bay. Like Maxwell, Hamilton had been squeezed out and was available for duty.[6] But on Easter Wednesday, 26 April, Asquith wrote to Kitchener who was now Secretary of State for War that;

> I think on the whole it would be better not to send [him] . . . to Dublin. There is a good deal of bitterness in Ireland about Suvla, etc., to which Redmond gave expression in the House this afternoon. . . . It is very desirable to send a competent man who so far as Ireland is concerned has no past record.[7]

By the merest coincidence Kitchener had just received a letter from Maxwell reporting that he was now medically fit for duty and seeking a post. Kitchener successfully recommended to Sir John Robertson, Chief of the Imperial General Staff, that

Maxwell be appointed Irish GOC with full authority to restore order, put down the rebellion and punish participants.[8]

Maxwell was confirmed in his post on Easter Thursday, 27 April, and he travelled immediately to Ireland. The following day he wrote to his wife:

> We arrived at 2 a.m. From the sea, it looked as if the entire city of Dublin was in flames, but when we got to North Wall it was not quite so bad as that, yet a great deal of the part north of the Liffey was burning. Bullets were flying about, the crackle of musketry and machine-gun fire breaking out every other minute. We were met by three motor cars and drove up to the Royal Hospital. The town is piquetted with soldiers and most of the rebels are in a ring fence and we are gradually closing in on them. I think after tomorrow it will be clearer, but a lot of men will be knocked over. These infernal rebels have got a lot of rifles and apparently a fair supply of ammunition. . . . It is strange coming back to Dublin and living in the Royal Hospital. Since I began this letter a good deal has happened; I think the signs are that the rebels have had enough of it. I will know for certain tonight.[9]

Maxwell had at his disposal between 18,000 and 20,000 troops in the capital, with substantially more due to arrive within the next forty-eight hours. Having consulted his commanding officers, he decided to isolate further the 'infectious patches'.[10] Lowe was ordered to close in on O'Connell Street and its bombardment by artillery was intensified, forcing the rebels to evacuate their headquarters. At the same time, the construction of a military cordon around the Four Courts was begun, and the existing one around the north side was extended southwards, to encircle the city, using the line of the Grand Canal. Incendiary warfare was the most effective and destructive weapon which was deployed by British troops to hasten the end of the Rising. Once Pearse had surrendered, his order to the other garrisons to follow suit removed the necessity of using force to compel their capitulation and the collapse of the rebellion on 29 and 30 April was speedy. By Sunday, Maxwell considered that 'the rebellion . . . [was] . . . practically crushed. . . . Rebels surrendering freely.' But he stressed that 'every precaution is being taken'. He still feared that there might be 'one or two Sidney Street affairs, as some of these devils are fairly desperate'. He suspended further reinforcements from England and though he continued to report sniping in Dublin until 4 May, none the less the city was 'reverting to the normal condition'.[11]

Throughout the suppression of the Rising Maxwell insisted that 'all surrenders must be absolutely unconditional' and in this he had the unwavering support of the Irish administration.[12] Nathan, for instance, had rejected out of hand a suggestion by the Lord Mayor of Dublin, James Gallagher, that a deputation of citizens should mediate with the rebels.[13] Likewise, on 28 April, Campbell, the Irish Attorney-General, wrote to Nathan that it was 'vital that no terms other than unconditional surrender should be offered to or accepted from anyone who has taken part in armed rebellion'.[14] This response was no doubt partly prompted by the widespread presumption of strong German involvement in the Rising, which Lord French considered was intended to prevent British reinforcements being sent to France. A cabinet paper argued that enemy intervention in Ireland was a calculated military response to the palpable failure of their attack on Verdun.[15] On the morning of Sunday 30 April Maxwell and Birrell learnt that the officer commanding the Queenstown garrison was agreeable to rebels in Tralee handing their arms over to some responsible person. He was also prepared to give guarantees that no action would be taken against anyone unless it was proved they had been in recent communication with Germany and that any arms surrendered would be returned at the end of the war unless the civil authorities declared otherwise. Just over two hours later Maxwell wired back that no terms or guarantees were to be offered to anyone found in arms and that all surrenders had to be unconditional.[16]

The Irish military historian Major-General Pat Hally has written that crushing the rebellion in less than a week in a built-up area, where defenders always hold the advantage, was a considerable military achievement.[17] This was true even though the insurgents were few in number and without machine guns and artillery. The performance of the British army is even more impressive when the youth and inadequate training of many soldiers, their ignorance of the geography of Dublin and their initial ignorance of the location, strength and weaponry of the rebels are all taken into account. Three-quarters of the Sherwood Foresters who fought at Mount Street Bridge had no more than three months' service and no training in street-fighting.[18] As well, many soldiers fought in scratch units under unfamiliar officers and something like two dozen regiments were estimated to be present in Portobello Barracks because men on Easter leave were unable to report back to their own depots.[19]

Errors of military judgement were, of course, made by the British commanders during Easter Week. The attempt to place a cordon around the Four Courts without adequate intelligence on rebel dispositions must have increased casualties. Hally has criticised the persistent attacks by Sherwood Foresters on Clanwilliam House, which he attributes to an ignorance of rebel strength and locations; he considers it all the more reprehensible given that within a few hundred yards, two alternative routes into the city lay open and undefended. However, the GOC Irish Command had given Maconchy, the commanding officer of the Sherwoods, very explicit instructions which stated :

The objective of the force is to clear the country of rebels between the area of Stillorgan, Donnybrook and Dublin roads. To effect this, every road and lane in that area must be traversed by patrols and the head of the columns will in no case advance beyond any house from which fire has been opened, until all the inhabitants of such houses have been destroyed or captured. Any man found in such a house bearing arms or not may be considered as a rebel.

Because opposition was anticipated beyond Donnybrook and Ballsbridge, troops were advised that machine guns should 'be carried close to the head of each column [and would] . . . prove of great value in street fighting'.[20] For this reason also they were not to advance beyond the area of Harcourt Street, Grafton Street and Stephen's Green where they were to receive further instructions.

From the early stages of the Rising power was increasingly concentrated in the hands of the military authorities. Wimborne, the Lord Lieutenant, declared martial law in Dublin City and County on the evening of Easter Tuesday, 25 April. Its operation was intended initially for a period of one month. Subsequently the cabinet became increasingly alarmed at military reports of risings in Galway, Clare, Cork and Wexford, attacks on police barracks and large columns marching on Athlone, Arklow and possibly Dublin. Accordingly, on 26 April, martial law was extended to the whole of Ireland, initially for a period of one month. On the following day Asquith informed parliament that General Maxwell was leaving for Ireland immediately, that he had been granted plenary powers and that the Irish administration was to place itself at his disposal.[21]

Maxwell's relations with the Irish administration were strained from the very start. After meeting Birrell and Wimborne for the first time on 28 April, he noted: 'They do not altogether appreciate going under my orders but I told them I did not mean to interfere unless it was necessary and I hoped they would do all I asked them to do.'[22] Soon after this meeting Birrell, Nathan and the Irish legal advisers registered their strong disapproval of the passage of power to the military authorities.

They telegrammed Asquith that;

All of us are strongly of opinion that for the moment the imminent proclamation of martial law for the whole of Ireland most inadvisable. First, all useful powers already exist under DORA . . . and recent proclamation abolishing civil trial. Secondly, we anticipate grave possibility of bad effects produced if martial law is extended to the very large areas which at present show no sign of disturbance. . . . Please consider this immediately.[23]

At a cabinet meeting later that afternoon Lloyd George feared that Ireland might be 'set ablaze by the unconsidered actions of some subordinate officer', but his anxious colleagues confirmed the extension of martial law.[24] They did, however, place restrictions on Maxwell's authority to delegate his powers to subordinate officers and Asquith urged him only to employ extreme measures in an emergency.[25]

Maxwell was not the stereotypical pro-Unionist bigot which he is often depicted as being. He believed that the cause of the current imbroglio lay in government appeasement of every political faction for years past. For this failure to enforce the law firmly and impartially he believed the Irish administration bore primary responsibility. Of Birrell he said, 'He is not as bad as is thought but like so many politicians he does not put into effect what he preaches.'[26] In particular Maxwell condemned the way in which militant Ulster Unionist resistance to the Third Home Rule bill between 1912 and 1914 was handled. He wrote, 'It is the government as a whole that are to blame. Ever since they winked at Ulster breaking the law they have been in difficulties and have hoped and hoped that something would turn up. . . . Wait and see. Well, we waited and now see the result, viz rebellion and loss of life.'[27]

Maxwell's distaste for what he regarded as political cravenness and ineptitude was echoed in the letters of serving soldiers. These reveal a desire for strongly repressive measures, but also cynicism about the will of politicians to enforce such a policy. One British officer wrote on 27 April that 'The daily papers made me pace with rage. . . . Is there no-one in England with any guts at all. This little Irish affair will wake them up. I suppose they will shamble and slither and compromise through it. . . . If they don't hang or shoot that d——d swine Casement, not one of them ever deserve to be spoken to again by any decent man. Lord, what a pack of invertebrate monkeys they are.' On 2 May, he noted: 'I wish they would send us to kill some of them [the rebels].'[28] Another soldier who had served in Dublin observed that 'I do not for a moment believe that with a firm and determined government resolved to win the war we should have been treated to this humiliating affair in Ireland.' He predicted cynically that Casement would either be acquitted or reprieved and released to resume his political career while the rebels would be bribed to keep the peace in future. 'They well know that the fate that they justly deserve would not be meted out to them.'[29]

But neither was Maxwell the man to carry through a policy of savage and blind repression. One Irish civil servant found him 'a clever man, broadminded and open to argument' and his private papers reveal him as a man with rather enlightened social opinions.[30] Maxwell regarded the poverty and squalor of the Dublin slums as an indictment of British rule in Ireland and he also condemned the callous neglect of absentee landlords, whom he regarded as a primary source of Irish disaffection. His favoured political system consisted of a strong executive which was responsive to the grievances of moderate opinion. Nevertheless, he was concerned not to promote any perception that violence would extract concessions and he was determined to crush revolutionary nationalism in Ireland and punish its instigators.[31] Soon after his arrival in Dublin, he predicted accurately that 'I do not think that Birrell will bother Ireland much more' and by 1 May 1916 the Chief Secretary had gone.[32] He was soon followed by Nathan, who resigned immediately after receiving Birrell's telegraph that 'P.M. thinks you must share my fate'.[33] Maxwell was convinced that 'we have narrowly missed a most serious rebellion',[34] an opinion which no doubt was largely derived from Sir Neville Chamberlain. The Inspector-General of the RIC had argued that if the Aud's arms and ammunition had been landed, the Volunteers outside Dublin would not have held back.[35]

Apart from those selected for a court-martial, rebels who surrendered were transported immediately to internment camps in England and by 3 May 300 had arrived at Knutsford and over 30 at Stafford.[36] Meanwhile, arrests of fugitive rebels continued and a street cordon was maintained in Dublin, quaysides were closely monitored and passengers could leave Ireland only via Dublin, Kingstown, Belfast and Greenore. One of Nathan's last acts was to recruit port watchers. Maxwell had dismissed any suggestion of clemency for rebels at a time when the British Empire was engaged in a great war and 'Dublin is still smouldering and the blood of the victims of this mad rebellion is hardly dry'.[37]

The selection of the most prominent rebels had been conducted in Richmond Barracks where, on arrival, prisoners were packed into billets with a few buckets to serve as latrines. There was hardly enough room to sit down and in one the men came to an arrangement that one half would tighten together standing while the others rested for a while. The mood was sombre as they conversed about their likely fate. Some thought they would be shipped to France as cannon fodder against the Germans and others believed that they would be transported to the colonies like the convicts of old, or even executed. But some just wanted to die. Con Colbert was still disorientated by the inexplicable turn of events and showed all the symptoms of post-traumatic shock.[38] His will to live had clearly drained away, as a member of his Marrowbone Lane garrison recalled:

He said that from his point of view he would prefer to be executed and said 'We are all ready to meet our God. We had hopes of coming out alive. Now that we are defeated, outside that barrack wall the people whom we have tried to emancipate have demonstrated nothing but hate and contempt for us. We would be better off dead as life would be a torture. We can thank the Mother of God for her kindness in her intercession for us that we have had the time to prepare ourselves to meet our Redeemer.' Colbert then called on us all to recite the Rosary for the spiritual and temporal welfare of those who fought in the cause of Irish Freedom, past, present and future generations.[39]

Next day guards distributed biscuits and tins of bully beef which when empty were used as mugs from which to drink tea. After relays had been taken to the latrines the men were paraded in the square where their names, addresses and occupations were taken from them. They were next marched into the gymnasium hall, a wooden building with a galvanised and glass roof. Inside they were ordered to sit on the floor in rows of ten, facing a partition half wood and half glass. Behind it they could see themselves being scrutinised by detectives from the G Division of the Dublin Metropolitan Police. After a while the detectives entered the gymnasium and walked among the prisoners, one of them carrying an ashplant walking stick and another an umbrella. As they went they ordered to one side prominent rebels such as MacDermott, Ceannt, Colbert and Major John MacBride.[40]

Meanwhile, with normality returning to the capital, British military platoons were dispatched to the provinces to reinforce the troops already stationed there. The army concentrated on areas which had shown recent signs of discontent, such as Limerick, Cork, Kilkenny and Athlone. Their primary purpose was to complete the pacification of the country by apprehending rebel bands still at large. They also co-operated closely with local police and intelligence personnel from Dublin to arrest suspects and compel the surrender of weapons. In addition, the troops carried out route marches with large numbers of men and heavy weaponry designed to 'make the rebels furiously to think'.[41] Smoke from the field kitchens caused them to be mistaken for 'poison gas machines'.[42] It was during one such clearing-up operation in County Cork on 2 May, at 3.45 a.m., that an RIC party went to Bawnard House, Castle Lyons, to arrest two prominent local dissidents, Thomas and David Kent. They lived in the family home with two other brothers, Richard and William, and their 84-year-old mother. Head Constable Rowe kicked at the front door which the occupants were ordered to open. According to police reports, a voice inside replied: 'We will not surrender, we will leave some of you dead' and three shots were fired, the last of which 'blew the face off' Rowe. In the ensuing gun battle David Kent was gravely injured until at 4.50 a.m. the family offered to surrender on condition that a priest was summoned. They subsequently threw out their arms, but there was a considerable delay whilst military assistance was summoned from Fermoy, 4 miles away, in order to prevent an escape. After the soldiers arrived at 6.00 a.m., the Kents emerged but Richard made a dash for freedom and was shot dead before he had gone 25 yards. Both Thomas and William Kent were subsequently court-martialled in Cork, and charged with having taken part in 'armed Rebellion'.[43]

A total of 3,430 men and 79 women were arrested after the Rising – a considerable number in relation to the scale of the outbreak. Of these, 1,424 men and 73 women were released after inquiry. The civil servant who assessed the women (apart from Markievicz) in Kilmainham Gaol who were suitable for release was met by behaviour which varied from truculence to tearfulness. He claimed that, apart from the five whom he decided to detain, none knew for what they were fighting but had been impelled to participate by poverty, a sense of 'excitement' and a feeling it was 'something to be in'.[44] Maxwell was delighted by this apparent absence of real ideological motivation because he had been at a loss as to what to do with 'all those silly little girls'.[45] He agreed to send them home while the handful kept in custody were soon transferred to England. Of the 1,836 men who were also sent to be interned in England, 1,272 were soon released after it was decided that they were low-level dupes of the rebel leadership. Most of the rest were freed by Christmas 1916 and the final batch were let out under a general amnesty in July 1917.[46]

There were 186 men and 1 woman, Markievicz, who had been selected for courts-martial, all but four of which took place in Dublin. Such trials were not a new experience for Irishmen in 1916, because out of 2,912 traceable death sentences passed by British courts-martial during the First World War 221 were passed on Irish soldiers. Even though they constituted only 2 per cent of the British Army,

Irishmen were the recipients of 8 per cent of the death sentences passed.[47] One historian has argued that this disproportionate harshness derived from a belief that the Irish 'needed firm, perhaps even harsh, handling. The Easter Rising . . . merely confirmed the British in their preconceived ideas, concerns and fears about Irish reliability.'[48] The Irish courts-martial of the rebels consisted of a panel of judges, comprising three officers who were not required to have been legally trained. Any death sentence passed by them required a unanimous verdict which could not be carried out until it had been confirmed by Maxwell. Before the accused knew their fate there would be an unavoidable delay which could last from a few hours to several days. Brigadier-General Charles Blackader presided at over half of the cases held in Dublin in which the death sentence was recommended and later confirmed. The prosecuting counsel was William Wylie, the son of an Ulster Presbyterian minister. Although he had helped suppress the Rising as a member of Trinity College's OTC, Wylie was strongly opposed to the speed and secrecy of the trials, but his proposal to allow defendants access to a defence counsel was rebuffed by the Irish Attorney-General. Nevertheless, after MacDonagh's trial on 2 May, he succeeded in enabling them to call witnesses.[49]

All but two of the courts-martial which resulted in execution took place at Richmond Barracks. This could accommodate a substantial number of prisoners and was also close to Maxwell's residence in the Royal Hospital. The two exceptions were Thomas Kent, who faced his charges in Cork Detention Barracks, and James Connolly, who, propped up in bed, was tried in the Red Cross Hospital at Dublin Castle after passing a medical examination. After what Maxwell described as an 'unavoidable delay', the courts-martial began on Tuesday 2 May, when thirty cases had been prepared for consideration.[50] Those of Pearse and MacDonagh were due to have been held on the previous day. The hearings in Richmond Barracks began in two adjacent rooms and one defendant described his court as 'crowded in a very small room, with quite a lot of

office furniture and the witnesses had to sidle in and out'.[51]
The trials of those later executed took place between 2 and 9
May, but in some cases the official court records either fail to
make clear the precise date or give more than one date.
Nevertheless, the sequence broadly followed the number
allocated to each of the accused (except Connolly) at
Richmond Barracks immediately after the surrender. These
suggest no obvious sequence – Daly was number 21, the lowest
apart from Patrick Pearse; Willie Pearse was 27, whilst
Connolly and MacDermott were 90 and 91 respectively, the
highest-numbered of the rebels to be executed and, of course,
the last. As far as can be determined, the trial dates were:
Patrick Pearse, MacDonagh and Clarke on 2 May; Daly, Willie
Pearse, O'Hanrahan and Plunkett on 3 May; MacBride, Kent
and Heuston on 4 May; Ceannt probably on 4 May; Mallin and
Colbert on 4 or 5 May; Connolly and MacDermott on 9 May.[52]

The official record of proceedings confirms that all faced
the same central charge, which in most if not all cases was
handed to them in advance of the trial. It alleged that they
'did an act, to wit did take part in an armed rebellion and in
the waging of war against His Majesty the King, such act
being of such a nature as to be calculated to be prejudicial to
the defence of the realm, being done with the intention and
for the purpose of assisting the enemy'. In several cases an
alternative charge was added that they 'did attempt to cause
disaffection among the civil population of His Majesty'.[53]
With the exception of Willie Pearse all of the defendants
pleaded not guilty. Ned Daly later explained to his sister that
'he had protested strongly against the part of the charge
about "assisting the enemy", that all he did . . . was for
Ireland, his own land'.[54] When one rebel attempted to plead
guilty to just one part of the charge ('did take part in an
armed rebellion'), he was told that this was inadmissible.[55]

Each of the fifteen was faced with broadly similar types of
evidence. The witnesses for the prosecution were frequently
military officers captured by the rebels during the Rising.
These were able to identify the accused and describe their
actions as well as detailing whether they were in positions of

command, had fired at Crown forces, etc. Others were able to testify whether at the time of surrender the defendant had been armed, had led out a body of men and what rank he had given to his captors. Police officers, and in McDermott's case a prison warder, were also called to provide information about the person's past involvement in extreme nationalism. This involvement could range from their participation in route marches to the frequency of their visits to Liberty Hall or the headquarters of the Irish Volunteers. Documentary evidence was also produced. This included dispatches sent during the Rising (such as one in which MacBride was designated 'Commandant'),[56] Connolly's note to Heuston ordering him to 'seize Mendicity at all costs',[57] Patrick Pearse's letter to his mother, dated 1 May, and the Proclamation itself.[58] Thomas Kent's trial in Cork was distinctive in that three of the RIC members involved in the gun battle at his home gave evidence, and also two of the military officers summoned by the police to supervise the family's surrender.[59]

The fifteen rebels responded in various ways to the prosecution evidence. A few called witnesses in their own defence. Most cross-examined the prosecution witnesses and invariably forced them to concede that, if they had been held captive, they had been well treated. The prosecution evidence was at times misleading and inaccurate. An army officer described seeing Ceannt at the head of rebels in St Patrick's Park after the surrender and describing himself as 'Commandant' and strongly implying that he had been active in Jacob's Factory. Ceannt had actually been in command at the South Dublin Union and among his three defence witnesses he called John MacBride who stated categorically that Ceannt had not been located in Jacob's during the Rising. Ceannt also denied assisting the enemy and argued that no evidence to support such a charge had been produced. He concluded with an appeal: 'I claim . . . there is reasonable doubt and the benefit of the doubt should be given to the accused.'[60] Ceannt appears to have decided to exploit every discrepancy in the prosecution case to achieve an acquittal on technical grounds. A member of his battalion records Ceannt coaching him and other prisoners in Richmond Barracks on how to rebut the cases against them.[61]

The evidence at MacBride's trial confirmed that he had no foreknowledge of the Rising. Two army officers noted that at the surrender in St Patrick's Park he was not in uniform and MacBride himself testified that he had left home on Easter Monday morning to meet his brother, at whose wedding he was to be best man. He said that at Stephen's Green he met a column of Volunteers led by MacDonagh, who told him that a rebellion was underway and invited him to participate. MacBride declared that, 'I knew there was no chance of success and I never advised or influenced any other person to join. [At Jacob's] I was appointed second in command and I felt it my duty to occupy that position.' He concluded by pointing out that 'I could have escaped from Jacob's Factory after the surrender had I desired, but I considered it a dishonourable thing to do.'[62] Blackader, who presided over the proceedings, thought him the 'most soldierly' of the defendants.[63] MacBride also called as a witness Mrs Fred Allan, his landlady for some years, who confirmed that he had left home on Easter Monday to meet his brother for lunch at the Wicklow Hotel.

Several rebel leaders made no statement in their defence. None is attributed to Sean MacDermott, and Con Colbert merely stated 'I have nothing to say.'[64] Clarke told his wife that he had made no statement from the dock and had treated the proceedings as a farce, and his icy contempt for his accusers is confirmed by Wylie who thought him 'calm and brave' throughout.[65] Plunkett, perhaps constrained by ill-health, likewise declared he had nothing to say in his defence and merely offered a brief clarification of a point about the Proclamation.[66] However, others made short statements from the dock. MacDonagh commented: 'I did everything I could to assist the officers in the matter of the surrender, telling them where the arms and ammunition were after the surrender was decided on.'[67] After reflecting on this speech he concluded that his words might be later misinterpreted as having been a plea for mercy and drew up a statement the following day which said that, 'I made no appeal, no recantation, no apology for my acts. In what I said I merely claimed that I acted honourably . . . in all that I set myself to do.'[68] In June 1916, 10,000 copies of a speech purporting to be that made by MacDonagh in court were produced in Dublin and led to prosecutions against three printers and a newsagent. The contents, however, appear to have been entirely bogus.[69] During his trial William Pearse was identified by a military officer held captive in the GPO as 'an officer, but I do not know his rank'.[70] Despite later assertions that he condemned himself in court by exaggerating his own role in the Rising, Willie is officially recorded as saying simply and honestly: 'I had no authority or say in the arrangements for the starting of the rebellion. I was throughout only a personal attaché to my brother, Patrick Pearse. I had no direct command.'[71] His sole distinction was that he pleaded guilty to the charges.

Judging by the official record, both Daly and Mallin made determined attempts to evade the bullets of a firing squad. But although they fought hard to save their lives, they adopted very different strategies to achieve this goal. Daly testified that he was pleading not guilty because he had no dealings with any outside forces. Furthermore, while he did not deny that he held the position of commandant at the Four Courts he depicted himself as having been taken completely by surprise when the Rising commenced. Once it had started he claimed that he only participated in the imbroglio through an overriding sense of loyalty. He told the court that he 'had no knowledge of the insurrection until Monday morning, April 24. The officers, including myself, when we heard the news, held a meeting, and decided that the whole thing was foolish but that being under orders we had no option but to obey.'[72] By contrast, Mallin's version of events portrays himself as a simple foot soldier, a silk weaver, band instructor and drill instructor in the Citizen Army. His statement, almost every word of which was untrue, sought to exculpate himself as someone who was simply following his superior's orders:

I had no command in the Citizen Army. I was never taken into the confidence of James Connolly. I was under the impression that we were going out for manoeuvres on Sunday, but something altered the arrangement and the manoeuvres were postponed till Monday. I had verbal instruction from James Connolly to take 36 men to St Stephen's Green and to report to the Volunteer officer there. Shortly after my arrival at St Stephen's Green, the firing started and the Countess of Markievicz [sic] ordered me to take command of the men. As I had been so long associated with them, I felt I could not leave them and from that time I joined the rebellion. I made it my business to save all the officers and civilians who were brought into Stephen's Green. I gave explicit orders to the men to make no offensive movement. I prevented them attacking the Shelbourne Hotel.[73]

L.J. Kettle, who had been kept prisoner in the College of Surgeons, was called as a defence witness and stated that he had been treated with every possible consideration when held captive, but also confirmed that 'Mallin appeared to be in command'.[74]

Mallin's testimony concerning Markievicz completely reversed the relationship which had actually existed between them during the Rising. It was also potentially lethal to her because it literally placed in the firing line someone who had served him loyally throughout Easter Week. In view of the grim predicament in which Mallin now found himself it is perfectly understandable that he would have manoeuvred desperately to save his life. Perhaps also, Mallin believed that if the court accepted his evidence, it would never execute a woman in his place. Nevertheless, it was a tremendous gamble with a comrade's life and hardly a chivalrous one. Another defendant who fought hard at his trial was Sean Heuston, who challenged the validity of the documentary evidence produced by the prosecuting counsel. He claimed that 'the message in the notebook produced saying "I hope we will be able to do better next time" is not mine. The order from Connolly addressed to "Captain Houston" is not addressed to me as my name is "Heuston".'[75] He also complained that he had received no intimation of the nature of the charge against him until that very morning. In the case of Thomas Kent in Cork, he denied all the charges relating to the gun battle at his home near Fermoy. He told the court that;

> On 2 May 1916 during the night I was awakened by the sound of firearms and I immediately went into my mother's room, where my brother William was. They were standing on the bed in the corner of the room. I immediately went into the corner where they were, where the three of us remained till the military officers arrived when we immediately surrendered. I never fired or had arms in my hand.[76]

He offered no explanation as to who had fired the fatal shots from the house. The remainder of the defendants issued impressive statements at their trials. Michael O'Hanrahan, who had been seen at Richmond Barracks after the surrender with his brother, crying together in each other's arms, stated boldly and simply, 'As a soldier of the Republican Army, acting under orders of that Republic duly constituted, I acted under orders of my superiors.'[77] It was appropriate that two of his 'superiors' should have made the most substantial declarations, James Connolly and Patrick Pearse.

The prosecution evidence against Connolly came from two military officers who had been prisoners in the Post Office throughout the Rising and described him as being in a position of command. Major de Courcy Wheeler also recounted Connolly's acceptance of Pearse's surrender order and two of his dispatches were also produced. When he had completed his cross-examination, Connolly produced a prepared hand-written statement, a copy of which he gave to his daughter, Nora, just before his execution. It read:

> I do not wish to make any defence except against charges of wanton cruelty to prisoners [one witness alleged that he

had been tied up in a telephone box for three hours]. These trifling allegations that have been made in that direction, if they record facts that really happened, deal only with the almost unavoidable incidents of a hurried uprising and overthrowing of long established authorities and nowhere show evidence of a set purpose to wantonly injure unarmed prisoners. We went out to break the connection between this Country and the British Empire and to establish an Irish Republic. We believe that the call we thus issued to the people of Ireland was a nobler call in a holier cause than any call issued to them during this war having any connection with the war. We succeeded in proving that Irishmen are ready to die endeavouring to win for Ireland their national rights which the British government had been asking them to die to win for Belgium. As long as that remains the case the cause of Irish freedom is safe. Believing that the British government has no right in Ireland and never had any right in Ireland and never can have any right in Ireland, the presence in any one generation of even a respectable minority of Irishmen ready to die to affirm that truth makes that government for ever a usurpation and a crime against human progress. I personally thank God that I have lived to see the day when thousands of Irishmen and boys and hundreds of Irish women and girls were equally ready to affirm that truth and seal it with their lives if necessary.[78]

Pearse was escorted from Arbour Hill Detention Barracks to Richmond Barracks for his trial on the morning of 2 May. The prosecution witnesses were a policeman who had seen him acting in command of Irish Volunteers and an army officer who had witnessed his surrender to General Lowe. Another officer testified that, on 1 May at Arbour Hill, he had seen Pearse write a letter which was now entered in evidence. Pearse had intended it for his mother but it had been withheld by the military authorities – a contingency he must surely have taken into account, but about which he obviously did not care. Those military authorities had underlined the section which stated 'I understand that the German expedition which I was counting on actually set sail but was defeated by the British.'[79] It was also clear from the document that it assumed that he would be executed but his brother Willie would survive. Pearse did not call any defence witnesses, but standing in his Volunteer uniform stated:

> My sole object in 'surrendering unconditionally' was to save the slaughter of the civilian population; and to save the lives of our followers, <u>who had been led into this thing by us</u>. It is my hope that the British government who has shown its strength will also be magnanimous and spare the lives and give an amnesty to my followers as I am one of the persons <u>chiefly responsible</u>, have acted as Commander in Chief and President of the Provisional Government. I am prepared to take the consequences of my act, but I should like my followers to have an amnesty. I went down on my knees as a child and told God that I would work all my life to gain the freedom of Ireland. I have divined it my duty as an Irishman to fight for the freedom of my Country. <u>I admit I have organised men to fight against Britain. I admit having opened negotiations with Germany. We have kept our word with her and as far as I can see she did her part to help us. She sent a ship with arms. Germany has not sent us gold.</u>[80]

The parts of his speech thought most incriminating were subsequently underlined by the military authorities. William Wylie later described it as a 'Robert Emmet type' speech.[81]

Pearse's fearlessness and eloquence clearly made a deep impression on the men who held his life in their hands. Blackader, who presided at his court-martial, dined occasionally with the Countess of Fingall, who found him a 'charming, sympathetic person, half French, very emotional, and terribly affected by the work he had to do'.[82] On one occasion he told her, in relation to Pearse, 'I have just done one of the hardest tasks I have ever had to do. I have had to condemn to death one of the finest characters I have ever come across. There must be something very wrong in the state of things that makes a man like that a rebel. I don't wonder that his pupils adored him.'[83] However, Brigadier Maconchy, who presided over the trials of Mallin, Plunkett, Heuston and Willie Pearse, was less impressed by the demeanour of the defendants. He later wrote:

> We tried a very large number. There could be no doubt, on the evidence before us, of the only sentence permissible but of course it rested with the confirming officer to decide as to the carrying out of the sentence and it is possible that referment was also made to the Cabinet in London. We could only recommend certain cases for mercy. When called on for their defence they generally only convicted themselves out of their own mouths, and in many cases I refused to put down what they said as it only made their case worse. During the trial of one of the ringleaders, his whole attitude seemed so strange to me that I asked him if he would mind telling me, quite apart from his trial, what he was fighting for. He drew himself up and said, 'I was fighting to defend the rights of the people of Ireland.' I then asked him if anyone was attacking these rights and he said, 'No, but they might have been.' This seemed a strange excuse for shooting down innocent citizens in the streets, but I presume that is the fashion in all rebellions against constitutional authority.[84]

The court-martial proceedings continued apace throughout much of May. The largest number, thirty-six, was held on 4 May, when Markievicz was tried. Wylie found her performance a repellent and undignified spectacle. She 'did not impress me and the court'. They had expected that she would make a scene and throw things at the Judge and counsel.

> In fact [Wylie adds] I saw the general getting out his revolver and putting it on the table beside him. But he need not have troubled for she curled up completely. 'I am only a woman,' she cried, 'and you cannot shoot a woman, you

must not shoot a woman.' She never stopping moaning the whole time she was in the courtroom. . . . She crumpled up . . . I think we all felt slightly disgusted, [at a person who] had been preaching to a lot of silly boys, death and glory, die for your Country etc., and yet she was literally crawling. I won't say anymore; it revolts me still.[85]

However, the official record of Markievicz's trial shows that she acted bravely and with characteristic defiance throughout. She pleaded not guilty to the charge that she 'did . . . take part in an armed rebellion . . . for the purpose of assisting the enemy', but guilty to having attempted 'to cause disaffection among the civilian population of His Majesty'. When speaking in her own defence, she retracted nothing, stating simply: 'I went out to fight for Ireland's freedom and it does not matter what happens to me. I did what I thought was right and I stand by it'.[86] Wylie's wilful and indeed scurrilous distortion of her response at her trial is difficult to interpret. It may reflect his own personal sense of irritation at her self-assurance and boldness, which he may have interpreted as an insult to the court. Perhaps it is indicative of deep-rooted sexual prejudice and rank misogyny on his part. More likely, his fictitious account sprang above all, from a feeling that the Countess had by her actions betrayed both her religion and her class – the Protestant Ascendancy; she had been presented at court to Queen Victoria during her Jubilee Year, 1887.

Of the 186 men and 1 woman court-martialled, 11 were acquitted and 176 convicted; of these the official courts martial registers contain details of 88 sentences of 'death by being shot'. The verdict in Markievicz's case was unique: 'Guilty. Death by being shot. The court recommends the prisoner to mercy solely and onlt on account of her sex'.[87] The final decision as to whether to confirm or commute the sentence of the court lay with Maxwell and he was under considerable pressure to impose severe punishment. The pro-Union *Irish Times* demanded that 'Sedition must be rooted out of Ireland once and for all' and the *Irish Independent*, voice of Catholic business interests, said, 'Let the worst of the ringleaders be singled out and dealt with.'[88] Maxwell was later castigated for a lack of wisdom and foresight and accused of having 'lost Ireland for the British'.[89] He certainly believed that the rebel leaders should be executed and wrote that 'some must suffer for their crimes'.[90] He told Asquith on 9 May that because of the rebellion's seriousness, the loss of life and destruction of property and the involvement of the Germans, he believed that it had been essential to 'inflict the most severe sentences on the known organizers of this detestable Rising. . . . It is hoped that these examples will be sufficient to act as a deterrent to intriguers and to bring home to them that the murder of His Majesty's subjects or other acts calculated to imperil the safety of the realm will not be tolerated.'[91] By 10 May Maxwell had confirmed in fifteen cases the court-martial verdict of death by firing squad.

Apart from Thomas Kent, everyone sentenced to death was transferred to Kilmainham Gaol to await Maxwell's confirmation or commutation of their sentence. Kilmainham Gaol had been built over a century before and although it had catered for common convicts the 'Irish Bastille' was closely linked with defeated and incarcerated Irish rebels. Its inmates had included Henry Joy McCracken, one of the leaders of the 1798 Rebellion, and Robert Emmet in 1803; and five Invincibles who had killed the Chief Secretary for Ireland in 1882 were executed in Kilmainham. The gaol had ceased to operate as a convict prison in 1911 and had been taken over by the army for use as a detention barracks for military prisoners. The prison lacked even basic amenities. The cells were almost devoid of furniture; there were ground-sheets on the floor, buckets for waste disposal, poor lighting from candles or naked gas flames and the walls were shabby and grey.[92] The most significant part of the gaol now was the former stonebreakers' yard where any executions would take place.

On 2 May Brigadier J. Young had laid down the procedure

by which any executions were to be conducted. He specified that the condemned men were to be segregated beforehand and that motor cars were to be provided, if desired, to bring relatives or friends to the condemned man's cell for a final farewell or a chaplain for religious comfort. All but the priest were to leave before 3.30 a.m. when the first firing squad would parade. The first prisoner was to be brought out at 3.45 a.m. Not every account of the final minutes of the condemned men is completely clear but it seems that as they reached a long corridor which ran down to the execution yard they were blindfolded, their hands were tied behind their backs and a white piece of cloth was pinned just above their hearts. This procedure was probably regarded as the most efficient because it prevented the condemned man from entering the execution yard unrestrained, seeing the firing party, panicking and putting up strong physical resistance. Instead they were to be guided to the end of the corridor and through the door into the stonebreakers' yard. Young's instructions confirm the veracity of the cinematic cliché that firing squads waiting there for the condemned men were never supposed to know who fired the fatal shot. The twelve soldiers were to have their rifles loaded behind their backs and one of the weapons was to have a blank cartridge inserted. The soldiers were to have this arrangement explained to them by the officer in charge of each of the four firing squads on duty who were to be arranged in two rows of six with the front row kneeling and the back row standing. They were to fire at a visual signal from the officer in charge and execute the condemned men at a distance of ten paces. At least some, and possibly all, were shot sitting on a soap-box. Afterwards they were to be certified as dead by a medical officer and have a name label pinned to their breasts. The bodies would then be removed immediately to an ambulance, which, when full, was to drive to Arbour Hill Barracks where they were to be put in a grave alongside one another, covered in quicklime and the grave filled. One of the officers with the party was to keep a note of the identity of each body that was placed in the grave and a priest was to attend the funeral service.[93] The stipulation about the remains came from the very top because, from the outset, Maxwell was determined that the bodies of the executed men would not be released to their families. He feared that, 'Irish sentimentality will turn those graves into martyrs' shrines to which annual processions etc will be made. [Hence] the executed rebels are to be buried in quicklime, without coffins.'[94]

Once Maxwell had confirmed the death sentence officers were dispatched to Kilmainham to inform the condemned men. They were allowed to write last letters to family and friends, to receive visits and to have religious comfort.

They were also allowed to hand over mementoes; both MacDermott and Daly, for instance, cut off buttons from their clothes. The conditions in the cells were very depressing. Daly's family arrived to find him sleeping on the floor with a dog biscuit lying beside him. One of Michael O'Hanrahan's sisters recalls that she;

> asked Michael had he had anything to eat. He said he had been given bully-beef at 4 o'clock. (That was some ten hours before.) I asked had he even had a drink of water. He hadn't. . . . I demanded – I was desperate – that a drink of water be brought to him. I was surprised at the speed with which my request was answered. One of the soldiers rushed off and came back in no time with water in a black billy-can. Michael drank it from the can.[95]

The first three, Pearse, Clarke and MacDonagh, had been brought to Kilmainham during the evening of 2 May and were kept in separate rooms under observation throughout the night. In his final hours Pearse received Holy Communion from Father Aloysius and was delighted to hear that Connolly had received Holy Communion. Pearse exclaimed: 'Thank God. It is one thing I was anxious about.'[96] Pearse then completed his correspondence. In a letter to Willie whom he clearly expected to survive, he said, 'No-one can ever have had so true a brother as you.'[97] Unlike others, Pearse received no visits from his family. In his last letter to his mother he wrote that he had been hoping to see her one last time but it appears that the military transport sent to collect her turned back because of the continuing unrest in the city. The letter concluded:

I have just received Holy Communion. I am happy except for the great grief of parting from you. This is the death I should have asked for if God had given me the choice of all deaths – to die a soldier's death for Ireland and for freedom.

We have done right. People will say hard things of us now, but later on they will praise us. Do not grieve for all this, but think of it as a sacrifice which God asked of me and of you.

Good-bye again, dear, dear Mother. May God bless you for your great love for me and for your great faith, and may He remember all that you have so bravely suffered. I hope soon to see Papa, and in a little while we shall all be together again.

Wow-Wow [Pearse's sister Margaret], Willie, Mary Brigid and Mother, good-bye. I have not words to tell my love of you, and how my heart yearns to you all. I will call to you in my heart at the last moment.[98]

Clarke was visited at the end by his wife, who found him 'in a most exalted state of mind' but still fulminating against the 'treachery' of MacNeill who had clearly replaced Hobson as his *bête noire*. He also spoke of his relief that he was to be executed because his great dread had been that he might be returned to prison to repeat the hell of his previous incarceration.[99] MacDonagh was visited by his sister and Father Aloysius who recorded that when she left she flung her rosary around his neck. Between 2 and 3 a.m. all visitors were told to leave, despite Aloysius's insistence that clergymen were excluded from the order. Next morning he lodged an official complaint that priests should be permitted to stay with the prisoners, be present at the execution and administer extreme unction. The protest was successful and his proposals were adopted at the remaining executions.[100]

These first three executions were conducted by Major H.

Heathcote, the officer in charge of prisoners There was a delay because Brigadier Maconchy, who was responsible for verifying that all papers were in order, discovered that they had not been signed. He refused to allow matters to continue until the signature of someone in authority had been secured. The executions finally got underway between 3.30 and 4.00 a.m. on 3 May, when it was as light as at 5.00 or 5.30 a.m. today. The brightness was due to the fact that daylight saving did not come into operation until 21 May 1916 and GMT was not introduced into Ireland until 1917. The hands of Pearse, Clarke and MacDonagh had been bound behind their backs and they had also been blindfolded. The firing squad which was provided by the 59th Division readied itself and then shot when ordered. The Division's official history records that the three men all met their fate bravely. For whatever reason, the instructions were not carried out to the letter and no labels were affixed to the bodies.[101]

On 3 May fifteen rebels were sentenced to death and Maxwell confirmed the verdict in the cases of Willie Pearse, Ned Daly, Michael O'Hanrahan and Joseph Plunkett. Each was attended by a priest prior to his execution. Willie Pearse, who was also visited by his mother and sister, had failed to see Patrick before his execution, though he heard the fatal volley.[102] Daly, who had fought hard and unsuccessfully for his life, had now reconciled himself to his fate, which he faced in the final hours with courage and dignity. He received three of his sisters, including Mrs Clarke, and they found him 'glad and proud to die for his country'.[103] As they departed a British officer told them that they had his deepest sympathy but that he simply could not understand their attitudes and behaviour. O'Hanrahan's sisters arrived at Kilmainham after receiving a message sent in error that their brother wanted to see them before being deported to England. Only when they arrived were they advised by the Dalys to prepare for the worst. Hours before his death Plunkett had married Grace Gifford, a former Protestant whom he had come to know well during 1915 through their shared and intense interest in Roman Catholicism, which had led to a breach with her parents. They had become engaged in December 1915 but when she suggested an Easter wedding Plunkett warned her that 'We may be running a revolution then.' Later he suggested Easter Sunday so that they could go into the Rising together but a friend had bungled the arrangements and the priest did not read the banns. After the surrender Plunkett wrote to Grace proposing that they get married by proxy so that she would inherit his possessions. However, when she heard of the first three executions she had a premonition that Joseph would also be shot so she hurriedly secured the requisite papers from a priest, got a ring and went to Kilmainham. She was taken to the chapel and placed in front of the altar till Plunkett was escorted in by British soldiers. She observed that he was calm and completely unfrightened. When his handcuffs were removed the chaplain conducted the ceremony but afterwards they were allowed no private conversation whatever; the handcuffs were replaced and Plunkett was taken away. Grace saw her husband briefly one last time that evening. A British guard who stood with a watch told them 'Ten minutes' but Grace's conversation ran out altogether. Just before his execution Plunkett was reportedly in high spirits. He is said to have informed a priest moments before stepping in front of the firing squad, 'Father, I am very happy. I am dying for the glory of God and the honour of Ireland.'[104]

All four men were executed between 4.00 a.m. and 4.30 a.m. on 4 May. Their bodies were then brought to Arbour Hill and buried against an east-facing wall, alongside the three leaders who had already been interred there the previous morning. Patrick Pearse's grave was first in line, followed by those of MacDonagh, Clarke, Daly, O'Hanrahan, Willie Pearse and finally Plunkett. This was probably also the sequence in which they had faced the firing squad.[105]

Major John MacBride, who was executed at 3.47 a.m. on 5 May, went to his death with the same stylish indifference which he had displayed ever since the surrender at Jacob's Factory. According to Father Augustine, who was with him at the end, his request not to be blindfolded or have his hands bound was rejected. Tom Kettle, who was close by at the time, then overheard MacBride saying to the soldiers, 'Fire away, I've been looking down the barrels of rifles all my life.' Kettle described the remark as 'a lie, but a magnificent lie. He had been looking down the necks of porter bottles all his life.'[106] MacBride's estranged wife, Maud Gonne, who was living with their son in Paris, was reported by the British Special Branch as having first learnt of his execution from the morning newspapers, after which she promptly donned mourning clothes.[107]

Sean Heuston, Michael Mallin, Con Colbert and Eamonn Ceannt were executed between 3.45 a.m. and 4.05 a.m. on Monday 8 May. They had been transported to Kilmainham after their trials, probably on the evening of 5 May. There they attended Holy Communion on Sunday and heard later that Maxwell had confirmed their death sentence. That night they occupied four adjacent cells on the ground floor of the central compound beside the execution yard and their religious needs were met by the Capuchin priests from Church Street.[108] Heuston was visited by members of his family shortly before his death and his cousin Theresa recorded that a 'soldier holding a lighted candle was in the cell with them. He was young and deeply affected. He was crying.'[109] They could also hear weeping in the adjoining cell where Mallin was taking farewell of his pregnant wife, his four children and his sister and brothers. His 12-year-old son Seamus recalled that when they reached the prison;

There was a big dark hall; policemen and soldiers all around us. There was hardly a word spoken, and when there was, it was very hushed. We were led through a low doorway on the left hand side, each door exactly like the other. I noticed a light, like a yellow candle-flame, behind a half-opened door and I heard mumbling as if the Rosary was being said.[110]

When they were shown in to Mallin's cell they saw him with a subdued smile on his face and a small blanket wrapped around his shoulders. A tall solemn priest, Father

Brown, was standing beside him. Mallin requested that they burn a woollen picture which he had made of the flags and drums of the Royal Fusiliers, the regiment in which he had spent twelve years as a drummer. However, when Brown, who found Mallin 'serene, though very much affected', said that one should only have charitable thoughts when going to meet God, Mallin laughed and immediately agreed.[111]

Colbert had retreated into his own private world and obviously believed that the only way to maintain control of his emotions was by avoiding highly charged scenes. He did not send for any of his family and in one of ten letters which he wrote in his last hours he explained to a sister that any meeting between them 'would grieve us both too much'.[112]

Eamonn Ceannt also faced death with courage and dignity, but with some regrets. In a statement, dated 7 May, he wrote, 'I leave for the guidance of other Irish Revolutionaries who may tread the path which I have trod this advice, never to treat with the enemy, never to surrender at his mercy, but to fight to a finish.'[113] He was calm when he received his family. His brother Michael recalled that he had never seen him looking so well in a Volunteer uniform, his moustache trimmed and his face tanned and healthy. The two sentries in the cell allowed Ceannt to spend most of the time talking to his wife and even to kiss her. A few minutes before their time was up, Ceannt mentioned that his priest, Father McCarthy, had hinted that there was hope of a reprieve and that sympathetic soldiers had said such remarks as 'It's a Long Way to Tipperary'. But it was clear to Michael that Ceannt, who was speaking in a matter-of-fact but strained manner, knew there was no hope and only wanted to keep his mother's spirits up. Finally the sentries mentioned kindly that the family had to leave and after a few more words Ceannt said he had asked for Father Augustine but that he had not yet come. When the sentry was told this he offered to intercede with his commander and this appeared to please Ceannt, who kissed his wife once more before they left. Michael later recalled that;

After we left the cell and before the sentry shut the door I looked back at poor Ned and that picture I shall bear with me to the end. He stood sideways, right side towards me, the candle showing him up clearly from the external darkness, looking down at the little table where he had been writing, wrapped in thought, silent, a pucker at the base of his forehead, just at the nose. My heart welled up with infinite pity for him.[114]

Before the door was closed Michael cried out, '*Beannacht de Leat*' (God's blessing with you) to which Ceannt replied, '*Go soirbhidh Dia duit.*' (May God favour you). Just before Ceannt was led out to be shot Father Augustine arrived and he said to Michael the following day that he had told Eamonn, 'When you fall, Eamonn, I'll run out and anoint you.' Ceannt replied, 'Oh, Oh. That will be a grand consolation, Father.'[115] Ceannt, who was asked to sit on a soap-box, was blindfolded and had his hands tied. He complied with a request from a British officer to stretch out his legs. Then the firing squad took aim and shot him dead. Augustine remembered that 'When poor Ceannt tumbled over from the soap-box I stooped to take the crucifix which he was bearing in his hands and I saw that it was spattered with blood.'[116]

Thomas Kent faced the firing squad at Cork Detention Barracks on 9 May, clasping a rosary in his bound hands.[117] Sean MacDermott and James Connolly were the last of the rebel leaders to be shot, both at Kilmainham and both confirmed by Maxwell on 10 May. MacDermott was executed at 3.45 a.m. on 12 May. He was in transcendently high spirits to the end and highly optimistic about the future. On 11 May he wrote to the veteran Fenian John Daly about his imminent death: 'I have nothing to say about this only that I look on it as a part of the day's work. We die that the Irish nation may live. Our blood will rebaptise and reinvigorate the old land. Knowing this it is superfluous to say how happy I feel.'[118] Some had hoped that because there had been a pause in the executions he and Connolly would be spared, but MacDermott never thought this likely. Before his court-martial he had said that they were the only 'Signatories . . . [of the Proclamation] left. We'll be shot.'[119] Those who saw him in his final hours reported that he 'talked to us in a way that was in no way sad . . . about everything under the sun. . . . We had a good laugh. . . . It was ridiculous in a way because there was no sign of mourning.'[120]

Connolly was also executed in the early hours of Friday 12 May. On the previous afternoon the Capuchin priest, Father Aloysius, had visited a feverish Connolly who told him that he had not slept the previous night. They agreed that Aloysius would return on Friday morning to hear Connolly's confession and give him Holy Communion. But at 9 p.m. on Thursday Aloysius was suddenly informed that his services would be needed for early Friday morning and a military vehicle came to collect him at 1 a.m. At the same time an army lorry brought Connolly's wife and his daughter Nora to Dublin Castle Hospital. Nora remembered an eerie journey through streets deserted because of the curfew and the smell of burning from O'Connell Street.

> When we were shown in Papa said: 'Well, Lily, I suppose you know what this means?' She said: 'Oh, no, Jim. Oh no!' and he said: 'Yes, lovie,' and then Mama broke down sobbing, with her head on the bed. Papa said, 'I fell asleep for the first time tonight and they wakened me up at eleven and told me I was to die at dawn.' Mama said: 'Oh no!' again, and then crying bitterly, 'But your beautiful life, Jim, your beautiful life!' and he said: 'Wasn't it a full life, Lily, and isn't this a good end?' And she still cried and he said: 'Look, Lily, please don't cry. You will unman me.'[121]

Connolly's isolation from the other leaders had kept him ignorant of their fate and he fell silent when he learnt of their executions; he had expected to be the first to face the firing squad. Eventually he told them: 'Well, I am glad that I am going with them.' When Nora told him that the papers were speculating that there would be no more executions Connolly replied, 'England's promises, Nora, you and I know what they mean.'[122]

In fact, Maxwell had been coming under increasing political pressure to stop the executions. On 9 May, the day of Connolly's trial, he had complained to his wife, 'Now that the rebellion is over . . . the government is getting very cold feet and afraid. They are at me every moment not to overdo the death sentences. I never intended to but some must suffer.'[123] An uneasy Asquith had already instructed him on 28 April not to use extreme measures except in emergency cases and after the first executions the Prime Minister indicated that he was a 'little surprised and perturbed by the drastic action of shooting so many rebel leaders'.[124] After eight rebels had been shot, Maxwell told the cabinet on 6 May of the situation in Ireland and disclosed that he had commuted Markievicz's death sentence to penal servitude for life. Afterwards, Asquith told King George V that Maxwell had been instructed not to execute any woman (Markievicz was the only woman court-martialled) but that he had been given a general discretion to act as he saw fit, provided that only ringleaders and murderers should be shot and that the executions should not be dragged out.[125] On 10 May Maxwell confirmed the courts-martial verdicts on Connolly and MacDermott, but Asquith, who travelled to Dublin on the night of 11 May intervened personally to suspend these executions for one day. Earlier on the 11th Kitchener had written to Maxwell that unless he heard to the contrary from Asquith he could carry out the sentences on the two men. Clearly no further stay of execution came and in both cases it would have been extremely difficult to have argued that Connolly and MacDermott were not ringleaders. Maxwell indeed regarded them as 'the worst of the lot'.[126]

After Father Aloysius had heard Connolly's confession and given him Holy Communion he withdrew while Connolly took a light meal. Just before they left for Kilmainham Aloysius asked Connolly to bear in mind that the men who would execute him were ordinary soldiers obeying orders and that he should feel no anger against them but forgive them. Connolly replied, 'I do, Father. I respect every man who does his duty.'[127] The priest then accompanied Connolly as he was carried in a stretcher down to the van which was to take him to his execution.

In view of Asquith's qualms, Maxwell submitted a memorandum to the Prime Minister to reassure him that the evidence of high crimes against all of the executed men was overwhelming. The document was based in part on the core prosecution evidence at the courts-martial, but information from Special Branch files had clearly been incorporated. Pearse was described as having taken an active role in the Volunteers from their inception, risen to the upper councils of the organisation, signed the Proclamation, was Commandant-General of the Army of the Irish Republic and had assumed the title President of the Provisional Government. His letter of 1 May to his mother was deemed proof that he had been in communication with Germany and that his object had been to defeat England. Clarke was said to have 'exercised a great influence on the younger members of the organization with which he was connected'. Plunkett was described as having misused his good education, because he had 'exercised a great influence for evil' within the Irish Volunteers.[128]

MacDonagh was stated to have been a prominent officer in the Irish Volunteers and a signatory of the Proclamation. He had also signed a document headed 'Army of the Irish Republic' in which he had described himself as 'Commandant-General and member of the Provisional Government of the Irish Republic'. Furthermore he had commanded the rebel garrison in Jacob's Factory.

James Connolly was listed as a prominent leader of the Citizen Army who had signed the Proclamation and in Easter Week had 'held the rank of Commandant General' of the Dublin section of the rebel army. MacDermott was described as 'one of the most prominent of the leaders of the Irish Volunteers' who had signed the Proclamation and in Easter Week had sent out mobilisation orders and dispatches, and had surrendered with a body of rebels in O'Connell Street. Ceannt was stated to be an extremist who was identified with all pro-German movements, was high in the Irish Volunteers and one of the signatories of the Proclamation. Though there had been some confusion in the evidence presented by the prosecution at the trial, it expressly stated that he 'held the rank of Commandant and was in command at the South Dublin Union', where 'British troops suffered heavily [and] . . . was armed at the time of his surrender'. Daly was regarded as one of the most prominent extremists, a commandant in charge at the Four Courts, 'where heavy fighting took place and casualties occurred'. It added that 'he admitted being at the meeting of officers which decided to carry out the orders of the executive council and commence the armed rebellion'.[129]

There has never been any doubt that if executions took place then the signatories of the Proclamation were certain to be shot. As a senior battalion commandant, Daly was also likely to be selected. Nevertheless, considerable controversy has always existed over the execution of the others. Maxwell's memorandum goes far to explain why they were chosen. It claimed that O'Hanrahan was employed at Irish Volunteer headquarters, was one of the organisation's most active members, 'a constant associate with the leaders of the rebellion' and an officer who had been arrested, armed and in uniform. Probably the clincher was that he was alleged to have been in command in an area where there had been heavy fighting and casualties among British troops. But O'Hanrahan had served in Jacob's Factory which had been notoriously inactive during the Rising and only by subsuming Jacob's into a wider area of conflict could Maxwell's statement have been remotely valid. William Pearse, it noted, was 'a brother of Patrick Pearse, the President of the Irish Republic', and it claimed, incorrectly, that he 'held the rank of Commandant in the rebel army' and was 'in the GPO during the fighting and surrendered with the rebels in Sackville Street'. MacBride's past clearly counted heavily against him in the eyes of the British military authorities. Maxwell noted that he had fought on the side of the Boers in command of the Irish Brigade in South Africa. He also alleged, incorrectly, that MacBride had been active in the Irish Volunteer movement when in fact he had never even been a member of the organisation. Maxwell claimed inaccurately that during Easter Week MacBride had held the rank of Commandant in an area where heavy fighting had occurred. He also claimed that it was clear from captured papers that MacBride had been in close touch with the other rebel leaders, sending and receiving dispatches. 'He voluntarily stated at his trial', it was noted, that he had been in 'command of a portion of the rebel forces.'[130]

Despite denials at his trial, Maxwell described Mallin as second-in-command of the Citizen Army, associated with it from the beginning and in command at Stephen's Green and the College of Surgeons, where 'there were many casualties amongst the military and civilians'. Maxwell also stated that Mallin had led the surrender of over 100 armed rebels. In the case of Heuston, Maxwell noted that though his small garrison had surrendered on Easter Wednesday substantial military casualties had been sustained in the fighting there. Colbert was described as one of the most active revolutionaries and a close associate of the rebel leadership. He had been prominent in organising the rebel army in which he had held the rank of captain. Maxwell's assessment of Thomas Kent was brief and specific. 'The man's crime was in effect the murder of a Head Constable . . . shots were fired from the house in the most deliberate manner.' Although in military terms Kent was completely insignificant, what almost certainly earned him the firing squad was that the shoot-out occurred after the rebel surrender. His execution probably served two purposes. It was punishment for an infraction of the rules of warfare and a warning to the population that now that the rebellion was crushed no further opposition would be tolerated.[131]

In view of the document's contents and the criteria by which Maxwell judged execution to be appropriate, de Valera was clearly fortunate to escape the firing squad. He held high rank in the Volunteers as a battalion commandant and his men at Mount Street Bridge had inflicted almost half of the British casualties in the entire Rising. He was lucky that he had been court-martialled as late as 8 May, when government pressure on Maxwell was mounting and representations by the United States Consul in Dublin that de Valera was an American citizen may also have helped. Wylie recorded a conversation with Maxwell who knew nothing of de Valera and asked if he would be likely to cause trouble in the future. Wylie replied, 'I wouldn't think so, sir. I don't think he's important enough. From what I can hear he's not one of the leaders.' Like Markievicz, de Valera was sentenced to death but had the sentence commuted to penal servitude for life.[132]

On 23 May Maxwell noted with evident relief: 'I have got some very tiresome courts-martial on hand but I have nearly got through with the rebels.'[133] The most significant case left was the trial of Eoin MacNeill. MacNeill had written to Maxwell on 2 May, offering to meet him to discuss how to prevent further conflict between Crown forces and the Irish Volunteers. Before establishing contact he had told Hobson that 'We would have no political future, if we were not arrested.'[134] He was granted his wish when he arrived at Maxwell's headquarters and was promptly conveyed to Arbour Hill. MacNeill was eventually tried by general court-martial because, in Maxwell's opinion, his case presented 'more difficult questions of law and . . . the admissability of evidence' than the others.[135] As a result, he was able to appoint his own counsel and he appeared before a judge advocate, Captain Kimber, and C.G. Blackader who presided, assisted by twelve other officers. The proceedings lasted from 22 to 24 May. MacNeill was charged on fifteen counts – in essence, that he had 'caused disaffection amongst the civilian population' through his role in the Irish Volunteers and in his public speeches, and had attempted to prejudice British military recruitment. MacNeill pleaded not guilty. Wylie, who prosecuted, claimed that 'The man who loads the rifles cannot clean his hands from the blood guiltiness of the discharge'.[136] But MacNeill insisted that he had tried to prevent the Rising and had almost succeeded with the Easter Sunday cancellation. Instead, he placed the responsibility for the rebellion on the government which he said had decided to suppress the Volunteers and so precipitated an armed response from the rebel leadership. MacNeill later said that he found Wylie fair but that the Judge Advocate Kimber had been prejudiced and constantly 'used every effort to weight the scales against me'. He was found guilty and sentenced to penal servitude for life.[137]

Overall, in fifteen of the ninety cases (16 per cent), in which the courts-martial had imposed the death sentence, Maxwell confirmed the verdict. He commuted the remaining seventy-five to varying terms of penal servitude, ranging from life in ten cases down to six months with hard labour in four cases. One can only speculate what would have happened without the constant pressure to desist, but the evidence suggests that, as he said, he had never intended to 'overdo' them. From the outset, he had overturned most of the death penalties imposed by the courts. By 3 May he had confirmed seven (24 per cent), out of twenty-seven, and by 5 May thirteen out of sixty-eight (19 per cent). The proportion executed consistently fell, as was to be expected, since the assumed 'ringleaders' were more likely to have been tried first. After Asquith came to Ireland on 12 May, largely to investigate the scale of the executions and imprisonments, he stated with evident relief, 'on the whole . . . there have been fewer bad blunders than one might have expected with the soldiery for a whole week in exclusive charge'.[138] Those whose death sentences had been revoked were, like the internees, transferred to England to serve their time.

In Ireland public sympathy for the rebels was already increasing. Quite possibly even without the death sentences and mass imprisonments, public attitudes would have changed. Tim Healy traced the origins of the change to the treatment of the surrendered prisoners at the Rotunda, in 'conditions which left a memory as bitter as that enkindled by the executions'.[139] By 29 May a British soldier in Ireland noted that 'People are already sympathising with the rebels and have forgotten the poor soldiers who have lost their lives through the wicked folly of the people. I am sorry the authorities put a stop to the shooting of prisoners found guilty.'[140] Two weeks later the

Inspector-General of the RIC had reported a reaction against the courts-martial, mass arrests and deportations, and said that many who had initially condemned the Rising had come to believe that unnecessary severity had been employed.[141] By late May, Maxwell himself recognised that, despite his best efforts, extreme nationalists were 'by no means cowed' and that 'a revulsion of feeling [had] set in'.[142] He believed that the first results of the punishments were good and the majority of people did not believe them excessive. However, 'misrepresentations' had caused growing popular sympathy for the rebels. 'Ireland is groaning under the tyranny of martial law. It is all eyewash for so far they have not felt it. But all the cranks and faddists scream before they are hurt. The dearly bought liberty of the subject is well in the limelight just now. Every rebel that was killed in Dublin they now say was murdered by soldiers in cold blood.' He noted that 'the Irish are beginning to think that all . . . should be let off . . . [and] the tendency of course is to make martyrs of all those who have been executed'.[143] Maxwell's list of the sources of the misrepresentation was a lengthy one and by implication an indictment of much of Irish society and culture. He thought some of the Catholic clergy were 'really intensely disloyal and . . . keep any sores there are open' and he was especially resentful of 'the infernal requiem masses for the repose of the souls of those who died and have been executed'.[144] He suggested that the Pope might be 'induced to prevent priests mixing themselves up in matters political'.[145]

For Maxwell, the changing content of the censored correspondence of the rebel prisoners provided a depressing barometer of the shifting climate of opinion in Ireland. He informed Asquith in mid-June that it 'showed a decided turn for the worse, for whereas in the first blush of captivity their letters were more or less apologetic and humble, now the tone is defiant and shows that they are not in the least repentant. In fact they think they are very gallant fellows.'[146] He was well aware of and indeed had foreseen his own growing unpopularity as a more personal measure of public attitudes. In June 1916 he wrote that 'I am getting dead sick of this job. I will be the best hated man wherever there are Irish.'[147]

A month later he observed wearily that 'Yes! Some of the Irish call me very nasty names. Bloody Butcher! and such like but my skin is thick.'[148] On 20 July he vented his frustration. 'Oh! these Irish are a truly wonderful people. It is difficult to take them seriously; they are likened to spoiled children.'[149] By now Maxwell believed Asquith was 'giving in all along the line' and he expressed concern that he himself might be 'chucked over anyday'.[150] The Prime Minster had written to him expressing the hope that there should be 'no incidents . . . I hope that the visits and searches are now practically over and that you may find it possible to go slowly for the next week or so.'[151]

Despite the sensitivity to opinion in Ireland the government decided that Casement should be executed. On 27 April 1916 ministers had agreed that he should face a civil trial rather than a court-martial. Two months later, on 29 June, at the High Court of Justice in London, he was convicted of high treason and sentenced to death. The Home Secretary, Herbert Samuel, considered that the full cabinet should determine whether the prerogative of mercy should be exercised. Some members believed that he should be kept in confinement as a criminal lunatic. However, expert opinion declared him to be 'abnormal but not certifiably insane' and the cabinet decided that he should be hanged.[152] The sentence was carried out on 3 August at Pentonville prison. Asquith would have preferred a reprieve based on medical evidence but in its absence he did not feel it right to treat Casement more leniently than his associates had been treated by Maxwell in Ireland. During these cabinet sessions in July it was also decided to postpone the Irish question until after the war.[153]

In his letter of 1 May to his mother Pearse had stated:

You must not grieve for all this. We have pursued Ireland's honour and our own. Our deeds last week were the most splendid in Ireland's history. People will say hard things of me now but we shall be remembered by posterity and blessed by unborn generations.[154]

Opinion in nationalist Ireland changed more quickly than he had foreseen. It had shifted measurably when on 15 July W.J. Lynas, a 27-year-old soldier from Belfast's dockland, wrote home to his wife from the Western Front. He described with a pride and passion comparable to Pearse's 'the gallantry of our boys' (the 36th Division) at the Somme. 'They did not disgrace the name of Ulster. Our boys mounted the top and made a name for Ulster that will never die in the annals of history. No doubt Belfast today and the rest of Ulster is in deep mourning for the dear ones . . . doing their duty for King and Country.'[155] At Easter 1916 the republican tradition was rejuvenated by the Rising and some weeks later the pride of northern Unionists was strengthened by the UVF's sacrifice at the Somme. More than any other, these two political movements were to shape Ireland's political destiny in the decades to come.

NOTES

The following abbreviations are used in these Notes:

CAB   Cabinet Papers
CO   Colonial Office Records
IWM Imperial War Museum, London
NAI   National Archives of Ireland
NLI   National Library of Ireland
PRO   Public Record Office, Kew, London
WO   War Office Records

1: THE PLANNING OF THE EASTER RISING. PART ONE

1. For this process see Bulmer Hobson, *Ireland: Yesterday and Tomorrow* (Anvil Books, Tralee, 1968) pp. 1–13.
2. Ibid. p. 2.
3. Ibid. p. 3.
4. The best sources for Clarke's early life are his autobiography *Glimpses of an Irish Felon's Prison Life* (National Publications Committee, Cork, 1970) and Louis le Roux, *Tom Clarke and the Irish Freedom Movement* (Talbot Press, Dublin, 1936).
5. Clarke, *Glimpses of an Irish Felon's Prison Life*, p. 12.
6. Francis Jones, *History of the Sinn Fein Movement and the Irish Rebellion of 1916* (P.J. Kenedy, New York, 1917) pp. 143–4.
7. Bulmer Hobson, 'Foundation and Growth of the Irish Volunteers, 1913–1914', in F.X. Martin (ed.), *The Irish Volunteers 1913–1915* (James Duffy, Dublin, 1963) p. 17. For Clarke rubbing his hands see p. 87.
8. Hobson, *Ireland: Yesterday and Tomorrow*, p. 43.
9. Martin, *The Irish Volunteers*, p. 49.
10. Hobson, *Ireland: Yesterday and Tomorrow*, pp. 52–3.
11. In a letter from Pearse to John Devoy, 12 August 1914, now in the Allen Library, Edmund Rice House, North Richmond Street, Dublin.
12. Hobson, *Ireland: Yesterday and Tomorrow*, p. 32.
13. Ibid. p. 52.
14. Garret FitzGerald, *Irish Times*, 14 November 1998.
15. For the growth and structure of the Irish Volunteers see Martin, *The Irish Volunteers 1913–1915*.
16. David Fitzpatrick in an article, 'The Overflow of the Deluge: Anglo-

Notes

Irish Relationships, 1914–1922' in Oliver MacDonagh (ed.), *Ireland and Irish-Australia: Studies in Cultural and Political History* (Croom Helm, Beckenham, Kent, 1986) p. 83.

17. In a report entitled 'The Sinn Fein or Irish Volunteers and the Rebellion' which was drawn up for the Chief Secretary. It is reproduced in Breandan Mac Giolla Choille, *Intelligence Notes 1913–1916* (State Paper Office, Dublin, 1966) p. 222.

18. Diarmuid Lynch, *The IRB and the 1916 Insurrection* (Mercier Press, Cork, 1957) pp. 25–6 and 131.

19. Austin Clarke, *A Penny in the Clouds: More Memories of Ireland and England* (Routledge and Kegan Paul, London, 1968) p. 26.

20. Maire Nic Shiubhlaigh, *The Splendid Years* (James Duffy, Dublin, 1955) pp. 147–8.

21. Ruth Dudley Edwards, *Patrick Pearse: The Triumph of Failure* (Gollancz, London, 1977) pp. 153–4.

22. Lynch, *The IRB*, pp. 25, 112 and 130–2.

23. For background see B.L. Reid, *The Lives of Roger Casement* (Yale University Press, New Haven, 1978); R. Sawyer, *Casement, the Flawed Hero* (Routledge and Kegan Paul, London, 1984); B. Inglis, *Roger Casement* (Hodder and Stoughton, London, 1973); Crime Branch Special file on Casement, PRO, CO 904/195.

24. For this and Casement's German mission in general see Reinhard Doerries, 'Die Mission Sir Roger Casements im Deutschen Reich 1914–1916' in *Historische Zeitschrift* (1976), pp. 586–625.

25. Sawyer, *Flawed Hero*, p. 115; Inglis, *Roger Casement*, p. 272.

26. Sawyer, *Flawed Hero*, p. 124.

27. Casement's disillusionment is clear from his diary comments in NLI MS 5244, 1689–90 and 17587.

28. A copy of the Ireland Report is in the Casement Papers, NLI MS 130855(5). When I first located this document and realised its historical importance I was thrilled by the discovery. Until, that is, I learnt that a number of German historians had already been working productively in this field and had got there before me. There are two publications which are of crucial importance. The first is a book by Hans-Dieter Kluge, *Irland in der deutschen Geschichtswissenschaft, Politik und Propaganda* (P. Lang, Frankfurt am Main, 1985). This is complemented by an article by Andreas Kratz entitled 'Die Mission Joseph Mary Plunketts im Deutschen Reich und ihre Bedeutung fur den Osteraufstand 1916', which was published in the journal *Historische Mitteilungen* (1995), pp. 202–20. Unfortunately neither work has been translated into English. Even so the lack of impact that the researches of Kluge and Kratz have made on Irish historians is puzzling and regrettable. (M.T.F.)

29. Sean Fitzgibbon dictated his account to Michael J. Lennon in a five-part series, 'The Easter Rising from the Inside'. The quotation is from Part I in the *Irish Times*, 18 April 1949.

30. Lynch, *The IRB*, pp. 29–30.

31. Colonel J.J. O'Connell, typescript of his History of the Irish Volunteers, Bulmer Hobson Papers, NLI MS 13168.

32. PRO WO904/99.

33. Florence O'Donoghue, 'Plans for the 1916 Rising', *University Review* (March 1963), p. 10.

34. Diarmuid Lynch, Recollections and Comments on the IRB, in Documents presented to the Bureau of Military History, NLI MS 11128.

35. For the various other meeting places see account by Mrs Ceannt, William O'Brien Papers, NLI MS 13978 and le Roux, *Tom Clarke*, p. 190.

36. Lynch, Recollections and Comments on the IRB.

37. O'Daly's account is given in a lengthy memorandum describing his involvement in the Irish Volunteers. He presented it to the Allen Library when he had later risen to the rank of major-general in the Irish Army. Hereafter, Daly, Irish Volunteers.

38. Lynch, *The IRB*, pp. 73 and 101–2.

39. William O'Brien, *Irish Press*, 25 January 1936. See also Lynch, *The IRB*, p. 73.

40. Joseph O'Connor, 'Boland's Mill Area', in *Capuchin Annual* (1966), p. 240.

41. Simon Donnelly, in a memorandum entitled 'THOU SHALT NOT PASS – Ireland's Challenge to the British forces at Mount Street Bridge, Easter Week, 1916' University College, Dublin. Hereafter, Donnelly, Easter Week, 1916.

2: THE PLANNING OF THE EASTER RISING. PART TWO

1. For a good study of Connolly see Austen Morgan, *James Connolly: A Political Biography* (Manchester University Press, Manchester, 1988).

2. There are accounts of the meeting by MacNeill in NLI MS 13174(15) and by F.X. Martin, 'Select Documents: Eoin MacNeill on the 1916 Rising', *Irish Historical Studies*, xii, 47 (March 1961), pp. 245–6. See also Hobson, NLI MS 13171 and 13174.

3. James A. Gubbins and A.J. O'Halloran, 'Limerick's Projected Role in Easter Week, 1916', in Colonel J.M. McCarthy (ed.), *Limerick's Fighting Story* (Anvil Books, Tralee, N.D.) pp. 31–2. See also A. Cotton, 'Kerry's Place in the General Plan, 1916', in *Kerry's Fighting Story 1916–1921* (The Kerryman, Tralee, N.D.) p. 51.

4. See James Connolly, *Revolutionary Warfare* (New Books Publication, Dublin, 1968).

5. William Oman, Account of his service in the Citizen Army, the Allen Library, Dublin. Hereafter, Oman, Citizen Army.

6. Joseph O'Connor, NLI MS 13735.

7. The message was sent to Casement in Berlin from Plunkett's father in Berne, Switzerland. See note 8.

8. Count Plunkett, acting as a courier for the Military Council, had dispatched a message to Casement giving the date of the Rising and

stipulating that it was 'imperative' that German officers should arrive with the arms shipment to assist the Volunteers and that a German submarine would be required in Dublin Harbour. The incredulous Germans rejected both demands out of hand.

9. For details of the plans for the Rising in the west see Gubbins and O'Halloran, 'Limerick's Projected Role in Easter Week, 1916', pp. 31–40. See also Cotton, 'Kerry's Place in the General Plan, 1916', pp. 46–53.

10. Denis McCullough, 'The Events in Belfast', in *Capuchin Annual*, (1966), pp. 381–4.

11. Fitzgibbon, 'The Easter Rising from the Inside', Part I.

12. Hobson, typescript memorandum on the Irish Volunteers sent to the Bureau of Military History, NLI MS 13170.

13. Hobson, History of the Irish Volunteers, NLI MS 121799.

14. Martin, 'Select Documents', p. 255. Martin dates the incident as happening on Sunday 5 September 1915.

15. Ibid. p. 256.

16. NLI MS 13171 and 13174.

17. For The O'Rahilly, see his son's biography, Aodogán O'Rahilly, *Winding the Clock: O'Rahilly and the 1916 Rising* (Lilliput Press, Dublin, 1991).

18. The talk was given by Pearse in Dublin on 6 February 1916 to C Company of the 2nd Battalion. It was published in the journal *Irish Volunteer*.

19. O'Connor, 'Boland's Mill Area', p. 241.

20. Oscar Traynor, in a biographical account written shortly before his death, at the request of President de Valera (de Valera Papers, Archives Department, University College, Dublin, P150/1527). Hereafter, Traynor, Biographical Account.

21. Helena Moloney, transcripts of interviews for a 1966 BBC programme on the Easter Rising, NLI MS 15015.

22. Lynch, Recollections and Comments on the IRB.

23. Hobson, NLI MS 13171 and 13174.

24. Account by Peadar Bracken of his experiences in the Irish Volunteers at Easter 1916, in the Allen Library, Dublin. Hereafter, Bracken, Easter Week, 1916.

25. Leon Ó Broin, *Dublin Castle and the 1916 Rising: the Story of Sir Matthew Nathan* (Helican, Dublin, 1966) p. 12.

26. Nathan Papers, the Bodleian, Oxford, MS 472.

27. Ibid. MS 478.

28. Ibid.

29. Ibid. MS 466.

30. PRO CO904/23/3.

31. Ibid.

32. Ibid.

33. Desmond Fitzgerald, *Memoirs of Desmond Fitzgerald, 1913–1916* (Routledge and Kegan Paul, London, 1968) p. 116.

34. le Roux, *Tom Clarke*, p. 188.
35. Fitzgerald, *Memoirs*, p. 118.
36. Lynch, Recollections and Comments on the IRB, and an account by Frank Robbins, NLI MS 10915.
37. O'Connor, 'Boland's Mill Area', p. 239.
38. This has been persuasively argued by Marcus Bourke in his article 'Thomas MacDonagh's Role in the Plans for the Easter Rising' in *Irish Sword*, 8 (1967–1968).
39. Martin, 'Select Documents', p. 254.
40. Clarke, *A Penny in the Clouds*, p. 25.
41. PRO CO 904/23/3.
42. O'Broin, *Dublin Castle and the 1916 Rising*, p. 149.
43. Fitzgibbon, 'The Easter Rising from the Inside', Part II, *Irish Times*, 19 April 1949.
44. Hobson, NLI MS 17613.
45. Hobson, Account of Events in Dublin in the days preceding Easter Week 1916, NLI MS 17613.
46. Hobson, NLI 13171 and 13174.
47. Fitzgibbon, 'The Easter Rising from the Inside', Part III, *Irish Times*, 20 April 1949.
48. Martin, 'Select Documents', p. 262.
49. There is a contradiction here between the recollections of MacNeill and Hobson. MacNeill asserted that he did go to Volunteer Headquarters, saw Hobson and told him the countermanding orders were of no avail; NLI MS 13174(15). Hobson was equally certain that they never met; NLI MS 13170. Hobson's memory was always sharper than MacNeill's and if a meeting had taken place its content would surely have been memorable. Yet MacNeill provided no further details of the alleged meeting.
50. Hobson, *Ireland: Yesterday and Tomorrow*, pp. 76–7.
51. Fitzgibbon, 'The Easter Rising from the Inside', Part IV, *Irish Times*, 21 April 1949.
52. le Roux, *Tom Clarke*, p. 186.
53. Kluge, *Irland in der deutschen Geschwichtissenschaft*, p. 142.
54. Ibid. p. 144.
55. Doerries, 'Die Mission Sir Roger Casements', pp. 616–17.
56. Ibid. p. 617.
57. For a painstakingly researched account of the voyage of the *Aud*, see John de Courcy Ireland, *The Sea and the Easter Rising* (Maritime Institute of Ireland, Dublin, 1966) pp. 9–26.
58. Stafford to HQ Irish Command, 22 April 1916, Nathan Papers, MS 476.
59. See note 8.
60. O'Donoghue, 'Plans for the 1916 Rising', p. 13.
61. Mortimer O'Leary, account deposited by him in the Allen Library.
62. Mannix Joyce, 'The Story of Limerick and Kerry in 1916', *Capuchin Annual* (1966), p. 352.

NOTES

63. Ibid.
64. Fitzgibbon, 'The Easter Rising from the Inside', Part II.
65. Ibid.
66. For The O'Rahilly's journey to the west see O'Rahilly, *Winding the Clock*, pp. 199–200.
67. Senator James Ryan, 'General Post Office Area', in *Capuchin Annual* (1966).
68. le Roux, *Tom Clarke*, p. 204.
69. Details of the frantic efforts to round up the members of the Military Council can be found in le Roux, *Tom Clarke*, pp. 205–6, and Eilis ni Chorra, 'A Rebel Remembers', in *Capuchin Annual* (1966), pp. 292–300.
70. Joyce, 'The Story of Limerick and Kerry in 1916', p. 353.
71. William O'Brien, Notes on the Citizen Army, Florence O'Donoghue Papers, NLI MS 15673(1).
72. O'Connor, 'Boland's Mill Area', pp. 241–2.
73. Donnelly, Easter Week, 1916.
74. Ibid.
75. le Roux, *Tom Clarke*, pp. 212–13.
76. For a good account by one of the audience see Margaret Skinnider, *Irish Press*, 9 April 1966.
77. NLI MS 13174(15).
78. Dudley Edwards, *Patrick Pearse*, p. 274.
79. Fitzgibbon, 'The Easter Rising from the Inside', Part II, 19 April 1949.
80. Martin, 'Select Documents', p. 270.
81. Fitzgerald, *Memoirs*, p. 128.
82. Nathan Papers, MS 466.
83. Ibid. MS 449.
84. On the following see a memo by Nathan, Nathan Papers, MS 476 and Ó Broin, *Dublin Castle and the 1916 Rising*, pp. 83–4.
85. Ibid. pp. 86–7.
86. Dorothy Stopford, Diary, April to May 1916, NLI MS 16063.
87. Imperial War Museum, London, 71/11/2.

3: THE FIRST MORNING OF THE RISING AND STEPHEN'S GREEN

1. For Nathan's activities on Easter Monday morning see Ó Broin, *Dublin Castle and the 1916 Rising*, pp. 87–92.
2. For accounts of the events of Easter Monday morning at Liberty Hall see Oman, Citizen Army, Nora Connolly O'Brien, *Portrait of a Rebel Father* (Talbot Press, Dublin and Cork, 1935) pp. 297–300 and Frank Robbins, *Under the Starry Plough: Recollections of the Irish Citizen Army* (Academy Press, Dublin, 1977) pp. 83–4. For Ceannt see Lily O'Brennan's article, 'The Dawning of the Day', in *Capuchin Annual* (1936) pp. 157–9.
3. Oman, Citizen Army.
4. Connolly O'Brien, *Portrait of a Rebel Father*, pp. 298–9.

5. O'Rahilly, *Winding the Clock*, p. 206.
6. Oman, Citizen Army.
7. Ibid.
8. Ibid.
9. Price in his evidence on 25 May 1916 to the Royal Commission on the Rebellion in Ireland, Minutes of Evidence CMD 8279.
10. O'Daly, Irish Volunteers.
11. Robbins, *Under the Starry Plough*, p. 70.
12. Account by Margaret Skinnider, *Irish Press*, 9 April 1966, and in her *Doing My Bit for Ireland* (Century Co., New York, 1917) passim; Mallin's evidence at his court martial, PRO WO71/353; 'St Stephen's Green' in *The Catholic Bulletin*, (1918) pp. 502–4.
13. Robbins, *Under the Starry Plough*, p. 85.
14. In list of 'persons killed or wounded by rebels' by Sergeant Michael Mannion, dated 27 July 1916, in PRO WO35/69; Skinnider, *Irish Press*, 9 April 1966; see account by Belfast solicitor in *Belfast Telegraph*, 1 May 1916.
15. Ibid.; see also Crime Branch Special files on Markievicz, PRO CO904/209 and PRO WO35/207.
16. Diary kept by Douglas Hyde during Easter Rising, 24 April 1916, now in Trinity College, Dublin, MS 10343/7.
17. Liam Ó Briain, 'The St Stephen's Green Area', in *Capuchin Annual* (1966) p. 224; Nora O'Daly, account in *An tOglac*, 3 April 1926.
18. Account by Frank Robbins, NLI MS 10915.
19. Elizabeth Bowen, *The Shelbourne, a Centre in Dublin Life for more than a Century* (Harrap, London, 1951) pp. 151–5.
20. James Stephens, *The Insurrection in Dublin* (Colin Smyth, Gerrards Cross, 1978) p. 9.
21. Robbins, *Under the Starry Plough*, p. 97.
22. See Breda Grace, 'I Don't Forget', in de Valera Papers, University College, Dublin, MSS 94/385.
23. Robbins, *Under the Starry Plough*, p. 94.
24. Stephens, *Insurrection in Dublin*, p. 19.
25. Ibid. p. 18.
26. Account by J. William G. Smith in NLI MS 24952; see also account by Powell, assistant manager, Shelbourne Hotel, May 1916, in PRO WO35/69.
27. See contemporary reports of incidents made to police and lists of casualty statistics at Dublin hospitals in list compiled by Sergeant M. Mannion, dated 29 May 1916, in ibid.; Smith, NLI MS 24952.
28. Robbins, *Under the Starry Plough*, pp. 107–8; list by Mannion of killed and wounded, 29 July 1916, in PRO WO35/69; *Irish Times*, 4 May 1916.
29. Robbins, *Under the Starry Plough*, p. 88.
30. Ibid. p. 88.
31. Ó Briain, 'Stephen's Green Area', p. 222.
32. Skinnider, *Irish Press*, 9 April 1966; O'Daly, 'The Women of Easter

Week: Cumann na mBan in St Stephen's Green, and in the College of Surgeons' in *An tOglac*, 3 April 1926; Ó Briain, 'Stephen's Green Area', pp. 225–6.

33. Hyde, Diary, morning of 25 April.
34. 'The Story of a Machine-gun Section' by the OC, in *Irish Life, Record of the Rebellion of 1916* (Dublin, 1916) p. 22; P.J. O'Connor's account, the midnight march, in NLI MS 10915.
35. 'Story of Machine-gun Section', OC, p. 24; see also 'Stephen's Green', in *Capuchin Annual* (1918) pp. 550–1.
36. Stephens, *Insurrection in Dublin*, p. 26.
37. Ibid. Stephens noted four dead and one gravely injured. See also Robbins, *Under the Starry Plough*. pp. 103–6.
38. O'Daly, 'The Women of Easter Week'.
39. 'Story of a Machine-gun Section', OC, pp. 24–5.
40. Bowen, *Shelbourne*, pp. 156–61.
41. Robbins, *Under the Starry Plough*, p. 100.
42. See reference to Kathleen Clarke's letter to *Sunday Press* (April 1963) in note headed 'Occupation of Stephen's Green' in Florence O'Donoghue Papers, NLI MS 31299(2).
43. *Irish Times*, 25 April 1916.
44. Robbins, *Under the Starry Plough*, p. 101.
45. Ó Briain, 'Stephen's Green Area', p. 227; Skinnider, *Irish Press*, 9 April 1966.
46. Robbins, *Under the Starry Plough*, p. 93.
47. Skinnider, *Irish Press*, 9 April 1966; O'Daly, 'The Women of Easter Week'.
48. R.M. Fox, *The History of the Irish Citizen Army* (J. Duffy, Dublin, 1943) p. 160; military situation reports for 27–8 April, in PRO WO35/69; see account in *Irish Independent*, 11 May 1916.
49. Robbins, *Under the Starry Plough*, p. 114.
50. Ibid. pp. 115–16; Skinnider, *Irish Press*, 9 April 1966; 'Story of a Machine-gun Section', OC, p. 24; Ó Briain, 'Stephen's Green Area', p. 231.
51. 'Women in the Fight, a Memoir by Countess Markievicz', in Roger McHugh, *Dublin, 1916* (Arlington Books, Dublin, 1966) p. 124.
52. Skinnider, *Irish Press*, 9 April 1966, and *Doing My Bit*, passim.
53. Hyde, Diary, 29 April; Oman, Citizen Army.
54. Ibid.
55. Robbins, *Under the Starry Plough*, p. 103; Ó Briain, 'Stephen's Green Area', pp. 288–9.
56. Ibid. p. 233; O'Daly, 'The Women of Easter Week'.
57. Smith, NLI MS 24952.
58. Hyde, Diary, 28 April.
59. Robbins, *Under the Starry Plough*, pp. 117–18. Between the outbreak of war and 15 April 1916, a total of 17,536 men had enlisted from Dublin in the British army. See *On the Rebellion in Ireland*, report of Royal Commission, Command Paper 8279, p. 125.

60. Stephens, *Insurrection in Dublin*, pp. 53 and 59.

61. Ó Briain, 'Stephen's Green Area', p. 231.

62. Ibid. p. 233; the diaries of Diarmuid Coffey and his mother record a doctor stating that there were cases of nervous breakdown in the college (NLI MS 21193).

63. Diary of John Clarke, NLI MS 10485.

64. Hyde, Diary, 30 April.

65. Pearas F. Mac Lochlainn, *Last Words: Letters and Statements of the Leaders Executed after the Rising at Easter 1916* (Stationery Office, Dublin, 1990) p. 186.

66. Robbins, *Under the Starry Plough*, p. 120; see also Ó Briain, 'Stephen's Green Area', p. 234.

67. H. de Courcy Wheeler's account of surrender, in *Irish Life, Record of the Rebellion of 1916*, pp. 26–32; Elizabeth O'Farrell, 'The Surrender', in *Capuchin Annual* (1917) pp. 329–30.

68. Robbins, *Under the Starry Plough*, p. 121.

69. Mary Donnelly, 'With the Citizen Army in St Stephen's Green', in *An Poblacht*, 19 April 1930.

70. Ó Briain, 'Stephen's Green Area', p. 236; Skinnider, *Doing My Bit*, p. 155; Oman, Citizen Army; Markievicz told her sister the rebels in the college could have held out for days, McHugh, *Dublin, 1916*, p. 310.

71. Ó Briain, 'Stephen's Green Area', p. 236.

72. Ibid. p. 234; de Courcy Wheeler, in *Irish Life*, p. 32.

73. Ibid.; Oman, Citizen Army.

74. Comment attributed to Kettle, in Coffey, Diary; he also stated he was well treated by rebels, referred to in Hyde, Diary, 2 May.

75. Mr Purser (who worked there) and his wife stated that the rebels 'never even misarranged a bottle or did any damage whatever in the College' in ibid., 2 May.

76. Ó Briain, 'Stephen's Green Area', p. 236.

77. De Courcy Wheeler, account in NLI MS 15000; Oman, Citizen Army, recalls that 'the mob attempted to attack us. The British officer displayed great courage.' O'Daly states 'I carried a Red Cross flag as some extraordinary stories were afloat, to account for the presence of women among the garrison', in 'The Women of Easter Week'.

78. Ibid.

79. Robbins, *Under the Starry Plough*, pp. 127–8.

80. Ibid., p. 128.

81. See Skinnider, *Irish Press*, 9 April 1966; Hyde, Diary, 1 May; notes on Markievicz in PRO WO35/207; also Johnson's diary, 27 April 1916, in J.A. Gaughan, *Thomas Johnson, 1872–1963: First Leader of the Labour Party in Dail Eireann* (Kingdom Books, Mount Merrion, 1980) p. 51.

82. 'Momentous days; occasional diaries of Frances Taylor', entry for 30 April 1916, in *Dublin Historical Record*, Vol. XLVII (1994) pp. 80–1.

NOTES

4: BOLAND'S BAKERY

1. Tim Pat Coogan, *De Valera* (Hutchinson, London, 1993) p. 57.
2. Donnelly, Easter Week, 1916.
3. O'Connor, 'Boland's Mill Area', p. 242. The poor turn-out is also noted in Donnelly, Easter Week, 1916.
4. Donnelly, Easter Week, 1916.
5. George Lyons, 'Occupation of Ringsend Area in 1916', in *An tOglac*, 10 April 1926. Lyons's marvellous three-part account (published on 10, 17 and 24 April 1926) of the fighting at Boland's bakery and Mount Street Bridge is perhaps the best by any participant in the Rising. It is remarkable for its descriptive power, frankness, honesty and fairness. Hereafter Lyons, 'Ringsend Area'.
6. Donnelly, Easter Week, 1916.
7. Ibid.
8. Lyons, 'Ringsend Area', 10 April 1926.
9. Donnelly, Easter Week, 1916.
10. Lyons, 'Ringsend Area', 10 April 1926.
11. Donnelly, Easter Week, 1916.
12. For the Volunteer Training Corps see PRO WO141/6 and the account by one of its members, Henry Hanna, Trinity College, Dublin, MS 10066/192. The relatives of those members killed fought a campaign for financial compensation until the government conceded that the men had been killed while on military duty.
13. Donnelly, Easter Week, 1916.
14. Lyons, 'Ringsend Area', 10 April 1926.
15. Ibid.
16. Donnelly, Easter Week, 1916.
17. O'Connor, 'Boland's Mill Area', p. 244.
18. An unpublished manuscript, the Memoirs of Brigadier E.W.S.K. Maconchy, 1860–1920, now in the British Army Museum, London.
19. Grace, I Don't Forget.
20. Tom Walsh, 'The Epic of Mount Street Bridge', in *Irish Press* 'Commemoration Supplement' (April 1966).
21. Account by Mrs Ismena Rohde, NLI MS 15415.
22. From a contemporary newspaper account by an English visitor: 'Dublin Rebellion: Prestonian's Thrilling Experiences' by J.F. Cronin. Reprinted in McHugh, *Dublin, 1916*, pp. 85–6.
23. Walsh, 'The Epic of Mount Street Bridge'.
24. Maconchy, Memoirs.
25. *The Catholic Bulletin* (December 1917).
26. Ibid.
27. Ibid.
28. Walsh, 'The Epic of Mount Street Bridge'.
29. These are the official figures but Maconchy in his unpublished memoirs gives significantly smaller casualties: 5 officers dead and 12 wounded, 25 other ranks dead and 118 wounded.

Whether the discrepancy is due to faulty memory on Maconchy's part is unclear.

30. O'Connor, 'Boland's Mill Area', p. 240.
31. 'Easter Week Diary of Miss Lilly Stokes', reprinted in McHugh, *Dublin, 1916*, p. 69.
32. Lyons, 'Ringsend Area', 17 April 1926.
33. Donnelly, Easter Week, 1916.
34. Lyons, 'Ringsend Area', 17 April 1926.
35. O'Connor, 'Boland's Mill Area', p. 249.
36. Lyons, 'Ringsend Area', 24 April 1926.
37. O'Connor, 'Boland's Mill Area', p. 251.
38. Donnelly, Easter Week, 1916.
39. Lyons, 'Ringsend Area', 24 April 1926.
40. Donnelly, Easter Week, 1916.
41. Lyons, 'Ringsend Area', 24 April 1926.
42. Ibid.
43. Donnelly, Easter Week, 1916.
44. Lyons, 'Ringsend Area', 24 April 1926.
45. Ibid. For the surrender see also O'Connor, 'Boland's Mill Area', pp. 250–2 and Donnelly, Easter Week, 1916.
46. Donnelly, Easter Week, 1916.
47. Lyons, 'Ringsend Area', 24 April 1926.

5: JACOB'S FACTORY AND THE SOUTH DUBLIN UNION

1. Ignatius Callender, 'A Diary of Easter Week', *Dublin Brigade Review* (National Assocation of Old I.R.A., Dublin, 1939).
2. For the hostile reaction to the occupation of Jacob's see the account by Michael Walker, a member of E Company, 2nd Battalion, in the Allen Library, Dublin. Also Peadar Kearney, Reminiscences of Easter Week, in the library of Trinity College Dublin, MS 3560.
3. Kearney, Reminiscences.
4. 'Jacob's and Stephen's Green Area', *The Catholic Bulletin* (September 1918).
5. Kearney, Reminiscences.
6. Ibid.
7. Oman, Citizen Army.
8. Ibid.
9. Kearney, Reminiscences.
10. Walker, Jacob's Factory.
11. Kearney, Reminiscences.
12. Shiubhlaigh, *The Splendid Years*, p. 13.
13. Nurse Elizabeth O'Farrell, 'Story of the Surrender', *The Catholic Bulletin* (April–May 1917).
14. Revd Father Aloysius, O.F.M. Cap., Memories of Easter Week, 1916, in the Allen Library, Dublin.
15. Shiubhlaigh, *The Splendid Years*, p. 184.

NOTES

16. Ibid.
17. The first quotation is from Shiubhlaigh, the second from Walker, Jacob's Factory.
18. Kearney, Reminiscences.
19. Ibid.
20. Ibid.
21. Ibid.
22. Ibid.; Walker, Jacob's Factory; and Padraig O'Ceallaigh, 'Jacob's Factory Area', in *Capuchin Annual* (1966), p. 217.
23. Aloysius, Memories of Easter Week.
24. Captain Tom Young, 'Fighting in South Dublin: With the Garrison in Marrowbone Lane during Easter Week, 1916', *An tOglac*, 6 March 1916.
25. Aloysius, Memories of Easter Week.
26. Walker, Jacob's Factory and Aloysius, Memories of Easter Week.
27. Thomas King Moylan, A Dubliner's Diary 1914 to 1918, NLI MS 9620.
28. Robert Holland, Lieutenant in F Company, 4th Battalion, an account of the action at Marrowbone Lane, in the Allen Library, Dublin. Hereafter, Holland, Marrowbone Lane.
29. For good descriptions of the layout of the South Dublin Union and the initial occupation by the Volunteers, see Joseph Doolan of A Company, 4th Battalion, NLI MS 10915 and a four-part account in *The Catholic Bulletin* (March, April, May and June 1918).
30. Young, 'Fighting in South Dublin'.
31. 'A Volunteer', 'South Dublin Union Area', in *Capuchin Annual* (1966) p. 206.
32. Ibid. p. 208.
33. Peadar Doyle, Reminiscences of Five Years' Service of an Irish Volunteer, in the Allen Library, Dublin. Doyle was Ceannt's staff orderly in the South Dublin Union.
34. 'A Volunteer', 'South Dublin Union Area', p. 211.
35. *The Catholic Bulletin* (June 1918) and Doyle, Reminiscences.
36. *The Catholic Bulletin* (May 1918) and 'A Volunteer', 'South Dublin Union Area', p. 209.
37. Doyle, Reminiscences.
38. Ibid.
39. This account is based substantially on Doolan's description of the South Dublin Union.
40. Doyle, Reminiscences.
41. Ibid.
42. Holland, Marrowbone Lane.
43. Ibid.
44. Ibid.
45. Ibid.
46. Ibid.
47. Ibid.

48. Ibid.
49. Ibid.
50. Ibid.
51. Ibid.
52. Ibid.
53. Ibid.
54. Ibid.
55. Ibid.
56. Ibid.
57. Ibid.
58. Memoirs of a female member of the Marrowbone Lane garrison in 1916, NLI MS 18556.
59. Holland, Marrowbone Lane.
60. Ibid.
61. Ibid.
62. Ibid.
63. Ibid.

6: THE FOUR COURTS

1. John J. Reynolds, 'The Four Courts and North King Street Area in 1916', *An tOglac*, 15 May, 22 May and 29 May 1926.
2. *Pictorial Review of 1916: An Historically Accurate Account of Events which occurred in Easter Week* (Parkgate Press, Dublin, 1966) p. 30.
3. Anon., A Company, 1st Battalion, Irish Republican Army, Historical sketch of the unit during the years 1913–1916– 1917–1923, in the Allen Library, Dublin; History of 'A' Company, Archives Department, University College, Dublin LA 9.
4. Ibid.; Piaras Beaslai, 'Edward Daly's Command, Easter Week, 1916', in McCarthy (ed.), *Limerick's Fighting Story*, pp. 139–46, and T.P. Kilfeather, 'Commandant Edward Daly', in ibid. pp. 137–9.
5. Beaslai, 'Edward Daly's Command', pp. 139–41; Patrick Holohan, 'The Four Courts Area', in *Capuchin Annual* (1966) pp. 181–3; see also references to Daly in a book by his sister, *Kathleen Clarke, Revolutionary Woman, 1878–1972, An Autobiography*, ed. Helen Litton (O'Brien, Dublin, 1991).
6. D.A. Chart, *The Story of Dublin* (Dent, London, 1907) p. 272; James J. Brennan, 'The Mendicity Institution Area', in *Capuchin Annual* (1966) pp. 189–90.
7. Diary of John Clarke, NLI MS 10485; also account by A. Hannant, IWM; for Heuston, see NLI MS 15382 and 10076; Matt Connolly, 'Dublin City Hall Area', in *Capuchin Annual* (1966) p. 196.
8. Reynolds, 'The Four Courts'. See also Clarke, Diary; Anon., A Company.
9. See Heuston court-martial, evidence by officers from Royal Dublin Fusiliers, in PRO WO71/351; Brennan, 'Mendicity Institution Area';

NOTES

John M. Heuston OP, *Headquarters Battalion, Easter Week, 1916* (Nationalist Printers, Carlow, 1966) passim.

10. See description in *Irish Times*, 5 May 1916.
11. *War History of the 6th Battalion South Staffordshire Regiment* (Heinemann, London, 1921) p. 149; Reynolds, 'The Four Courts'; Holohan, 'Four Courts Area', p. 183.
12. Account by Liam Archer, Events at Easter Week, 1916, in Mulcahy Papers, Archives Department, University College, Dublin, P7/D/23); see 'A Letter by Professor George O'Neill, SJ, Easter Tuesday, April 25 1916', in McHugh, *Dublin, 1916*, pp. 184–5.
13. Clarke, Diary.
14. Ibid.
15. Beaslai, 'Edward Daly's Command', p. 147.
16. See account by Paddy Holohan in NLI MS 10915.
17. Ibid.; Reynolds, 'The Four Courts'; military situation reports for 25/26 April in PRO WO35/69; Clarke, *A Penny in the Clouds*, p. 34.
18. Sean Coady, 'Remembering St John's Convent', in *Capuchin Annual* (1966) p. 279.
19. Brennan, 'Mendicity Institution Area', pp. 190–1; notes made by Heuston, used in evidence in court-martial, PRO WO71/351.
20. Evidence given by Lieutenant A.P. Lindsay at Daly's court-martial, in PRO WO71/344.
21. Brighid Thornton, quoted in *Curious Journey, an Oral History of Ireland's Unfinished Revolution*, ed. K. Griffith and E. O'Grady (Hutchinson, London, 1982) p. 70.
22. Reynolds, 'The Four Courts' and Holohan, 'Four Courts Area', pp. 184–5.
23. Quoted in *Pictorial Review of 1916*, p. 32.
24. Lindsay stated in his court-martial evidence that Daly told him that he 'intended to make a counter-attack as the position was hopeless . . . he said he could not surrender without orders from his superiors'; PRO WO71/344.
25. Reynolds, 'The Four Courts'.
26. Daly, Irish Volunteers.
27. See description given to police, May 1916, by Lieutenant Mills, in PRO WO35/69.
28. Brennan, 'Mendicity Institution Area', p. 191; also evidence of prosecution witnesses in PRO WO71/351.
29. Ibid.
30. Archer, Events.
31. W.G. Smith (District Superintendant, No. 12 District), *Report of work done by St John's Ambulance Brigade during the Sinn Fein Rebellion April–May, 1916* (John Falconer, Dublin, 1916) p. 7.
32. Clarke, Diary.
33. See Christine O'Gorman, list (drawn up 29 May 1929) of those who 'received first aid in Father Mathew Hall', 26–9 April, NAI D/T S6023; Beaslai, 'Daly's Command' p. 143.

34. See the eye-witness account by John J. O'Leary published by the *Dublin Saturday Post* after the Rising in a composite edition for 29 April, 6 May and 13 May 1916 published after the Rising.

35. Clarke, Diary.

36. Message from Jervis Street Hospital to Nathan, 11.25 a.m., 28 April, in the Nathan Papers, MS 476; see also list of casualties in Dublin hospitals during Easter Week, dated 29 May 1916, by Sergeant Michael Mannion in PRO WO35/69.

37. Eilis Bean Ui Chonail, 'A Cumann na mBan recalls Easter Week', in *Capuchin Annual* (1966), pp. 271–8; also comments by Brighid Thornton in *Curious Journey*, passim.

38. Reynolds, 'The Four Courts'.

39. G.I. Edmunds, *2/6 Battalion, Sherwood Foresters, 1914–18: its Part in the Defeat of the Irish Rebellion, 1916* (Wilfred Edmonds, Chesterfield, 1960) unpaginated; Reynolds, 'The Four Courts'.

40. Ibid.

41. Ibid.

42. Account by A. Hannant, IWM; Edmunds, *2/6 Battalion, Sherwood Foresters*.

43. *1916 Rebellion Handbook*, introduction by Declan Kiberd (Mourne River Press, Dublin, 1998) p. 25.

44. *History of the 6th South Staffs*, pp. 149–50.

45. Ibid.; Holohan, 'Four Courts Area', p. 185.

46. Ibid.; Reynolds, 'The Four Courts'.

47. Ibid.

48. Ibid.; Holohan, 'Four Courts Area', pp. 185–6; John J. Reynolds, *A Fragment of 1916 History* (Sinn Fein Press, Dublin, 1919) pp. 4–31; see also report by A.E. Sandbach, commander of troops, Dublin area, 27 May 1916, in PRO WO35/67.

49. Quoted in Reynolds, *A Fragment*, p. 5; Holohan, 'Four Courts Area', pp. 185–6; *History of 6th South Staffs*, p. 151; Reynolds, 'The Four Courts'.

50. Ibid.; History of A Company.

51. Reynolds, 'The Four Courts'. Report of telephone call at 10.10 a.m., 28 April, in Nathan Papers, MS 476.

52. O'Gorman, list of casualties at Father Mathew Hall, in NAI D/T S6023; also account by D. Coffey, NLI MS 21193.

53. Archer, Events. For the final phase of the fighting, see Aloysius, Memories of Easter Week.

54. Daly told Lindsay he 'did not expect anyone who took part . . . would come back alive. . . . The object was to save the lives of as many people as possible in the building: PRO WO71/344; Reynolds, 'The Four Courts'.

55. Thornton's comments in *Curious Journey*, p. 75.

56. O'Farrell, 'The Surrender', in McHugh, *Dublin, 1916*, p. 211; account of final action and surrender also in Major H. de Courcy Wheeler, NLI MS 15000.

NOTES

57.   Thornton in *Curious Journey*, p. 75.

58.   Ibid. p. 77.

59.   Ibid. p. 76.

60.   Beaslai, 'Edward Daly's Command', p. 146.

61.   Holohan, 'Four Courts Area', pp. 187–8; Coady 'St John's Convent', p. 279.

62.   *History of 6th South Staffs*, pp. 151–2; Bean Ui Chonail, 'A Cumann na mBan recalls', pp. 275–6.

7: THE GENERAL POST OFFICE

1.   Dudley Edwards, *Patrick Pearse*, pp. 277 and 359.

2.   Lynch, 'Report of Operations, Easter Week, 1916', in *The IRB and the 1916 Insurrection*, p. 157.

3.   W.J. Brennan-Whitmore, *Dublin Burning* (Gill and Macmillan, Dublin, 1996) p. 37.

4.   Lynch, 'Report of Operations', p. 157.

5.   From a diary of events in the GPO which was reconstructed during his subsequent internment by Dick Humphries, NLI MS 18829. Hereafter, Humphries, GPO Diary.

6.   M.J. Staines and M.W. Reilly, 'The Defence of the GPO', in *An tOglac*, 23 January 1926.

7.   For a good account of the Proclamation see Liam de Paor, *On the Easter Proclamation and other Declarations* (Four Courts Press, Dublin, 1997).

8.   Corporal Liam Byrne, 'Wireless and 1916', *An Cosantoir* (April 1991).

9.   For the fighting at Hopkins & Hopkins see Cormac Turner, 'The Defence of Messrs Hopkins and Hopkins, O'Connell Street, Dublin', in *An tOglac*, 5 June 1926. For the fighting at Kelly's see Bracken, Easter Week, 1916.

10.   Bracken, Easter Week.

11.   Liam Ó Briain, *Ciumhni Cinn*, (Sairseal agus Dill, Dublin, 1974) pp. 70 and 73.

12.   Lynch, Recollections and Comments on the IRB.

13.   Humphries, GPO Diary.

14.   Frank Thornton, in the Humphries Papers, Archives Department, University College, Dublin, P67/45.

15.   Traynor, Biographical Account.

16.   Sean T. O'Kelly in his account of his Easter Week experiences, *Irish Press*, 6–9 August 1961.

17.   Joe Good, *Enchanted by Dreams: The Journals of a Revolutionary* (Brandon Books, Dingle, 1996).

18.   Brennan-Whitmore, *Dublin Burning*, pp. 52–3.

19.   Good, *Enchanted by Dreams*, p. 30.

20.   O'Kelly, Easter Week experiences.

21.   NLI MS 13170.

22.   Humphries, GPO Diary.

23. Staines and Reilly, 'The Defence of the GPO'.
24. Joe Sweeney in a deposition made in 1934 describing his experiences in the GPO, Personal Narratives of the Rising of 1916, NLI MS 10915.
25. Staines and Reilly, 'The Defence of the GPO'.
26. Thornton, statement of Easter Rising experiences.
27. For the occupation of the Metropole Hotel, see Commandant Charles Saurin, 'Hotel Metropole Garrison', *An tOglac*, 13 and 20 March 1926.
28. Traynor, Biographical Account.
29. Bracken, Easter Week.
30. Ibid.
31. Humphries, GPO Diary.
32. Traynor, Biographical Account.
33. Ibid.
34. Humphries, GPO Diary.
35. Staines and Reilly, 'The Defence of the GPO'.
36. Ryan, 'General Post Office Area'.
37. Ibid.
38. Desmond Fitzgerald, *Memoirs*, p. 148.
39. Lynch, 'Report of Operations', p. 172.
40. Staines and Reilly, 'The Defence of the GPO'.
41. Thornton, statement of Easter Rising experiences.
42. Saurin, 'Hotel Metropole Garrison'.
43. Good, *Enchanted by Dreams*, p. 45.
44. Humphries, GPO Diary.
45. Good, *Enchanted by Dreams*, p. 50.
46. Humphries, GPO Diary.
47. Ibid.
48. Commandant P. Colgan, 'Maynooth Volunteers and 1916', *An tOglac*, 8 May 1926.
49. Humphries, GPO Diary.
50. Ibid.
51. Saurin, 'Hotel Metropole Garrison'.
52. Humphries, GPO Diary.
53. Traynor, Biographical Account.
54. Humphries, GPO Diary.
55. Staines and Reilly, 'The Defence of the GPO'.
56. Humphries, GPO Diary.
57. Ibid.
58. Sean MacEntee, *Episode at Easter* (Gill and Macmillan, Dublin, 1966) p. 157.
59. Joyce, 'The Story of Limerick and Kerry', p. 362.
60. Traynor, Biographical Account.
61. MacEntee, *Episode at Easter*, p. 154.
62. Traynor, Biographical Account and Saurin, 'Hotel Metropole Garrison'.

63. Ryan, 'General Post Office Area'.
64. Lynch, 'Report of Operations', p. 175.
65. Good, *Enchanted by Dreams*, p. 50.
66. Joyce, 'The Story of Limerick and Kerry', p. 363.
67. Thornton, statement of Easter Rising experiences.
68. Humphries, GPO Diary.
69. Accounts by Jack Plunkett of events 1914–22, NLI MS 11397.
70. MacEntee, *Episode at Easter*, p. 158.
71. Ibid.
72. Good, *Enchanted by Dreams*, p. 53.
73. Lynch, 'Report of Operations', p. 175.
74. Good, *Enchanted by Dreams*, pp. 53–4.
75. Saurin, 'Hotel Metropole Garrison'; Traynor, Biographical Account; and Good, *Enchanted by Dreams*, p. 42.
76. Staines and Reilly, 'The Defence of the GPO'.
77. Ibid.
78. Lynch, 'Report of Operations', p. 179.
79. Sean MacEntee, 'Easter Week in the GPO', *The Irish Digest* (May 1944).
80. Diarmuid Lynch, Roll of Honour, Florence O'Donoghue Papers, NLI MS 31409.
81. Good, *Enchanted by Dreams*, p. 56.
82. Traynor, Biographical Account.
83. Bracken, Easter Week.
84. Good, *Enchanted by Dreams*, pp. 57–8.
85. O'Farrell, 'The Surrender'.
86. Lieutenant Charles Steinmeyer, 'The Evacuation of the GPO', *An tOglac*, 27 February 1926.
87. Good, *Enchanted by Dreams*, p. 60.
88. Traynor, Biographical Account.
89. Ibid.
90. Good, *Enchanted by Dreams*, p. 63.
91. Ryan, 'The General Post Office Area'.
92. Good, *Enchanted by Dreams*, p. 64.
93. Nurse Julia Grenan, 'Story of the Surrender', *The Catholic Bulletin* (June 1917).
94. O'Farrell, 'The Surrender'.
95. Ibid.
96. Ryan, 'The General Post Office Area'.
97. Ibid.
98. Plunkett, Events 1914–22.
99. Traynor, Biographical Account.
100. Good, *Enchanted by Dreams*, p. 66.
101. Plunkett, Events 1914–22.
102. Good, *Enchanted by Dreams*, p. 71.
103. Grenan, 'Story of the Surrender'.
104. Ibid.

105. Traynor, Biographical Account.
106. Grenan, 'Story of the Surrender'.

8: A CITY AT WAR

1. O'Daly, 'The Women of Easter Week'.
2. Lyons, 'Ringsend Area', 10, 17 and 24 April 1926.
3. Donnelly, Easter Week, 1916.
4. A Company (Allen Library).
5. Christina Doyle Collection, NLI MS 5816–17.
6. Papers of Reverend Patrick J. Doyle, P.P., NLI MS 13561(12)
7. Holohan, 'Four Courts Area'.
8. Ó Briain, 'Stephen's Green Area'.
9. *History of the 6th South Staffs*, p. 145.
10. Good, *Enchanted by Dreams*, p. 30.
11. Ó Briain, 'Stephen's Green Area'.
12. Holohan, 'Four Courts Area'.
13. Walsh, 'The Epic of Mount Street Bridge'.
14. Good, *Enchanted by Dreams*, p. 31.
15. Griffith and O'Grady (eds), *Curious Journey*, pp. 58–9.
16. Lieutenant Jameson's letters to his family have been presented to the Imperial War Museum, London.
17. For Begley's desertion see O'Connor, 'Boland's Mill Area'. For M'Carthy see Holland, Marrowbone Lane.
18. Donnelly, Easter Week, 1916.
19. Jameson, Letters.
20. A memoir by Patrick Rankin of his participation in the occupation of the GPO, NLI MS 22251.
21. The pleas of the two young Volunteers, Byrne and Rowe, to be allowed to remain were rejected by Malone. Grace, 'I Don't Forget'.
22. Lyons, 'Ringsend Area'.
23. Frances Downey, diary for 22–7 April 1916, Trinity College, Dublin, MS 10066/193. Hereafter, Downey, Diary.
24. Griffith and O'Grady (eds), *Curious Journey*, p. 57.
25. Jameson, Letters.
26. Ibid.
27. Robbins, NLI MS 10915 and *Under the Starry Plough*, pp. 111–12.
28. Archer, Events.
29. Saurin, 'Hotel Metropole Garrison'.
30. Connolly, 'Dublin City Hall Area'.
31. *The Catholic Bulletin* (September 1916).
32. Griffith and O'Grady (eds), *Curious Journey*, p. 79.
33. Holland, Marrowbone Lane.
34. O' Daly, 'The Women of Easter Week'.
35. O'Gorman, list of those who 'received first aid in Father Mathew Hall' in Easter Week, NAI D/T S6023.
36. Connolly, 'Dublin City Hall Area'.

Notes

37. Ó Briain, 'Stephen's Green Area'.
38. See, for instances, Good, *Enchanted by Dreams*, p. 44.
39. Griffith and O'Grady (eds), *Curious Journey*, p. 66.
40. Good, *Enchanted by Dreams*, pp. 58–9; Saurin, 'Hotel Metropole Garrison'; and Traynor, Biographical Account.
41. Good, *Enchanted by Dreams*, pp. 39–40.
42. Clarke, *A Penny in the Clouds*, pp. 34–5.
43. Ó Briain, 'Stephen's Green Area'.
44. Walsh, 'The Epic of Mount Street Bridge'.
45. Account by James A. Glen, Trinity College, Dublin, MS 4456. In 1966 Nelson's Pillar was bombed and partially demolished by republicans. Because of safety fears the demolition was completed by army engineers.
46. For the different flags see Lynch, NLI MS 31409.
47. Sweeney, Personal Narratives of the Rising.
48. Humphries, GPO Diary.
49. Fitzgerald, *Memoirs*, p. 134.
50. Sweeney, Personal Narratives of the Rising.
51. Jameson, Letters. Jameson was to find out for himself the conditions on the Western Front to which he was transferred soon after the Easter Rising. He was killed in the summer of 1916.
52. Good, *Enchanted by Dreams*, pp. 42–3.
53. Ó Briain, 'Stephen's Green Area'.
54. The ruse is described in Lyons, 'Ringsend Area' and Donnelly, Easter Week, 1916.
55. Turner, 'Hopkins and Hopkins'.
56. Nathan Papers, MS 477.
57. Lord Dunsany, 'Recollections of 1916', *Irish Digest* (April 1939).
58. Holohan, 'Four Courts Area', p. 184 and Griffith and O'Grady (eds), *Curious Journey*, p. 70.
59. *Irish Times*, 9 May 1916.
60. Dunsany, 'Recollections of 1916'.
61. Holohan, 'Four Courts Area'.
62. Nathan Papers, MS 477.
63. File on unarmed victims, PRO WO 35/69.
64. Father Flanagan, 'The General Post Office Area', *Catholic Bulletin* (August 1918).
65. Lyons, 'Ringsend Area'.
66. Lynch, Report on Operations, Easter Week, pp. 178–9.
67. Rankin, GPO. For the bag of ammunition left in Lansdowne Road see Denis Johnston, Diary of his experiences during the Easter Rising, Trinity College, Dublin, MS 10066/179.
68. Maconchy, Memoirs.
69. Elsie Mahaffy, Diary, Trinity College, Dublin, MS 2074.
70. Jameson, Letters.
71. Mrs A.H. Norway, *The Sinn Fein Rebellion as I saw it* (Smith, Elder, London, 1916) p. 48.

72. Kearney, Reminiscences.
73. Johnston, Diary.
74. Walsh, 'The Epic of Mount Street Bridge'.
75. Coffey, Diary, NLI MS 21193.
76. Griffith and O'Grady (eds), *Curious Journey*, p. 72.
77. Clarke, *A Penny in the Clouds*, p. 33.
78. Humphries, GPO Diary.
79. Walter Starkie, *Scholars and Gypsies* (John Murray, London, 1963) p. 148. In 1916 Starkie was a student at Trinity College, Dublin where he subsequently became Professor of Spanish.
80. E.U. Bradbridge, *The 59th Division 1915–1918* (Wilfred Edmunds, Chesterfield, 1928) p. 37.
81. Lieutenant-Colonel W.C. Oates, *The Sherwood Foresters in the Great War 1914–1919* (T. Forman and Sons, Nottingham, 1920) p. 42.
82. NLI MS 24952.
83. Diary of Mrs Augustine Henry (she was married to a British army officer) for the period October 1915 to June 1916, NLI MS 7984.
84. Hyde, Diary, 24 April 1916.
85. File on unarmed victims, PRO WO35/69.
86. Ibid.
87. Ibid.
88. Downey, Diary, April 1916.
89. Nathan Papers, MS 477.
90. Brennan, 'Mendicity Institution Area', p. 191.
91. Nathan Papers, MS 476.
92. Henry, Diary.
93. Griffith and O'Grady (eds), *Curious Journey*, p. 66.
94. Robert Hogan and Michael O'Neill, *Joseph Holloway's Irish Theatre* (Dixon, California, 1967) p. 182.
95. Jameson, Letters.
96. Nathan Papers, MS 476.
97. Reynolds, *A Fragment of 1916 History*, pp. 7–8.
98. Ibid., pp. 26–7.
99. PRO WO35/67/3.
100. Edmunds, *2/6 Battalion, Sherwood Foresters, 1914–18*, p. 45.
101. Maxwell to his wife Louise, 18 May 1916, Sir John Maxwell Papers, CO583, Princeton University Library, Box 6/9.
102. Maxwell in an undated letter to Kitchener, Maxwell Papers, Box 30/107.
103. PRO WO904/215.
104. File on the Sheehy-Skeffington affair, PRO WO30/67.
105. Ibid.
106. Ibid.
107. Ibid.
108. Ibid.
109. 4 June 1916, Maxwell Papers.
110. File on the Sheehy-Skeffington affair, PRO WO30/67.

111. Ibid.
112. Ibid.
113. NLI MS 15415.
114. Account by Nellie O'Brien of her experiences during Easter Week, Trinity College, Dublin, MS 10343/1.
115. Michael Kent, Diary, NLI MS 15292.
116. Fox, *History of the Irish Citizen Army*, pp. 172–4.
117. Gaughan, *Thomas Johnson*, p. 48; the book contains Johnson's diary of Easter Week.
118. Starkie, *Scholars and Gypsies*, pp. 144–5.
119. Hyde, Diary, 30 April 1916.
120. Starkie, *Scholars and Gypsies*, p. 144.
121. Starkie, ibid.; Norway, *The Sinn Fein Rebellion*, pp. 38–9.
122. Good, *Enchanted by Dreams*, p. 35.
123. Stopford, Diary.
124. Henry, Diary.
125. Ibid.
126. Lyons, 'Ringsend Area'.
127. *Irish Times*, 9 May 1916.
128. For the various measures to alleviate the food shortage see Nathan Papers, MS 476; *Irish Times*, 2 May 1916; and a record of the activities of the Society of St Vincent de Paul, NLI MS 13737.
129. NLI MS 24952.
130. Ibid.
131. Lyons, 'Ringsend Area'.
132. O'Leary, *Dublin Saturday Post* (compendium edn for 29 April, 6 May and 13 May).
133. Ibid.
134. Aloysius, Memories of Easter Week.
135. Flanagan, 'The General Post Office Area'. All the quotations in the subsequent account of Flanagan's experiences are from this source.
136. Mrs A. Mitchell, NLI MS 24553.
137. Henry, Diary.
138. Lieutenant A.A. Luce, 12th Royal Irish Rifles, Recollections of Easter 1916, Trinity College, Dublin, MS 4874.
139. Army Field Message Book of Major H.E. de Courcy Wheeler, recording events connected with the surrender of the insurgents in Dublin, 29 April to 1 May 1916, NLI microfilm, n5670, p5892.
140. Rankin, GPO.
141. Holland, Marrowbone Lane.
142. Kent, Diary.
143. Robbins, *Under the Starry Plough*, p. 127.
144. Doyle, description of the South Dublin Union.
145. Army Field Message Book of de Courcy Wheeler.
146. Lyons, 'Ringsend Area'.
147. Brighid Thornton in Griffith and O'Grady (eds), *Curious Journey*, p. 77. See also 'list of persons killed or wounded' brought to Dublin

hospitals, which was compiled by Sergeant Michael Mannion, 29 May 1916, PRO WO 35/69.

148. Griffith and O'Grady (eds), *Curious Journey*, pp. 69–70.
149. Archer, Events.
150. Account by J.W. Rowarth, IWM 80/40/1; the list drawn up by Christine O'Gorman, 29 May 1929, of those who 'received first aid in Father Mathew Hall' in Easter Week, refers to three arrested as spies, NAI SD/T S6023; the police recorded growing militancy in the North King Street area for two to three months before the Rising. See the report by Major-General Sandbach, 25 May 1916, in PRO WO35/67.
151. Archer, Events. See also the statement by Hannant on the experience of the Lancers in IWM.
152. Nathan Papers MS 467.
153. Archer, Events. See also Bean Ui Chonaill, 'A Cumann na mBan recalls', p. 276.
154. Coady, 'St John's Convent', p. 279; Adrian and Sally Warwick-Haller, *Letters from Dublin, Easter 1916: Alfred Fannin's Diary of the Rising* (Irish Academic Press, Blackrock, 1995) pp. 32–3.
155. Archer, Events.
156. Documents on the Rising, NLI MS 13668.
157. Clarke, Diary.
158. Mahaffy, Diary.
159. Birrell to Nathan, 3 May 1916, Nathan Papers, MS 477.
160. Daly, Irish Volunteers.
161. Jameson, Letters.
162. Stopford, Diary.
163. O'Leary, *Dublin Saturday Post* (compendium edn).
164. Ibid.
165. Report of a meeting between the Home Secretary and a Dublin deputation headed by the Lord Mayor after the Rising, J. Brennan Papers, NLI MS 26178.
166. Mahaffy, Diary.
167. Henry, Diary.
168. Nathan Papers, MS 477.

9: THE RISING OUTSIDE DUBLIN

1. For the Rising outside Dublin see Joyce, 'The Story of Limerick and Kerry in 1916'; and Seumas O'Dubhghaill, 'Activities in Enniscorthy', Mattie Nielan, 'The Rising in Galway' and Liam Ruiseal, 'The Position in Cork', all published in *Capuchin Annual* (1966).
2. Paddy Houlihan, The Battle of Ashbourne, NLI MS 18098. There is also a good account by Colonel Joe Lawless, 'The Fight at Ashbourne', in *Capuchin Annual* (1966) pp. 307–16.
3. Ibid.

4.   Jerry Golden, The Story of the Fight at Rath Cross Roads or The Battle of Ashbourne, Allen Library, Dublin.

5.   A memorandum from Sergeant O'Connell, the RIC officer who had gone ahead with the warning (Mulcahy Papers, UCD).

6.   Lawless, 'The Fight at Ashbourne', p. 313.

7.   Golden, The Story of the Fight at Rath Cross Roads.

8.   Ibid.

9.   PRO WO35/69.

10.   Houlihan, The Battle of Ashbourne.

10: SUPPRESSION, COURTS-MARTIAL AND EXECUTIONS

1.   This discussion of military aspects of the Rising is based mainly on the following: situation reports, PRO WO35/69; *On the Rebellion in Ireland*, report of Royal Commission (HMSO, London, 1916), Command Papers 8279, 8311; Major-General J.P. Hally, 'The Easter Rising in Dublin; the Military Aspects', Part 1, in *The Irish Sword*, Vol. 7 (1966) pp. 213–16, and Part 2 in Vol. 8 (1967) pp. 48–57; Colonel E. O'Neill, 'The Battle of Dublin, 1916', in *An Cosantoir* (May 1966), pp. 211–22; 'General Maxwell's Reports' in *An tOglac*, 19 June 1926; undated report for Chief Secretary, entitled 'The Sinn Fein or Irish Volunteers and the Rebellion' in NAI DFA/IFS, Box 6 No. 134 Part 5.

2.   Ibid. pp. 31–2; Hally, 'The Easter Rising', Part 2, pp. 48–51.

3.   Wimborne to Birrell, at 12.58 p.m., 25 April 1916, Asquith Papers, MS 41–3 (Bodleian Library, Oxford).

4.   Report by Nathan, at 5.15 p.m., 26 April 1916, in PRO WO35/69.

5.   Report at 10.55 p.m., 26 April, in ibid.

6.   Ó Broin, *Dublin Castle and the 1916 Rising*, pp. 114–16; Sir George Arthur, *General Sir John Maxwell* (London, 1932) pp. 245–8 and passim.

7.   Kitchener Papers PRO 30/57/55; see also Asquith to King George V, 27 April, in PRO CAB37/146 and cabinet discussion in PRO CAB41/37.

8.   Maxwell to Kitchener, 21 April, and Kitchener to Robertson, 26 April, in PRO 30/57/55; Arthur, *Maxwell*, pp. 247–8.

9.   Maxwell Papers, Box 6/9.

10.   Arthur, *Maxwell*, p. 249.

11.   See reports, 30 April and 2 May, in PRO WO35/69, and letter to wife, 30 April, Maxwell Papers, Box 6/9.

12.   Report 2 May, PRO WO35/69.

13.   See comment dated 27 April 1916, in Nathan Papers, MS 476.

14.   Ibid.

15.   PRO CAB37/147, Paper no. 34 forwarded by Esme Howard; see also Ó Broin, *Dublin Castle and the 1916 Rising*, p. 114.

16.   The wire was sent at 9.15 a.m. and the reply at 11.30 a.m., 30 April: Nathan Papers, MS 477.

17. Hally, 'The Easter Rising', Part 2, p. 51.
18. Oates, *The Sherwood Foresters in the Great War*, p. 39.
19. Account by Lieutenant Henry Douglas (Sherwood Foresters), NLI MS 4796.
20. Instructions issued on 25 April to troops arriving at Kingstown on 26 April, in PRO WO35/69.
21. Asquith to King George V, 27 April, in PRO CAB37/146.
22. To his wife, Maxwell Papers, Box 6/9.
23. PRO CAB42/12, appendix 83A1.
24. Ibid. and supporting papers in PRO CAB37/146.
25. Ibid.
26. To his wife, 4 May, Maxwell Papers, Box 6/9.
27. Ibid.
28. Letters dated 27 April and 2 May, by Captain H. Peel, in IWM P391.
29. Letter by A.L. Franklin, IWM 93/25/1.
30. Leon Ó Broin, *WE Wylie and the Irish Revolution, 1916–21* (Gill and Macmillan, Dublin, 1989) p. 29.
31. Arthur, *Maxwell*, p. 269; Maxwell Papers, passim, Boxes 1–6.
32. To his wife, early May, Maxwell Papers, Box 6/9; Ó Broin, *Dublin Castle and the 1916 Rising*, pp. 120–4.
33. In Nathan Papers, 3 May, MS 476.
34. Maxwell memorandum, dated 13 May, Asquith Papers, MS 41–3.
35. Inspector General's Confidential Report for 1 April–31 May, dated 15 June 1916, in PRO CO904/99.
36. Report at 11.00 a.m. on 3 May, PRO WO35/69.
37. Arthur, *Maxwell*, p. 264.
38. Statement by Robert Holland, the Allen Library, Dublin.
39. Ibid.
40. Ibid.; see reports by Major-General S. MacSuibhne and P.J. O'Mara in NLI MS10915; also account by Jack Plunkett, NLI MS 11397.
41. Comment by Lieutenant-Colonel J.N. Galloway in IWM 87/45/1.
42. Lieutenant-Colonel J.P.W. Jamie, MC, *The 177th Brigade 1914–18* (W. Thornley, Leicester, 1931) p. 14; Lieutenant W. Meakin, *The Fifth North Staffs. and the North Midland Territorials, 1914–19* (Hughes and Harber, Longton, 1920) p. 73 records a similar experience.
43. See proceedings of Kent's court-martial in PRO WO71/356.
44. Ó Broin, *Wylie and the Irish Revolution*, p. 36.
45. Ibid.
46. Report for the Chief Secretary, 'The Sinn Fein or Irish Volunteers', in NAI DFA/IFS, Box 6, no. 134, Part 5.
47. Gerard Oram, *Worthless Men: Race, Eugenics and the Death Penalty in the British Army during the First World War* (Boutle, London, 1998) p. 69.
48. Ibid., pp. 72–3; see also his *Death Sentences passed by Military Courts of the British Army, 1914–24* (Boutle, London, 1998) pp. 13–16.
49. Ó Broin, *Wylie and the Irish Revolution*, p. 23.
50. Reports, 2 and 3 May, PRO WO35/69. Dr. R.F. Tobin (St Vincent's

Hospital) and Dr P.J. O'Farrell declared Connolly to be 'fit to undergo his trial. . . . His mind, memory and understanding [were] entirely unimpaired': PRO WO71/354.

51. Account by Jack Plunkett, NLI MS 11397.
52. Official reports of court-martial proceedings of rebel leaders, PRO WO71/344–58.
53. Ibid.
54. Mac Lochlainn, *Last Words*, p. 171.
55. See account by Maurice Brennan in NLI MS 10915.
56. PRO WO71/350.
57. PRO WO71/351.
58. PRO WO71/345.
59. PRO WO71/356.
60. PRO WO71/348.
61. Account by Patrick Doyle in the Allen Library, Dublin.
62. PRO WO71/347.
63. Ó Broin, *Wylie and the Irish Revolution*, p. 27. Blackader also described him as 'a brave man', p. 26.
64. PRO WO71/355, 352.
65. Ó Broin, *Wylie and the Irish Revolution*, p. 23.
66. PRO WO71/349.
67. PRO WO71/346.
68. Mac Lochlainn, *Last Words*, p. 62.
69. Ibid. pp. 54–60.
70. PRO WO71/358.
71. Ibid.
72. PRO WO71/344.
73. PRO WO71/353.
74. Ibid.
75. PRO WO71/351.
76. PRO WO71/356.
77. PRO WO71/357.
78. PRO WO71/354.
79. PRO WO71/345.
80. Ibid.
81. Ó Broin, *Wylie and the Irish Revolution*, p. 21.
82. Countess of Fingall, *Seventy Years Young: Memories of Elizabeth, Countess of Fingall* (Lilliput, Dublin, 1991) p. 376.
83. Ibid.
84. Maconchy, Memoirs.
85. Ó Broin, *Wylie and the Irish Revolution*, p. 27.
86. Official Record of trial, 4 May 1916, PRO HO144/1580/316818; *see also* Brian Barton, *From Behind a Closed Door: Secret Court Martial Records of The Easter Rising* (The Blackstaff Press, Belfast, 2002), pp. 72–82.
87. PRO HO144/1580/316818.
88. Griffith and O'Grady (eds), *Curious Journey*, p. 248; Eoin Neeson, *Birth of a Republic* (Prestige Books, Dublin, 1998) pp. 175–6.

89. Hally, 'The Easter Rising', Part 2, p. 53.
90. To his wife, 9 May, Maxwell Papers, Box 6/9.
91. Maxwell to Asquith, 9 May, Asquith Papers, MS 41–3.
92. Mac Lochlainn *Last Words*, passim;
    P. Cooke, *A History of Kilmainham Jail, 1796–1924* (Stationery Office, Dublin, 1995); Jack Plunkett described it as 'lamentably lacking in the necessary amenities'. NLI MS 11397.
93. In PRO WO35/67/1.
94. Ó Broin, *Dublin Castle and the 1916 Rising*, p. 139.
95. Mac Lochlainn, *Last Words*, p. 84.
96. Aloysius, Memories of Easter Week.
97. Mac Lochlainn, *Last Words*, p. 31.
98. Ibid. p. 33.
99. Ibid. p. 44.
100. Aloysius, Memories of Easter Week.
101. Note by A. Lee, dated 4 May 1916, in PRO WO35/67/1; Bradbridge, *The 59th Division 1915–1918*, p. 43; Mac Lochlainn, *Last Words*, pp. 31–2.
102. Ibid. p. 78.
103. Mac Lochlainn, *Last Words*, p. 70.
104. Ibid. p. 96; accounts by Grace Plunkett, NLI MS 21598–9.
105. PRO WO71/344, 347.
106. J.B. Lyons, *The Enigma of Tom Kettle: Irish Patriot, Essayist, Poet, British Soldier, 1880–1916* (Glendale Press, Dublin, 1983) p. 294.
107. Crime Branch Special Report, 28 September 1916, in PRO CO904/208.
108. Mac Lochlainn, *Last Words*, passim.
109. Ibid. p. 112.
110. Ibid. pp. 124–6.
111. Ibid. p. 127.
112. Ibid. p. 146.
113. Ibid. p. 136.
114. Account by Michael Kent, NLI MS 15292.
115. Ibid.
116. Mac Lochlainn, *Last Words*, p. 143.
117. Ibid. p. 156.
118. Ibid. p. 171.
119. Ibid. p. 167.
120. Ibid. p. 172.
121. Ibid. p. 191.
122. Account by Nora and Lily Connolly, NLI MS 13947.
123. To his wife, Maxwell Papers, Box 6/9.
124. Ó Broin, *Dublin Castle and the 1916 Rising*, p. 130.
125. See report of 6 May in PRO CAB41/37.
126. Maxwell to his wife, 12 May, Maxwell Papers, Box 6/9.
127. Aloysius, Memories of Easter Week.
128. Maxwell memorandum in Asquith Papers, MS 41–3, entitled 'Brief

history of rebels on whom it has been necessary to inflict the supreme penalty'.

129. Ibid.

130. Ibid.

131. Ibid.; also Maxwell to Bonham-Carter, 25 May.

132. Ó Broin, *Wylie and the Irish Revolution*, p. 32.

133. To his wife, Maxwell Papers, Box 6/9.

134. Michael Tierney, *Eoin MacNeill: Scholar and Man of Action, 1867–1945* (Clarendon Press, Oxford, 1980) p. 222.

135. Ibid. p. 227.

136. Ibid. p. 233.

137. Ibid. p. 239.

138. Roy Jenkins, *Asquith* (Collins, London, 1964) p. 398; for full list and dates of court martials held, see PRO WO213/8.

139. Ó Broin, *Wylie and the Irish Revolution*, p. 10.

140. Percy A. Bick to P.M. Yearsley in IWM 27/11/2.

141. Inspector-General's Confidential Report, dated 15 June, in PRO CO904/99; the Hyde Diary, 1 May, records the police back on the streets then for the first time since the Rising. They were described as 'running for their life. Two old men . . . cried out to accelerate their pace "Howl that fella! Howl that fella!"'

142. Arthur, *Maxwell*, p. 268; and Maxwell to his wife, 30 May, Maxwell Papers, Box 6/9.

143. Ibid.

144. Ibid. To his wife, 30 May, 19 June.

145. Arthur, *Maxwell*, p. 261.

146. Maxwell to Asquith, 15 June, Maxwell Papers, Box 2/8.

147. To his wife, 1 June, Maxwell Papers, Box 6/9.

148. Ibid. 5 July.

149. Ibid. 20 July.

150. Ibid. 1, 23 June.

151. Asquith to Maxwell, 27 May, Maxwell Papers, Box 2/8.

152. Asquith to King George V, 26 July, in PRO CAB41/37.

153. Ibid. see Asquith's correspondence with King George V, late July and early August; Jenkins, *Asquith*, pp. 403–4.

154. PRO WO71/345.

155. Lynas correspondence in IWM 89/7/1.

BIBLIOGRAPHY

A complete guide to the sources is to be found in the footnotes. The following list comprises only the major collections and some useful secondary accounts of the Easter Rising or specific aspects of the event.

Primary Sources

National Library of Ireland
Roger Casement papers
John Clarke diary
Augustine Henry diary
Bulmer Hobson papers
Dick Humphries diary
Diarmuid Lynch papers
Eoin MacNeill papers
Florence O'Donoghue papers
Dorothy Stopford diary

Trinity College Dublin
Douglas Hyde diary
Peadar Kearney papers
Elsie Mahaffy diary

Allen Library, Edmund Rice House, North Richmond Street, Dublin
Depositions by Father Aloysius, Peadar Bracken, Paddy Daly, Peadar Doyle, Jerry Golden, Robert Holland, William Oman and Michael Walker

University College, Dublin
Depositions by Liam Archer, Simon Donnelly, Frank Thornton and Oscar Traynor

Public Record Office, London
Kitchener papers
Cabinet papers
Colonial Office papers
War Office papers

Imperial War Museum
P.A. Bick papers

BIBLIOGRAPHY

A. Hannant papers
A.M. Jameson papers

British Army Museum, London
E.W.S.K. Maconchy memoirs
Bodleian Library, Oxford
Asquith papers
Nathan papers

Princeton University
Sir John Maxwell papers

Secondary Sources

Books

Caulfield, Max *The Easter Rebellion* (New English Library, London, 1965)
Dangerfield, George *The Damnable Question: A Study in Anglo-Irish Relations* (Constable, London, 1977)
Dudley Edwards, Ruth *Patrick Pearse: The Triumph of Failure* (Gollancz, London, 1977)
Duff, Charles *Six Days to Shake an Empire* (Dent, London, 1966)
Foster, R.F. *Modern Ireland 1600–1972* (Penguin, London, 1989)
Fox, R.M. *The History of the Irish Citizen Army* (James Duffy, Dublin, 1943)
McHugh, R. *Dublin, 1916* (Arlington Books, Dublin, 1966)
Hobson, Bulmer *Ireland:Yesterday and Tomorrow* (Anvil Books, Tralee, 1968)
Holt, Edgar *Protest in Arms 1916–1923* (Putnam, London, 1960)
Kluge, Hans-Dieter *Irland in der deutschen Geschichtswissenschaft, Politik und Propaganda* (P. Lang, Frankfurt am Main, 1985)
Lyons, F.S.L. *Ireland since the Famine* (Fontana, London, 1986)
Lynch, Diarmuid *The I.R.B. and the 1916 Insurrection* (Mercier Press, Cork, 1957)
Martin, F.X. *The Irish Volunteers, 1913–1915* (James Duffy, Dublin, 1963)
Martin, F.X. *The Easter Rising and University College, Dublin* (Browne & Nolan, Dublin, 1966)
Martin, F.X. *Leaders and Men of the Easter Rising* (Methuen, London, 1967)
Mac Lochlainn, Piaras F. *Last Words: Letters and Statements of the Leaders Executed after the Rising at Easter 1916* (Stationery Office, Dublin, 1990)
Morgan, Austen *James Connolly: A Political Biography* (Manchester University Press, Manchester, 1988)
Ó Broin, Leon *Dublin Castle and the 1916 Rising: the Story of Sir Matthew Nathan* (Helican, Dublin, 1966)
O'Rahilly, Aodogán *Winding the Clock: O'Rahilly and the 1916 Rising* (Lilliput Press, Dublin, 1991)
Reid, B.L. *The Lives of Roger Casement* (Yale University Press, New Haven, 1978)
le Roux, Louis *Tom Clarke and the Irish Freedom Movement* (Talbot Press, Dublin, 1936)

Ryan, Desmond *The Rising: The Complete Story of Easter Week* (Golden Eagle Books, Dublin, 1949)

Stephens, James *The Insurrection in Dublin* (Colin Smyth, Gerrards Cross, 1978)

Taillon, Ruth *The Women of 1916* (Beyond the Pale Publications, Belfast, 1996)

Thompson, William *The Imagination of an Insurrection: Dublin, Easter 1916* (Oxford University Press, 1967)

Articles

Doerries, Reinhard, 'Die Mission Sir Roger Casements im Deutschen Reich 1914–1916', in *Historische Zeitschrift* (1976)

Kratz, Andreas, 'Die Mission Joseph Mary Plunketts im Deutschen Reich und ihre Bedeutung fur den Osteraufstand 1916', in *Historische Mitteilungen* (1995)

Martin, F.X., 'Select Documents: Eoin MacNeill on the 1916 Rising', *Irish Historical Studies*, vol. xii, no. 47(March 1961)

Martin, F.X., 'Myth, Fact and Mystery', *Studia Hibernica*, no. 7, 1967

Martin, F.X., 'The 1916 Rising – A Coup d'Etat or a "Bloody Protest"?', *Studia Hibernica*, no. 8, 1968

O'Donoghue, Florence, 'Plans for the 1916 Rising', *University Review*, March 1963

The Commemorative issue of the *Capuchin Annual* (1966) contains many interesting articles on the Easter Rising.

INDEX